SELF-CRITICISM
AND
SELF-ENHANCEMENT

SELF-CRITICISM
AND
SELF-ENHANCEMENT

Theory, Research, and Clinical Implications

Edited by
Edward C. Chang

American Psychological Association
Washington, DC

Published by
American Psychological Association
750 First Street, NE
Washington, DC 20002
www.apa.org

To order
APA Order Department
P.O. Box 92984
Washington, DC 20090-2984
Tel: (800) 374-2721; Direct: (202) 336-5510
Fax: (202) 336-5502; TDD/TTY: (202) 336-6123
Online: www.apa.org/books/
E-mail: order@apa.org

In the U.K., Europe, Africa, and the Middle East, copies may be ordered from
American Psychological Association
3 Henrietta Street
Covent Garden, London
WC2E 8LU England

Typeset in Goudy by Stephen McDougal, Mechanicsville, MD

Printer: Maple-Vail Book Manufacturing, Binghamton, NY
Cover Designer: Naylor Design, Washington, DC
Technical/Production Editor: Tiffany L. Klaff

The opinions and statements published are the responsibility of the authors, and such opinions and statements do not necessarily represent the policies of the American Psychological Association.

Library of Congress Cataloging-in-Publication Data

Self-criticism and self-enhancement : theory, research, and clinical implications / edited by Edward C. Chang.
    p. cm.
  Includes bibliographical references and index.
  ISBN-13: 978-1-4338-0115-0
  ISBN-10: 1-4338-0115-9
  1. Criticism, Personal. 2. Self-perception. I. Chang, Edward C. (Edward Chin-Ho)

BF637.C74S45 2008
155.2'5—dc22   2007016026

British Library Cataloguing-in-Publication Data
A CIP record is available from the British Library.

Printed in the United States of America
First Edition

To my dear parents, Tae Myung-Sook and Chang Suk-Choon, who taught me well as a child that self-criticism and self-enhancement are not givens; rather, they are privileged choices one can make use of in life. To my wife, who, like myself, works hard for everyone but herself. Not self-criticism, not self-enhancement, but self-sacrifice! She was taught by the best—her loving and hardworking dad. To my 6-year-old Princess Olivia Dae Chang. In less than a year, I have learned so many things from you, from designing a Polly Pocket™ hotel that will one day rival the life-renewing Four Seasons Resort in Wailea, to snorkeling with fishes at Molikini Crater and Castaway Cay, to picking up my old Rossignol F200. But, most of all, you have taught me to always appreciate how lucky I am to have such a sweet, intelligent, and creative daughter as you in my world. You inspire me, like the music of Vienna Teng, to change the routine scripts of my life so that I may grow anew each day. When I was a young boy, I could not fully appreciate why my parents sacrificed so much of their lives for their children. Now, of course, the answer is as clear as the smile on my daughter's face when she hands me one of her poems, colorful drawings, or sheets of completed math and spelling problems. On that note, thank you, Mr. Schwartz, for letting parents like myself share the adventures of reading (and of life) with your first graders. You have shown us how group-enhancing activities can simultaneously be self-enhancing. Finally, I would like to dedicate this book to C. R. Snyder and William Dember. Rick and Bill were individuals who selflessly helped many of us develop both personally and professionally. They were model mentors and kind souls to those who had the honor and privilege of knowing them. In their own ways, they kept the science, practice, and teaching of psychology a very positive human endeavor.

CONTENTS

CONTRIBUTORS

Raymond M. Bergner, PhD, Illinois State University, Normal
Jonathon D. Brown, PhD, University of Washington, Seattle
Patrick J. Carroll, PhD, The Ohio State University, Lima
Edward C. Chang, PhD, University of Michigan, Ann Arbor
Rita Chang, MA, University of Michigan, Ann Arbor
C. Randall Colvin, PhD, Northeastern University, Boston, MA
Katrina L. Cooper, PhD, Bethany College, Bethany, WV
Robert Griffo, MA, Northeastern University, Boston, MA
Takeshi Hamamura, MA, University of British Columbia, Vancouver,
  Canada
Steven J. Heine, PhD, University of British Columbia, Vancouver,
  Canada
Christian Holle, PhD, William Paterson University, Wayne, NJ
Jill M. Holm-Denoma, PhD, University of Vermont, Burlington
Rick Ingram, PhD, University of Kansas, Lawrence
Thomas E. Joiner Jr., PhD, Florida State University, Tallahassee
Allison M. Kade, BA, University of Michigan, Ann Arbor
William M. P. Klein, PhD, University of Pittsburgh, Pittsburgh, PA
Michelle Luke, PhD, University of Southampton, Southampton, England
Margaret A. Marshall, PhD, Seattle Pacific University, Seattle, WA
Julie K. Norem, PhD, Wellesley College, Wellesley, MA
Ainhoa Otamendi, PhD, University of Malaga, Malaga, Spain
Christopher Peterson, PhD, University of Michigan, Ann Arbor
James L. Pretzer, PhD, Case Western Reserve University, Cleveland,
    OH; Cleveland Center for Cognitive Therapy, Beachwood, OH
Abbey R. Roach, MA, University of Kentucky, Lexington
Lawrence J. Sanna, PhD, University of North Carolina at Chapel Hill

Constantine Sedikides, PhD, University of Southampton, Southampton, England
Suzanne C. Segerstrom, PhD, University of Kentucky, Lexington
James A. Shepperd, PhD, University of Florida, Gainesville
Kate Sweeny, MS, University of Florida, Gainesville

FOREWORD

CHRISTOPHER PETERSON

One approach to psychological theory and research is to begin with the assumption that things are very simple. This strategy may produce a short-term splash, or even a long-term one (witness Skinner), but it is ultimately doomed because it is flat-out wrong. Human conduct is never very simple.

Another approach is to begin with the assumption that things are very complex. This strategy produces no kind of splash at all because it is immediately doomed as a guide to research or practice.

There is a third approach, rare but reasonable, and that is to assume that things are complex but to take a further step and articulate the parameters and circumstances that allow us to make sense of the complexity. The work of my colleague Edward C. Chang has long embodied this third approach. In this volume, he and his colleagues tackle from this perspective the related topics of self-criticism and self-enhancement.

What is psychologically beneficial about self-criticism and self-enhancement, and what is psychologically damaging? And what are the factors that frame and lead to these good or bad effects? One important theme running through the book is that of culture, and how a psychological stance that makes sense and pays dividends in one setting may have very different effects in another. Psychologists are not the only ones who have something to learn from this work.

Chang and his colleagues are to be commended for moving beyond a one-size-fits-all approach to their topics. This is a good and interesting book, informed by philosophical arguments as well as empirical data. I repeat my highest praise: It recognizes complexity without becoming mired in it.

PREFACE

Life is complex. I say this not only because I grew up in the hustle and bustle of New York City but also because I grew up as an immigrant from a very different cultural heritage. The confluence of these factors forced me to be accepting of all sorts of possibilities, including those of self-criticism and self-enhancement. Accordingly, this volume represents an attempt to share with interested readers a way not only to recognize complexity in our lives but also to embrace it.

Several years ago, I edited a volume focused on optimism and pessimism, titled *Optimism and Pessimism: Implications for Theory, Research, and Practice.* My goal was simple in design, to get some of the leading scholars, researchers, and practitioners working on optimism and pessimism to talk with one another and with readers about the complexities of these two constructs. I wanted readers to walk away with the idea that optimism is not always functionally good and pessimism is not always functionally bad. A few years later, a dear colleague and I followed up with a volume titled *Virtue, Vice, and Personality: The Complexity of Behavior.* This time, the focus was on the functional complexities of key personality variables. Now, in the present volume, I seek to situate some of the discussions that have been presented in these earlier works and in the extant literature under the broader framework of self-criticism and self-enhancement.

It seems like it is always about good versus evil. Let me expand on this. In contrast to a tradition of negative psychology that has focused on studying the function of "negative" variables like neuroticism, pessimism, perfectionism, and rumination, there has been a growing push in recent years for a positive psychology that focuses on studying the function of "positive" variables like optimism, personal control, self-esteem, and personal striving. In essence, these self-referent variables (and the many others studied by psychologists) represent those that either involve a negative bias toward *self-criticism*, as indicated by an explicit or an implicit tendency to focus on negative self-referent information or perceptions, or involve a positive bias toward *self-enhancement,* as indicated by an explicit or an implicit tendency to focus on positive self-referent information or perceptions. A deeper understanding of how negative and positive psychological variables may function as a virtue in one situation and as vice in another situation can be obtained by using a framework involving self-criticism and self-enhancement. Put another way, many negative and positive psychological variables can be understood as a function of self-criticism and self-enhancement, respectively. Moreover, this framework provides a powerful way to understand the basic motivational mechanisms that determine complex group behavior. For example, some have suggested that Westerners are motivated by a pattern of behavior most consistent with self-enhancement, whereas Easterners are motivated by a pattern of behavior most consistent with self-criticism. Thus, a framework involving self-criticism and self-enhancement represents a wide-ranging conceptual tool for understanding differences in individuals and groups. Accordingly, this volume will focus on a balanced discussion of the diverse costs and benefits of self-criticism and self-enhancement on our lives, and the need to think more complexly about these core meaning-making variables as we try like Nietzsche to get beyond the convention of good versus evil.

Unlike most scholarly works, I believe that this volume has great far-reaching potential and offers an optimal balance between theory, research, and practice. The contributors are world-renowned experts on the topic of self-criticism and self-enhancement. And although each of the chapter contributors have been asked to focus their writings on a core conceptual idea, all of the present contributors share a deep and open appreciation for the rich complexity of self-criticism and self-enhancement as multifaceted and multidetermined variables that involve and evoke different outcomes in different contexts. Thus, my overarching goal for this volume is to challenge readers to think more richly and complexly about self-criticism and self-enhancement as powerful frameworks for understanding and changing human behavior, including one's own.

I would like to thank the many individuals who have played a valuable role in assisting me with this volume. First, and foremost, I would like to thank the contributors of this volume for making this exciting work come to fruition. Without their support, this volume would not have been possible. I also would like to thank the development and production editors at the American Psychological Association (APA), Emily Leonard and Tiffany Klaff, who helped ensure that this book was complete and ready for publication each and every step of the way, and the many students who offered their assistance with this project. In addition, I would like to thank my little editorial assistant, Olivia Chang, for helping me to collate and package the final chapters prior to submission. And last, but not least, I would like to thank Susan Reynolds at the APA for giving me the opportunity to edit this volume and for her generous patience and support throughout this project.

SELF-CRITICISM
AND
SELF-ENHANCEMENT

1

INTRODUCTION TO SELF-CRITICISM AND SELF-ENHANCEMENT: VIEWS FROM ANCIENT GREECE TO THE MODERN WORLD

EDWARD C. CHANG

> The fool doth think he is wise, but the wise man knows himself to be a fool.
>
> —William Shakespeare, *As You Like It*

> I'm bad.
>
> —LL Cool J, *I'm Bad*

Most pop psychology books in America focus on ways to foster some form of self-enhancement (e.g., feeling good about oneself, increasing one's self-image, obtaining greater personal wealth, living the life one wants to live). Indeed, a quick search at Amazon.com identified over 39,000 books that focus on self-help, most of which seem, according to their titles, to focus on various ways to improve oneself or one's condition. In addition, many psychological interventions focus on ways to overcome some form of self-criticism (e.g., expecting too much from oneself, feeling bad about oneself, having little personal confidence). But is self-enhancement always a good thing, and is self-criticism always a bad thing? And what are *self-enhancement* and *self-criticism*? The answers to these questions depend on many factors.

SOME EARLY PHILOSOPHICAL NOTIONS OF (FUNCTIONAL) SELF-CRITICISM AND (DYSFUNCTIONAL) SELF-ENHANCEMENT

If one were to take a historical look at how self-criticism and self-enhancement were viewed during the times of the ancient Greeks, one would find that self-criticism was not necessarily attached to notions of vice and negative functioning, and self-enhancement was not necessarily attached to notions of virtue and positive functioning.

How Self-Criticism Leads to True Understanding: A Look at Plato's Allegory of the Cave

Many scholars consider Plato to be the first and greatest philosopher to have ever lived. Indeed, Alfred Whitehead (1929), the famous philosopher, logician, and mathematician, argued that much of Western philosophy represented merely a series of footnotes to the works of Plato. He said this because Plato, using the voice of his mentor Socrates, wrote about many diverse topics in great style and detail, from complex topics on metaphysics to fundamental questions about ethics and justice. The value of Plato's works is so wide-ranging that some have even considered them to represent an important source of self-therapy (Marinoff, 1999). Indeed, the notion of self-criticism involving a process of not blindly accepting one's own opinions (or those of others) as true was central to Plato's use of the Socratic method and his view that the unexamined life was not worth living. And perhaps this notion is no better illustrated than in his famous allegory of the cave (Heidegger, 1931/2002).

In Plato's *Republic*, Socrates tried to convey to his colleague Glaucon the difference between opinions and truth by describing a situation in which adults, imprisoned since childhood, were living in a cave. For these individuals, the world that existed was limited to seeing moving shadows of objects along the cave walls and never the objects that were the real cause of those shadows. Hence, these individuals lived in a world of mere opinions and distortions. Although this situation would normally distress any adult, these prisoners were not necessarily disturbed by their illusory existence because they had lived in this underground world of shadows and distortions for most of their mortal existence. In essence, they had gotten too accustomed to these distortions and never had reason to question or doubt their understanding of the world. Then one day, according to Socrates, these prisoners were released from the cave. As they ascended to the opening of the cave, they experienced acute pain as they were struck by the brilliance of the sunlight. Thus, engaging oneself in the self-critical process of discovering truth was an act that Plato appreciated as central to living a worthwhile life but that was also necessarily challenging and even threatening to most. Only as time passed did these former prisoners begin to realize that they had falsely perceived shadows as objects, rather than as the reflections of objects. This self-critical process ultimately involves an emerging sense of enlightenment and true awareness of the self and world. Although the meaning of this story has multiple layers and dimensions, one can clearly see how the allegory represents Plato's great appreciation for the value of self-critique as a way for rational individuals to obtain true and essential knowledge of themselves and the world around them. In that regard, self-criticism is a constructive process, rather than a destructive one.

The Problem of Unbound Self-Enhancement: Aristotle's Theory of the Golden Mean

Just as for Plato an absence of self-criticism was a major limitation to truly knowing oneself, an excess of self-enhancement can be said to have been a similar concern for Aristotle in the search for the good life. Among his contemporaries were Epicurus and his followers, who held the view that individuals were largely constituted by appetites and passions. According to Epicurus, the path to the good life was determined by maximizing pleasurable experiences over painful experiences. Thus, a key focus was on promoting and garnering positive experiences for the self (Jones, 1989). In contrast to those who followed Epicurus and emphasized the maximization of pleasure or self-enhancing experiences, Aristotle emphasized the importance of keeping such self-enhancing pursuits and activities in check by emphasizing balance and right proportion. This focus is most clearly represented in Aristotle's *Nicomachean Ethics*.

In the *Nicomachean Ethics*, Aristotle began with the question, What is the end of man? His answer: an activity of soul that is in conformity with virtue, with the end being happiness. For Aristotle, living a virtuous life was central to the pursuit of individual happiness. But, how does one live virtuously? Aristotle began with the notion that there are several identifiable virtues of man. Among them, he noted the virtues of courage, liberality, pride, friendliness, wittiness, justice, and temperance.

For Aristotle, not only a lack or deficiency of character but also an excess of character could prevent one from living a life in accordance with virtue. Thus, consider the notion of courage as a virtue. On the one hand, if one runs away or avoids a challenge that one is more than able to handle, then it may be said that one possesses cowardice. For example, a man who quickly runs away when he is teased or made a joke of by lesser others may be said to show cowardice because he does not stand up and respond to such inappropriate actions even though he is capable of doing so. On the other hand, if a person stands firm in the face of a challenge he or she does not have resources to handle, then it may be said that the individual is rash or foolish. For example, a man who refuses to flee a situation in which he is about to be physically threatened by a mob of individuals would be said to exhibit foolishness. Within Aristotle's doctrine of the mean, therefore, the truly courageous individual is one who demonstrates the ability to engage in the proper proportion or amount of courageousness as determined by the context and resources at hand. Thus, the virtue of courage resides between the vice of cowardice (not having or demonstrating sufficient courage in appropriate situations) and the vice of foolhardiness (having or demonstrating too much courage in inappropriate situations). What is important is that for Aristotle, the pursuit of *eudaimonea*, in contrast to the Epicurean pursuit of pleasure, required individuals to keep self-enhancing tendencies bounded and in check by evaluating the goodness of those characteristics against the outcomes they produced (Barnes, 1982). Yet, it is worth noting that some self-critical tendencies were also considered to represent potential virtues. For example, Aristotle considered shame as a virtue that resided between the extremes of disgrace (showing too much shame) and shamelessness (showing too little shame) when bad actions are committed by a good man. In these ways, Aristotle appreciated the possibility that all virtues could easily become vices if the proper amount was not expressed in different situations.

MODERN VIEWS OF (DYSFUNCTIONAL) SELF-CRITICISM AND (FUNCTIONAL) SELF-ENHANCEMENT

Whereas classical views may have been more open to the idea of self-criticism and self-enhancement as being adaptive and maladaptive, respectively, modern views have tended to reflect the opposite idea (see Figure 1.1).

From Psychoanalysis to Cognitive Theory: The Tyranny of the Bad and Negative Self

In modern times, many leading psychological theories of psychopathology hold that negative schemas of the self are a major contributor to or cause of mental illness. Within classical psychoanalytic theory, Freud (1933/1965, 1940/1964) believed the psyche comprised three distinct functions: the id, the ego, and the superego. When these different functions operate without extreme conflict, then anxiety is avoided. However, in some cases, intrapsychic conflict arises and anxiety or neurosis can result. Thus, a strict and unforgiving superego that quickly squelches individual passions and desires to attain a desired object can lead to emotional disturbance. Indeed, several psychodynamic theorists following Freud expanded on this point, arguing that self-critical behaviors were the root of psychopathology. For example, Horney (1950) referred to the "tyranny of the should" and argued that individuals become neurotic when they are driven by critical inner commands to satisfy some idealized image of the self. Along those lines, humanistic psychologists have also focused on how negative perceptions of the self as deficient, undesirable, or unworthy lead to poor health and an inability to reach one's maximum potential (Maslow, 1954; Rogers, 1951, 1961).

In addition to psychodynamic and humanistic theories, modern cognitive theories have tended to emphasize self-critical behaviors, broadly de-

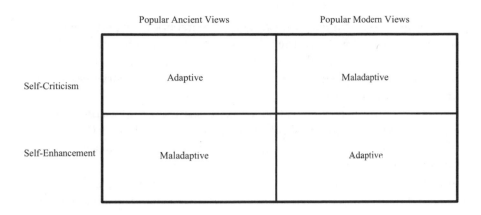

	Popular Ancient Views	Popular Modern Views
Self-Criticism	Adaptive	Maladaptive
Self-Enhancement	Maladaptive	Adaptive

Figure 1.1. An example of how views of self-criticism and self-enhancement have changed across the ages.

fined, as antecedents to mental disturbance. For example, Beck (1976) proposed that a pessimistic triad involving negative schemas about the self, future, and the world was causally related to emotional disorders. Over the years, however, cognitive models have tended to focus most of their attention on negative schemas involving the self. For example, over three decades, works by Seligman and his colleagues (Garber & Seligman, 1980; Peterson, Maier, & Seligman, 1993; Seligman, 1975) have shown that holding a pessimistic explanatory style for understanding why events happen to individuals has an impact on psychological and physical well-being. Beyond a pessimistic explanatory style, researchers have also found other negative self-schemas involved in instigating, intensifying, or reinforcing the experience of various emotional disturbances (e.g., Blatt, 2004; Ellis, 1962, 2001; Nolen-Hoeksema, 2003). In all, growing evidence points to self-critical behaviors as a cause of or concomitant with maladjustment and negative emotional outcomes.

Thinking Positively and Feeling Good: The Emergence of Positive Psychology

Just as researchers have found self-criticism to represent a maladaptive force in modern life, other researchers have found self-enhancement to represent an adaptive force linked to good health and well-being (Taylor, 1989). In that regard, Taylor and Brown's (1988) seminal review of the empirical literature on self-enhancement has become the center of much interest and discussion over the past two decades. On the basis of their review, these researchers found that healthy individuals, in contrast to unhealthy or distressed individuals, often engage in a variety of self-enhancing behaviors (e.g., overly positive self-evaluations, exaggerated perceptions of personal control, and unrealistic optimism for the self). As a result, self-enhancement has become a prominent psychological variable for understanding why and how individuals remain positive and resilient to negative experiences (Hoyle, Kernis, Leary, & Baldwin, 1999).

The importance of self-enhancement has been underscored in more recent years with the emergence of a positive focus in psychology (Carr, 2004). Building on earlier works that focused on trying to understand ways in which individuals may optimally develop and interact with their changing environments (e.g., Antonovsky, 1979; Jahoda, 1958; Maslow, 1954; Rogers, 1961), Seligman and Csikszentmihalyi (2000) argued for the development of a positive psychology that had as its aim "to begin to catalyze a change in the focus of psychology from preoccupation only with repairing the worst things in life to also building positive qualities" (p. 5). Similar points have also been raised by other researchers interested in studying positive aspects of human behavior and functioning (e.g., McCullough & Snyder, 2000; Sheldon & King, 2001; cf. Chang & Sanna, 2003). From the standpoint of positive psychology, it is crucial not only to study factors that are related to psychological dysfunction but also to study self-enhancement variables such as optimism and hope that have been related to positive psychological functioning and to other character strengths (Aspinwall & Staudinger, 2003; Peterson, 2006; Peterson & Seligman, 2004; Snyder & Lopez, 2007). Moreover, there has been growing interest in positive psychological applications to foster greater happiness and well-being in individuals, groups, and communities (Linley & Joseph, 2004).

CULTURE'S MANY LENSES: A DIFFERENT LOOK AT SELF-CRITICISM AND SELF-ENHANCEMENT

The modern notion of self-criticism as bad and self-enhancement as good may be more common in the West and less common in the East (Kitayama, Markus, Matsumoto, & Norasakkunkit, 1997; cf. Takano & Osaka, 1999). Western cultures are typically considered to be individualistic given their emphasis on attending to the needs of the self over others (Greenwald, 1980; Weisz, Rothbaum, & Blackburn, 1984). Thus, for most Westerners the attainment of personal happiness rather than group happiness is highly regarded and sought after, as codified and expressed in historical works such as the Declaration of Independence of the United States. Therefore, it is not too surprising that in Western cultures, maybe especially in the United States (Brandt, 1970; Held, 2002), conditions associated with a lack of self-interest, such as anhedonia, an inability to experience personal pleasures, and dependency, a condition defined by a tendency to subordinate one's needs to those of others, are seen typically as signs of psychological dysfunction or mental illness (American Psychiatric Association, 2000). Self-enhancement for Westerners is thus believed to represent a constructive process that allows them to maintain and support the independent self (Taylor & Brown, 1988).

Eastern cultures (i.e., cultures found in many Asian countries) have been considered collectivist, given their focus on fostering a view of the self as fundamentally interrelated with significant others (Doi, 1971/1973; Markus & Kitayama, 1991). Hence, attending to significant others, harmonious interdependence with them, and fitting in not only are valued but also are often strongly expected among members living within these cultures. Thus, for example, in contrast to many Western psychological approaches that focus largely on treating and strengthening internal attributes of an independent self (Prilleltensky, 1989; Sarason, 1981), a key objective of some indigenous Japanese therapies is to help clients overcome and transcend a focus on the immediate and independent self (e.g., Morita, 1928/1998). One finds that the self fostered in Eastern cultures, as in Japan, is interdependent with significant others, such that important others "participate actively and continuously in the definition of the interdependent self" (Markus & Kitayama, 1991, p. 227). Therefore, self-criticism for Easterners is believed to represent a constructive process that allows them to maintain and support the interdependent self or the group. Taken together, these culturally different patterns indicate a need to consider more inclusive models and a need to situate the field's understanding of self-criticism and self-enhancement.

OVERVIEW OF THE PRESENT VOLUME

What this brief philosophical and historical examination of self-criticism and self-enhancement shows is that self-criticism and self-enhancement represent patterns of thought found throughout history. In addition, it also shows that "negative" constructs such as self-criticism may not always be bad and "positive" constructs such as self-enhancement may not always be good (Chang, 2001). With that in mind, the contributors to this volume were asked to reflect on different and complex (sometimes complementary, sometimes competing) truths regarding the usefulness of self-criticism and self-enhancement on the basis of their own theoretical approaches, scientific investigations, and clinical work involving these robust psychological constructs.

The present volume consists of three main parts. Part I focuses on popular notions of self-enhancement as good and self-criticism as bad. In chapter 2, Margaret A. Marshall and Jonathon D. Brown start with a new look at Taylor and Brown's (1988) original contention that self-enhancement behaviors, or positive illusions, are psychologically beneficial. They then provide a careful review and evaluation of recent findings related to the study of positive illusions and show how these findings are consistent with a causal model of adaptation, resilience, and growth involving positive affective states, interpersonal relationships, and coping. In chapter 3, Suzanne C. Segerstrom and Abbey R. Roach focus on the important role of self-enhancement in physical health. Their review of the literature shows that self-enhancement variables such as self-esteem, optimism, and control are frequently linked to a wide range of positive health outcomes, including lower cardiovascular reactivity, better recovery from surgery, and greater longevity. In chapter 4, Christian Holle and Rick Ingram focus on the psychological hazards of self-criticism. On the basis of a review of major clinical models of self-criticism, these authors discuss how and why self-criticism is so strongly linked to affective disorders. These authors specifically examine commonalities between popular cognitive and psychodynamic models of depression, as well as note the importance of recent works on perfectionism. In chapter 5, Jill M. Holm-Denoma, Ainhoa Otamendi, and Thomas E. Joiner Jr. focus on examining the damaging effects of self-criticism in the interpersonal realm. They discuss why self-critical individuals often experience struggles in a variety of social domains, including marital and romantic relationships and parent–child dyads, and consider possible mechanisms that might account for these damaging effects.

Complementing the first part, Part II focuses on the less popular but equally compelling notions of self-criticism as good and self-enhancement as bad. In chapter 6, Julie K. Norem focuses on the construct of defensive pessimism as a positive self-critical tool. Her review of the literature on defensive pessimism shows that it is linked to positive outcomes for individuals by helping them to generate the necessary motivation and energy to pursue a variety of performance goals. In chapter 7, Takeshi Hamamura and Steven J. Heine focus on an intriguing discussion of the positive functions of self-criticism in non-Westerners. These authors argue that for Japanese, self-criticism is strongly and positively tied to self-improvement and face-maintenance processes, which are different from the function of self-criticism found in Westerners. That is, for Japanese, unlike North Americans, self-criticism is often used to improve themselves to avoid potential negative outcomes, including critical evaluations from others. In chapter 8, C. Randall Colvin and Robert Griffo focus on the potential costs of self-enhancement. These authors begin with a discussion of the different conceptualizations of self-enhancement in the literature and end with a review of recent findings pointing to various situations in which self-enhancement has been found to be associated with narcissism and poor psychological adjustment. In chapter 9, William M. P. Klein and Katrina L. Cooper focus on the physical health costs of self-enhancement. These authors begin with an examination of some of the methodological problems that have existed in past studies on the link between self-enhancement and health outcomes, review findings regarding the effect of self-enhancement on health outcomes, and end with a discussion of potential factors that may moderate the link between self-enhancement biases and negative health outcomes.

To integrate the rich and diverse views represented in the previous two parts, Part III focuses on an appreciation of self-criticism and self-enhancement as both good and bad. In chapter 10, James A. Shepperd, Patrick J. Carroll, and Kate Sweeny examine the function of self-enhancement and self-criticism as it changes across different (temporal) contexts. In chapter 11, Constantine Sedikides and Michelle Luke provide a broad conceptual framework for understanding the complex conditions around which self-criticism and self-enhancement processes may operate in a constructive or symbiotic fashion, and when they may operate in a destructive—whether parasitic or antisymbiotic—fashion.

Part IV addresses some of the clinical implications of self-criticism and self-enhancement. In chapter 12, James L. Pretzer focuses on ways to help clients who have little to no self-esteem. He begins with an emphasis on the need to understand the client's conceptualization of self-esteem-related problems and then moves on to a careful discussion of how therapists may help their clients to develop a more healthy perception of themselves. In chapter 13, Raymond M. Bergner focuses on ways to promote adaptive versus maladaptive self-criticism. He begins with an examination of self-criticism as represented within the clinical context and then moves on to a discussion of different clinical strategies that may be used by therapists to foster more adaptive outcomes, including concepts and skills related to adaptive forms of self-criticism.

The volume concludes with a look to the future. In chapter 14, myself, Rita Chang, Lawrence J. Sanna, and Allison M. Kade discuss potential new directions in the study of self-enhancement and self-criticism. They focus on the need to incorporate more inclusive and integrative frameworks that may generate new models of self-criticism and self-enhancement in future research and practice. As a starting point, they explore recent works related to the study of perfectionism and contingencies of self-worth.

LEARNING FROM THE PAST AND PRESENT

Before concluding this section, I would like to share two experiences I had, one involving a patient and the other involving a student, that helped transform my appreciation of self-criticism and self-enhancement as interesting theoretical constructs into a personal recognition of these processes as meaningful, embodied, and involving social consequences.

The Patient and the Student

As part of my training in the doctoral clinical psychology program at the State University of New York at Stony Brook, I had to complete a 1-year internship at an American Psychological Association–accredited site. I was fortunate enough and honored to have been selected to do my internship at Bellevue Hospital Center–New York University Medical Center (the same place my father had worked at as a forensic chemist during my childhood). During my year, I had opportunities to work with a wide variety of patients, from children with severe school problems associated with attention-deficit/hyperactivity disorder to adults dealing with debilitating depression and chronic medical illness. But, of all my patients during my clinical training year, one stood out: Ms. X. Ms. X was the first hospital patient I was assigned to at Bellevue. She was a young lady of Asian decent, and she was particularly interested in working with an Asian intern or therapist. What made this case particularly intriguing for me was that I could not fully understand why she had been coming to Bellevue for psychological treatment for 4 years. She was originally admitted with a presentation of depressed mood and anxiety. Later, during the course of her first year of treatment, she was diagnosed with dysthymic disorder, a condition indicated by chronic depressed mood. Indeed, Ms. X reported that her self-confidence was always a bit shaky and that she often found herself dwelling on negative aspects of herself and her decisions, which in turn led to frequent creative blocks. But, what was so difficult for me to clinically grasp was that Ms. X was an artist, a very successful one at that. Despite having only recently graduated from art school, she had already been selected for a number of prestigious awards and fellowships in the arts, and her works were exhibited with some regularity at major galleries in and outside the United States.

The student, Mr. Y, was in the process of finishing a degree from a highly selective Ivy League school when he applied for admission into the clinical program of a leading university, where I was a member of the admissions committee. He had excellent academic marks and showed great promise of becoming a stellar researcher (e.g., numerous research awards, a few authored peer-reviewed journal publications, several scientific conference presentations). The supporting letters for him by well-known and highly regarded researchers were among the best I have ever read. I was so impressed by everything I saw and read about this individual that I was ready to welcome him to our program. But some of the other members had very different perceptions. In describing himself, Mr. Y talked about how he was often "self-critical," not being very satisfied with his efforts until his goals or objectives were satisfactorily reached. Some of the members took this personal disclosure of self-criticism as a potential red flag and thought this applicant would be a liability if we were to accept him. They viewed Mr. Y as a negative person who would have a potential negative or disruptive influence on peers, faculty, and the program itself. This perception emerged among some of the members of the committee despite the fact that there was not a single piece of evidence to base such predictions on.

What the patient and the student have in common is that they embodied for me the clear and present danger of living in a modern world in which people (no matter how intelligent) hold singular views about self-criticism as always maladaptive and self-enhancement as always adaptive. (I return to Ms. X and Mr. Y in the final chapter of this volume.)

Final Remarks

It is clear from past and present notions of self-criticism and self-enhancement that these constructs involve complex ideas that are sometimes competing and sometimes complementary. Because these notions represent theoretical constructions, caution, if not skepticism, is needed regarding any singular meaning or value of self-criticism and self-enhancement across different contexts. As a result, this volume's central goal is to make more explicit some of the complexities and commonalities related to understanding how, when, and why self-criticism and self-enhancement play a central role in the way people shape and direct their lives each day. All of the contributors of this volume are to be congratulated for not only providing clear and compelling discussions of each construct from their particular perspective but also appreciating alternative, often competing, views. Indeed, the works presented in this volume are a testimony to the fact that greater appreciation for these constructs can be garnered to yield a better understanding of them in both future research and practice.

REFERENCES

American Psychiatric Association. (2000). *Diagnostic and statistical manual of mental disorders* (4th ed., text rev.). Washington, DC: Author.

Antonovsky, A. (1979). *Health, stress and coping.* San Francisco: Jossey-Bass.

Aspinwall, L. G., & Staudinger, U. M. (Eds.). (2003). *A psychology of human strengths: Fundamental questions and future directions for a positive psychology.* Washington, DC: American Psychological Association.

Barnes, J. (1982). *Aristotle.* New York: Oxford University Press.

Beck, A. T. (1976). *Cognitive therapy and the emotional disorders.* New York: International Universities Press.

Blatt, S. J. (2004). *Experiences of depression: Theoretical, clinical, and research perspectives.* Washington, DC: American Psychological Association.

Brandt, L. W. (1970). American psychology. *American Psychologist, 25,* 1091–1093.

Carr, A. (2004). *Positive psychology: The science of happiness and human strengths.* New York: Brunner-Routledge.

Chang, E. C. (Ed.). (2001). *Optimism and pessimism: Implications for theory, research, and practice.* Washington, DC: American Psychological Association.

Chang, E. C., & Sanna, L. J. (Eds.). (2003). *Virtue, vice, and personality: The complexity of behavior*. Washington, DC: American Psychological Association.

Doi, T. (1973). *The anatomy of dependence* (J. Bester, Trans.). Tokyo, Japan: Kodansha. (Original work published in 1971)

Ellis, A. (1962). *Reason and emotion in psychotherapy*. Oxford, England: Lyle Stuart.

Ellis, A. (2001). *Overcoming destructive beliefs, feelings, and behaviors: New directions for rational emotive behavior therapy*. Amherst, NY: Prometheus Books.

Freud, S. (1964). *The standard edition of the complete psychological works of Sigmund Freud: Vol. 23. An outline of psychoanalysis*. (J. Strachey, Ed. & Trans.). London: Hogarth Press. (Original work published 1940)

Freud, S. (1965). *New introductory lectures on psychoanalysis*. New York: Norton. (Original work published 1933)

Garber, J., & Seligman, M. E. P. (Eds.). (1980). *Human helplessness: Theory and applications*. New York: Academic Press.

Greenwald, A. G. (1980). The totalitarian ego: Fabrication and revision of personal history. *American Psychologist, 35,* 603–618.

Heidegger, M. (2002). *The essence of truth: On Plato's cave allegory and Theaetetus* (T. Sadler, Trans.). New York: Continuum. (Original work published 1931)

Held, B. S. (2002). The tyranny of the positive attitude in America: Observation and speculation. *Journal of Clinical Psychology, 58,* 965–991.

Horney, K. (1950). *Neurosis and human growth: The struggle toward self-realization*. New York: Norton.

Hoyle, R. H., Kernis, M. H., Leary, M. R., & Baldwin, M. W. (1999). *Selfhood: Identity, esteem, regulation*. Boulder, CO: Westview Press.

Jahoda, M. (1958). *Current concepts of positive mental health*. New York: Basic Books.

Jones, H. (1989). *The Epicurean tradition*. London: Duckworth.

Kitayama, S., Markus, H. R., Matsumoto, H., & Norasakkunkit, V. (1997). Individual and collective processes in the construction of the self: Self-enhancement in the United States and self-criticism in Japan. *Journal of Personality and Social Psychology, 72,* 1245–1267.

Linley, P. A., & Joseph, S. (Eds.). (2004). *Positive psychology in practice*. Hoboken, NJ: Wiley.

Marinoff, L. (1999). *Plato not Prozac! Applying eternal wisdom to everyday problems*. New York: HarperCollins.

Markus, H. R., & Kitayama, S. (1991). Culture and the self: Implications for cognition, emotion, and motivation. *Psychological Review, 98,* 224–253.

Maslow, A. (1954). *Motivation and personality*. New York: Harper & Row.

McCullough, M. E., & Snyder, C. R. (2000). Classical sources of human strength: Revisiting an old home and building a new one. *Journal of Social and Clinical Psychology, 19,* 1–10.

Morita, S. (1998). *Morita therapy and the true nature of anxiety-based disorders (shinkeishitsu)* (A. Kondo, Trans.). New York: State University of New York Press. (Original work published in 1928)

Nolen-Hoeksema, S. (2003). *Women who think too much: How to break free of overthinking and reclaim your life*. New York: Holt.

Peterson, C. (2006). *A primer in positive psychology*. New York: Oxford University Press.

Peterson, C., Maier, S. F., & Seligman, M. E. P. (1993). *Learned helplessness: A theory for the age of personal control*. New York: Oxford University Press.

Peterson, C., & Seligman, M. E. P. (2004). *Character strengths and virtues: A handbook and classification*. Washington, DC: American Psychological Association; and New York: Oxford University Press.

Prilleltensky, I. (1989). Psychology and the status quo. *American Psychologist, 44,* 795–802.

Rogers, C. (1951). *Client-centered therapy: Its current practice, implications, and theory*. Boston: Houghton Mifflin.

Rogers, C. (1961). *On becoming a person*. Boston: Houghton Mifflin.

Sarason, S. B. (1981). An asocial psychology and a misdirected clinical psychology. *American Psychologist, 36,* 827–836.

Seligman, M. E. P. (1975). *Helplessness: On depression, development, and death*. San Francisco: Freeman.

Seligman, M. E. P., & Csikszentmihalyi, M. (2000). Positive psychology: An introduction. *American Psychologist, 55,* 5–14.

Sheldon, K. M., & King, L. A. (2001). Why positive psychology is necessary. *American Psychologist, 56,* 216–217.

Snyder, C. R., & Lopez, S. J. (2007). *Positive psychology: The scientific and practical explorations of human strengths*. Thousand Oaks, CA: Sage.

Takano, Y., & Osaka, E. (1999). An unsupported common view: Comparing Japan and U.S. on individualism/collectivism. *Asian Journal of Social Psychology, 2,* 311–341.

Taylor, S. E. (1989). *Positive illusions: Creative self-deception and the healthy mind*. New York: Basic Books.

Taylor, S. E., & Brown, J. D. (1988). Illusion and well being: A social psychological perspective on mental health. *Psychological Bulletin, 103,* 193–210.

Weisz, J. R., Rothbaum, F. M., & Blackburn, T. C. (1984). Standing out and standing in: The psychology of control in America and Japan. *American Psychologist, 39,* 955–969.

Whitehead, A. N. (1929). *Process and reality: An essay in cosmology*. New York: Macmillan.

I

SELF-ENHANCEMENT
AS GOOD,
SELF-CRITICISM AS BAD

2

ON THE PSYCHOLOGICAL BENEFITS OF SELF-ENHANCEMENT

MARGARET A. MARSHALL AND JONATHON D. BROWN

Nothing is easier than self-deceit. For what each man wishes, he also believes to be true.

—Demosthenes, c. 383–322 BCE

How well do people know themselves? Are they equally aware of their strengths and faults, or do they exaggerate their virtues and dismiss their shortcomings? And what should they think? Are they better off knowing what they are really like or are they better served by embellishing themselves? In 1988, Taylor and Brown examined these questions. Following a comprehensive review of the literature, they reached two conclusions. First, most people do not hold accurate views of themselves. Instead, they inflate their virtues, exaggerate their ability to bring about desired outcomes, and believe their future will be rosier than base rate data can justify. Second, if not too extreme, these biases are generally advantageous, promoting a variety of criteria normally associated with adaptation and health. Taylor and Brown (1988) coined the term *positive illusions* to refer to these beliefs. The term *illusion* was chosen to highlight a simple fact: In many cases, these beliefs are simply too good to be true. As an example, consider that 75% of American newlyweds believe their marriage will last throughout their lives, yet the divorce rate in America exceeds 50% (Heaton & Albrecht, 1991).

The thesis put forth by Taylor and Brown (1988) garnered a great deal of attention and generated a good deal of controversy (Colvin & Block, 1994;

Shedler, Mayman, & Manis, 1993; Taylor & Brown, 1994a, 1994b). Our goal in this chapter is to review some of this research and integrate the more recent findings with Taylor and Brown's original position.

THE CASE FOR ACCURACY

Accurate self-knowledge has long been seen as essential for effective functioning. For example, Jahoda (1958) defined the mentally healthy person as one who is capable of perceiving the self as it actually is, without distorting one's perceptions to fit one's wishes, and Maslow (1950) wrote that healthy individuals are able to accept themselves and their own nature, with all of its discrepancies from their ideal image.

It is easy to see how such a thesis developed. Grossly inaccurate self-views are detrimental to well-being. People who hallucinate or experience delusions of grandeur are not paragons of mental health. Whether other, less extreme divergences from reality are detrimental to well-being is another matter. Taylor and Brown's theory applies only to mildly distorted self-views that paint a self-portrait just slightly better than reality warrants. At no time did they state or imply that excessive self-enhancement is better than moderate self-enhancement. This point is often overlooked by those who have criticized their approach (e.g., Colvin & Block, 1994).

BENEFITS OF POSITIVE ILLUSIONS

Theoretical positions aside, testing whether positive illusions have costs or benefits requires that one first establish standards for judging what's good or bad. Taylor and Brown (1988) dealt with this issue by identifying four commonly agreed on criteria of mental health: (a) subjective feelings of happiness, life satisfaction, and contentment; (b) the ability to engage in meaningful and productive work; (c) the ability to form stable and fulfilling interpersonal relationships; and (d) the capacity to face life's challenges and potentially grow from them.

Of the four criteria, achievement-related outcomes appear to provide the weakest support for Taylor and Brown's formulation. Although some studies find that positive beliefs in one's ability promote task performance, other studies find no effect or the opposite to be true (Aspinwall & Taylor, 1992; Robins & Beer, 2001; Wright, 2000). Marshall and Brown (2004) argued that some of this inconsistency may be due to the difficulty of the task. Positive beliefs in one's ability ought to influence task performance by affecting how long and hard people try (Bandura, 1997). Easy tasks require little in the way of effort and persistence, so positive beliefs in one's ability ought to have little effect on performance of easy tasks. Extremely difficult tasks may also

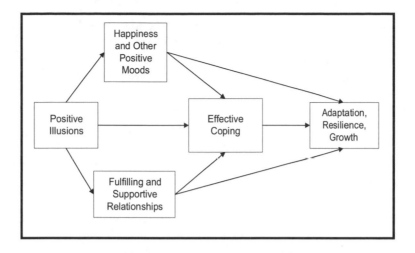

Figure 2.1. Positive illusions and psychological well-being.

fail to reveal the power of positive beliefs if people can't succeed no matter how hard or long they try. As a consequence, moderately difficult tasks would seem to provide the proper forum for testing the positive-illusions framework.

Evidence for the other three criteria (i.e., happiness, satisfying interpersonal relationships, and adaptation and growth) is clearer and more abundant. Figure 2.1 presents a heuristic device for organizing research in this area. The figure shows that positive illusions promote adaptation, resilience, and growth indirectly, via their influence on positive affective states, interpersonal relationships, and coping. In the sections that follow, we review evidence pertinent to this model.

Positive Illusions, Happiness, and Well-Being

After years of focusing on the "negative" side of psychological life, psychologists have recently turned their attention to studying psychological health and well-being (Seligman & Csikszentmihalyi, 2000; Sheldon & King, 2001). Among the many topics being examined are happiness, contentment, and life satisfaction (Diener & Seligman, 2002). Across cultures, the way people evaluate themselves predicts these emotional states (Diener & Diener, 1995). People who think well of themselves, believe they are capable of bringing about desired outcomes, and are optimistic about the future are happier and more satisfied with their lives than are those who lack these perceptions, even when these perceptions are illusory.

Positive emotion, in turn, promotes adaptation and well-being. Compared with unhappy people, happy people are more creative, sociable, and energetic, and more caring, helpful, and involved in community affairs

(Lyubomirsky, King, & Diener, 2005). They also live longer. Danner, Snowdon, and Friesen (2001) examined autobiographies of 180 Catholic nuns, composed when the nuns were in their early 20s. Each sister was asked to write a short sketch of her life at the time she entered the convent, and these autobiographies were later coded for the presence of positive emotional content. Women who expressed the most positive emotion lived nearly 7 years longer than did those who expressed the least positive emotion. It is especially notable that these effects appeared more than 50 years after the essays were written.

Frederickson's (1998, 2001) build-and-broaden model seeks to explain why positive emotional states are beneficial. The model proposes that positive emotional states promote well-being (a) by leading people to think more flexibly and creatively, (b) by increasing activity level and social contacts, and (c) by directly reducing cardiovascular reactivity to stressful life events. In combination, these processes help happy people cope better with life stress than those who are more dysphoric or dyspeptic (Folkman & Moskowitz, 2000).

Positive Illusions, Social Relationships, and Well-Being

When Taylor and Brown published their findings in 1988, there was virtually no research on the role of illusions in romantic relationships. Since then, research in this area has proliferated, and three findings have emerged. First, people view their relationship partners in unrealistically positive terms. They believe their partner is better than most other people, and they view their partner more positively than their partners view themselves or are viewed by others (Gagné & Lydon, 2004; Murray & Holmes, 1997; Murray, Holmes, & Griffin, 1996a, 1996b). Second, couples view their relationship in unrealistically positive terms. They believe their love is stronger than other people's love and that the problems that beset other people's relationships, such as poor communication skills or incompatible interests, pose less of a threat to their own relationship (Buunk & van der Eijnden, 1997; Rusbult, Van Lange, Wildschut, Yovetich, & Verette, 2000). Third, couples believe that they have more control over their relationship's outcomes than do most other people and that they are more apt to remain together than are most other couples (Fowers, Lyons, Montel, & Shaked, 2001; Murray & Holmes, 1997). Moreover, this relationship superiority bias occurs across cultures (Endo, Heine, & Lehman, 2000). In short, when thinking about their relationships, people exhibit the same three biases Taylor and Brown (1988) identified as being characteristic of self-perceptions: They view their relationship in overly positive terms, exaggerate their ability to bring about desired outcomes, and are unrealistically optimistic.

These tendencies predict relationship success. People who idealize their partner and view their relationship in overly positive terms are more satisfied with their relationship, more committed to it, and more apt to remain to-gether than are those who are more accurate and balanced (Murray & Holmes, 1993, 1997, 1999; Murray et al., 1996a, 1996b). The effect is strongest when both partners exhibit these tendencies, providing evidence for an effect we call *illusion collusion*. Simply put, happy, satisfied, and committed couples support one another's positive biases and illusions.

Doing so benefits not only the relationship but also health and well-being. A wealth of evidence shows that relationships are good medicine. People who turn to someone in times of trouble cope better than do those who go it alone (Cohen & Wills, 1985). When it comes to buffering the adverse effects of stress, the perception of support seems to be most impor-tant. Those who believe they are loved and supported are better able to with-stand life stress than are those who feel unloved and unsupported. Positive illusions predict these perceptions. People who think well of themselves and are optimistic are especially apt to perceive their relationships as being strong and supportive (Bonanno, Rennicke, & Dekel, 2005; see also Brissette, Scheier, & Carver, 2002).

Positive Illusions, Stress, and Coping

Most people face trouble in their lives at one point or another. They may lose their jobs, confront a natural disaster, be victimized by crime, or grieve the loss of a loved one. The manner in which people deal with stress-ful events like these has been a hotbed of research activity for nearly 50 years. The upshot of this research is that people are exceptionally resilient. Although many people are initially shaken when stressful life events occur, most recover in a relatively short time (Brickman, Coates, & Janoff-Bulman, 1978; Diener, 1994; Schulz & Decker, 1985; Taylor, 1983). Some even re-port that their lives changed for the better. For example, many cancer pa-tients feel a greater sense of purpose, increased spirituality, and more appre-ciation for friends and family (Carver & Antoni, 2004; Taylor, 1983; Taylor, Kemeny, Bower, Gruenewald, & Reed, 2000). Of course, not everyone copes well with adversity, and some people require counseling or other forms of treatment to help them adjust, but most people who face major life events return to a level of psychological functioning that is at least as positive as the one they enjoyed before the event occurred.

Coping with traumatic experiences often involves restoring a positive sense of self-worth, reasserting control over one's life, finding meaning in the experience, and reclaiming an optimistic view of the future. In other words, recovery from traumatic events often involves restoring the positive illusions that were in place prior to the experience. Positive illusions drive the recov-ery process. People regain a favorable self-image, recapture perceived con-trol, and reclaim optimism by construing events in overly positive ways. For example, they believe that they are coping better than are most other victims and have more control over the course of their disease than they actually do. They also construct a view of the future that is unrealistically optimistic in light of their condition. These illusions are subtle and are responsive to the realities of the situations individuals face, but they are also at least somewhat unrealistic (Taylor et al., 2000).

The benefits of positive illusions are strongest when self-reports of distress are gathered, but the effect also occurs when more objective indicators are examined. Bonanno and colleagues explored coping and adaptation in a group of civilians exposed to urban combat during Bosnia's civil war (Bonanno, Field, Kovacevic, & Kaltman, 2002). Mental health professionals examined each participant, and their ratings of psychological well-being were correlated with the participants' tendency to view themselves in overly positive terms. A positive relationship emerged, indicating that self-enhancement biases predicted well-being under times of stress. A second study found a similar pattern among people coping with the premature death of a spouse, and a follow-up study found a similar effect among New Yorkers coping with the aftermath of the 9/11 terrorist attacks (Bonanno et al., 2005).

Research on optimism and coping provides additional evidence for the link between illusions and well-being. A large body of research shows that optimism plays a key role in how people cope with life-threatening experiences (Carver et al., 1993). For example, in one study of men undergoing coronary artery bypass surgery, Scheier and colleagues (1989) found that optimists recovered more quickly from surgery and were faster to resume their normal activities than were pessimists.

Other studies have found that optimism confers benefits even when it is unrealistic. Taylor et al. (1992) studied 550 gay men who had tested for the presence of the AIDS virus (HIV). About half of the men were HIV positive; the other half were HIV negative. After receiving their test results, the men were asked to indicate their agreement with a number of statements (e.g., "I feel safe from AIDS because I've developed an immunity"; "I think my immune system [is] more capable of fighting the AIDS virus than are the immune systems of other gay men"). These items were combined to create an index of how optimistic the men were that they would not develop AIDS. In realistic terms, people who are HIV positive are much more likely to develop AIDS than are people who are HIV negative. Nevertheless, men who knew they were HIV positive were significantly more optimistic about not developing AIDS than were men who knew they were HIV negative. Moreover, this optimism was linked with lower levels of psychological distress and the adoption of health-promoting behaviors, such as a proper diet, exercise, and rest. In this study, then, even unrealistic optimism was beneficial.

Lazarus and his colleagues have provided a useful framework for understanding these effects (Lazarus & Folkman, 1984; Lazarus & Launier, 1978). These investigators have identified two types of coping strategies. One coping strategy, termed *problem-focused coping*, involves taking active steps to deal with the source of stress. For example, a person who is laid off from work may immediately start looking for another job. This coping style is problem-focused because the person's efforts are directed at resolving the source of stress. A second coping strategy, termed *emotion-focused coping*, attempts to manage the emotional distress that arises from a stressful experience. Sometimes emotion-focused coping is constructive (e.g., under stressful circumstances, a person may exercise to alleviate anxiety); other times it is destructive (e.g., a person under stress can abuse alcohol or drugs in an effort to reduce anxiety).

Which of these strategies do optimists use? Numerous studies have found that optimists are more inclined than pessimists to use problem-focused coping strategies (Aspinwall & Brunhart, 1996; Carver et al., 1993; Scheier et al., 1989; Scheier, Weintraub, & Carver, 1986). When faced with a stressful situation, optimists seek out relevant information and actively attempt to solve their problems, either by directly attacking the source of distress or by looking at the situation in ways that cast things in the most positive light (e.g., believing they have learned a lot from the experience and are a better person for having gone through it).

In summary, the picture that emerges from the research we have been discussing is not one of an optimistic person who blithely assumes everything will be fine and then does nothing to bring about this state of affairs. Instead, optimists adopt constructive, problem-focused coping strategies. They set goals and then actively set about to attain them. They look at their situation in the most positive terms and attempt to construe benefit from tragedy. In colloquial terms, they "make lemonade out of lemons."

THE NEGATIVE SIDE OF POSITIVE ILLUSIONS

Positive illusions are not always adaptive. In this section, we review three circumstances that pose potential problems.

Positive Illusions and Interpersonal Evaluations

Modesty is generally valued in our culture, and people who publicly "blow their horn" risk opprobrium and rejection. At the same time, people enjoy the company of those who are optimistic and exhibit a strong sense of personal agency. For these reasons, we should not be surprised to find that the evidence linking self-enhancing illusions to interpersonal evaluations is mixed. Some studies find a negative correlation between self-enhancement and interpersonal evaluations (Colvin, Block, & Funder, 1995; John & Robins, 1994; Paulhus, 1998), whereas others find the opposite to be true (Brendgen, Vitaro, Turgeon, Poulin, & Wanner, 2004; Taylor, Lerner,

Sherman, Sage, & McDowell, 2003b). Still others have found that self-enhancing people make a positive first impression but are later disliked (Paulhus, 1998), or are disliked only if they have recently been threatened or thwarted (Heatherton & Vohs, 2000; Vohs & Heatherton, 2001). In short, whether self-enhancement engenders interpersonal acceptance or rejection is uncertain. One thing is clear, however: Self-enhancing people perceive their relationships as being more supportive and fulfilling than do those who are more balanced or self-deprecating (Bonanno et al., 2005; Dougall, Hyman, Hayward, McFeeley, & Baum, 2001). Insofar as perceived support from others is a valuable resource in times of stress, these positive beliefs would seem to have salutary consequences.

Illusions, Narcissism, and Aggression

The link between illusions and aggression is also of interest. Although low self-esteem and negative self-views are risk factors for real-world aggression (Donnellan, Trzesniewski, Robins, Moffitt, & Caspi, 2005), some laboratory studies have found that people with inflated self-views are prone to aggression when their feelings of self-worth are threatened (Baumeister, Smart, & Boden, 1996; Bushman & Baumeister, 1998). In these studies, self-enhancement is generally measured with the Narcissistic Personality Inventory, a measure of narcissistic tendencies in the general population (Raskin & Terry, 1988). Narcissism is a multifaceted construct, characterized not only by self-aggrandizement but also by an exaggerated sense of entitlement, a lack of empathy, and a tendency to exploit others for personal gain. To date, researchers have not firmly established which of these dimensions predicts aggression, although it appears that tendencies toward exploitation and entitlement are more directly linked with aggression than is self-aggrandizement (Washburn, McMahon, King, Reinecke, & Silver, 2004).

Positive Illusions and Decision Making

Critics of the positive-illusions approach have pointed to situations in which people make important life decisions, such as deciding whether to have a medical procedure or where to invest their retirement. People need to be attentive to the costs and benefits of their choices in situations like these, and some studies have found that people who exaggerate their belief to bring about desired outcomes make poorer choices when making decisions under uncertainty (Fenton-O'Creevy, Nicholson, Soane, & Willman, 2003). Optimism has also been linked to gambling and an inability to learn from contingent feedback when risks are unlikely to pan out (Gibson & Sanbonmatsu, 2004). In situations like these, positive illusions appear to be a liability.

Not all evidence supports this conclusion, however. Other studies find that people who exhibit self-enhancing illusions pay attention to negative information when it's likely to be useful and are highly sensitive to the contingencies between their actions and outcomes (Aspinwall & Brunhart, 1996; McFarlin, Baumeister, & Blascovich, 1984). Like the gambler in the Kenny Rogers song, self-enhancing people seem to "know when to hold 'em, know when to fold 'em" (Aspinwall, Richter, & Hoffman, 2001). The key variable seems to be the objective contingency between actions and outcomes. If the task is uncontrollable (as is true in many artificial laboratory settings), positive illusions may well prove maladaptive, as people will persist in courses of action that are destined to fail. If, however, people have some control over the outcome (as is usually true in the real world), positive illusions will probably be beneficial, as people who are efficacious and optimistic will work hard to bring about a desired outcome (Fournier, de Ridder, & Bensing, 2002).

This flexibility underscores another important point about the nature of positive illusions. Some researchers view positive illusions as having a trait-like quality. From this perspective, across situations, some people are self-enhancing, some are accurate, and some are self-deprecating. Others reject this claim, arguing that self-enhancement is sensitive to subtle situational variations and contingencies, showing a great deal of situational specificity (see Taylor et al., 2003b; Taylor, Lerner, Sherman, Sage, & McDowell, 2003b, for a discussion of these positions). One way to resolve these competing positions is to assume that self-enhancement is a trait that incorporates flexibility and a keen awareness of when self-enhancement biases are apt to be advantageous and when they are likely to be ineffective (Aspinwall & Staudinger, 2003). Rather than rigidly adhering to one approach or another, people rely on an armamentarium of self-enhancement devices to offset threatening life events. Sometimes these devices will entail direct efforts to alter the event and sometimes they will involve efforts designed to alleviate distress.

CONCLUDING REMARKS AND RECOMMENDATIONS FOR FUTURE RESEARCH

In 1988, Taylor and Brown surveyed the literature on accuracy and self-knowledge and reached two conclusions: Most people regard themselves in overly positive terms and, under many circumstances, doing so is a benefit, not a liability. Support for their first conclusion is overwhelming (Brown, 1986, 1991, 1998). Hundreds of studies have found that people view themselves, their ability to bring about desired outcomes, and their future in terms that are too good to be true. Of course, not everyone exhibits these tendencies and situational factors can attenuate or even eliminate them, but the tendency is a general one, even in cultures that put a premium on modesty and humility (Brown, 2003; Brown & Kobayashi, 2002; Kurman, 2001; Mezulis, Abramson, Hyde, & Hankin, 2004; Sedikides, Gaertner, & Toguchi, 2003).

Although the evidence relating illusions to well-being is less consistent, we believe the preponderance supports Taylor and Brown's (1988) claim. Under most situations, people who regard themselves in positive terms believe they are in control of their lives and look forward to a bright and prosperous future fare better than do those who lack these perceptions. To be sure, excessively positive self-relevant beliefs can be problematic, but this fact was never in dispute. As noted earlier, Taylor and Brown never claimed that the more self-aggrandizement, the better.

In this regard, we think it would be fruitful to consider the relation between illusions and self-esteem. People who think well of themselves generally feel good about themselves, which raises the possibility that self-esteem underlies the effects attributed to positive thinking. Indeed, many researchers use the term *positive self-concept* as a synonym for high self-esteem, and *negative self-concept* as a synonym for low self-esteem, and some of the research that has been conducted to test Taylor and Brown's formulation has examined self-esteem as a proxy for positive illusions. We think using self-esteem as a substitute for positive thinking is inadvisable. Although they are highly correlated, people's thoughts and feelings about themselves are distinguishable and have different origins and consequences (Bernichon, Cook, & Brown, 2003; Brown, 1993; Brown & Marshall, 2001, 2006; Dutton & Brown, 1997).

This distinction may be particularly important when considering the costs and benefits of positive illusions. Although research in this area is just beginning, early findings suggest that positive illusions are beneficial when they are accompanied by high self-esteem but detrimental when they are accompanied by low self-esteem (Barry, Frick, & Killian, 2003; Nathanson, Kurt, & Paulhus, 2005; Paulhus, Robins, Trzesniewski, & Tracy, 2004; Sedikides, Rudich, Gregg, Kumashiro, & Rusbult, 2004).

We also believe that progress could be made by changing the methodological approach that dominates research in this area. Virtually all investigations that have tested Taylor and Brown's formulation have calculated a predictor variable by combining perception with reality. For example, Colvin, Block, and Funder (1995) asked participants to evaluate themselves. Later the participants were evaluated by a group of observers, and a self-enhancement index was formed by subtracting the observer ratings from the self-ratings. This discrepancy score was then used as a predictor variable. This approach assumes that people who view themselves as positively as they are viewed by others are equivalent to those who view themselves as negatively as they are viewed by others (i.e., both groups receive a difference score = 0.00). We doubt that people who know they are well-liked are psychologically equivalent to those who know they are disliked.

The use of difference scores also means that only people who lack talent, attractiveness, or intelligence can be classified as self-aggrandizing. Assuming that "being bad" at something has negative consequences, this prop-

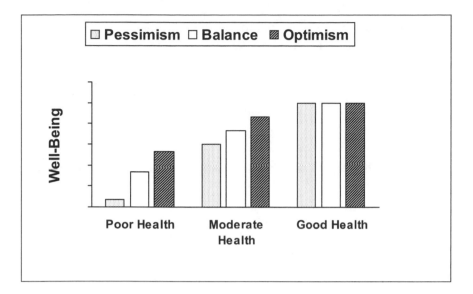

Figure 2.2. Hypothetical relationship between optimism, health, and well-being.

erty of difference scores virtually guarantees a negative correlation between self-enhancement and some criterion.

John and Robins (1994) attempted to avoid these problems by calculating a residual score rather than a difference score (see also Kwan, John, Kenny, Bond, & Robins, 2004; Paulhus, 1998). In their research, they first regressed self-evaluations on peer ratings and then used the residual as a predictor variable in further analyses. The residual represents the amount of variance in self-evaluations that cannot be explained by peer evaluations. This approach avoids the pitfalls of a difference score, but it does not fully capture the complexity of the relationship between truth, fiction, and well-being. A residual score is akin to examining a main effect term in a regression equation that controls for other predictors. As such, it fails to consider the possible interaction between self-views and reality.

Figure 2.2 illustrates why this issue is important to consider. The figure shows a hypothetical data pattern regarding the relation between actual health, optimism, and well-being. A Health × Optimism interaction is present, such that beliefs don't matter much when health is good, matter a little when health is moderate, and matter a great deal when health is poor. Obviously, these data are only hypothetical, and we are only speculating that this pattern best describes the relation among health, perception, and well-being. The important point, however, is that none of the investigations we reviewed in this chapter would have detected such an effect, because none included separate estimates of reality and self-perception.

As we see it, the issue here is not simply a methodological one. At the heart of the Taylor and Brown model is the claim that positive beliefs, even if somewhat illusory, are beneficial to well-being. This claim can properly be tested only by considering the interaction between self-views and objective reality. Doing so will yield greater insight into the truth about fiction.

REFERENCES

Aspinwall, L. G., & Brunhart, S. M. (1996). Distinguishing optimism from denial: Optimistic beliefs predict attention to health threats. *Personality and Social Psychology Bulletin, 22,* 993–1003.

Aspinwall, L. G., Richter, L., & Hoffman, R. R. (2001). Understanding how optimism "works": An examination of optimists' adaptive moderation of belief and behavior. In E. C. Chang (Ed.), *Optimism and pessimism: Theory, research, and practice* (pp. 217–238). Washington, DC: American Psychological Association.

Aspinwall, L. G., & Staudinger, U. M. (2003). A psychology of human strengths: Some central issues of an emerging field. In L. G. Aspinwall & U. M. Staudinger (Eds.), *A psychology of human strengths: Fundamental questions and future directions for a positive psychology* (pp. 9–22). Washington, DC: American Psychological Association.

Aspinwall, L. G., & Taylor, S. E. (1992). Modeling cognitive adaptation: A longitudinal investigation of individual differences and coping on college adjustment and performance. *Journal of Personality and Social Psychology, 63,* 989–1003.

Bandura, A. (1997). *Self-efficacy: The exercise of control.* New York: Freeman.

Barry, C. T., Frick, P. J., & Killian, A. L. (2003). The relation of narcissism and self-esteem to conduct problems with children: A preliminary investigation. *Journal of Clinical Child and Adolescent Psychology, 32,* 139–152.

Baumeister, R. F., Smart, L., & Boden, J. M. (1996). Relation of threatened egotism to violence and aggression: The dark side of high self-esteem. *Psychological Review, 103,* 5–33.

Bernichon, T., Cook, K. E., & Brown, J. D. (2003). Seeking self-evaluative feedback: The interactive role of global self-esteem and specific self-views. *Journal of Personality and Social Psychology, 84,* 194–204.

Bonanno, G. A., Field, N. P., Kovacevic, A., & Kaltman, S. (2002). Self-enhancement as a buffer against extreme adversity: Civil war in Bosnia and traumatic loss in the United States. *Personality and Social Psychology Bulletin, 28,* 184–196.

Bonanno, G. A., Rennicke, C., & Dekel, S. (2005). Self-enhancement among high-exposure survivors of the September 11th terrorist attack: Resilience or social maladjustment? *Journal of Personality and Social Psychology, 88,* 984–998.

Brendgen, M., Vitaro, F., Turgeon, L., Poulin, F., & Wanner, B. (2004). Is there a dark side of positive illusions? Overestimation of social competence and subsequent adjustment in aggressive and nonaggressive children. *Journal of Abnormal Child Psychology, 32,* 305–320.

Brickman, P., Coates, D., & Janoff-Bulman, R. J. (1978). Lottery winners and accident victims: Is happiness relative? *Journal of Personality and Social Psychology, 36*, 916–927.

Brissette, I., Scheier, M. F., & Carver, C. S. (2002). The role of optimism in social network development, coping, and psychological adjustment during a life transition. *Journal of Personality and Social Psychology, 82*, 102–111.

Brown, J. D. (1986). Evaluations of self and others: Self-enhancement biases in social judgments. *Social Cognition, 4*, 353–376.

Brown, J. D. (1991). Accuracy and bias in self-knowledge. In C. R. Snyder & D. F. Forsyth (Eds.), *Handbook of social and clinical psychology: The health perspective* (pp. 158–178). New York: Pergamon Press.

Brown, J. D. (1993). Self-esteem and self-evaluation: Feeling is believing. In J. Suls (Ed.), *Psychological perspectives on the self: Vol. 4. The self in social perspective* (pp. 27–58). Hillsdale, NJ: Erlbaum.

Brown, J. D. (1998). *The self*. New York: McGraw-Hill.

Brown, J. D. (2003). The self-enhancement motive in collectivistic cultures: The rumors of my death have been greatly exaggerated. *Journal of Cross-Cultural Psychology, 34*, 603–605.

Brown, J. D., & Kobayashi, C. (2002). Self-enhancement in Japan and America. *Asian Journal of Social Psychology, 5*, 145–167.

Brown, J. D., & Marshall, M. A. (2001). Self-esteem and emotion: Some thoughts about feelings. *Personality and Social Psychology Bulletin, 27*, 575–584.

Brown, J. D., & Marshall, M. A. (2006). The three faces of self-esteem. In M. Kernis (Ed.), *Self-esteem: Issues and answers* (pp. 4–9). New York: Psychology Press.

Bushman, B. J., & Baumeister, R. F. (1998). Threatened egotism, narcissism, self-esteem, and direct and displaced aggression: Does self-love or self-hate lead to violence? *Journal of Personality and Social Psychology, 75*, 219–229.

Buunk, B. P., & van der Eijnden, R. J. J. M. (1997). Perceived prevalence, perceived superiority, and relationship satisfaction: Most relationships are good, but ours is the best. *Personality and Social Psychology Bulletin, 23*, 219–228.

Carver, C. S., & Antoni, M. H. (2004). Finding benefit in breast cancer during the year after diagnosis predicts better adjustment 5 to 8 years after diagnosis. *Health Psychology, 23*, 595–598.

Carver, C. S., Pozo, C., Harris, S. D., Noriega, V., Scheier, M. F., Robinson, D. S., et al. (1993). How coping mediates the effects of optimism on distress: A study of women with early stage breast cancer. *Journal of Personality and Social Psychology, 65*, 375–390.

Cohen, S., & Wills, T. A. (1985). Stress, social support, and the buffering hypothesis. *Psychological Bulletin, 98*, 310–357.

Colvin, C. R., & Block, J. (1994). Do positive illusions foster mental health? An examination of the Taylor and Brown formulation. *Psychological Bulletin, 116*, 3–20.

Colvin, C. R., Block, J., & Funder, D. C. (1995). Overly positive self-evaluations and personality: Negative implications for mental health. *Journal of Personality and Social Psychology, 68,* 1152–1162.

Danner, D. D., Snowdon, D. A., & Friesen, W. V. (2001). Positive emotions in early life and longevity: Findings from the nun study. *Journal of Personality and Social Psychology, 80,* 804–813.

Diener, E. (1994). Assessing subjective well-being: Progress and opportunities. *Social Indicators Research, 31,* 103–157.

Diener, E., & Diener, M. (1995). Cross-cultural correlates of life satisfaction and self-esteem. *Journal of Personality and Social Psychology, 68,* 653–663.

Diener, E., & Seligman, M. E. P. (2002). Very happy people. *Psychological Science, 13,* 81–84.

Donnellan, M. B., Trzesniewski, K. H., Robins, R. W., Moffitt, T. E., & Caspi, A. (2005). Low self-esteem is related to aggression, antisocial behavior, and delinquency. *Psychological Science, 16,* 328–335.

Dougall, A. L., Hyman, K. B., Hayward, M. C., McFeeley, S., & Baum, A. (2001). Optimism and traumatic stress: The importance of stress and coping. *Journal of Applied Social Psychology, 31,* 223–245.

Dutton, K. A., & Brown, J. D. (1997). Global self-esteem and specific self-views as determinants of people's reactions to success and failure. *Journal of Personality and Social Psychology, 73,* 139–148.

Endo, Y., Heine, S. J., & Lehman, D. R. (2000). Culture and positive illusions in close relationships: How my relationships are better than yours. *Personality and Social Psychology Bulletin, 26,* 1571–1586.

Fenton-O'Creevy, M., Nicholson, N., Soane, E., & Willman, P. (2003). Trading on illusions: Unrealistic perceptions of control and trading performance. *Journal of Occupational and Organizational Psychology, 76,* 53–68.

Folkman, S., & Moskowitz, J. T. (2000). Positive affect and the other side of coping. *American Psychologist, 55,* 647–654.

Fournier, M., de Ridder, D., & Bensing, J. (2002). Optimism and adaptation to chronic disease: The role of optimism in relation to self-care options of Type I diabetes mellitus, rheumatoid arthritis and multiple sclerosis. *British Journal of Health Psychology, 7,* 409–432.

Fowers, B. J., Lyons, E., Montel, K. H., & Shaked, N. (2001). Positive illusions about marriage among married and single individuals. *Journal of Family Psychology, 15,* 95–109.

Fredrickson, B. L. (1998). What good are positive emotions? *Review of General Psychology, 2,* 300–319.

Fredrickson, B. L. (2001). The role of positive emotions in positive psychology: The broaden-and-build theory of positive emotions. *American Psychologist, 56,* 218–226.

Gagné, F. M., & Lydon, J. E. (2004). Bias and accuracy in close relationships: An integrative review. *Personality and Social Psychology Review, 8,* 322–338.

Gibson, B., & Sanbonmatsu, D. M. (2004). Optimism, pessimism, and gambling: The downside of optimism. *Personality and Social Psychology Bulletin, 30,* 149–160.

Heatherton, T. F., & Vohs, K. D. (2000). Interpersonal evaluations following threats to self: Role of self-esteem. *Journal of Personality and Social Psychology, 78,* 725–736.

Heaton, T. B., & Albrecht, S. L. (1991). Stable unhappy marriages. *Journal of Marriage and the Family, 53,* 747–758.

Jahoda, M. (1958). *Current concepts of positive mental health.* New York: Basic Books.

John, O. P., & Robins, R. W. (1994). Accuracy and bias in self-perception: Individual differences in self-enhancement and the role of narcissism. *Journal of Personality and Social Psychology, 66,* 206–219.

Kurman, J. (2001). Self-enhancement: Is it restricted to individualistic cultures? *Personality and Social Psychology Bulletin, 12,* 1705–1716.

Kwan, V. S. Y., John, O. P., Kenny, D. A., Bond, M. H., & Robins, R. W. (2004). Reconceptualizing individual differences in self-enhancement bias: An interpersonal approach. *Psychological Review, 111,* 94–110.

Lazarus, R. S., & Folkman, S. (1984). *Stress, adaptation, and coping.* New York: Springer Publishing Company.

Lazarus, R. S., & Launier, R. (1978). Stress-related transactions between person and environment. In L. A. Pervin & M. Lewis (Eds.), *Perspectives in interactional psychology* (pp. 287–327). New York: Plenum Press.

Lyubomirsky, S., King, L., & Diener, E. (2005). The benefits of frequent positive affect: Does happiness lead to success? *Psychological Bulletin, 131,* 801–855.

Marshall, M. A., & Brown, J. D. (2004). Expectations and realizations: The role of expectancies in achievement settings. *Motivation & Emotion, 28,* 347–361.

Maslow, A. H. (1950). Self-actualizing people: A study of psychological health. *Personality Symposia: Symposium No. 1 on Values* (pp. 11–34). New York: Grune & Stratton.

McFarlin, D. B., Baumeister, R. F., & Blascovich, J. (1984). On knowing when to quit: Task failure, self-esteem, advice, and nonproductive assistance. *Journal of Personality, 52,* 138–155.

Mezulis, A. H., Abramson, L. Y., Hyde, J. S., & Hankin, B. L. (2004). Is there a universal positivity bias in attributions? A meta-analytic review of individual, developmental, and cultural differences in the self-serving attributional bias. *Psychological Bulletin, 130,* 711–747.

Murray, S. L., & Holmes, J. G. (1993). Seeing virtues in faults: Negativity and the transformation of interpersonal narratives in close relationships. *Journal of Personality and Social Psychology, 65,* 707–722.

Murray, S. L., & Holmes, J. G. (1997). A leap of faith? Positive illusions in romantic relationships. *Personality and Social Psychology Bulletin, 23,* 586–604.

Murray, S. L., & Holmes, J. G. (1999). The (mental) ties that bind: Cognitive structures that predict relationship resilience. *Journal of Personality and Social Psychology, 77,* 1228–1244.

Murray, S. L., Holmes, J. G., & Griffin, D. W. (1996a). The benefits of positive illusions: Idealization and the construction of satisfaction in close relationships. *Journal of Personality and Social Psychology, 70*, 79–98.

Murray, S. L., Holmes, J. G., & Griffin, D. W. (1996b). The self-fulfilling nature of positive illusions in romantic relationships: Love is not blind, but prescient. *Journal of Personality and Social Psychology, 71*, 1155–1180.

Nathanson, C., Kurt, A., & Paulhus, D. L. (2005, January). *Interpersonal consequences of insecure high self-esteem.* Paper presented at the annual meeting of the Society for Personality and Social Psychology, New Orleans, LA.

Paulhus, D. L. (1998). Interpersonal and intrapsychic adaptiveness of trait self-enhancement: A mixed blessing? *Journal of Personality and Social Psychology, 74*, 1197–1208.

Paulhus, D. L., Robins, R. W., Trzesniewski, K. H., & Tracy, J. L. (2004). Two replicable suppressor situations in personality research. *Multivariate Behavioral Research, 39*, 303–328.

Raskin, R., & Terry, H. (1988). A principal-components analysis of the Narcissistic Personality Inventory and further evidence of its construct validity. *Journal of Personality and Social Psychology, 54*, 890–902.

Robins, R. W., & Beer, J. S. (2001). Positive illusions about the self: Short-term benefits and long-term costs. *Journal of Personality and Social Psychology, 80*, 340–352.

Rusbult, C. E., Van Lange, P. A. M., Wildschut, T., Yovetich, N. A., & Verette, J. (2000). Perceived superiority in close relationships: Why it exists and persists. *Journal of Personality and Social Psychology, 79*, 521–545.

Scheier, M. F., Matthews, K. A., Owens, J. F., Magovern, G. J., Sr., Lefebvre, R. C., Abbott, R. A., & Carver, C. S. (1989). Dispositional optimism and recovery from coronary artery bypass surgery: The beneficial effects on physical and psychological well-being. *Journal of Personality, 57*, 1024–1040.

Scheier, M. F., Weintraub, J. K., & Carver, C. S. (1986). Coping with stress: Divergent strategies of optimists and pessimists. *Journal of Personality and Social Psychology, 51*, 1257–1264.

Schulz, R., & Decker, S. (1985). Long-term adjustment to physical disability: The role of social support, perceived control, and self-blame. *Journal of Personality and Social Psychology, 48*, 1162–1172.

Sedikides, C., Gaertner, L., & Toguchi, Y. (2003). Pancultural self-enhancement. *Journal of Personality and Social Psychology, 84*, 60–79.

Sedikides, C., Rudich, E. A., Gregg, A. P., Kumashiro, M., & Rusbult, C. (2004). Are normal narcissists psychologically healthy? Self-esteem matters. *Journal of Personality and Social Psychology, 87*, 400–416.

Seligman, M. E. P., & Csikszentmihalyi, M. (2000). Positive psychology: An introduction. *American Psychologist, 55*, 5–14.

Shedler, J., Mayman, M., & Manis, M. (1993). The illusion of mental health. *American Psychologist, 48*, 1117–1131.

Sheldon, K. M., & King, L. (2001). Why positive psychology is necessary. *American Psychologist, 56,* 216–217.

Taylor, S. E. (1983). Adjustment to threatening events: A theory of cognitive adaptation. *American Psychologist, 38,* 1161–1173.

Taylor, S. E., & Brown, J. D. (1988). Illusion and well-being: A social psychological perspective on mental health. *Psychological Bulletin, 103,* 193–210.

Taylor, S. E., & Brown, J. D. (1994a). Positive illusions and well-being revisited: Separating fact from fiction. *Psychological Bulletin, 116,* 21–27.

Taylor, S. E., & Brown, J. D. (1994b). Illusion of mental health does not explain positive illusions. *American Psychologist, 49,* 972–973.

Taylor, S. E., Kemeny, M. E., Aspinwall, L. G., Schneider, S. G., Rodriguez, R., & Herbert, M. (1992). Optimism, coping, psychological distress, and high-risk sexual behavior among men at risk for acquired immunodeficiency syndrome (AIDS). *Journal of Personality and Social Psychology, 63,* 460–473.

Taylor, S. E., Kemeny, M. E., Bower, J. E., Gruenewald, T. L., & Reed, G. M. (2000). Psychological resources, positive illusions, and health. *American Psychologist, 55,* 99–109.

Taylor, S. E., Lerner, J. S., Sherman, D. K., Sage, R. M., & McDowell, N. K. (2003a). Are self-enhancing cognitions associated with healthy or unhealthy biological profiles? *Journal of Personality and Social Psychology, 85,* 605–615.

Taylor, S. E., Lerner, J. S., Sherman, D. K., Sage, R. M., & McDowell, N. K. (2003b). Portrait of the self-enhancer: Well-adjusted and well-liked or maladjusted and friendless? *Journal of Personality and Social Psychology, 84,* 165–176.

Vohs, K. D., & Heatherton, T. F. (2001). Self-esteem and threats to self: Implications for self-construals and interpersonal perceptions. *Journal of Personality and Social Psychology, 81,* 1103–1118.

Washburn, J. J., McMahon, S. D., King, C. A., Reinecke, M. A., & Silver, C. (2004). Narcissistic features in young adolescents: Relations to aggression and internalizing symptoms. *Journal of Youth and Adolescence, 33,* 247–260.

Wright, S. S. (2000). Looking at the self in a rose-colored mirror: Unrealistically positive self-views and academic performance. *Journal of Social and Clinical Psychology, 19,* 451–462.

3

ON THE PHYSICAL HEALTH BENEFITS OF SELF-ENHANCEMENT

SUZANNE C. SEGERSTROM AND ABBEY R. ROACH

Ample evidence suggests that people believe that they have more positive qualities than others believe that they do, that their futures will be more positive than is likely to transpire, and that they have more control over their environments than they actually do (Taylor & Brown, 1988). These positive illusions may involve idealistically favorable views of self, unrealistic optimism about the likelihood of future events, and inflated perceptions of personal control. This chapter examines the relationship between self-enhancement in three specific domains—self, future, and control—and physical health. In general, the evidence shows that across all three domains, self-enhancement is associated with better physiological functioning as well as health outcomes. However, in each domain are also contradictory findings that suggest the need for a reexamination of the hypothesis that self-enhancement is always adaptive for physical health. This research literature, therefore, reveals not only what the effects of self-enhancement on health may be but also perhaps something about self-enhancement itself.

Although almost everyone has a self-enhancing view of the future, degree of self-enhancement varies. These individual differences are reflected in personality traits including self-esteem, which captures individual differences in self-enhancement; dispositional optimism, which captures individual differences in positive expectancies for the future; and mastery and locus of control, which capture individual differences in degree of control attributed to the self. Attributional style, which is a person's habitual way of explaining positive and negative events, also reflects these three domains in the causal dimensions of locus (cause located in self or other), stability (likelihood of the cause persisting in the future), and control (ability to modify the cause). Although studies have experimentally manipulated self-enhancement, primarily control beliefs, the majority of the empirical evidence for the relationship between self-enhancement and health that was reviewed addresses the question of whether individual differences in self-enhancement systematically associate with better health.

Greater self-enhancement benefits psychological adjustment; in fact, people with depression may lack these illusions (Taylor & Brown, 1988). When the physical health consequences of self-enhancement are evaluated, it is important to recognize that self-reported health may be more attributable to psychological states than to physiological states (Watson & Pennebaker, 1989). Therefore, the focus of the chapter is on the relationship between self-enhancement and "hard" physiological and health outcomes such as immune function, blood pressure, disease progression, and mortality. Perceptions of health as reflected in self-report are important: They influence one's sense of well-being as well as behaviors such as usage of medical care. In the interest of separating perceptions of health from biological outcomes, this chapter focuses on physiological or biological evidence rather than self-reported health.

SELF-ESTEEM

The Benefits of Self-Esteem

People who believe in their own high worth and abilities—that is, who have high self-esteem—are definitely happier, likely engage in more efficient self-regulation, and may perform better than do people with low self-esteem (Baumeister, Campbell, Krueger, & Vohs, 2003). In addition to positive effects on psychological functioning, higher levels of self-esteem appear also to benefit health and especially longevity. Older adults who had positive views of their aging selves survived longer than did those who did not have positive views: Over a 23-year follow-up period, the average longevity of participants with positive self-perceptions was 7.5 years longer than that of participants with less positive self-perceptions. This effect was independent of the participants' age, sex, and functional health (Levy, Slade, Kunkel, & Kasl, 2002). This study also found that in addition to the direct effect of positive self-perceptions of aging on longevity, positive self-perceptions also had indirect effects on longevity via a stronger will to live, which also predicted longer survival. In another study, self-esteem predicted reduced mortality among older adults residing in a nursing home, a relationship that was stronger than those between mortality and other potential predictors such as life satisfaction (O'Connor & Vallerand, 1998). A third study examined self-esteem and survival among 123 leukemia and lymphoma patients treated with bone marrow transplants (BMTs). BMT poses a series of risks even after successful transplantation (i.e., the marrow generates new cells), including infections, graft versus host disease (in which the newly produced cells attack their host), and relapse. In this study, patients in the lowest quartile of self-esteem lived approximately 250 days posttransplant; those in the next highest quartile lived over 1,000 days. Again, self-esteem predicted survival where other potential predictors, such as quality of life, did not (Broers et al., 1998).

There is also evidence for a protective effect of self-esteem with regard to physiological reactivity to stressors, particularly in terms of the release of stress hormones such as cortisol. Cortisol is a steroid hormone whose acute release during stressors mobilizes energy resources for fight or flight; however, its prolonged release can have negative consequences including immunosuppression, loss of insulin sensitivity (a risk for adult-onset diabetes), decreased muscle and bone mass, and damage to hippocampal neurons (Sapolsky, 1994). Excess cortisol secretion therefore provides a plausible physiological mechanism by which low self-esteem could translate into health outcomes. Several studies have found an association between lower self-esteem and higher cortisol reactivity to stressors such as mental arithmetic tasks, among both college-age and older (ages 70–79) participants (Kirschbaum et al., 1995; Pruessner, Hellhammer, & Kirschbaum, 1999; Seeman et al., 1995). In a similar manner, students who tended to see themselves more positively than they saw their peers had lower cardiovascular reactivity to a stressor as reflected by smaller increases in systolic blood pressure, heart rate, and the rate pressure product, an indirect measure of total circulatory output. However, cortisol reactivity did not differ between high and low self-enhancers. The cardiovascular effects were attributable to self-enhancement rather than actual characteristics of the participants because friends' ratings could not account for the effects: How positively people saw themselves was more important than how others saw them (Taylor, Lerner, Sherman, Sage, & McDowell, 2003).

One naturalistic study found that higher self-esteem was associated with higher basal levels of cortisol among young psychologically and physically healthy men (Zorrilla, DeRubeis, & Redei, 1995). However, this finding should not be taken to mean that higher self-esteem was associated with greater physiological vulnerability, because samples were taken in the morning hours. Basal cortisol is released in a circadian rhythm that ideally peaks within an hour of waking and reaches a nadir in the evening hours. Disruptions of this rhythm typically manifest as a flattening of this slope via elevation of evening levels, suppression of morning levels, or both. Although evening cortisol was not measured in this study, it is possible that elevated morning cortisol associated with self-esteem reflects a steeper negative diurnal slope, a pattern that is associated with better physiological regulation and health. Finally, men in this study with higher self-esteem also had more positive affect, but affect did not account for the relationship between self-esteem and cortisol. This result, together with the findings in older adults that the longevity benefits of self-esteem were independent of life satisfaction or quality of life, suggests that the effects of self-esteem are not mediated by constructs related to mood or adjustment.

The Limits of Self-Esteem

Study of the psychological effects of self-esteem has generally turned away from a main-effects model of self-esteem (in which self-esteem is presumed to be beneficial) toward a search for moderating factors and dynamic properties of self-esteem. Evidence in the psychophysiological domain is likewise indicating that self-esteem may only sometimes have beneficial effects on health. In one of the reactivity studies, cortisol increased only in participants who had both low self-esteem and high external locus of control, which suggests that low self-esteem may be most hazardous in the absence of other potentially protective factors such as a sense of control (Pruessner et al., 1999). Another important moderator of the effects of self-esteem has to do with the dynamics of self-esteem. People with stable self-esteem have few short-term fluctuations around their mean level of self-esteem, whereas people with unstable self-esteem have a great deal of fluctuation. Instability may leave people psychologically vulnerable even when average levels of self-esteem are high (Baumeister, Smart, & Boden, 1996). Both stable low self-esteem and self-esteem instability were associated with increased total peripheral resistance, a measure of vasoconstriction, and lower cardiac output, a measure of the amount of blood pumped by the heart, after failure feedback from a task in which participants completed either an easy or a difficult version of the Remote Associates Test. Any benefit of high self-esteem may therefore be restricted to high, stable self-esteem (Seery, Blascovich, Weisbuch, & Vick, 2004). Overall, self-esteem generally seems to have protective effects against stressors and beneficial effects for health, but these effects may occur primarily when self-esteem is both high and stable.

OPTIMISM

The Benefits of Optimism

Optimism, as defined by positive outcome expectancies, is consistently associated with better psychological health (see Carver & Scheier, 1999, for a review), more active coping with stressors (see Solberg Nes & Segerstrom, 2006, for a review), and more persistence in mastering difficult tasks (e.g., Solberg Nes & Segerstrom, 2006). Several studies now suggest that optimists' better psychological adaptation is reflected in better physical health. More optimistic cardiac bypass patients recovered better from surgery and were less likely to be rehospitalized than were their more pessimistic counterparts (Fitzgerald, Tennen, Affleck, & Pransky, 1993; Scheier et al., 1989, 1999). In two independent studies, more optimistic cancer patients lived longer (albeit in one study, only the younger patients lived longer; Allison, Guichard, Fung, & Gilain, 2003; Schulz, Bookwala, Knapp, Scheier, & Williamson, 1996). In many of these studies, optimism predicted health outcomes after initial health was controlled for, which suggests that better initial health was not a third variable that predicted both optimism and later health. Further evidence in this regard is provided by a study of heart transplant outcomes. The success of a heart transplant is not related to heart function before the transplant (as that heart is now gone), a phenomenon called the *blank slate*. Nonetheless, more presurgically optimistic patients recovered better from transplant surgery and were more resistant to postsurgical infection than were less optimistic patients (Leedham, Meyerowitz, Muirhead, & Frist, 1995). It may even be beneficial to be born to an optimist. Pregnant women who were more optimistic experienced less stress during pregnancy and had longer pregnancies and larger babies. Birth weight is an important pregnancy outcome: Larger babies are less prone to perinatal and neonatal complications (Lobel, DeVincent, Kaminer, & Meyer, 2000; Rini, Dunkel-Schetter, Wadhwa, & Sandman, 1999).

Optimism has also demonstrated positive relationships with physiological parameters that could account for better health. More optimistic members of a community sample had lower ambulatory blood pressure than did their more pessimistic counterparts (Räikkönen, Matthews, Flory, Owens, & Gump, 1999). Optimism has also been associated with better immune status during chronic infections with human papilloma virus and HIV (Byrnes et al., 1998; Milam, Richardson, Marks, Kemper, & McCutchan, 2004). Overall, a substantial body of evidence links positive expectations for the future to better physiological functioning in the present and a healthier future.

The Limits of Optimism

Although these studies provide substantial evidence of health benefits accompanying optimism, a number of studies also fail to demonstrate beneficial effects of optimism in almost all the same domains: recovery from cardiac surgery (Contrada et al., 2004), survival with cancer (Schofield et al., 2004), gestational age and birth weight (Snedeker, Spencer, Solberg Nes, Miller, & Segerstrom, 2005), and immune function, symptom onset, and survival in HIV seropositive gay men (Reed, Kemeny, Taylor, & Visscher,

1999; Reed, Kemeny, Taylor, Wang, & Visscher, 1994; Tomakowsky, Lumley, Markowitz, & Frank, 2001). Although demographic and disease variables could account for these divergent findings (e.g., optimism predicted survival only for younger cancer patients and HIV progression only for demographically diverse samples), psychoneuroimmunological research suggests that optimism does not always have healthy consequences.

Both experimental and naturalistic studies of optimism and immune parameters suggest that when stressors are straightforward, more optimism is associated with higher immune parameters, but when stressors are difficult, more optimism is associated with lower immune parameters. Difficult stressors have included laboratory stressors that were uncontrollable or became more difficult with better performance (Segerstrom, Castaneda, & Spencer, 2003; Sieber, Rodin, Larson, Ortega, & Cummings, 1992) and naturalistic stressors that were prolonged or arose from goal conflict (Cohen et al., 1999; Segerstrom, 2001, 2006). In each case, optimism interacted with stressor difficulty to predict cellular immune parameters (number of T cells, natural killer cell cytotoxicity, and delayed-type hypersensitivity), which reflect the ability of the immune system to fight viral and some kinds of bacterial infections.

It is tempting to attribute these effects to vulnerability arising from self-enhancement: Believing in a positive future leads to collapse when that future fails to manifest itself. However, direct tests of this possibility uniformly found that premorbid optimism did not increase psychological vulnerability when the future turned out to be negative rather than positive (e.g., Helgeson, 2003). Furthermore, negative affect, which would be predicted from such vulnerability, did not mediate the relationship between optimism and immune function (e.g., Segerstrom, 2006). Instead, it is more likely that optimistic beliefs lead the people who hold them to engage and persist in trying to overcome difficult stressors, whereas people holding pessimistic beliefs are more likely to disengage and give up (Carver & Scheier, 1999). Consistent with this interpretation, conscientiousness, a personality dimension related to persistence and hard work, replicated the effects of optimism in combination with difficult mental arithmetic (Segerstrom et al., 2003). Likewise, optimism led to more persistence at a difficult anagram task but also to higher indices of physiological stress afterward (skin conductance and salivary cortisol; Solberg Nes et al., 2005).

If the negative consequences of optimism are related to engagement and persistence with goals and stressors, it is likely that these immediate negative effects may be replaced with positive effects in the long run. Some health costs of engagement in the short term reverse in the long term, when disengagement becomes more costly (Suls & Fletcher, 1985). If optimism has both physiological and health-related costs and benefits, it makes sense that the health outcomes have been mixed. However, it is telling that no studies of clinical health outcomes have shown negative consequences of optimism, which suggests that the benefits outweigh the costs.

Little Optimism Versus Big Optimism

Most of the aforementioned studies focused on *big optimism*, or generalized expectancies for the future. However, a number of studies have examined the effects of *little optimism*, or expectancies about specific events or domains (Peterson, 2000). These studies suggest that little optimism has health effects that are both more robust and less diverse than those of big optimism. In the same populations in which big optimism has null or mixed effects, little optimism consistently predicts better health. This is true of HIV seropositive gay men, among whom more positive expectancies about future health predicted later symptom onset and longer survival after AIDS diagnosis (Reed et al., 1994, 1999). It is also true among law students, among whom big optimism interacted with high and low goal conflict to predict cellular immunity (Segerstrom, 2001, 2006). In the same samples, more positive expectancies about law school predicted higher helper T cell counts and natural killer cell cytotoxicity (Segerstrom, Taylor, Kemeny, & Fahey, 1998). Situation-specific, or little, optimism is likely to be more closely related to cognitive, behavioral, and emotional responses to the relevant situation or stressor (e.g., disease threat, law school stress) and therefore to physiological responses, making it a more robust predictor than is big optimism.

CONTROL

The Benefits of Control

Being able to control the environment means the ability to bring about desirable circumstances and events and avoid undesirable ones, including those that might adversely affect health. Perception of low control over one's environment has been linked to both poor health and psychological distress such as anxiety. Workers who could exercise more control over their jobs, potentially matching their workload to their energy levels and avoiding or preempting stressors, had lower risk of coronary heart disease than did those who could exercise less control (Karasek, Baker, Marxer, Ahlbom, & Theorell, 1981).

Belief in one's ability to control the environment, even without effecting change, may be sufficient to gain a health advantage. In a classic test of this hypothesis, Langer and Rodin (1976; Rodin & Langer, 1977) drew nursing home residents' attention to ways that their lives could be fuller and more interesting: for example, by having a nice room, by visiting other residents, by owning a plant, and by attending movie night (the latter two activities were provided by the experimenters). For half of the residents, personal choice and control in these decisions and activities was emphasized, whereas for the other half (the comparison group), staff responsibility for these decisions and activities was emphasized. Three weeks after the intervention, those in the group for whom control was emphasized were happier, more active, more alert, and more sociable than were those in the comparison group; 18 months after the intervention, the control group had a mortality rate of 15% compared with 30% in the comparison group. Although the benefits offered to the residents were equivalent, increased perception of control over the environment appeared to affect both quality of life and longevity.

Experimental studies have also manipulated participants' perceptions of control, often without giving them any actual control. One such study randomly assigned male participants to one of four conditions. In an "escapable noise" condition, participants could push buttons to terminate a loud, intermittent noise. In an "inescapable noise with response" condition, participants thought they could push buttons to terminate the noise, but this response was inert, and their actual noise exposure was yoked to the first group. In an "inescapable noise without response" condition, participants were told to sit and listen to the noise. Only those in the last condition had declines in natural killer cell cytotoxicity over the 24 hours following the stressor (Sieber et al., 1992). Therefore, belief in control was as effective as actual control in ameliorating the effects of the stressor on the immune system.

Another laboratory study manipulated perceptions of predictability, which is likely to be beneficial because of the generally greater ability to control that which can be predicted. One group of undergraduates read scenarios and wrote about the predictable aspects of college life, one read scenarios and wrote about the unpredictable aspects of college life, and the control group read and wrote about physical aspects of the campus environment. Participants for whom unpredictable (and hence uncontrollable) aspects of college life were made salient had greater blood pressure reactivity during a subsequent thought listing task than did those for whom predictable aspects were made salient (Pham, Taylor, & Seeman, 2001).

Manipulation of control perceptions is not the only route by which to examine the health benefits of self-enhanced views of control. People naturally differ in the degree to which they believe that they, rather than other people, chance, or fate, determine important outcomes, a belief typically referred to as *internal locus of control* or *mastery* (Pearlin & Schooler, 1978; Rotter, 1966). In a 17-year study of Norwegian adults, external locus of control (compared with internal locus of control) predicted greater mortality from causes other than cardiovascular disease and cancer (Dalgard & Haheim, 1998). In a sample of 49 acute coronary syndrome patients, more perceived control was significantly negatively correlated with percentage of monocytes (Gidron, Armon, Gilutz, & Huleihel, 2003). Monocytes initiate inflammatory responses that are associated with negative health outcomes, including cardiovascular disease. A lower number of monocytes might reduce inflammatory responses and predict better health outcomes for patients with higher control beliefs.

An experimental study demonstrated that individual differences in perceived control moderated stress responses in much the same way as did manipulated perceptions of control. High school teachers were randomly assigned to either a task condition in which they were asked to solve a three-dimensional puzzle that they were predetermined to fail or a no-task condition in which they read a magazine. Those who perceived the task as less controllable had fewer T lymphocytes, T helper cells, and B cells compared with those who perceived it to be more controllable (Brosschot et al., 1998).

The Limits of Control

As with other forms of self-enhancement, control beliefs sometimes fail to show a positive relationship with health. Perceived control and locus of control were not associated with survival among two samples of cancer patients (Jamison, Burish, & Wallston, 1987; Richardson, Zarnegar, Bisno, & Levine, 1990). Researchers have suggested that these results might have been influenced by factors such as type of cancer, stage of cancer when diagnosed, or restricted range of adjustment. Nonetheless, although control is advantageous to physical health in many instances, there is evidence that the nature of the relationship between control and health may sometimes rely on other factors.

Although studies that manipulated perceived control and those that exploited individual differences in control beliefs all suggested that more control is better, several of these studies also showed that the effect of bestowing a perception of control depends on the individual's control beliefs: Perceived control is best for people who believe in their own abilities to exert control. In two experimental studies, manipulated perceptions of control buffered against neuroendocrine and immunological consequences of stressors only when participants also had loci of control that were more internal (Bollini, Walker, Hamann, & Kestler, 2004; Sieber et al., 1992). *Self-efficacy*, the confidence a person has in his or her ability, also moderates the relationship between perceived control and physiological indices of stress. Researchers manipulated controllability by randomly assigning participants to either self-paced (high control) or externally paced (low control) mental arithmetic tasks. Low control was associated with higher blood pressure and heart rate reactivity during the task compared with high control. However, participants in the high control condition who also had high self-efficacy had lower blood pressure and heart rate than did all other groups (i.e., participants in the high control condition who had low self-efficacy and participants in the low control condition regardless of self-efficacy; Gerin, Litt, Deich, & Pickering, 1995). Again, the effect of perceived control was greatest for people with naturally self-enhancing beliefs. Thus, the most positive health outcomes accrue to people who have not only a sense of control over a situation but also confidence in their ability to exercise it.

Furthermore, self-enhancing beliefs may not be helpful in situations in which little control is available. In the study reviewed earlier, the high self-efficacy, low control group had no advantage over the low self-efficacy, low control group (Gerin et al., 1995). Although internal locus of control enhanced the immunological protection afforded by perceived control, when control was not available, a locus of control that was more internal predicted lower natural killer cytotoxicity, enhancing the negative effects of uncontrollability (Sieber et al., 1992).

One question that arises from this finding has to do with developmental interactions with control beliefs. As people age, their ability to control many important aspects of their lives may decline: They may have more uncontrollable health problems, have limited mobility that limits their choices, or experience uncontrollable stressors such as bereavement. Furthermore, perceived control also may decline with age. In one study of coronary artery bypass graft surgery patients, older patients perceived less control over their disease than did the younger patients and attributed the cause of their disease to external factors such as old age. Younger patients, however, were more likely to feel that their own health decisions caused their illness (Gump et al., 2001). This developmental change in perception of control suggests that older people might not benefit as much as would younger people from manipulations to increase their perceived control. However, the classic nursing home studies (Langer & Rodin, 1976; Rodin & Langer, 1977) would suggest otherwise. The interaction between individual differences in perceived control and manipulations to increase perceived control will require further study as it pertains to developmental changes in control beliefs.

GLOBAL SELF-ENHANCEMENT

Although most studies have examined the individual effects of self-esteem, optimism, and control-relevant traits, some studies have examined the global effects of self-enhancing cognitive styles on health. Helgeson (2003) examined the effects of self-enhancing cognitive styles on disease outcomes among angioplasty patients, using a composite measure of dispositional self-esteem, optimism, and mastery and parallel measures specific to heart disease. Consistent with the beneficial effects of individual components of self-enhancement, this composite, measured at the time of initial angioplasty, dramatically predicted rehospitalization during the subsequent 4 years: An increase of 1 point in the self-enhancement composite (about 1/6 of 1 standard deviation) decreased the likelihood of hospitalization for cardiac reasons by 38%. Another striking demonstration of the health effects of composite self-enhancement came from a study of survival with amyotrophic lateral sclerosis (ALS), colloquially known as Lou Gehrig's disease (McDonald, Wiedenfeld, Hillel, Carpenter, & Walter, 1994). ALS is a neuromuscular disease that causes progressive paralysis, leading to respiratory weakness and death, usually within 3 to 5 years of diagnosis. Among a sample of 144 ALS patients, psychosocial adjustment, including indices of optimism and control, significantly influenced mortality. Patients with the best adjustment had a median survival time of >1,200 days, whereas those with the worst adjustment had a median survival time of 333 days. Furthermore, the worst-adjusted patients were almost 7 times more likely to die during the 1,200-day follow-up period.

Another measure of global self-enhancement is provided by *attributional* or *explanatory style*, a measure of the ways that people perceive the causes of positive and negative events in their lives. Optimistic or self-enhancing attributional styles emerge when people perceive the causes of positive events to be *internal* (good things come from them), *stable* (good things will continue in the future), and *global* (good things will arise in lots of different areas) and the causes of negative events to be *external* (bad things come from someone or something else), *unstable* (bad things won't necessarily repeat themselves), and *specific* (bad things are self-contained anomalies). Some studies also measure controllability of the cause; consistent with the original learned helplessness formulation, uncontrollable causes for negative events are thought to be particularly detrimental.

A number of studies, mostly by Peterson, Seligman, and their colleagues, have linked attributional style to health and longevity. Optimistic attributions made by 1940s Harvard graduates at the age of 25 predicted better health during the subsequent 3 decades, optimistic attributions made by members of the Baseball Hall of Fame before the age of 35 correlated with greater longevity, and optimism derived from the Minnesota Multiphasic Personality Inventory predicted lower mortality 30 years later in a large group of medical patients (Maruta, Colligan, Malinchoc, & Offord, 2000; Peterson & Seligman, 1987; Peterson, Seligman, & Vaillant, 1988).

In one analysis, global attributions for negative events made in childhood were associated with earlier death during a nearly 60-year follow-up; this was particularly true for death as a consequence of accident or violence (Peterson, Seligman, Yurko, Martin, & Friedman, 1998). The emphasis on accidental or violent death suggests a behavioral mechanism for the effects of self-enhancing attributions, but studies of blood pressure and immune function offer additional physiological pathways by which optimistic explanations might translate into greater longevity. For example, low socioeconomic status (SES) is a major risk factor for cardiovascular diseases, including hypertension (Steptoe et al., 2003), but in a study of 37 postmenopausal women, low SES women with optimistic attributional styles had blood pressure equally as low as that of high SES women; only low SES women who were pessimistic had significantly higher ambulatory blood pressure (Grewen et al., 2000).

Likewise, aging is a major risk factor for immunosuppression, but optimistic older adults had higher immune parameters (e.g., lymphocyte proliferation) than did pessimistic older adults (Kamen-Siegel, Rodin, Seligman, & Dwyer, 1991). Finally, HIV seropositive gay men who made optimistic attributions lost helper T cells more slowly than did their pessimistic counterparts; helper T cell loss is the major pathology of HIV infection (Segerstrom, Taylor, Kemeny, Reed, & Visscher, 1996). These studies suggest that self-enhancing attributions can be physiologically protective, potentially contributing to greater longevity. As was true of dispositional optimism, however, the opposite effect has been reported: Optimistic attributional style was associated with faster T cell loss in another sample of HIV seropositive gay men (Tomakowsky et al., 2001).

One element of the attributional style literature that poses problems is the variety of dimensions that have been linked to physiology and health. First, in many of these studies, the various dimensions have been measured together, but only a few studies have examined effects of individual dimensions. A second problem is that those studies diverge significantly in the "active ingredient": Internal attributions predicted helper T cell changes in one study (Segerstrom et al., 1996), stable attributions predicted blood pressure differences in another (Grewen et al., 2000), and global attributions predicted early mortality in yet another (Peterson et al., 1998). For attributional style studies to be captured in the nomological net of self-enhancing cognition, examination of the specific components in future studies will be important.

CONCLUSION

Both laboratory research and naturalistic research show that traits that reflect self-enhancement, including self-esteem, dispositional optimism, internal locus of control, mastery, and attributional style, associate with physiological parameters that could affect physical health, such as immune function, blood pressure, and neuroendocrine responses. In general, the direction of this association appears salubrious: Greater self-enhancement is accompanied by higher immune function and lower blood pressure and cortisol. In fact, even the exceptions to these directional relationships may be salubrious. In the case in which self-esteem was associated with higher cortisol, cortisol was measured in the morning when high cortisol levels are more desirable than low levels that flatten the diurnal slope (Zorrilla et al., 1995). Where control was associated with lower numbers of immune cells, the cells were monocytes that mediate inflammatory responses associated with poorer health outcomes (Gidron et al., 2003).

However, these associations were not universally found. Although such a criticism could be leveled at almost any literature, the research also suggests that there may be boundary conditions under which self-enhancement is helpful. Self-esteem may promote cardiovascular health only when self-esteem is both high and stable; optimism may promote higher immunity during stressors only when they are uncomplicated; and control over the environment may be beneficial only in the presence of traits such as mastery or internal locus of control. Nonetheless, it is important to note that it is very rare to find that self-enhancing cognitions or traits actually harm health: The worst outcome is typically a neutral relationship, particularly in investigations of arguably the most important health parameter, longevity. Although some studies have not found a significant effect of self-enhancement on survival, to our knowledge no studies show that people with greater tendencies to self-enhance die earlier. In general, self-enhancement seems unlikely to harm and has the potential to help one's physical health.

The effects of self-enhancement on health appear to be relatively independent of psychological adjustment. Although self-esteem, optimism, and mastery are generally associated with better psychological adjustment, where adjustment was tested as a mediator, it generally did not account for the effects of self-enhancement. One possibility is that some third variable affected by self-enhancement influences adjustment and physiology, although the two are not necessarily related to each other. Perhaps the lives of those who self-enhance run more smoothly or, as suggested by the data on perceived control, self-enhancement permits one to take full advantage of opportunities to control one's environment. Another possibility is the existence of alternative pathways between self-enhancement and physiology. For example, motivational states are not always well reflected in affect but can have physiological consequences (Segerstrom, 2006). The independent effects of self-enhancement on adjustment and physiology reveal the existence of two pathways toward well-being that may allow people to live both longer and better.

REFERENCES

Allison, P. J., Guichard, C., Fung, K., & Gilain, L. (2003). Dispositional optimism predicts survival status 1 year after diagnosis in head and neck cancer patients. *Journal of Clinical Oncology, 21*, 543–548.

Baumeister, R. F., Campbell, J. D., Krueger, J. I., & Vohs, K. D. (2003). Does high self-esteem cause better performance, interpersonal success, happiness, or healthier lifestyles? *Psychological Science in the Public Interest, 4*, 1–44.

Baumeister, R. F., Smart, L., & Boden, J. M. (1996). Relation of threatened egotism to violence and aggression: The dark side of high self-esteem. *Psychological Review, 103*, 5–33.

Bollini, A. M., Walker, E. F., Hamann, S., & Kestler, L. (2004). The influence of perceived control and locus of control on cortisol and subjective responses to stress. *Biological Psychology, 67*, 245–260.

Broers, S., Hengeveld, M. W., Kaptein, A. A., LeCessie, S. L., van de Loo, F., & de Vries, T. (1998). Are pretransplant psychological variables related to survival after bone marrow transplantation? A prospective study of 123 consecutive patients. *Journal of Psychosomatic Research, 45*, 341–351.

Brosschot, J. F., Godaert, G. L., Benschop, R. J., Olff, M., Ballieux, R. E., & Cobi, J. (1998). Experimental stress and immunological reactivity: A closer look at perceived uncontrollability. *Psychosomatic Medicine, 60*, 359–361.

Byrnes, D. M., Antoni, M. H., Goodkin, K., Efantis-Potter, J., Asthana, D., Simon, T., et al. (1998). Stressful events, pessimism, natural killer cell cytotoxicity, and cytotoxic/suppressor T cells in HIV+ Black women at risk for cervical cancer. *Psychosomatic Medicine, 60*, 714–722.

Carver, C. S., & Scheier, M. F. (1999). Optimism. In C. R. Snyder (Ed.), *Coping: The psychology of what works* (pp. 182–204). New York: Oxford University Press.

Cohen, F., Kearney, K. A., Zegans, L. S., Kemeny, M. E., Neuhaus, J. M., & Stites, D. P. (1999). Differential immune system changes with acute and persistent stress for optimists vs. pessimists. *Brain, Behavior, and Immunity, 13*, 155–174.

Contrada, R. J., Goyal, T. M., Cather, C., Rafalson, L., Idler, E. L., & Krause, T. J. (2004). Psychosocial factors in outcomes of heart surgery: The impact of religious involvement and depressive symptoms. *Health Psychology, 23*, 227–238.

Dalgard, O., & Haheim, L. (1998). Psychosocial risk factors and mortality: A prospective study with special focus on social support, social participation, and locus of control in Norway. *Journal of Epidemiology and Community Health, 52*, 476–481.

Fitzgerald, T. E., Tennen, H., Affleck, G., & Pransky, G. S. (1993). The relative importance of dispositional optimism and control appraisals in quality of life after coronary artery bypass surgery. *Journal of Behavioral Medicine, 16*, 25–43.

Gerin, W., Litt, M., Deich, J., & Pickering, T. (1995). Self-efficacy as a moderator of perceived control effects on cardiovascular reactivity: Is enhanced control always beneficial? *Psychosomatic Medicine, 57*, 390–397.

Gidron, Y., Armon, T., Gilutz, H., & Huleihel, M. (2003). Psychological factors correlate meaningfully with percent monocytes among acute coronary syndrome patients. *Brain, Behavior, and Immunity, 17*, 310–315.

Grewen, K., Girdler, S. S., West, S. G., Bragdon, E., Costello, N., & Light, K. C. (2000). Stable pessimistic attributions interact with socioeconomic status to influence blood pressure and vulnerability to hypertension. *Journal of Women's Health and Gender-Based Medicine, 9*, 905–915.

Gump, B., Matthews, K., Scheier, M., Schulz, R., Bridges, M., & Magovern, G. (2001). Illness representations according to age and effects on health behaviors following coronary artery bypass graft surgery. *Journal of American Geriatrics, 49*, 284–289.

Helgeson, V. S. (2003). Cognitive adaptation, psychological adjustment, and disease progression among angioplasty patients: 4 years later. *Health Psychology, 22*, 30–38.

Jamison, R. N., Burish, T. G., & Wallston, K. A. (1987). Psychogenic factors in predicting survival of breast cancer patients. *Journal of Clinical Oncology, 5,* 768–772.

Kamen-Siegel, L., Rodin, J., Seligman, M. E. P., & Dwyer, J. (1991). Explanatory style and cell-mediated immunity in elderly men and women. *Health Psychology, 10,* 229–235.

Karasek, R., Baker, D., Marxer, F., Ahlbom, A., & Theorell, T. (1981). Job decision latitude, job demands, and cardiovascular disease: A prospective study of Swedish men. *American Journal of Public Health, 71,* 694–705.

Kirschbaum, C., Pruessner, J. C., Stone, A. A., Federenko, I., Gaab, J., Schommer, D., et al. (1995). Persistent high cortisol responses to repeated psychological stress in a subpopulation of healthy men. *Psychosomatic Medicine, 57,* 468–474.

Langer, E. J., & Rodin, J. (1976). The effects of choice and enhanced personality responsibility for the aged: A field experiment in an institutional setting. *Journal of Personality and Social Psychology, 34,* 191–198.

Leedham, B., Meyerowitz, B. E., Muirhead, J., & Frist, W. H. (1995). Positive expectations predict health after heart transplantation. *Health Psychology, 14,* 74–79.

Levy, B., Slade, M., Kunkel, S., & Kasl, S. (2002). Longevity increased by positive self-perceptions of aging. *Journal of Personality and Social Psychology, 83,* 261–270.

Lobel, M., DeVincent, C. J., Kaminer, A., & Meyer, B. A. (2000). The impact of prenatal maternal stress and optimistic disposition on birth outcomes in medically high-risk women. *Health Psychology, 19,* 544–553.

Maruta, T., Colligan, R. C., Malinchoc, M., & Offord, K. P. (2000). Optimists vs. pessimists: Survival rate among medical patients over a 30-year period. *Mayo Clinic Proceedings, 75,* 140–143.

McDonald, E. R., Wiedenfeld, S. A., Hillel, A., Carpenter, C. L., & Walter, R. A. (1994). Survival in amyotrophic lateral sclerosis: The role of psychological factors. *Archives of Neurology, 51,* 17–23.

Milam, J. E., Richardson, J. L., Marks, G., Kemper, C. A., & McCutchan, A. (2004). The roles of dispositional optimism and pessimism in HIV disease progression. *Psychology and Health, 19,* 167–181.

O'Connor, B. P., & Vallerand, R. J. (1998). Psychological adjustment variables as predictors of mortality among nursing home residents. *Psychology and Aging, 13,* 368–374.

Pearlin, L. I., & Schooler, C. (1978). The structure of coping. *Journal of Health and Social Behavior, 19,* 2–21.

Peterson, C. (2000). The future of optimism. *American Psychologist, 55,* 44–55.

Peterson, C., & Seligman, M. E. P. (1987). Explanatory style and illness. *Journal of Personality, 55,* 237–265.

Peterson, C., Seligman, M. E. P., & Vaillant, G. E. (1988). Pessimistic explanatory style is a risk factor for physical illness: A thirty-five-year longitudinal study. *Journal of Personality and Social Psychology, 55,* 23–27.

Peterson, C., Seligman, M. E. P., Yurko, K. H., Martin, L. R., & Friedman, H. S. (1998). Catastrophizing and untimely death. *Psychological Science, 9,* 127–130.

Pham, L. B., Taylor, S. E., & Seeman, T. E. (2001). Effects of environmental predictability and personal mastery on self regulatory and physiological processes. *Personality and Social Psychology, 27,* 611–620.

Pruessner, J. C., Hellhammer, D. H., & Kirschbaum, C. (1999). Low self-esteem, induced failure and the adrenocortical stress response. *Personality and Individual Differences, 27,* 477–489.

Räikkönen, K., Matthews, K. A., Flory, J. D., Owens, J. F., & Gump, B. B. (1999). Effects of optimism, pessimism, and trait anxiety on ambulatory blood pressure and mood during everyday life. *Journal of Personality and Social Psychology, 76,* 104–113.

Reed, G. M., Kemeny, M. E., Taylor, S. E., & Visscher, B. R. (1999). Negative HIV-specific expectancies and AIDS-related bereavement as predictors of symptom onset in asymptomatic HIV-positive gay men. *Health Psychology, 18,* 354–363.

Reed, G. M., Kemeny, M. E., Taylor, S. E., Wang, H. Y. J., & Visscher, B. R. (1994). Realistic acceptance as a predictor of decreased survival time in gay men with AIDS. *Health Psychology, 13,* 299–307.

Richardson, J., Zarnegar, Z., Bisno, B., & Levine, A. (1990). Psychosocial status at initiation of breast cancer treatment and survival. *Journal of Psychosomatic Research, 34,* 189–201.

Rini, C. K., Dunkel-Schetter, C., Wadhwa, P. D., & Sandman, C. A. (1999). Psychological adaptation and birth outcomes: The role of personal resources, stress, and sociocultural context in pregnancy. *Health Psychology, 18,* 333–345.

Rodin, J., & Langer, E. J. (1977). Long-term effects of a control-relevant intervention with the institutionalized aged. *Journal of Personality and Social Psychology, 35,* 897–902.

Rotter, J. B. (1966). Generalized expectancies for internal versus external control of reinforcement. *Psychological Monographs, 80*(1, Whole No. 609).

Sapolsky, R. M. (1994). *Why zebras don't get ulcers.* New York: Freeman.

Scheier, M. F., Matthews, K. A., Owens, J. F., Magovern, G. J., Lefebvre, R. C., Abbott, R. A., et al. (1989). Dispositional optimism and recovery from coronary artery bypass surgery: The beneficial effects on physical and psychological well-being. *Journal of Personality and Social Psychology, 57,* 1024–1040.

Scheier, M. F., Matthews, K. A., Owens, J. F., Schulz, R., Bridges, M. W., et al. (1999). Optimism and rehospitalization after coronary artery bypass graft surgery. *Archives of Internal Medicine, 159,* 829–835.

Schofield, P., Ball, D., Smith, J. G., Borland, R., O'Brien, P., et al. (2004). Optimism and survival in lung carcinoma patients. *Cancer, 100,* 1276–1282.

Schulz, R., Bookwala, J., Knapp, J. E., Scheier, M., & Williamson, G. M. (1996). Pessimism, age, and cancer mortality. *Psychology and Aging, 11,* 304–309.

Seeman, T. E., Berkman, L. F., Gulanski, B. I., Robbins, R. J., Greenspan, S. L., Charpentier, P. A., et al. (1995). Self-esteem and neuroendocrine response to challenge: MacArthur studies of successful aging. *Journal of Psychosomatic Research, 19,* 69–84.

Seery, M. D., Blascovich, J., Weisbuch, M., & Vick, S. B. (2004). The relationship between self-esteem level, self-esteem stability, and cardiovascular reactions to performance feedback. *Journal of Personality and Social Psychology, 87,* 133–145.

Segerstrom, S. C. (2001). Optimism, goal conflict, and stressor-related immune change. *Journal of Behavioral Medicine, 24,* 441–467.

Segerstrom, S. C. (2006). How does optimism suppress immunity? Evaluation of three affective pathways. *Health Psychology, 25,* 653–657.

Segerstrom, S. C., Castaneda, J. O, & Spencer, T. E. (2003). Optimism effects on cellular immunity: Testing the affective and persistence models. *Personality and Individual Differences, 35,* 1615–1624.

Segerstrom, S. C., Taylor, S. E., Kemeny, M. E., & Fahey, J. L. (1998). Optimism is associated with mood, coping, and immune change in response to stress. *Journal of Personality and Social Psychology, 74,* 1646–1655.

Segerstrom, S. C., Taylor, S. E., Kemeny, M. E., Reed, G. M., & Visscher, B. R. (1996). Causal attributions predict rate of immune decline in HIV seropositive gay men. *Health Psychology, 15,* 485–493.

Sieber, W. J., Rodin, J., Larson, L., Ortega, S., & Cummings, N. (1992). Modulation of human natural killer cell activity by exposure to uncontrollable stress. *Brain, Behavior, and Immunity, 6,* 141–156.

Snedeker, J. L., Spencer, T. E., Solberg Nes, L., Miller, F. C., & Segerstrom, S. C. (2005). *Optimism and coping in early pregnancy: Effects on anxiety and birth outcomes.* Unpublished manuscript, University of Kentucky, Lexington.

Solberg Nes, L., & Segerstrom, S. C. (2006). Dispositional optimism and coping: A meta-analytic review. *Personality and Social Psychology Review, 10,* 235–251.

Solberg Nes, L., Segerstrom, S. C., & Sephton, S. E. (2005). Engagement and arousal: Optimism's effects during a brief stressor. *Personality and Social Psychology Bulletin, 31,* 111–120.

Steptoe, A., Kunz-Ebrecht, S., Owen, N., Feldman, P. J., Willemsen, G., Kirschbaum, C., et al. (2003). Socioeconomic status and stress-related biological responses over the working day. *Psychosomatic Medicine, 65,* 461–470.

Suls, J., & Fletcher, B. (1985). The relative efficacy of avoidant and nonavoidant coping strategies: A meta-analysis. *Health Psychology, 4,* 249–288.

Taylor, S. E., & Brown, J. (1988). Illusion and well-being: A social psychological perspective on mental health. *Psychological Bulletin, 103,* 193–210.

Taylor, S. E., Lerner, J. S., Sherman, K. D., Sage, R. M., & McDowell, N. K. (2003). Are self-enhancing cognitions associated with healthy or unhealthy biological profiles? *Journal of Personality and Social Psychology, 85,* 605–615.

Tomakowsky, J., Lumley, M. A., Markowitz, N., & Frank, C. (2001). Optimistic explanatory style and dispositional optimism in HIV-infected men. *Journal of Psychosomatic Research, 51,* 577–587.

Watson, D., & Pennebaker, J. W. (1989). Health complaints, stress, and distress: Exploring the central role of negative affectivity. *Psychological Review, 96,* 234–254.

Zorrilla, E. P., DeRubeis, R. J., & Redei, E. (1995). High self-esteem, hardiness and affective stability are associated with higher basal pituitary-adrenal hormone levels. *Psychoneuroendocrinology, 20,* 591–601.

4

ON THE PSYCHOLOGICAL HAZARDS OF SELF-CRITICISM

CHRISTIAN HOLLE AND RICK INGRAM

Self-criticism in psychopathology can include such elements as negative and critical thoughts directed toward one's own personal or physical characteristics, excessive self-blame for shortcomings, the inability to accomplish goals and tasks in accordance with unrealistically high standards, and the low regard with which individuals believe they are being appraised by others. Such self-critical thoughts, beliefs, and attributions have been linked to the etiology or maintenance of several forms of psychopathology including depression (Beck, 1987; Blatt, 1995), social anxiety (L. A. Clark, Watson, & Mineka, 1994), substance abuse (Blatt, Rounsaville, Eyre, & Wilber, 1984), and eating disorders (Lehman & Rodin, 1989; Steiger, Gauvin, Jabalpurwila, Seguin, & Stotland, 1999). Self-criticism in psychopathology is quite pervasive.

Despite the pervasiveness of self-criticism across various forms of psychopathology, it has been particularly strongly linked both empirically and theoretically to affective disorders. In this chapter we explore self-criticism as it relates specifically to depression. In this regard, two theoretical approaches that have examined negative self-referent cognitions and attitudes are discussed as they pertain to self-criticism in depression. As the information-processing paradigm has long examined negative biases in clinical disorders, including perception, attention, and memory (e.g., Mathews, Ridgeway, & Williamson, 1996; Mogg, Mathews, & Eysenck, 1992; Williams, Watts, MacLeod, & Mathews, 1997), a specific model from this paradigm is discussed in relation to self-criticism. In particular, we examine Beck's cognitive model of depression as it pertains to self-criticism. Next, a well-established psychodynamic approach developed by Blatt that uses self-criticism as a key factor in its conceptualization is also discussed. Finally, perfectionism, a construct that spans both models, is examined.

COGNITIVE APPROACHES TO DEPRESSION AND SELF-CRITICISM

Because cognitive models have been conceptualized in information-processing terms, a brief description of the information-processing paradigm is helpful. This paradigm focuses largely on the structures and operations within the system and how they function in the selection, transformation, encoding, storage, retrieval, and generation of information and behavior. Information processing constitutes a framework for examining the cognitive mechanisms that underlie and mediate cognition, affect, and behavior. Thus, information processing provides a conceptual umbrella over a confluence of constructs sharing similar assumptions concerning the functioning of human cognition (Ingram & Kendall, 1986).

Cognitive clinical conceptualizations of psychopathology typically share the proposition that cognitions such as dysfunctional thoughts, beliefs, and attributions are related to affective and behavioral dysfunctions. Cognitive models have proven particularly useful for conceptualizing psychological processes in depression (Alloy, 1988; Segal & Dobson, 1992), and a central feature among most cognitive models is an emphasis on cognitive structures (e.g., Beck, 1967; Segal, 1988) or networks (e.g., Ingram, 1984; Teasdale, 1983; Teasdale & Barnard, 1993) that may play a role in the onset and maintenance of depression. Moreover, negative self-evaluation, particularly in the case of self-critical thoughts, beliefs, and attitudes, has been a central feature in the construction of a number of cognitive models of depression along with other themes such as loss, separation, disappointment, and rejection (e.g., Abramson, Seligman, & Teasdale, 1978; Beck, 1967, 1976; Bower, 1981; Teasdale & Dent, 1987). Indeed, psychological treatments for depression based on various cognitive models have focused on the distorted and critical views of the self as a key aspect of treatment (e.g., DeRubeis et al., 1990). Arguably the most influential cognitive model of depression is based on Beck's work.

Self-Criticism in Beck's Cognitive Model of Depression

Although many theorists have noted that individuals with depression appraise themselves in a negative manner, Beck (1967) was among the first to recognize that negative views of the self reflect a core symptom of depression. In Beck's model, these negative views are theorized to result from faulty information processing that leads to errors in thinking and interpreting experiences and in generating inappropriately self-critical thoughts. In what Beck (1967) termed a *negative cognitive triad*, he observed individuals with depression not only hold critical views regarding the self but also tend to evidence negative views of the world and the future. This conceptualization suggests that self-critical beliefs are not solely about current experiences but also reflect a global view of the world and also extend into the future (Burns, 1980). In this model, reality is distorted and self-interpretations of one's life and experiences are systematically biased in the direction of emphasizing negative features and information (Beck, 1967). This distortion leads to self-criticism by the individual who has depression that fosters a view of the self as deficient, inadequate, or unworthy. Furthermore, people with depression selectively attend to the negative even when alternative positive interpretations are reasonable and valid, thus maintaining a harsh and critical view of themselves while minimizing positive aspects of the self (Beck, 1976). These negative biases are organized within depressive cognitive schemas.

Schemas are basic information-processing structures in humans that allow data to be quickly and efficiently processed so that individuals can attend to relevant and important information (Segal, 1988). Schemas also tend to fill in missing gaps in knowledge and, as such, guide the search for information based on what is consistent with the beliefs and structure of the schema itself. Beck (1967) adapted the idea of schemas to understand depression and suggested that individuals with depression possess dysfunctional self-schemas that contain preexisting critical and negative beliefs that lead individuals with depression to pay attention to information that supports these beliefs while ignoring disconfirming positive information. Viewed as a stable information-processing structure composed of negative self-representations, the negative self-schema is thought to dominate cognition during episodes of affective distress and produce dysfunctional information-processing patterns. Moreover, Beck argued that the self-critical thoughts generated by schemas are automatic in that they occur without conscious effort or choice (Beck, 1976).

Since Beck (1967) first invoked the idea of a schema and notions of faulty information processing, the schema construct has generated considerable theoretical and empirical work in depression (Beck, Rush, Shaw, & Emery, 1979; Hollon, Kendall, & Lumry, 1986; Ingram, Miranda, & Segal, 1998; Williams et al., 1997). Data suggest that, once activated, schemas consist of pervasive negative beliefs and dysfunctional assumptions about the self and its relation to the world and the future. Thus, a pervasively negative self-schema in a person with depression would likely contain critical and disparaging beliefs about the self and would generate self-critical thoughts congruent with these beliefs and propositions. These self-critical beliefs have been found to be relatively enduring despite contrary information and positive experiences that the person with depression may encounter (Beck, 1976). The negative self-schema is the organizing principle underlying many of the cognitive approaches to depression (e.g., Beck, 1976, 1983, 1987; Ingram, 1984; Teasdale & Barnard, 1993).

Cognitive–Behavioral Treatment

Originally developed by Beck (1976), cognitive treatments for depression typically focus on maladaptive cognitions and beliefs that are thought to have a role in the onset and maintenance of depression. Most cognitive therapies also include behavioral techniques in the treatment of depression, such as addressing reduced positive reinforcement in the environment of the person with depression, providing training to improve social skills deficits, and correcting deficiencies in the ability to regulate self-reinforcement (e.g., Lewinsohn, Clarke, Hops, & Andrews, 1990; Rehm, Fuchs, Roth, Kornblith, & Romano, 1979).

Central to most cognitive–behavioral therapies is a focus on changing the dysfunctional and automatic thoughts that are theorized to stem from maladaptive schemas (e.g., DeRubeis & Feeley, 1990; Hollon & Kendall, 1980). Working with the therapist, clients are taught to monitor their thinking and become aware of their depressogenic automatic thoughts. Once dysfunctional cognitions are identified, clients are instructed in ways to challenge and dispute the validity of these self-critical thoughts and beliefs (Hollon & Beck, 1994). Clients are taught not to accept self-criticisms as being true, but to regard them as hypothetical propositions and, with the aid of the therapist, to examine the evidence for the validity of such faults and shortcomings in their life or behavior (DeRubeis et al., 1990). The goal of cognitive–behavioral therapy is to ultimately replace self-critical thoughts and beliefs with more rational and realistic cognitions that will make it more likely for the client to engage in healthy positively reinforced behaviors not previously attempted (Jacobson et al., 1996). Homework and behavioral exposures are often used in this type of therapy to obtain additional evidence and practice to challenge and dispute faulty self-criticisms (Addis & Jacobson, 1996). Cognitive–behavioral therapies place an emphasis on targeting dysfunctional thoughts not only because of the function they are believed to play in mediating dysfunctional mood and behavior but, more important, because such thoughts also reveal core assumptions and beliefs that stem from the client's maladaptive schemas (e.g., Beck et al., 1979; Ingram & Holle, 1992; Jacobson et al., 1996).

Young, Weinberger, and Beck (2001) identified several maladaptive schemas, the majority of which are theorized to have developed early in life. Two such identified schemas, "Defectiveness and Shame" and "Unrelenting Standards," are relevant to this discussion of self-criticism. The former is composed of a collection of self-critical beliefs holding that the person with depression is inferior or defective in several important respects. Individuals with this type of schema tend to be hypersensitive to criticism from others and constantly compare themselves negatively with those around them (Young et al., 2001). The latter schema contains themes relating to excessively high internal standards of behavior that the individual often cannot meet. It is ironic that although these standards are set high in an attempt to avoid criticism from others, the result is often an increase in self-criticism by the person with depression. Individuals with this type of maladaptive schema seldom find satisfaction in accomplishments and rarely slow down and relax, thus significantly reducing the enjoyment they obtain from life (Young, Klosko, & Weishaar, 2003).

The efficacy of cognitive–behavioral treatments for depression has been well documented (see Beck, 2005). Studies comparing such treatments with medication or with other forms of psychotherapy for depression have shown mixed results and have led to much discussion in the literature (e.g., Dobson, 1989; Jacobson & Hollon, 1996). However, substantive evidence supports the contention that cognitive–behavioral treatments are at least comparable if not superior to other types of treatment for depression, particularly when symptom reduction and relapse prevention is examined (Evans et al., 1992; Hollon, Shelton, & Loosen, 1991).

Accuracy of Self-Criticism

Cognitive–behavioral treatment of depression is based on the supposition that self-critical thoughts and beliefs are a consequence of a negative self-referent cognitive bias produced by a systematic distortion of reality. According to this view, individuals with depression do not view themselves and their behavior in an accurate fashion. Although several researchers support this view (e.g., Teasdale & Barnard, 1993; Williams, Watts, MacLeod, & Mathews, 1997), Beck's (1967) traditional position that people with depression distort the processing of information in systematically negative ways has also been challenged by several sources (e.g., Alloy & Abramson, 1979; Lewinsohn, Mischel, Chaplin, & Barton, 1980; Sackeim, 1983). Thus, there has been disagreement in the depression literature pertaining to the relative accuracy or distortion of cognition in depression. In general, studies investigating this issue have shown mixed results, suggesting that sometimes individuals with depression distort information (e.g., Nelson & Craighead, 1977, reinforcement condition; Gotlib, 1983) and sometimes they do not (Nelson & Craighead, 1977, punishment condition). These mixed results therefore strongly suggest that the accuracy of information processing in depression is determined by a number of complex factors and that general conclusions about distortion or accuracy are probably premature. One area that appears to have strong evidence of depressive realism arises from studies on contingency judgment tasks in which an objective measure of reality is compared with judgments made by people with depression (Ackermann & DeRubeis, 1991; D. A. Clark, Beck, & Alford, 1999; Dobson & Franche, 1989).

In more fundamental terms, although accuracy can be operationalized easily in laboratory situations, the notion of accuracy and distortion has not been adequately defined conceptually (Roth & Ingram, 1985). Beck's (1967) contention, for example, implied a "distortion by commission" definition in which individuals with depression somehow change positive or neutral information into negative information to fit their depressive schema. An equally likely but very different definition of distortion is a "distortion by omission" notion. In such a case, individuals with depression may process negative information and fail to recognize positive data (the converse may be just as likely for individuals without depression). The overall effect of this processing style thus would be distortion, because of the imbalance of information attended to relative to information available. Whether this or other conceptualizations of distortion are useful, it is important for future research to reach some degree of consensus about what constitutes distortion or accuracy before the phenomenon can be examined and conclusions drawn (see Haaga, Dyck, & Ernst, 1991, for a more extensive review).

PSYCHODYNAMIC APPROACHES TO DEPRESSION AND SELF-CRITICISM

From a psychoanalytic perspective, perhaps the most well known theory of self-criticism as it relates to depression can be seen in the work of Blatt (1974). In a combination of theories taken from both psychoanalytic and cognitive developmental domains, Blatt and colleagues (Blatt, 1974; Blatt, D'Afflitti, & Quinlan, 1976; Blatt, Quinlan, Chevron, McDonald, & Zuroff, 1982) proposed the existence of two broad types of depression: *anaclitic* and *introjective*. Anaclitic depression is characterized by feelings of helplessness, weakness, and loneliness. Individuals with this type of depression have intense and chronic fears of being abandoned and left unprotected by others (Blatt, 1974, 1995). However, introjective depression is characterized by feelings of worthlessness, inferiority, guilt, and a sense of having failed to live up to the expectations and standards of oneself and others. Because individuals with introjective depression have a strong fear of losing the approval of significant others, they engage in harsh self-criticism and evaluation. Blatt (1974) argued that people with introjective depression strive for excessive achievement and perfection as a result of their perceived inferiority coupled with a fear of disapproval from others they care about. Although they are typically highly competitive and often accomplish a great deal, they obtain little satisfaction from their success (Blatt, 1974, 1995).

Blatt and colleagues (Blatt, D'Afflitti, & Quinlan, 1976) subsequently developed the labels of *dependent* and *self-critical* for anaclitic and introjective depression, respectively. These labels were based on a factor analysis of a set of items thought to represent what individuals with depression commonly experience. Two factors emerged: dependence (including issues relating to abandonment, feeling lonely and helpless, and dependency on others) and self-criticism (including self-criticism, fear of disapproval, and failure to meet expectations and standards; Blatt et al., 1976).

Self-critical depression is thought to develop from early developmental experiences as a result of an individual's attempt to cope with severe disruptions of the normal developmental process (Blatt & Shichman, 1983). As a result, this form of depression is believed to develop as a result of the individual attempting to maintain a sense of the self as separate, autonomous, and positively valued. When these strategies fail, as they frequently do, these individuals experience depression along with other possible forms of psychopathology (Blatt & Shichman, 1983). Those who experience self-critical depression are reported to have a number of interpersonal difficulties. These include lower social support (e.g., Dunkley, Zuroff, & Blankstein, 2003; Mongrain, 1998; Priel & Besser, 2000) and impaired relationships with significant others (e.g., Mongrain, Lubbers, & Struthers, 2004; Santor & Zuroff, 1997; Thompson & Zuroff, 1998; Zuroff & Duncan, 1999).

Blatt (1995) described self-critical people with depression as having strong needs to succeed that drive them to strive for goals and accomplishments that are often overreaching. Coupled with this drive to perform is a desire to not appear weak or deficient to others. Thus they are both vulnerable to the criticisms of others and highly self-critical of themselves. Much of this self-criticism, Blatt (1995) argued, arises from an irrational desire for perfection and unrealistically high standards of achievement that the individual cannot meet. Moreover, because of interpersonal difficulties, they are either unable or unwilling to turn to others for help (Blatt, 1995; Blatt et al., 1982).

Research has also identified a number of other problematic areas that self-critical people with depression experience; issues of self-worth, self-esteem, failure, and guilt are particularly prominent (Zuroff, Igreja, & Mongrain, 1990). As introjective depression is characterized by high self-criticism and feelings of guilt and worthlessness, this form of depression is also thought to hold an increased risk for suicide attempts (Blatt, 1974, 1995; Blatt et al., 1982).

Introjective depression is theorized to occur from early experience with harsh, demanding, and critical parents. This exposure leads to the child internalizing these attitudes and ultimately they become part of the child's personality structure. Incorporation of these attitudes is thought to bring about a degradation in the child's feelings of self-worth and produce excessive self-criticism as an adult (Blatt, 1974). Thus, psychodynamic treatment attempts to first form a solid and supportive therapeutic relationship with the patient who is depressed and then gradually change the maladaptive and rigid internalized structures developed in childhood (Auerbach & Blatt, 2001). In a successful treatment outcome, the patient will be able to identify and incorporate the more loving and forgiving and less critical aspects of the parents. Positive structural reorganization can also occur through transference in sessions with the therapist.

Analyses of outpatient treatment data indicate that brief treatment for self-critical depression is ineffective, probably because of the harsh, critical, and judgmental characteristics of this form of depression (Blatt et al., 1995, 1996). In addition, perfectionism, a characteristic of self-critical depression, appears to be a central component in treatment response to brief therapy. In particular, those patients with relatively low levels of perfectionism are comparatively more responsive to various forms of brief treatment modalities than are those with high levels of perfectionism (Blatt et al., 1995, 1996).

These findings led Blatt and colleagues (1998) to suggest that introjective, self-critical patients may require more long-term, intensive, psychodynamically oriented therapy to change entrenched negative mental self-representations. Furthermore, Blatt suggested that people with introjective depression who are concerned about issues of autonomy and control react negatively to predetermined limitations on the therapeutic process in brief sessions and that they may respond more constructively to a treatment process in which they participate in deciding when to terminate. Likewise, Blatt has argued (e.g., Blatt & Felsen, 1993) that individuals dealing with issues of self-definition and self-worth, as is the case with the self-critical form of depression, typically have greater intellectual capabilities and are more self-reflective than are those with the dependent form of depression and thus are more suited to long-term, intensive psychoanalytic treatment. Indeed, clinical data have consistently indicated significantly greater clinical improvement in self-critical patients with depression in long-term therapy relative to dependent patients with depression (Blatt & Ford, 1994).

COMPARISON OF APPROACHES TO DEPRESSION AND SELF-CRITICISM

At first glance, Beck's and Blatt's conceptualizations of depression as they relate to self-criticism appear quite different. In Beck's model (1967, 1987), self-criticism stems from activation of schemas that produce negative self-referent thoughts and beliefs. Thus Beck (1983) argued that people can appear quite different depending on whether they are depressed or in remission, with the frequency of self-critical thoughts substantially higher in a depressed state. This proposition is supported by a number of studies that have found that negative self-referent thinking and critical beliefs tend to occur only as long as the depressive episode persists (Dobson & Shaw, 1987; Dohr, Rush, & Bernstein, 1989; Hasher, Rose, Zacks, Sanft, & Doren, 1985; Lewinsohn, Steinmetz, Larson, & Franklin, 1981; but see Ingram et al., 1998, and Segal & Ingram, 1994, for an explanation of the diathesis-stress perspective on the enduring nature of depressive schemas and self-critical thinking). In contrast, Blatt's introjective self-critical form of depression appears to represent relatively enduring personal characteristics more approximating that of a personality trait; the self-criticism appears to be long lasting and rooted in early childhood experiences (Blatt & Maroudas, 1992) and not in current stressors or life situations, as in Beck's model.

Despite originating from different theoretical perspectives, both models share some similarities in many respects, particularly as Beck has continued to modify his theory. In particular, Beck's (1983) reformulated theory distinguishes between two modes of depression: a *sociotropic* (socially dependent) depression and an *autonomous* (socially independent) depression. Beck's (1983) autonomous depression and Blatt's (1974) self-critical depression have much conceptual overlap. For instance, the mode of individuality (autonomy), according to Beck (1983), refers to independence and freedom of choice with an emphasis on action to attain meaningful goals. Beck argued that a person with autonomous depression is achievement-oriented and continually facing themes of failure and defeat when obligations are not fulfilled. Thus, people with autonomous depression try to manipulate others or their environment to lessen the possibility of failure and criticism from others and themselves. This conceptualization is very similar to Blatt's self-critical depression. Another similarity resides in the notion of perfectionism.

Perfectionism

The construct of perfectionism has been strongly linked with self-criticism in a number of studies that span both cognitive (e.g., Frost, Marten, Lahart, & Rosenblate, 1990) and psychodynamic (e.g., Blatt, 1995) approaches to depression. Perfectionism has varying definitions in the literature, such as those definitions emphasizing the holding of impossibly high standards in terms of productivity and accomplishment (Burns, 1980) or the overly critical self-evaluation of meeting such high self-standards (Frost et al., 1990). Behavioral and self-regulation models have conceptualized perfectionism as a pursuit of unattainable standards that, when not accomplished, generates self-criticism and leads to generalized negative self-evaluations of many aspects of the self (e.g., Carver & Ganellen, 1983; Rehm, 1977), often without a reduction in the attempt to achieve the unattainable goals (Carver & Scheier, 1986).

Perfectionism has been increasingly viewed as a multidimensional construct by a number of investigators (e.g., Frost et al., 1990; Hewitt & Flett,

1991), many of whom have found that subsets of this construct correlated with self-criticism and related concepts. The Multidimensional Perfectionism scale, which was created by Frost and colleagues (Frost et al., 1990) to assess dimensions of perfectionism, has found a number of dimensions related to negative self-evaluation, such as an overconcern for making mistakes, doubting the quality of one's work, and excessively high standards. Hewitt and Flett (1991) similarly proposed that perfectionism contains three distinct types: *other-oriented perfectionism, self-oriented perfectionism,* and *socially prescribed perfectionism.* Echoing many of Frost and colleagues' (1990) dimensions of perfectionism, self-oriented perfectionism also relates strongly to negative self-evaluation. This subtype involves unrealistically high standards, attempts to avoid failure, and a nonacceptance of one's faults (Hewitt & Flett, 1991).

In a more direct link between perfectionism and self-criticism, Dunkley and colleagues (Dunkley, Zuroff, & Blankstein, 2003) identified two primary dimensions of perfectionism: *personal standards perfectionism* and *self-critical perfectionism.* Although the dimension personal standards perfectionism involves the setting of high standards and goals for oneself, it is seen as containing positive and adaptive elements compared with self-critical perfectionism (Dunkley et al., 2003). According to Dunkley and colleagues (2003), people with self-critical perfectionism are in a constant state of critical examination of their behavior coupled with a harsh self-examination that prevents them from obtaining satisfaction from those performances that are done well. Although both dimensions engage in negative self-evaluation, self-critically perfectionistic individuals react to stressful and problematic situations in a helpless manner and tend to focus inward on their own shortcomings and deficiencies. Dunkley and colleagues also argued that people with self-critical perfectionism tend to back off and avoid situations that may appear threatening because of a preoccupation with their own deficiencies. Thus, these individuals lack the ability and motivation to actively cope with a wide array of situations they presume are too difficult and resort to habitual avoidance (Dunkley et al., 2003).

It should be noted, however, that not all the data on perfectionism support its existence as an entirely negative construct (Flett & Hewitt, 2002). Following a factor analysis of two perfectionism scale scores, Frost, Heimberg, Holt, Mattia, and Neubauer (1993) found a factor strongly associated with positive or adaptive aspects of perfectionism in addition to a factor that has typically been associated with negative or maladaptive aspects of this construct. The primary difference between the adaptive and maladaptive aspects of perfectionism appears to center on whether the high standards set by an individual are achievable or not, and how the individual reacts to mistakes when these standards are occasionally not met (Enns & Cox, 2002). Thus, adaptive perfectionism is theorized to be motivated by the desire for positive rewards and orderliness as contrasted with an excessive concern and avoidance of failure when performance does not meet unrealistically high standards, as is construed to be the case with maladaptive perfectionism (Rice, Ashby, & Slaney, 1998).

In sum, perfectionism is a construct that is closely tied to various ideas about depression and that embodies the self-critical aspects of depression. Because of the mismatch between perfectionistic personality dimensions and unrealistically high standards, and the inability of most individuals to consistently meet these high standards, perfectionism is seen as a dimension that underlies and gives rise to self-criticism. Although deriving from different theoretical perspectives than either Beck's or Blatt's original models, perfectionism is a construct that fits easily within these models. Indeed, both models of depression include the role of perfectionism in the genesis of depression.

Final Thoughts

In this chapter, we briefly examined the information-processing framework that underlies cognitive models of depression and then discussed what is arguably the most prominent cognitive mode of depression: the cognitive model proposed by Beck. The central organizing concept of this model is the cognitive schema, which, as we have shown, gives rise to, among other cognitions, self-critical thoughts. After his original proposals, Beck modified his theory of depression to suggest two different subtypes of depression: autonomous and sociotropic. Both types of depression are precipitated by events that match the cognitive characteristics of these subtypes.

Although Beck's and Blatt's models differ in a number of important respects, Beck's concepts of autonomy and sociotropy do share considerable similarities with Blatt's more psychodynamically inspired model of depression—in particular, the concepts of dependent and self-critical depression subtypes. In a more general way, both Beck's and Blatt's ideas resemble many aspects of perfectionism—a concept that suggests that some people exhibit unrealistically high standards, and that when these standards are not met, a self-critical form of depression is likely to ensue. Self-criticism is thus a concept that is inherent in depression theories and is a mechanism that may serve to maintain depression; individuals who respond to adverse life events by being unrealistically critical of themselves are prone to continue experiencing a negative affective state.

Of course, the role of self-criticism and psychopathology is more complex in both its antecedents and consequences as pertaining to depression. In this chapter we were able to touch on only a few of the elements of self-criticism, and only in one specific disorder, namely depression. Without a doubt, self-criticism, to varying degrees, plays a role in other forms of psychopathology and is certainly worthy of both theoretical discussion and empirical investigation in all areas of psychopathology.

REFERENCES

Abramson, L. Y., Seligman, M. E., & Teasdale, J. D. (1978). Learned helplessness in humans: Critique and reformulation. *Journal of Abnormal Psychology, 87*, 49–74.

Ackermann, R., & DeRubeis, R. J. (1991). Is depressive realism real? *Clinical Psychology Review, 10*, 565–584.

Addis, M. E., & Jacobson, N. S. (1996). Reasons for depression and the process and outcome of cognitive–behavioral psychotherapies. *Journal of Consulting and Clinical Psychology, 64*, 1417–1424.

Alloy, L. B. (Ed.). (1988). *Cognitive processes in depression*. New York: Guilford Press.

Alloy, L. B., & Abramson, L. Y. (1979). Judgment of contingency in depressed and nondepressed students: Sadder but wiser? *Journal of Experimental Psychology: General, 108*, 441–485.

Auerbach, J. S., & Blatt, S. J. (2001). Self-reflexivity, intersubjectivity, and therapeutic change. *Psychoanalytic Psychology, 18*, 427–450.

Beck, A. T. (1967). *Depression: Clinical, experimental, and theoretical aspects*. New York: Harper & Row.

Beck, A. T. (1976). *Cognitive therapy and the emotional disorders*. New York: International Universities Press.

Beck, A. T. (1983). Cognitive therapy of depression: New perspectives. In P. J. Clayton & J. E. Barret (Eds.), *Treatment of depression: Old controversies and new approaches* (pp. 265–290). New York: Raven Press.

Beck, A. T. (1987). Cognitive models of depression. *Journal of Cognitive Psychotherapy: An International Quarterly, 1*, 5–37.

Beck, A. T. (2005). The current state of cognitive therapy: A 40-year retrospective. *Archives of General Psychiatry, 62*, 953–959.

Beck, A. T., Rush, A. J., Shaw, B., & Emery, G. (1979). *Cognitive therapy of depression*. New York: Guilford Press.

Blatt, S. J. (1974). Levels of object representation in anaclitic and introjective depression. *Psychoanalytic Study of the Child, 29*, 107–157.

Blatt, S. J. (1995). The destructiveness of perfectionism: Implications for the treatment of depression. *American Psychologist, 49*, 1003–1020.

Blatt, S. J., D'Afflitti, J. P., & Quinlan, D. M. (1976). Experiences of depression in normal young adults. *Journal of Abnormal Psychology, 85*, 383–389.

Blatt, S. J., & Felsen, I. (1993). Different kinds of folks may need different kinds of strokes: The effect of patients' characteristics on therapeutic process and outcome. *Psychotherapy Research, 3*, 245–259.

Blatt, S. J., & Ford, R. Q. (1994). *Therapeutic change: An object relations perspective*. New York: Plenum Press.

Blatt, S. J., & Maroudas, C. (1992). Convergences among psychoanalytic and cognitive-behavioral theories of depression. *Psychoanalytic Psychology, 9*, 157–190.

Blatt, S. J., Quinlan, D. M., Chevron, E. S., McDonald, C., & Zuroff, D. C. (1982). Dependency and self-criticism: Psychological dimensions of depression. *Journal of Consulting and Clinical Psychology, 50,* 113–124.

Blatt, S. J., Quinlan, D. M., Pilkonis, P. A., & Shea, T. M. (1995). Impact of perfectionism and need for approval on the brief treatment of depression: The National Institute of Mental Health Treatment of Depression Collaborative Research Program revisited. *Journal of Consulting and Clinical Psychology, 63,* 125–132.

Blatt, S. J., Rounsaville, B., Eyre, S. L., & Wilber, C. (1984). The psychodynamics of opiate addiction. *Journal of Nervous and Mental Disease, 172,* 342–352.

Blatt, S. J., & Shichman, S. (1983). Two primary configurations of psychopathology. *Psychoanalysis and Contemporary Thought, 6,* 187–254.

Blatt, S. J., Zuroff, D. C., Bondi, C. M., Sanislow C., & Pilkonis, P. (1998). When and how perfectionism impedes the brief treatment of depression: Further analyses of the National Institute of Mental Health Treatment of Depression Collaborative Research Program. *Journal of Consulting and Clinical Psychology, 66,* 423–428.

Blatt, S. J., Zuroff, D. C., Quinlan, D. M., & Pilkonis, P. (1996). Interpersonal factors in brief treatment of depression: Further analyses of the National Institute of Mental Health Treatment of Depression Collaborative Research Program. *Journal of Consulting and Clinical Psychology, 64,* 162–171.

Bower, G. H. (1981). Mood and memory. *American Psychologist, 36,* 129–148.

Burns, D. D. (1980). *Feeling good: The new mood therapy.* New York: Morrow.

Carver, C. S., & Ganellen, R. (1983). Depression and components of self-punitiveness: High standards, self-criticism, and overgeneralization. *Journal of Abnormal Psychology, 92,* 330–337.

Carver, C. S., & Scheier, M. F. (1986). Self and the control of behavior. In L. Hartman & K. Blankstein (Eds.), *Perception of self in emotional disorder and psychotherapy* (pp. 5–35). New York: Plenum Press.

Clark, D. A., Beck, A. T., & Alford, B. A. (1999). *Scientific foundation of cognitive theory and therapy of depression.* New York: Wiley.

Clark, L. A., Watson, D., & Mineka, S. (1994). Temperament, personality, and the mood and anxiety disorders. *Journal of Abnormal Psychology, 103,* 103–116.

DeRubeis, R. J., Evans, M. D., Hollon, S. D., Garvey, M. J., Grove, W. M., & Tuason, V. B. (1990). How does cognitive therapy work? Cognitive change and symptom change in cognitive therapy and pharmacotherapy for depression. *Journal of Consulting and Clinical Psychology, 58,* 862–869.

DeRubeis, R. J., & Feeley, M. (1990). Determinants of change in cognitive therapy for depression. *Cognitive Therapy and Research, 14,* 469–482.

Dobson, K. (1989). A meta-analysis of the efficacy of cognitive therapy for depression. *Journal of Consulting and Clinical Psychology, 57,* 414–419.

Dobson, K., & Franche, R. L. (1989). A conceptual and empirical review of the depressive realism hypothesis. *Canadian Journal of Behavioral Sciences, 21,* 419–433.

Dobson, K. S., & Shaw, B. F. (1987). Specificity and stability of self-referent encoding in clinical depression. *Journal of Abnormal Psychology, 96,* 34–40.

Dohr, K. B., Rush, A. J., & Bernstein, I. H. (1989). Cognitive biases and depression. *Journal of Abnormal Psychology, 98,* 263–267.

Dunkley, D. M., Zuroff, D. C., & Blankstein, K. R. (2003). Self-critical perfectionism and daily affect: Dispositional and situational influences on stress and coping. *Journal of Personality and Social Psychology, 84,* 234–252.

Enns, M. W., & Cox, B. (2002). The nature and assessment of perfectionism: A critical analysis. In G. L. Flett & P. L. Hewitt (Eds.), *Perfectionism: Theory, research, and treatment* (pp. 33–62). Washington, DC: American Psychological Association.

Evans, M. D., Hollon, S. D., DeRubeis, R. J., Piasecki, J. M., Grove, M. J., & Tuason, V. B. (1992). Differential relapse following cognitive therapy and pharmacotherapy for depression. *Archives of General Psychiatry, 49,* 802–808.

Flett, G. L., & Hewitt, P. L. (2002). Perfectionism and maladjustment: An overview of theoretical, definitional, and treatment issues. In G. L. Flett & P. L. Hewitt (Eds.), *Perfectionism: Theory, research, and treatment* (pp. 5–32). Washington, DC: American Psychological Association.

Frost, R. O., Heimberg, R. G., Holt, C. S., Mattia, J. L., & Neubauer, A. L. (1993). A comparison of two measures of perfectionism. *Personality and Individual Differences, 14,* 119–126.

Frost, R. O., Marten, P. A., Lahart, C. M., & Rosenblate, R. (1990). The dimensions of perfectionism. *Cognitive Therapy and Research, 14,* 449–468.

Gotlib, I. H. (1983). Perception and recall of interpersonal feedback: Negative bias in depression. *Cognitive Therapy and Research, 7,* 399–412.

Haaga, D. A., Dyck, M. J., & Ernst, D. (1991). Empirical status of cognitive therapy of depression. *Psychological Bulletin, 110,* 215–236.

Hasher, L., Rose, K. C., Zacks, R. T., Sanft, H., & Doren, B. (1985). Mood, recall, and selectivity effects in normal college students. *Journal of Experimental Psychology: General, 114,* 104–118.

Hewitt, P. L., & Flett, G. L. (1991). Dimensions of perfectionism in unipolar depression. *Journal of Abnormal Psychology, 100,* 98–101.

Hollon, S. D., & Beck, A. T. (1994). Cognitive and cognitive-behavioral therapies. In A. E. Bergin & S. L. Garfield (Eds.), *Handbook of psychotherapy and behavior change* (4th ed., pp. 428–466). Oxford, England: Wiley.

Hollon, S. D., & Kendall, P. C. (1980). Cognitive self-statements in depression: Development of an Automatic Thoughts Questionnaire. *Cognitive Therapy and Research, 4,* 383–395.

Hollon, S. D., Kendall, P. C., & Lumry, A. (1986). Specificity of depressotypic cognitions in clinical depression. *Journal of Abnormal Psychology, 95,* 52–59.

Hollon, S. D., Shelton, R. C., & Loosen, P. T. (1991). Cognitive therapy and pharmacotherapy for depression. *Journal of Consulting and Clinical Psychology, 59*, 88–99.

Ingram, R. E. (1984). Toward an information-processing analysis of depression. *Cognitive Therapy and Research, 8*, 443–447.

Ingram, R. E., & Holle, C. (1992). The cognitive science of depression. In D. J. Stein & J. E. Young (Eds.), *Cognitive science and clinical disorders* (pp. 187–209). Orlando, FL: Academic Press.

Ingram, R. E., & Kendall, P. C. (1986). Cognitive clinical psychology: Implications of an information processing perspective. In R. E. Ingram (Ed.), *Information processing approaches to clinical psychology* (pp. 3–21). London: Academic Press.

Ingram, R. E., Miranda, J., & Segal, Z. V. (1998). *Cognitive vulnerability to depression.* New York: Guilford Press.

Jacobson, N. S., Dobson, K. S., Truax, P. A., Addis, M. E., Koerner, K., Gollan, J. K., et al. (1996). A component analysis of cognitive–behavioral treatment for depression. *Journal of Consulting and Clinical Psychology, 64*, 295–304.

Jacobson, N. S., & Hollon, S. D. (1996). Cognitive-behavior therapy versus pharmacotherapy: Now that the jury's returned its verdict, it's time to present the rest of the evidence. *Journal of Consulting and Clinical Psychology, 64*, 74–80.

Lehman, A. K., & Rodin, J. (1989). Styles of self-nurturance and disordered eating. *Journal of Consulting and Clinical Psychology, 57*, 117–122.

Lewinsohn, P. M., Clarke, G., Hops, H., & Andrews, J. A. (1990). Cognitive-behavioral treatment for depressed adolescents. *Behavior Therapy, 21*, 385–401.

Lewinsohn, P. M., Mischel, W., Chaplin, W., & Barton, R. (1980). Social competence and depression: The role of illusory self-perceptions? *Journal of Abnormal Psychology, 89*, 203–212.

Lewinsohn, P. M., Steinmetz, J. L., Larson, D. W., & Franklin, J. (1981). Depression-related cognitions: Antecedent or consequence? *Journal of Abnormal Psychology, 90*, 213–219.

Mathews, A., Ridgeway, V., & Williamson, D. A. (1996). Evidence for attention to threatening stimuli in depression. *Behaviour Research and Therapy, 34*, 695–705.

Mogg, K., Mathews, A., & Eysenck, M. (1992). Attentional bias to threat in clinical anxiety states. *Cognition and Emotion, 6*, 149–159.

Mongrain, M. (1998). Parental representations and support-seeking behaviors related to dependency and self-criticism. *Journal of Personality, 66*, 151–173.

Mongrain, M., Lubbers, R., & Struthers, W. (2004). The power of love: Mediation of rejection in roommate relationships of dependents and self-critics. *Personality and Social Psychology Bulletin, 30*, 94–105.

Nelson, R. E., & Craighead, W. E. (1977). Selective recall of positive and negative feedback, self-control behaviors, and depression. *Journal of Abnormal Psychology, 86*, 379–388.

Nietzel, M. T., & Harris, M. J. (1990). Relationship of dependency and achievement/autonomy to depression. *Clinical Psychology Review, 10,* 279–297.

Priel, B., & Besser, A. (2000). Dependency and self-criticism among first-time mothers: The roles of global and specific support. *Journal of Social and Clinical Psychology, 19,* 437–450.

Rehm, L. P. (1977). A self-control model of depression. *Behavior Therapy, 8,* 787–804.

Rehm, L. P., Fuchs, C. Z., Roth, D. M., Kornblith, S. J., & Romano, J. M. (1979). A comparison of self-control and assertion skills treatments of depression. *Behavior Therapy, 10,* 429–442.

Rice, K. G., Ashby, J. S., & Slaney, R. B. (1998). Self-esteem as a mediator between perfectionism and depression: A structural equations analysis. *Journal of Counseling Psychology, 45,* 304–314.

Roth, D. L., & Ingram, R. E. (1985). Factors in the Self-Deception Questionnaire: Associations with depression. *Journal of Personality and Social Psychology, 48,* 243–251.

Sackeim, H. A. (1983). Self-deception, self-esteem, and depression: The adaptive value of lying to oneself. In J. Masling (Ed.), *Empirical studies of psychoanalytical theories* (pp. 101–157). Hillsdale, NJ: Analytic Press.

Santor, D. A., & Zuroff, D. C. (1997). Interpersonal responses to threats to status and interpersonal relatedness: Effects of dependency and self-criticism. *British Journal of Clinical Psychology, 36,* 521–542.

Segal, Z. V. (1988). Appraisal of the self-schema construct in cognitive models of depression. *Psychological Bulletin, 103,* 147–162.

Segal, Z. V., & Dobson, K. S. (1992). Cognitive models of depression: Report from a consensus conference. *Psychological Inquiry, 3,* 225–229.

Segal, Z. V., & Ingram, R. E. (1994). Mood priming and construct activation in tests of cognitive vulnerability to unipolar depression. *Clinical Psychology Review, 14,* 663–695.

Steiger, H., Gauvin, L., Jabalpurwila, S., Seguin, J., & Stotland, S. (1999). Hypersensitivity to social interactions in bulimic syndromes: Relationship to binge eating. *Journal of Consulting and Clinical Psychology, 67,* 765–775.

Teasdale, J. D. (1983). Negative thinking in depression: Cause, effect, or reciprocal relationship? *Advances in Behaviour Therapy and Research, 5,* 3–25.

Teasdale, J. D., & Barnard, P. J. (1993). *Affect, cognition, and change.* Hillsdale, NJ: Erlbaum.

Teasdale, J. D., & Dent, J. (1987). Cognitive vulnerability to depression: An investigation of two hypotheses. *British Journal of Clinical Psychology, 26,* 113–126.

Thompson, R., & Zuroff, D. C. (1998). Dependent and self-critical mothers' responses to adolescent autonomy and competence. *Personality and Individual Differences, 24,* 311–324.

Williams, J. M., Watts, F. N., MacLeod, C., & Mathews, A. (1997). *Cognitive psychology and emotional disorder.* Chichester, England: Wiley.

Young, J. E., Klosko, J. S., & Weishaar, M. E. (2003). *Schema therapy: A practitioner's guide*. New York: Guilford Press.

Young, J. E., Weinberger, A. D., & Beck, A. T. (2001). Cognitive therapy for depression. In D. H. Barlow (Ed.), *Clinical handbook of psychological disorders: A step-by-step treatment manual* (3rd ed., pp. 264–308). New York: Guilford Press.

Zuroff, D. C., & Duncan, N. (1999). Self-criticism and conflict resolution in romantic couples. *Canadian Journal of Behavioural Science, 31*, 137–149.

Zuroff, D. C., Igreja, I., & Mongrain, M. (1990). Dysfunctional attitudes, dependency, and self-criticism as predictors of depressive mood states: A 12-month longitudinal study. *Cognitive Therapy and Research, 14*, 315–326.

5

ON SELF-CRITICISM AS INTERPERSONALLY MALADAPTIVE

JILL M. HOLM-DENOMA, AINHOA OTAMENDI,
AND THOMAS E. JOINER JR.

Among the potentially damaging effects of self-criticism is interpersonal strife. Individuals who are highly critical of themselves often experience struggles in many social domains, including relationships with romantic partners, family members, and friends. These interpersonal difficulties may result from the hypothesized insecurities that self-critical individuals have about attachment and social rank, their tendency to make few requests for social support, their relative lack of interpersonal goals, and the little pleasant affect they feel when acting communally. It is interesting that self-criticism appears to increase the frequency of negative interpersonal events and to increase subjective distress associated with interpersonal stressors. In this chapter we discuss the dynamic function of self-criticism, mediators between self-criticism and interpersonal difficulties, and how self-criticism affects particular interpersonal relationships (e.g., marriages and friendships).

THE GENERAL CONTEXT OF SELF-CRITICISM

Self-criticism is conceptualized as a continuous personality dimension that concerns one's self-appraisal. On the positive end of this continuum, self-criticism influences how one achieves a positive, realistic, and cohesive sense of oneself (Bagby & Rector, 1998; Rosenfarb, Becker, Khan, & Mintz, 1994). For people with healthy levels of this trait, being self-critical is an affirming, inspiring factor that helps them to achieve their goals. For example, an aspiring athlete may use constructive self-criticism to achieve success in the form of self-feedback in the development of skills, disciplined training regimens, and competitive tactics. In this sense, self-criticism works much like adaptive perfectionism might in an ideal environment.

However, for some people, self-criticism is an unhealthy, destructive force that leaves them feeling frustrated and discouraged. This discontentment occurs because some self-critical individuals become disapproving of themselves when they fail to achieve internalized standards and goals. For example, if the aspiring athlete mentioned earlier berated him- or herself for not meeting goals instead of seeing progress as a step in the right direction, and focused on imperfections instead of potential strengths, the end result might be aggravation and dissatisfaction. Thus, the athlete's self-criticism would likely thwart the attainment of his or her ultimate goals.

When self-criticism is manifested negatively, it often affects not only the self-critic but also interpersonal relationships. Self-critics have been described as ambivalent about interpersonal relationships, as they desire others' respect and approval while simultaneously fearing disapproval, loss of control, and their own autonomy (Blatt & Shichman, 1983). Previous research teams have described people with unhealthy levels of self-criticism as having poor mood management skills (Fichman, Koestner, Zuroff, & Gordon, 1999), high levels of negative affect (Mongrain & Zuroff, 1995), and maladaptive relationship schemas (Zuroff & Duncan, 1999).

ETIOLOGY AND FUNCTION OF SELF-CRITICISM

Before we consider the lifelong interpersonal effects of self-criticism, it is interesting to speculate on its origins. Some psychoanalysts have hypothesized that self-criticism is a result of a child's concern about losing the approval of cold, harsh, demanding, and judgmental parents (e.g., Blatt, 1974). They have specifically suggested that self-criticism is an internalization of rejecting and restrictive parenting. This hypothesis was empirically examined in a prospective longitudinal study of children ages 5 to 12 (Koestner, Zuroff, & Powers, 1991). Results indicated that within same-sex parent–child relationships, restrictive and rejecting parenting styles at age 5 predicted self-critical behaviors in offspring at age 12. A follow-up assessment revealed that self-criticism at age 12 predicted personal and social maladjustment at age 31 and that, for those self-critics who had children at age 31, self-criticism was negatively correlated with satisfaction with parenting.

Other studies have also shown that self-critical behaviors in offspring may be a result of parents who put a high emphasis on achievement and control (McCranie & Bass, 1984; Whiffen & Sasseville, 1991). These results support the idea that early parenting behaviors may play a role in both the development and maintenance of a self-critical personality style and inter-personal difficulties. They also indicate that self-criticism may be passed, genetically and environmentally, from one family member to the next.

In light of the fact that self-critical processes appear to originate in early life and continue throughout development, it is interesting to consider their impact. It is easy to imagine that having a self-critical personality style would negatively influence social interactions and possibly break social mo-res. Some researchers have gone so far as to assert that self-critics may even defy evolutionary processes such as altruism and social reciprocity. For ex-ample, Zuroff, Moskowitz, and Cote (1999) found that self-critical adults experienced less pleasant affect when acting communally than did those who were non-self-critical. Santor and Zuroff (1998) have also demonstrated that when interpersonal relatedness is threatened, self-critical women pro-mote their status by controlling a shared resource, even at the expense of a close friend. Because self-critics do not experience a great deal of reinforce-ment for acting altruistically and fear disapproval and rejection (Blatt & Shichman, 1983), they are probably less likely than uncritical people to act altruistically.

INTERPERSONAL CORRELATES OF SELF-CRITICISM

Many negative interpersonal correlates of self-criticism have been iden-tified. These correlates may appear early in life. For instance, retrospective self-reports from women indicate that self-criticism may be linked to a perceived difficulty in affective bonds with peers and fathers during childhood (Rosenfarb et al., 1994). During adolescence and young adulthood, self-criticism appears to affect rates of conflict and mood regulation. For example, Fichman, Koestner, and Zuroff (1994) reported that adolescent self-critics are too con-trolling in social interactions and thus incur an increased rate of social prob-lems. Self-critical young adults have also been found to experience more negative affect and less positive affect during social interactions and to set fewer interpersonal goals when compared with noncritical young adults (Mongrain & Zuroff, 1995). Self-report studies indicate that college-age self-critics report having fewer friends and being less satisfied with their social support in comparison with noncritics (Moskowitz & Zuroff, 1991).

As life progresses for self-critical individuals, many of their interper-sonal problems continue. For instance, adult self-critics have been described as having poor social acuity, being insensitive to nonverbal cues (Aube &

Whiffen, 1996), experiencing elevated levels of hostility in conflict-resolution situations (Zuroff & Duncan, 1999), reporting lower levels of trust and self-disclosure (Zuroff & Fitzpatrick, 1995), being relatively vindictive and socially avoidant (Alden & Bieling, 1996), and exhibiting lower intimacy motivation (Mongrain & Zuroff, 1995). Objective judges also rate self-critics as less likable than noncritical individuals (Zuroff, Moskowitz, Wielgus, Powers, & Franko, 1983). Thus, self-criticism appears to be correlated with a variety of negative interpersonal exchanges, poor social skills, and relatively unsatisfying relationships over the life span.

SELF-CRITICISM MODERATING AND MEDIATING MODELS

Although correlational data offer some insight into the way self-criticism may be associated with interpersonal problems, they do not offer explanations for the relationship between self-criticism and troubled social relationships. Some researchers have attempted to identify social context variables that appear to moderate a self-critic's emotions and actions. For example, Coyne and Whiffen (1995) and Robins (1995) have described the congruency hypothesis, which suggests that self-critical individuals will report increased levels of distress, as compared with people with low levels of self-criticism, when they experience certain types of environmental stressors (i.e., those that specifically impinge on or are congruent with their self-critical vulnerability). In this theory, self-criticism moderates the relationship between external stressors and subjective distress. Thus, self-critics play passive roles in their social context, as they appear to react only to stressful events and not affect their occurrence. Not much empirical data have supported this hypothesis.

In contrast to a moderating model, a mediating model would assume that self-critical individuals actually affect stressful events, which may subsequently increase subjective distress. Many mediating models of self-criticism have been posited. For example, Hewitt and Flett (1991) have hypothesized that self-critics may, in an attempt to meet their achievement goals, become actively overloaded. This overloading may increase their chances of failure and also may create interpersonal stress or erode social support (Helgeson, 1994). In other words, self-criticism is a vulnerability that may generate stress and decrease social support over time, which may lead to increased distress for the self-critical individual. Initial support for this mediation model was found in a longitudinal study of young adults (Priel & Shahar, 2000). Other researchers have also detailed possible mediation models that have received some empirical support. For example, Zuroff, Stotland, Sweetman, Craig, and Koestner (1995) suggested that self-critics create their social worlds by selecting unpleasant, self-critical people with whom to socialize and may engage in behaviors that evoke critical reactions in others. As is discussed more thoroughly later in the chapter, evidence supports this theory (e.g., in romantic relationships; Vettese & Mongrain, 2000).

Whiffen and Aube (1999) articulated that moderating and mediating models of self-criticism may complement each other, rather than being mutually exclusive. They have posited that self-critics likely play an active role in creating interpersonal environments, but also that the negative behavior of others likely exacerbates and maintains this personality style. Therefore, they suggest that an interactionist account of how self-criticism functions on an interpersonal level may be important to consider. Thus, when examining self-critical interpersonal contexts, one must observe the perceptions not only of self-critics but also of their social partners.

SELF-CRITICISM AS NEGATIVE IN ROMANTIC RELATIONSHIPS

Data from studies of romantic partners appear to support Whiffen and Aube's (1999) account of how self-criticism may predispose negative interactions between the self-critic and his or her significant other. For example, in a study of 65 women and their partners, Vettese and Mongrain (2000) assessed how self-criticism affects interpersonal communication. When self-critics were asked to appraise their own and their partner's performance on a conflict-resolution task, they made proportionately more negative than positive statements about both their behavior and their partner's behavior. This behavior had the effect of eliciting more negative feedback about the self-critic from the partner. One posited explanation for why this process may occur is based on self-verification theory (Swann, 1990). The authors suggested that women who truly are critical of themselves may act in such a way so as to draw out critical comments from others in their social environment.

Other researchers have also reported the trend that self-critics tend to engage in negative conversations with their partners, especially in the presence of unfavorable feedback from outsiders. For example, Santor, Pringle, and Israeli (2000) conducted a study in which dating couples viewed and assessed interpersonal vignettes. Following the assessment, they were given bogus feedback from the experimenter about their accuracy in appraisal. For couples given unfavorable feedback, self-criticism predicted a decrease in agreeable comments and an increase in blaming one another. Thus, people who are self-critical appear to engage in negative communication styles with romantic partners following a stressful event. It is interesting to consider related work that stems from more recent research on individuals with depressive symptoms. Casbon, Burns, Bradbury, and Joiner (2005) showed that when individuals with depression received direct, negative feedback from their partners, they responded by seeking further negative feedback. In light of the link between self-criticism and depression (Blatt, 1974; Blatt & Zuroff,

1992), it is possible that self-critics elicit negative communication and criticism from their romantic partners.

An interesting question to consider at this point is as follows: Is there any evidence that self-critics have reason to be so critical? To our knowledge, no studies have directly examined this topic. Preliminary work suggests that self-critical individuals tend to have romantic partners who have many complaints about them (Whiffen & Aube, 1999). This type of information provides support for the previously described mediational process, such that self-critical individuals tend to have marriages that are characterized by self-criticism and complaints about the spouse by both partners. As a result of this tendency, self-critics may report feeling maritally distressed (Whiffen, Aube, Thompson, & Campbell, 2000). In another perspective, Coyne and Whiffen (1995) suggested that self-criticism is a reflection of a stressful interpersonal situation, such as an unsatisfying marriage. Finally, Whiffen and Aube (1999) have shown that spousal criticism actually elevates rates of self-criticism, which may in turn elicit depressogenic symptoms from the self-critic. Thus, some indirect support exists that shows self-criticism may be a realistic response to a distressing marital context.

Why might self-critical individuals report feeling dissatisfied in their romantic relationships? One reason may be the tendency for self-critics to exhibit a submissive–cold interpersonal style and report feeling anxious about attachment figures (Whiffen et al., 2000). In addition, researchers have suggested that self-critical participants react in overtly hostile (Zuroff & Duncan, 1999) and less loving (Mongrain, Vettese, Shuster, & Kendal, 1998) ways when engaging in conflict-resolution tasks with a romantic partner. These facts suggest that self-critical individuals may interpersonally precipitate an atmosphere that is unlikely to result in complete relationship satisfaction.

SELF-CRITICISM AS NEGATIVE IN FRIENDSHIPS AND PEER RELATIONSHIPS

We have previously discussed how self-criticism negatively affects romantic relationships, but how does it affect friendships and other peer relationships? It is interesting that self-criticism appears to function somewhat differently in nonromantic relationships. As early as 1955, Goffman suspected that self-critical individuals may elicit overt support and reassurance from others through their negative self-statements. Within decades, however, other researchers noted that although self-critical behavior may elicit overt support initially, it may also bring forth covert negative feelings and long-term rejection from others (Gergen & Wishnov, 1965; Platt, 1977).

In a study examining these possibilities, self-critical individuals were shown to receive more overt public support and to be more socially desirable than people who were considered either self-enhancers or neutral (Powers &

Zuroff, 1988). It is interesting that in this same study, self-critics were also covertly perceived to be less socially competent, more anxious, and more depressed than were people in the other two categories. Thus, it appears that self-critics may elicit both outward support and covert negativity from people in their social network. This trend is interesting to consider in light of related studies on reassurance seeking. In other words, self-critical comments may initially have the effect of eliciting reassurance from others. However, if a self-critic's reassurance seeking behavior becomes excessive, it puts him or her at a heightened risk of increasing interpersonal stress and eroding his or her social support network (Potthoff, Holahan, & Joiner, 1995).

Self-critical individuals have also been shown to emphasize achievement at the expense of interpersonal relationships (Helgeson, 1994). This type of behavior may have the effect of eroding social support and increasing interpersonal stress over time, which increases the self-critic's perceived distress even further (Priel & Shahar, 2000).

SELF-CRITICISM, IN RELATIONSHIP WITH DEPRESSION, AS INTERPERSONALLY MALADAPTIVE

Many studies have shown that a relationship exists between feelings of dysphoria and self-critical behaviors (Blatt, D'Afflitti, & Quinlan, 1976; Gudleski & Shean, 2000; Robins & Block, 1988). For example, self-critical women exhibited greater depressive symptoms, including anhedonia, than did other women when interacting with significant others (Mongrain et al., 1998). It has also been consistently demonstrated that self-criticism is a personality characteristic dimension associated with depression (e.g., Clark, Watson, & Mineka, 1994; Mongrain, 1993; Mongrain & Zuroff, 1995). Finally, self-criticism has been linked to suicidality (a symptom of depression), such that self-critics demonstrate greater lethality and a greater intent to die than do non-self-critics (Fazaa & Page, 2003). But how exactly is the relationship between depression or dysphoria and self-criticism explained?

One possibility originates from the fact that self-critics seek to gain approval of others through success (e.g., in academic or professional settings). When these people encounter life events that thwart their goals, they evaluate themselves harshly, a process that may serve as a catalyst of depression. Blatt and Zuroff (1992) have suggested that self-critical people experience introjective depression (characterized by feelings of guilt and worthlessness) when they fail to achieve internalized standards or goals. Self-criticism has also been related to dysfunctional mood regulation techniques, such as venting and social isolation (ineffective mood regulation processes hypothesized to prolong negative affect; Fichman et al., 1999; Larsen, 1993). Powers, Zuroff, and Topciu (2004) reported that both overt and covert expression of self-criticism independently predict depression. In light of this evidence, self-criticism is likely one contributing force in the onset of depression, which in turn leads to many negative interpersonal consequences (e.g., excessive reassurance seeking and negative feedback seeking; cf. Joiner, 2002).

It appears that self-critics may begin to experience interpersonal stressors before they develop depression. In a longitudinal study by Shahar, Joiner, Zuroff, and Blatt (2004), results indicated that self-critics both reacted to interpersonal stressors poorly and created interpersonal stressors (e.g., depleted social support networks), which had the effect of making the self-critic more vulnerable to developing depression. In this account, interpersonal stressors are the factors that mediate the link between self-criticism and depression.

Important to note in this context is that self-critical individuals are said to experience higher rates of introjective (as opposed to anaclitic) depression (Blatt, 1974). It is hypothesized that this type of depression is initiated when feelings of low self-worth are activated (whereas anaclitic depression is said to be caused by intense feelings of loneliness or loss). Self-critical people are more likely than noncritical people to experience feelings of low self-worth following stressors, which makes them more likely to then experience introjective depression, which often results in problematic social functioning. Of the two proposed types of depression, the introjective type has been linked to more negative interpersonal functioning, including self-denigrating and negative-feedback-seeking behaviors (Vettese & Mongrain, 2000).

SELF-CRITICISM, IN RELATIONSHIP WITH SOCIAL PHOBIA, AS INTERPERSONALLY MALADAPTIVE

Self-criticism has not been uniquely linked to depressive psychopathology. Blatt (1991) suggested that rather than being related only to depression, self-critical behaviors may also predispose a person to mental disorders such as obsessive–compulsive disorder (OCD). Other researchers have begun to apply Blatt's hypothesized link between self-criticism and OCD to other anxiety disorders. For example, in a study by Cox et al. (2000), individuals with social phobia were found to exhibit high levels of self-criticism. Although these individuals with social phobia were not found to have levels of self-criticism higher than those found in people with depression, they were found to exhibit self-critical behaviors at almost three times the rate of people with panic disorder. Cox, Walker, Enns, and Karpinski (2002) also reported that self-criticism was related to the severity of social phobia symptoms.

Enns and Cox (1997) attempted to describe how self-critics may encounter negative interpersonal environments as follows: A self-critic may blame him- or herself for relationship problems and attribute these difficulties to personal inadequacy. People with social phobia may also assume that others share their less-than-flattering self-views (Leary & Kowalski, 1995). When these two ideas are combined, the result may be an individual who is socially phobic and self-critical who believes that he or she is interpersonally inadequate. These beliefs will undoubtedly affect the nature of his or her interpersonal relationships.

In addition to being linked with the symptoms of social phobia, self-criticism has also been identified as a prognostic indicator of social phobia treatment. Cox et al. (2002) reported that decreases in self-criticism during the course of treatment were significantly associated with positive responses to cognitive–behavioral therapy for social phobia, even when depressive symptoms were controlled for. The authors suggested that their findings are indicative of the fact that self-critical people with social phobia experience fears not only of negative evaluation but also of social interactions and interpersonal performance. It is important to note the relationship between self-criticism and social phobia, as social phobia is known to be a disorder that very negatively affects one's social behaviors and relationships.

SELF-CRITICISM AS INTERPERSONALLY POSITIVE

As previously discussed, self-critics experience and engage in a plethora of negative interpersonal interactions. For example, they have been shown to be very concerned with how others perceive them, which influences how they interact with others and often has the effect of the self-critic publicly expressing critical self-views or requesting reassurance from others (Blatt, 1974; Coyne, 1976; Joiner, Alfano, & Metalsky, 1992; Joiner & Metalsky, 2001; Joiner, Metalsky, Katz, & Beach, 1999; Powers & Zuroff, 1988). This type of behavior has consistently been shown to negatively impact social relationships (e.g., Joiner, 2002). If there are so many negative consequences of self-critical behavior, why do certain people continually engage in it?

This type of question is difficult to answer, as most psychological phenomena result from complex interplays of positive and negative effects. Some theories have tried to explain the positive interpersonal consequences that self-critical individuals experience and their motivation for eliciting these social responses. Some explanations say that self-critical behaviors actually generate positive interpersonal responses, at least for a time (Coyne, 1976; Goffman, 1955; Jones & Pittman, 1982; Powers & Zuroff, 1988). Goffman, for example, posited that self-critical individuals elicit responses of overt support and reassurance from others because others attempt to "preserve the face" of both individuals and to avoid discomfort or the rupture of the relationship. Goffman, as well as Jones and Pittman, thought that self-criticism is a strategy to avoid attack and ensure that one receives positive reinforcement from others.

In a similar way, Coyne's theory on the interactional nature of depression (1976) clearly specifies how certain people tend to seek reassurance from their significant others when feeling down or depressed. The significant others, at least initially, respond in a reassuring manner, which provides the self-critic with support from the environment. However, as discussed earlier, the initially positive consequences of reassurance-seeking tend to disappear once the reassurance-seeking behavior becomes excessive (Potthoff, Holahan, & Joiner, 1995). As self-critics increasingly seek reassurance from others, they are likely to experience an erosion of their social support networks.

Other empirical studies have shown that self-critical people are so hard on themselves that people around them often offer spontaneous social support as an attempt to provide comfort. A study by Powers and Zuroff (1988) demonstrated that when people interacted with self-critical individuals who performed poorly in a task, they tended to be more overtly supportive than when they interacted with others who were in self-enhancement or neutral conditions. These results replicated those of Gergen and Wishnov (1965) and Platt (1977), as they reported that subjects who had to perform a task with self-critical individuals tended to offer more overt social support to self-critical partners than to partners who were more self-enhancers or neutral individuals. It appears that the initial offering of overt social support may reinforce a self-critic's behaviors.

Finally, it is possible that self-critics use their behavior as a way to gain the approval and respect of others (Alden & Bieling, 1996). Although, to our knowledge, the specifics of this process have not been elucidated, it is plausible to hypothesize that a self-critic may elicit the respect of others if he or she appears to be always striving for the best. For example, imagine that a self-critic makes statements about his or her performance that reflect personal dissatisfaction. If others view the self-critic's performance positively and observe the self-critic still feeling unsatisfied with his or her work (e.g., expressing unhappiness with a less-than-perfect product), they may look at the self-critic as someone who strives to always perform at a higher level. This externally observed perfectionistic behavior may elicit feelings of respect from others.

Although self-critics appear to elicit initially positive and overt feedback from others, many researchers point out that, eventually, self-criticism generates negative responses from the social environment (Coyne, 1976; Gergen & Wishnov, 1965; Jones & Pittman, 1982; Platt, 1977). Thus, reactions to self-criticism are both positive and negative, and it is difficult to determine when or how changes from positive to negative reactions may occur. In general, it appears that although self-criticism initially generates positive interpersonal reactions (in the form of both direct and indirect social support), when people in the social environment of the self-critical individual get too tired or too uncomfortable with this behavior, they display negative social responses.

CONCLUDING REMARKS

In this chapter, self-criticism has been presented as a construct that often manifests itself as interpersonally maladaptive. This dynamic trait has been shown to both influence and be influenced by one's social environment. Furthermore, it may negatively affect one's most important relationships, including close friendships and romantic relationships, by sacrificing intimacy for achievement and through the use of negative communication styles. In light of its complex interpersonal nature, it is no wonder that self-critical behavior often initially evokes support from others, whereas with time, it leads to the erosion of relationships. For individuals who frequently exhibit self-critical behaviors, it may be difficult to disentangle the mixed interpersonal messages that they receive from others.

REFERENCES

Alden, L. E., & Bieling, P. J. (1996). Interpersonal convergence of personality constructs in dynamic and cognitive models of depression. *Journal of Research in Personality, 30,* 60–75.

Aube, J., & Whiffen, V. E. (1996). Depressive styles and social acuity: Further evidence for distinct interpersonal correlates of dependency and self-criticism. *Communication Research, 23,* 407–424.

Bagby, R. M., & Rector, N. A. (1998). Self-criticism, dependency, and the five factor model of personality in depression: Assessing construct overlap. *Personality and Individual Differences, 24,* 895–897.

Blatt, S. J. (1974). Levels of object representation in anaclitic and introjective depression. *The Psychoanalytic Study of the Child, 24,* 107–157.

Blatt, S. J. (1991). A cognitive morphology of psychopathology. *Journal of Nervous and Mental Disease, 179,* 449–458.

Blatt, S. J., D'Afflitti, J. P., & Quinlan, D. M. (1976). Experiences of depression in normal young adults. *Journal of Abnormal Psychology, 85,* 383–389.

Blatt, S. J., & Shichman, S. (1983). Two primary configurations of psychopathology. *Psychoanalysis and Contemporary Thought, 6,* 187–254.

Blatt, S. J., & Zuroff, D. (1992). Interpersonal relatedness and self-definition: Two prototypes for depression. *Clinical Psychology Review, 12,* 527–562.

Casbon, T. S., Burns, A. B., Bradbury, T. N, & Joiner, T. E. (2005). Receipt of negative feedback is related to increased negative feedback seeking among individuals with depressive symptoms. *Behaviour Research and Therapy, 43,* 485–504.

Clark, L. A., Watson, D., & Mineka, S. (1994). Temperament, personality, and the mood and anxiety disorders. *Journal of Abnormal Psychology, 103,* 103–116.

Cox, B. J., Rector, N. A., Bagby, R. M., Swinson, R. P., Levitt, A. J., & Joffe, R. T. (2000). Is self-criticism unique for depression? A comparison with social phobia. *Journal of Affective Disorders, 57,* 223–228.

Cox, B. J., Walker, J. R., Enns, M. W., & Karpinski, D. C. (2002). Self-criticism in generalized social phobia and response to cognitive-behavioral treatment. *Behavior Therapy, 33,* 479–491.

Coyne, J. C. (1976). Toward an interactional description of depression. *Psychiatry, 39,* 28–40.

Coyne, J. C., & Whiffen, V. E. (1995). Issues in personality diathesis for depression: The case of sociotropy-dependency and autonomy-self-criticism. *Psychological Bulletin, 118,* 358–378.

Enns, M. W., & Cox, B. J. (1997). Personality dimensions and depression: Review and commentary. *Canadian Journal of Psychiatry, 42,* 274–284.

Fazaa, N., & Page, S. (2003). Dependency and self-criticism as predictors of suicidal behavior. *Suicide and Life Threatening Behavior, 33,* 172–185.

Fichman, L., Koestner, R., & Zuroff, D. C. (1994). Depressive styles in adolescence: Assessment, relation to social functioning, and developmental trends. *Journal of Youth and Adolescence, 23,* 315–330.

Fichman, L., Koestner, R., Zuroff, D. C., & Gordon, L. (1999). Depressive styles and the regulation of negative affect: A daily experience study. *Cognitive Therapy and Research, 23,* 483–495.

Gergen, K., & Wishnov, B. (1965). Others' self-evaluations and interaction anticipation as determinants of self-presentation. *Journal of Personality and Social Psychology, 2,* 348–358.

Goffman, E. (1955). On facework: An analysis of ritual elements in social interaction. *Psychiatry, 18,* 213–231.

Gudleski, G. D., & Shean, G. D. (2000). Depressed and nondepressed students: Differences in interpersonal perceptions. *The Journal of Psychology, 134,* 56–62.

Helgeson, V. S. (1994). Relation of agency and communion to well-being: Evidence and potential exploration. *Psychological Bulletin, 116,* 412–428.

Hewitt, P. L., & Flett, G. L. (1991). Dimensions of perfectionism in unipolar depression. *Journal of Abnormal Psychology, 100,* 98–101.

Joiner, Jr., T. E. (2002). Depression in its interpersonal context. In H. Gotlib & C. Hammen (Eds.), *Handbook of depression* (pp. 295–313). New York: Guilford Press.

Joiner, Jr., T. E., Alfano, M. S., & Metalsky, G. I. (1992). When depression breeds contempt: Reassurance-seeking, self-esteem, and rejection of depressed college students by their roommates. *Journal of Abnormal Psychology, 101,* 165–173.

Joiner, Jr., T. E., & Metalsky, G. I. (2001). Excessive reassurance seeking: Delineating a risk factor involved in the development of depressive symptoms. *Psychological Science, 12,* 371–378.

Joiner, Jr., T. E., Metalsky, G. I., Katz, J., & Beach, S. R. H. (1999). Depression and excessive reassurance seeking. *Psychological Inquiry, 10,* 269–278.

Jones, E. E., & Pittman, T. S. (1982). Toward a general theory of strategic self-presentation. In J. Suls (Ed.), *Psychological perspectives on the self: Vol. 1. The self in social perspective* (pp. 231–262). Hillsdale, NJ: Erlbaum.

Koestner, R., Zuroff, D. C., & Powers, T. A. (1991). Family origins of adolescent self-criticism and its continuity into adulthood. *Journal of Abnormal Psychology, 100,* 191–197.

Larsen, R. (1993, August). *Emotion regulation in everyday life: An experience sampling method.* Paper presented at the 101st Annual Convention of the American Psychological Association, Toronto, Ontario, Canada.

Leary, M. R., & Kowalski, R. M. (1995). The self-presentation model of social phobia. In R. Heimberg (Ed.), *Social phobia: Diagnosis, assessment, and treatment* (pp. 94–112). New York: Guilford Press.

McCranie, E. W., & Bass, J. D. (1984). Childhood family antecedents of dependency and self-criticism: Implications for depression. *Journal of Abnormal Psychology, 93,* 3–8.

Mongrain, M. (1993). Dependency and self-criticism located within the five-factor model of personality. *Personality and Individual Differences, 15,* 455–462.

Mongrain, M., Vettese, L. C., Shuster, B., & Kendal, N. (1998). Perceptual biases, affect, and behavior in the relationships of dependents and self-critics. *Journal of Personality and Social Psychology, 75,* 230–241.

Mongrain, M., & Zuroff, D. C. (1995). Motivational and affective correlates of dependency and self-criticism. *Personality and Individual Differences, 18,* 347–354.

Moskowitz, D. S., & Zuroff, D. C. (1991). *Contributions of personality and environmental factors to positive and negative affect in an adult community sample.* Poster session presented at the meeting of the Canadian Psychological Association, Calgary, Alberta, Canada.

Platt, B. (1977). *Perceived adjustment and positivity of self-presentation as determinants of others' public and private evaluation.* Unpublished doctoral dissertation, Miami University, Oxford, OH.

Potthoff, J. G., Holahan, C. J., & Joiner, T. E. (1995). Reassurance-seeking, stress generation, and depressive symptoms: An integrative model. *Journal of Personality and Social Psychology, 68,* 664–670.

Powers, T. A., & Zuroff, D. C. (1988). Interpersonal consequences of overt self-criticism: A comparison with neutral and self-enhancing presentations of self. *Journal of Personality and Social Psychology, 54,* 1054–1062.

Powers, T. A., Zuroff, D. C., & Topciu, R. A. (2004). Covert and overt expressions of self-criticism and perfectionism and their relations to depression. *European Journal of Personality, 18,* 61–72.

Priel, B., & Shahar, G. (2000). Dependency, self-criticism, social context and distress: Comparing moderating and mediating models. *Personality and Individual Differences, 28,* 515–525.

Robins, C. J. (1995). Personality-event interaction models of depression. *European Journal of Personality, 9,* 367–378.

Robins, C. J., & Block, P. (1988). Personal vulnerability, life events, and depressive symptoms: A test of a specific interactional model. *Journal of Personality and Social Psychology, 54,* 847–852.

Rosenfarb, I. S., Becker, J., Khan, A., & Mintz, J. (1994). Dependency, self-criticism, and perceptions of socialization experiences. *Journal of Abnormal Psychology, 103,* 669–675.

Santor, D. A., Pringle, J. D., & Israeli, A. L. (2000). Enhancing and disrupting cooperative behavior in couples: Effects of dependency and self-criticism following favorable and unfavorable performance feedback. *Cognitive Therapy and Research, 24,* 379–397.

Santor, D. A., & Zuroff, D. C. (1998). Controlling shared resources: Effects of dependency, self-criticism, and threats to self-worth. *Personality and Individual Differences, 24,* 237–252.

Shahar, G., Joiner, T. E., Zuroff, D. C., & Blatt, S. J. (2004). Personality, interpersonal behavior, and depression: Co-existence of stress-specific moderating and mediating effects. *Personality and Individual Differences, 36,* 1583–1596.

Swann, W. B. (1990). To be known or adored: The interplay of self-enhancement and self-verification. In E. Higgins & R. Sorrentino (Eds.), *Handbook of motivation and cognition: Vol. 2. Foundations of social behavior* (pp. 408–448). New York: Guilford Press.

Vettese, L. C., & Mongrain, M. (2000). Communication about the self and partner in the relationships of dependents and self-critics. *Cognitive Therapy and Research, 24,* 609–626.

Whiffen, V. E., & Aube, J. A. (1999). Personality, interpersonal context, and depression in couples. *Journal of Social and Personal Relationships, 16,* 369–383.

Whiffen, V. E., Aube, J., Thompson, J., & Campbell, T. L. (2000). Attachment beliefs and interpersonal contexts associated with dependency and self-criticism. *Journal of Social and Clinical Psychology, 19,* 184–205.

Whiffen, V. E., & Sasseville, T. M. (1991). Dependency, self-criticism, and recollections of parenting: Sex differences and the role of depressive affect. *Journal of Social and Clinical Psychology, 10,* 121–133.

Zuroff, D. C., & Duncan, N. (1999). Self-criticism and conflict resolution in romantic couples. *Canadian Journal of Behavioural Science, 31,* 137–149.

Zuroff, D. C., & Fitzpatrick, D. K. (1995). Depressive personality styles: Implications for adult attachment. *Personality and Individual Differences, 18,* 253–265.

Zuroff, D. C., Moskowitz, D. S., & Cote, S. (1999). Dependency, self-criticism, interpersonal behaviour and affect: Evolutionary perspectives. *British Journal of Clinical Psychology, 38,* 231–250.

Zuroff, D. C, Moskowitz, D. S., Wielgus, M. S., Powers, T. A., & Franko, D. L. (1983). Construct validation of the Dependency and Self-Criticism Scales of the Depressive Experiences Questionnaire. *Journal of Research in Personality, 17,* 226–241.

Zuroff, D. C., Stotland, S., Sweetman, E., Craig, J. A., & Koestner, R. (1995). Dependency, self-criticism, and social interactions. *British Journal of Clinical Psychology, 34,* 543–553.

II

SELF-CRITICISM AS GOOD, SELF-ENHANCEMENT AS BAD

6

DEFENSIVE PESSIMISM AS A POSITIVE SELF-CRITICAL TOOL

JULIE K. NOREM

There is no doubt that people can be too self-critical and too pessimistic—just as they can talk too much, eat too much, exercise too much, or work too much. The potential for excess and its related negative consequences, however, does not itself constitute an automatic indictment of a basic process. Ceasing to eat is not an adaptive response to eating too much; rather, those who eat too much probably need to change how, how much, and what they eat. Of course, the analogy cannot be pushed too far: It would be ridiculous to argue that self-criticism is vital to adaptation in the same way that eating is. Nevertheless, the analogy can be helpful in that it points to the importance of thinking about the different forms and functions self-criticism may take.

In this chapter, I argue that individuals who use defensive pessimism as a strategy are able to use both pessimism and self-criticism in amounts and forms that are relatively adaptive. To be more precise, I consider the ways in which self-criticism can be particularly adaptive when used as part of defensive pessimism.

DEFENSIVE PESSIMISM AS A STRATEGY:
NUANCED NEGATIVITY

Defensive pessimism is a strategy typically used by people who feel anxious and out of control (Norem, 2001a; Norem & Cantor, 1986a, 1986b). Individuals using the strategy set low expectations and reflect extensively on what might go wrong in particular situations. They mentally rehearse both what might happen and what they could do to prepare for, mitigate, or prevent the negative outcomes they imagine. Much of the research on defensive pessimism contrasts it with *strategic optimism*. Individuals using strategic optimism set high expectations and actively avoid thinking about possible outcomes.

Using their preferred strategy, defensive pessimists find that they feel less anxious, anxiety is less likely to interfere with their performance, and they feel more in control. Their performance when they use their strategy is generally equivalent to that of nonanxious individuals using an optimistic strategy. Their performance is also better when they use their strategy than when they do not. Thus, experimental manipulations that succeed in making defensive pessimists more optimistic, more cheerful, or less reflective result in poorer performance (Norem & Illingworth, 1993; Sanna, 1998; Spencer & Norem, 1996). Similar results have been found in naturalistic and field studies that examined how individuals pursue their goals outside of the laboratory (Tomaya, 2005). Finally, as I discuss later, anxious individuals who use defensive pessimism fare better across a variety of outcomes than do anxious individuals who do not use defensive pessimism (Elliot & Church, 2003; Eronen, Nurmi, & Salmela Aro, 1998; Norem & Burdzovic Andreas, 2007).

One of the major psychological drawbacks to pessimism is that it can be demotivating. If one believes that bad things are certain to happen, there would seem to be little point in working to prevent them from happening, and one may very well conclude that giving up is the only reasonable option. Withdrawal and avoidance in anticipation of negative outcomes may be especially likely when the feared outcomes directly implicate the self.

Rather than being certain that something bad will happen, however, defensive pessimists are typically uncertain about what will happen. Under those circumstances, the belief that negative things might happen can lead to a productive and motivating search for ways to prevent bad things from happening or to prepare to cope if they do (Norem, 2001a). Pessimism can thus provide a useful impetus for exerting control over one's environment in positive ways, and that is how it appears to function for those using defensive pessimism. By anticipating what might go wrong using extensive, concrete, and specific imagery, defensive pessimists, rather than dwelling on their anxiety, motivate themselves to act effectively to avoid negative outcomes and pursue the goals that are important to them (W. C. Chang & Sivam, 2004; Schoneman, 2002; Showers, 1992; Showers & Reuben, 1990).

In addition to instigating a search for means to control and change one's environment, defensive pessimism has the potential to help people control and change themselves. It is virtually a truism that to change, a person needs to want to change. The logical antecedent to wanting to change something is identifying what particular characteristics or behaviors are problematic, particularly if one is to move beyond wishful thinking. Of course, it can be aversive to think about what one might want to change about oneself, because doing so requires recognizing one's shortcomings. Indeed, the negative affect generated by self-criticism, particularly among those prone to rumination about the past, may be counted as a significant potential short-term and long-term cost of self-criticism (Cox, McWiliams, Enns, & Clara, 2004).

Nevertheless, there are numerous circumstances in which a person may be willing to tolerate short-term emotional discomfort as a precursor to or part of the process of self-change; psychotherapy is an obvious and not uncommon example of this. Even outside of formal therapy, however, people work to change themselves. Those for whom self-change goals are salient may be willing to tolerate short-term discomfort to progress toward their long-term goals. In other words, if changing oneself is sufficiently important to a person, the negative affect involved in the process may be a small price to pay.

Some evidence shows that defensive pessimists are less focused on affective outcomes and more focused on performance and improvement than are some other individuals (Sanna, 1998). Sanna (1996), among other researchers, discussed two major functions that mental simulation may serve: preparatory and affective. Thinking through (mentally simulating) an event can help people prepare for similar events in the future; mental simulation can also influence moods. Imagining negative outcomes before the fact or thinking about how things could have turned out better after the fact may increase negative mood, whereas imagining positive outcomes before the fact or thinking about how things might have been worse after the fact may increase positive mood. Sanna found that defensive pessimists are more likely to engage in upward prefactual simulations and less likely to engage in downward counterfactual simulations than are strategic optimists. Upward prefactuals are mental simulations before an event of what might go wrong, whereas downward counterfactuals are mental simulations after the fact of worse outcomes than those that actually occurred. Sanna argued that defensive pessimists may be most concerned with or able to use the preparative function of downward prefactuals: That is, they think through possible negative outcomes to prepare themselves, because being prepared is their most salient goal (Kelly et al., 2003; Norem, 2003). In contrast, strategic optimists may be more concerned with creating or maintaining positive mood; thus, they are more likely to avoid thinking about possible negative outcomes before the fact, and more likely to imagine how things might have been worse after the fact, which should increase their positive reaction to or minimize the negative impact of their actual outcomes.

Other data support the suggestion that defensive pessimists may be able to tolerate the negative affect associated with negative thinking and to use self-criticism as an effective tool as they pursue their goals. Sanna (1996) found that defensive pessimists generally prefer not to engage in either upward or downward counterfactual thinking: In other words, when left to their own devices, they do not dwell on what has already happened. Showers and Reuben (1990) similarly found that the defensive pessimists' "thinking through" does not resemble depressogenic rumination, in that it does not persist once a situation is over. In fact, defensive pessimism is actually related to less recall of unsuccessful performances among anxious individuals (Schoneman, 2002). These findings paint a picture of individuals whose negative focus is primarily future-oriented, in service of their desire to manage their anxiety and to exert control to prepare and improve themselves. A similar portrait emerges in the following discussion of the goals defensive pessimists set, how they appraise those goals, and how they think about themselves.

SELF-ESTEEM, SELF-KNOWLEDGE, AND SELF-CHANGE AMONG DEFENSIVE PESSIMISTS

Defensive pessimism is moderately negatively correlated with self-deception and impression management tendencies (Norem, 2005), which suggests that those who use defensive pessimism are less motivated to deceive themselves about themselves or to make a positive impression on others than are those who are more optimistic. In a similar way, defensive pessimists tend not to use self-enhancing attributions when they succeed or self-protective attributions when they do less well (Norem, 2001a; Norem & Cantor, 1986a).

This lack of concern with protecting themselves from negative feedback can also be seen in a study of social performance (Norem, 2001b). In this study, participants made a "dating service"-type videotape of themselves. Observers who were unaware of the strategies the participants were using rated the videotapes on a number of dimensions. Observers thought the videos made by each group were similar overall and did not rate them differently in terms of the positivity of the impression they conveyed. There were, however, significant differences between the defensive pessimists and strategic optimists in both their self-ratings and in their reactions to positive and negative feedback. (All participants received identical feedback as part of the study so that recall of feedback type could be compared.) Strategic optimists remembered the negative feedback as less negative than it was, although their memories of positive feedback were relatively accurate. In contrast, defensive pessimists remembered the positive feedback as less positive than it was, but were more accurate in their recall of the negative feedback.

Although there was no direct measure of attention in this study, the results suggest that the defensive pessimists were more oriented toward the negative information about themselves than toward the positive information. Defensive pessimists also seemed more critical of their own performances: Prior to receiving feedback about their performance, they rated themselves higher in "need for improvement" than the observers rated them, whereas strategic optimists rated themselves lower on this measure than the observers rated them.

These findings are important because they begin to provide a context for considering some of the other data related to defensive pessimists' self-beliefs and self-evaluations. They reinforce the idea that defensive pessimists' negative perspective on themselves may be in active service of their performance goals, rather than a more pervasive passive or fatalistic negative view.

Further reinforcement for this view comes from the initial experiment in an ongoing series of studies examining relations between social support and strategies among dating couples. In this study, one member of a dating couple was assigned to prepare and deliver a videotaped speech. In a separate room, the other member of the couple was asked to copy in his or her own handwriting a pre-prepared note of social support. The notes contained one of two kinds of social support: either informational support, such as suggestions for improving the speech, or emotional support, such as reassurance that the speech would go well. Observers who were unaware of the speaker's strategy subsequently rated the videotaped speeches or the social support received. According to these ratings, defensive pessimists performed better when they received informational support, rather than emotional encouragement or compliments, from their romantic partner before a performance. They also subsequently evaluated their relationship more positively in the informational support condition, possibly because they felt their partners knew them well when their partners were able to supply support that fit their preferred strategy. Preliminary analyses of results from a second study show that when defensive pessimists and strategic optimists describe the kinds of social support they would prefer to receive from others, defensive pessimists prefer informational support that helps them prepare for a performance rather than reassurance or emotion-focused encouragement (Gagne & Norem, 2005).

There is considerable evidence that defensive pessimists evaluate themselves more negatively than do more optimistic individuals. Defensive pessimism is negatively correlated with self-esteem (Norem, 2001b). Defensive pessimists also have a higher ratio of negative to positive content in their self-descriptions than do strategic optimists (Yamawaki, Tschanz, & Feick, 2004), and observers rate defensive pessimists' actual self-descriptions as less positive than the descriptions generated by strategic optimists (Norem, 2005). Studies that rely on measurement at a single point in time and global self-evaluations will virtually always find results similar to these. These global and one-time measurements, however, do not provide much insight into how defensive pessimists may be able to use their negative self-appraisals to motivate effective positive change. For that, more knowledge is needed about the content of defensive pessimists' beliefs about themselves and about the function their self-beliefs serve.

In a 5-year longitudinal study of female college students, defensive pessimists' self-evaluations and self-perceptions showed significant changes over time. There were also some intriguing contrasts in self-knowledge between defensive pessimists and other anxious individuals. For this study, participants completed a lengthy questionnaire at the beginning of their first year in college about their backgrounds, goals, actual self-concepts, possible selves, and other personality characteristics, in addition to reporting on their characteristic strategies in social and academic domains.

Using tripartite splits on a trait anxiety measure, in conjunction with the Defensive Pessimism Questionnaire (Norem, 2001b), I identified three groups among the participants in this study: strategic optimists, defensive pessimists, and those who were as anxious as the defensive pessimists (and thus significantly more anxious than the strategic optimists) but did not use defensive pessimism ("anxious others").

At the beginning of the study, a number of interesting differences among these groups were seen. Both the defensive pessimists and the anxious others reported lower self-esteem than that of the strategic optimists. Across their 4 years in college, however, latent individual growth curve analysis indicated that defensive pessimists showed significant increases in self-esteem, so that by the end of their 4 years their level of self-esteem was approximately equivalent to that of the optimists (who showed no significant change). In contrast, the other anxious individuals showed a small decrease in self-esteem during college (Norem & Burdzovic Andreas, 2007).

When one looks at the different aspects of the defensive pessimists' self-knowledge, one can begin to see how their self-criticism—their recognition of negative aspects of themselves—co-occurs with a focus on the potential for positive change. In the longitudinal study, participants described their actual selves; their ideal, ought, and feared possible selves; and the aspects of themselves they were "working on changing." They also rated how important each characteristic of each self was, and how likely they thought it was that that they would develop or change that characteristic.

At the beginning of the study, the discrepancy between actual self and both ideal and ought selves was significantly greater for the defensive pessimists and the other anxious participants than it was for the strategic optimists, and both anxious groups gave higher importance ratings to their feared possible selves than the strategic optimists did to theirs. The defensive pessimists, however, rated both their ideal and their ought possible selves as more likely to develop than did the anxious participants who were not defensive pessimists. Defensive pessimists also rated the characteristics they listed as "working on changing" as more likely to change than did the other anxious participants; they also indicated that this aspect of their self-concept was more important to them than did either the other anxious group or the strategic optimists considered the characteristics they were "working on changing" (Norem, 2005).

Approximately 6 months after they started college, participants in the study rated the amount of change in the actual self and "working on changing" characteristics they had generated initially. Defensive pessimists reported more positive change than did either the strategic optimists or the other anxious group, and less negative change than did the other anxious participants. Latent individual growth curve analyses on actual–ideal self-discrepancies also showed that defensive pessimists significantly reduced the discrepancy between their actual and ideal selves during their time in college. In contrast, the other anxious participants moved further away from their ideal selves during college.

In sum, these data suggest defensive pessimists are motivated to improve themselves and that they are able to focus on negative aspects of both situations and themselves without becoming debilitated or demoralized. Instead, this focus on the potential for improvement appears to lead to significant positive change among defensive pessimists in both global self-evaluations and specific self-perceptions.

USING NEGATIVE MOOD: SPECIFICITY IN SELF-CRITICISM AND GOAL SETTING

Defensive pessimism, and pessimism more generally, are typically associated with negative mood (Norem & Illingworth, 2004). Negative mood, including pessimism, can lead to avoidance or withdrawal from goal pursuit, as individuals try to escape situations that make them feel bad. Beyond potentially negative motivational consequences, negative mood also has characteristic influences on the ways in which people think. Negative mood often leads to detail-oriented, concrete, and specific thinking styles, in contrast to the more heuristic, "big picture" thinking associated with positive mood (Isen, 1987).

Whether positive or negative mood leads to better outcomes is likely to be a function of the particular tasks and contexts involved. For example, a study of mood and creativity found that those in a positive mood were more creative, when creativity was measured by the number and diversity of the products generated. When, however, creativity was measured by the usefulness and originality of the products generated, those in the negative mood condition were more creative (Vosberg, 1998).

With respect to thinking about self, the effects of a concrete and specific style are likely to vary depending on an individual's perception of the valence of self-characteristics. Just as attributing positive events to more global, as opposed to specific, causes is likely to lead to more positive affect, construing positively evaluated self-characteristics in broader ways is likely to lead to more positive global self-evaluations and to increased positive affect when reflecting on the self (Peterson, 1991). When thinking about negative aspects of the self, however, construing one's characteristics in a broad or abstract way may increase negative self-evaluation and consequent negative affect. An analogy to attributional style is helpful here, too, in that more global attributions for negative events are related to more negative affect generally, and potentially related to feelings of helplessness.

From this perspective, it would seem that the particular kind of negative perspective characteristic of defensive pessimism would be useful for identifying specific and concrete things about oneself that one wants to change. Overall, defensive pessimism shows a small negative correlation with the tendency to make global attributions; that is, defensive pessimists tend to make specific attributions for both positive and negative events (Norem, 2001b). Moreover, the actual self characteristics listed by defensive pessimists and strategic optimists do differ significantly in breadth: Defensive pessimists tend to give more specific, more concrete descriptions (e.g., "punctual" rather than "conscientious") than do strategic optimists for both positive and negative aspects of the self (Norem, 2005). Although this specific focus may decrease the overall impact of the positive self-characteristics the defensive pessimists identify, it also seems likely to curtail the negative impact of self-criticism. It is less overwhelming, for example, for someone to recognize that he or she "has trouble getting started on projects" than to conclude that he or she is generally irresponsible or inept.

Just as important, thinking about the aspects of self that one wants to change may be much less daunting if the focus is on narrowly construed, specific characteristics, because the more specific the characteristic, the closer one is to identifying specific behaviors that one needs to adjust to succeed in changing that characteristic. Research on goal pursuit suggests that people are more likely to succeed if they identify specific and concrete goals, breaking down large goals into smaller, more manageable chunks that include specific plans—"implementation intentions," in the words of one researcher (Gollwitzer, 1999). Taking the first step toward the goal of "becoming more organized" is much easier (and more likely) when that broad goal is broken into smaller chunks such as "at 2 p.m. I will begin sorting the pile closest to the door into three categories: trash, immediate action, and file." When people identify "baby steps" toward change, they are less likely to be anxious and intimidated by its prospect, and more likely to believe that they can actually do what is required. This seems to be the case for defensive pessimists, who believe that they are more likely to be able to move toward their ideal and ought selves, and more likely to be successful in changing the aspects of themselves that they are trying to change, than other anxious individuals believe themselves to be.

Thus, even though it may be hedonically unpleasant, the negative affect induced by pessimistic expectations may lead to cognitive processing that facilitates change. The defensive pessimists may experience more positive self-change than might other anxious individuals because they are able successfully to identify specific characteristics with clearly associated behavioral referents that are amenable to change (Showers & Reuben, 1990). In an almost ironic sense, the negative affect and reflectivity associated with the defensive pessimists' strategy may make trying to change less intimidating to contemplate.

NEGATIVE AFFECT, PLANNING, AND RESILIENCE IN THE FACE OF SETBACKS

As noted previously, the defensive pessimists' detailed mental rehearsal can help them to anticipate difficulties that might arise and to prepare for them. Norem and Illingworth (2004), drawing on the mood-as-information model (Martin, Ward, Achee, & Wyer, 1993), argued that negative mood serves as a cue for continued vigilance and effort for defensive pessimists working toward their goals, which is why defensive pessimists actually perform less well when they are in a more positive mood than when they are in a more negative mood (see also Sanna, 1998).

This planning may serve defensive pessimists especially well when they are working on changing themselves. We human beings are often derailed in our efforts to change because the environment or the people with whom we interact resist or ignore our efforts. Others treat us as they always have, failing to recognize (and thus failing to reinforce) that we are behaving differently: For example, coworkers cajole us to try their "famous" home-baked cookies, even as we protest that we have just begun a new diet. When they encounter such (almost inevitable) roadblocks to self-change, defensive pessimists are likely to be prepared for them and unlikely to be demoralized by temporary setbacks or minor difficulties. They are used to persevering even when (or especially when) they are in a negative mood.

This ability to persevere may explain why defensive pessimists in the longitudinal study previously described reported significantly more progress toward their goals and more satisfaction with their goal pursuits during college than did other anxious individuals. Defensive pessimists were also significantly less likely than were other anxious individuals to report having dropped goals that they had previously set for themselves (Norem, 2005).

There is also some more direct evidence that defensive pessimists are able to respond flexibly to obstacles. As part of a longitudinal study of adjustment during college in the mid-1980s, students participated in an hour-long semistructured one-on-one problem-solving interview (Cantor & Norem, 1989; Cantor, Norem, Niedenthal, & Langston, 1987; Norem, 1988). Trained clinical interviewers presented participants with vignettes describing problem situations, such as balancing the increasingly complex demands of college life with parental expectations, or obtaining help from an intimidating professor in a course that was not going well. Participants were then asked to generate a plan of action that they would use to address the problem described in each vignette. After the participants finished describing their plans, the interviewer threw a curve into that plan: The interviewer asked the participant how he or she would respond to contingencies that the participants had not previously considered, and probed for alternative plans he or she would use should the original plan fail.

These videotaped interviews were then coded by two coders who counted the number of distinct components in the plans generated during the interview, as well as the number of components in the responses to the challenges to those plans posed by the interviewer. (Interrater reliability was 91% for this component of coding.) Results showed that defensive pessimists generated significantly more components in their original plans than did other participants. Defensive pessimists also responded with more alternative plans when asked about what they would do if their original plans went awry.

One must, of course, be cautious in assuming that plans generated in response to hypothetical situations have the same characteristics as those that individuals generate in real-life situations. Nevertheless, the situations chosen for this study were highly relevant for college students in general; indeed, they were developed from previously collected data on the challenges and stressful situations students reported facing during the months immediately prior to the study.

In addition, these data converge with the results already discussed, all of which support the argument that defensive pessimists are able to structure their self-criticism and manage negative affect in ways that contribute positively to goal pursuit and efforts toward self-change. Defensive pessimists recognize significant negative aspects of themselves that they would like to change, and the negative characteristics they report are specific and concrete. Their self-concepts are not monolithically negative, however; instead, their perceptions of negative self-aspects are embedded within positive self-knowledge, and defensive pessimists typically believe their negative characteristics are potentially changeable. Thus, in several ways, defensive pessimists are well poised to pursue effective self-help because they are able to recognize (rather than deny or dismiss) negative aspects of themselves, and to do so without becoming depressed or demoralized.

Defensive pessimists perceive the potential for positive self-change, and they may be able to confine their self-criticism within specific goal pursuits and self-change attempts. In other words, if defensive pessimists are self-critical only or primarily in the context of consciously trying to change things they do not like about themselves, or when they are focused on improving specific skills or performances, they may be able to avoid most of the potential negative effects of self-criticism. When defensive pessimists engage in negative thinking more generally, their focus is on what might go wrong in an impending situation. They do not, however, continue to ruminate about situations that have already happened: They are able to stop thinking negatively when there is no longer a preparatory benefit of doing so. Defensive pessimists' effective self-regulation of their negative thinking prevents them from falling into the kind of negative ruminative cycle that is a risk factor for depression (Norem & Smith, 2006). This same ability to stop the spread of negativity when it threatens to become pervasive or debilitating allows defensive pessimists to use self-criticism effectively rather than simply dwelling on their mistakes or perceived inadequacies.

CULTURAL, SITUATIONAL, INTERPERSONAL, AND PERSONAL INFLUENCES ON EFFECTIVE USE OF SELF-CRITICISM

Defensive pessimists seem to be able to use self-criticism effectively as part of their efforts at self-improvement. It does not follow from research on defensive pessimism, however, that self-criticism will always be a useful or constructive tool. Indeed, considering self-criticism specifically within the context of defensive pessimism as a strategy helps to highlight some of the varied influences that should be taken into consideration in any evaluation of the effects of self-criticism.

Cultural sensibilities are apt to have substantial influence on the typical consequences of self-criticism, as they do for other psychological processes (see chap. 7, this volume). Evidence continues to accumulate that optimism and pessimism are differently related to coping and mental health, depending on cultural contexts: For example, among Asian Americans, pessimism is related to active problem-solving coping strategies and emotion expression, and not related to depression, as it often is in Caucasian samples (E. C. Chang, 1996).

In cultural contexts in which there is relatively less emphasis on self-promotion and lack of positive affect is not considered abnormal, self-criticism, like pessimism, may be less likely to be met with concern or dismay from others than in the United States. When self-promotion and self-confidence are highly valued in social interactions, such as at work or in other situations in which competence expectations are salient, self-criticism may lead directly to more negative appraisals from others who infer from an individual's self-criticism that he or she is indeed less than competent. In an indirect way, individuals who continually hear a colleague engage in self-criticism may develop negative perceptions of that individual because of negative affect contagion, or because they resent the time and attention a self-criticizing colleague seems to demand.

The previously reviewed data from the study of social support in romantic relationships suggest that defensive pessimists are not looking for, and indeed prefer not to receive, reassurance from their significant others when they are in the midst of their negative thinking and self-critiques. It seems likely, however, that many people often perceive that those who criticize themselves during interpersonal interactions are implicitly asking for reassurance. This assumption may lead others to try to provide social support that actually interferes with whatever the defensive pessimist is trying to do, and may even impair relationships between defensive pessimists and those who offer such support. These negative effects of self-criticism are most likely to occur in relatively short-term or superficial relationships in which there is less tolerance of or awareness of individual differences; indeed, defensive pessimists' long-term friendships and romantic relationships do not vary in satisfaction from those of strategic optimists, and they are typically more satisfying than are those of other anxious individuals (Norem, 2005).

Self-criticism may also be more risky at some points in development than in others. Young adolescents may not have developed the mental self-regulation skills and capacities or the kind of detailed self-knowledge that permits them to use self-criticism diagnostically to select personal characteristics to work on improving without leaping to more generally negative self-evaluations. They might have difficulty regulating the negative affect generated by thinking about negative self-characteristics. Research suggests that girls, at least in the United States, may be more at risk than boys of getting trapped in negative cycles of self-criticism that put them at risk of depression (Shahar, Blatt, Zuroff, Kuperminc, & Leadbeater, 2004). Young girls' greater vulnerability to eating disorders and distorted tyrannies of perfectionism may combine to make constructive self-criticism less feasible or less likely to occur without outside intervention (Harter, Waters, & Whitesell, 1998).

Defensive pessimists use self-criticism in service of their goals: Their orientation is toward making themselves better and avoiding negative outcomes. This motivation for self-criticism may be one of the primary reasons that defensive pessimists' self-criticism works for them in positive ways. However, other motivations driving self-criticism may lead to less salutary effects. Gilbert and colleagues, for example, described a variety of self-criticism that is driven by self-hatred or feelings of disgust concerning the self. Self-criticism motivated by the desire to punish the self seems highly unlikely to have many positive consequences (Gilbert, Clearke, Hempel, Miles, & Irons, 2004).

CONSIDERING THE COMPLEXITY OF SELF-CRITICISM

Much of the research that considers self-criticism as a risk factor for depression focuses on particular kinds of self-criticism, or particular combinations of self-criticism and other characteristics, that seem quite different from the self-improvement-focused self-criticism used by those using defensive pessimism. For example, one influential perspective considers self-critical tendencies, in conjunction with excessive autonomy, to be a risk factor for depression (Robins, Bagby, & Rector, 1997). Another notes that self-criticism puts individuals at risk when socially prescribed perfectionism is activated (Powers, Keoestner, & Topciu, 2005). Defensive pessimism provides an illustrative counterexample that reinforces the importance of avoiding overly facile or automatic assumptions that psychological processes that operate within the normal range of individual differences are equivalent to those that may be implicated in the development or maintenance of pathology (Coyne, Thompson, & Whiffen, 2004).

Congruent with the aims of this volume, I would argue that it is extremely important to distinguish among different kinds of self-criticism when considering its implications. Defensive pessimism is a useful part of this consideration because the data show that those using defensive pessimism are able to be self-critical without succumbing to perfectionism, without being excessively autonomous, and without putting themselves at risk for depression.

Perhaps just as important is the need to distinguish between active self-criticism in the service of self-improvement goals, and relatively passive or static negative self-evaluations, such as those that may characterize those with chronically low self-esteem. The defensive pessimists' ongoing efforts at self-improvement—even if they are partially motivated by the desire to avoid becoming what they fear becoming—represent active goal engagement. The defensive pessimists' negativity functions within a complex worldview that combines recognition of the possibility that negative events will happen with belief in one's personal responsibility to try to prevent those events and the usefulness of efforts to exert personal control. This perspective contrasts vividly with a more fatalistic view that the self is somehow fatally or irredeemably flawed or that there is little possibility of positive change.

Defensive pessimists are able to confront negative aspects of themselves that they want to change by considering very narrow and specific self-characteristics and by making detailed plans for how they are going to pursue the goals they set for themselves. Understanding how the defensive pessimist's variety of self-criticism works may provide some insight into how to help those who struggle with less adaptive forms of self-criticism. Rather than promoting self-enhancement, or trying to convince someone who is excessively self-critical that he or she is in fact a likable or valuable person with something to contribute, those who try to help might be able to adapt worst-case analysis techniques to help globally self-critical individuals focus on specific characteristics that they want to change about themselves. Doing so may facilitate positive action, and action, in turn, is a powerful antidote to debilitating rumination.

The field's understanding of self-criticism and self-enhancement will be greatly enriched to the extent that researchers consider how these processes operate within individuals with varying other characteristics and motivations, and across varied social situations, across the life span and across cultural contexts. Defensive pessimism provides a vivid example of the use of self-criticism as an effective tool for self-change. Its value as an example lies both in specific research results that help those in the field understand this particular mode of self-criticism and in the challenge that this body of research offers to conventional wisdom about self-criticism more generally.

REFERENCES

Cantor, N., & Norem, J. K. (1989). Defensive pessimism and stress and coping. *Social Cognition, 7*, 92–112.

Cantor, N., Norem, J. K., Niedenthal, P. M., & Langston, C. A. (1987). Life tasks, self-concept ideals, and cognitive strategies in a life transition. *Journal of Personality and Social Psychology, 53*, 1178–1191.

Chang, E. C. (1996). Cultural differences in optimism, pessimism, and coping: Predictors of subsequent adjustment in Asian American and Caucasian American college students. *Journal of Counseling Psychology, 43*, 113–123.

Chang, W. C., & Sivam, R. W. (2004). Constant vigilance: Heritage values and defensive pessimism in coping with severe acute respiratory syndrome in Singapore. *Asian Journal of Social Psychology, 7*, 35–53.

Cox, B. J., McWiliams, L. A., Enns, M. W., & Clara, I. P. (2004). Broad and specific personality dimensions associated with major depression in a nationally representative sample. *Comprehensive Psychiatry, 45*, 246–253.

Coyne, J., Thompson, R., & Whiffen, V. (2004). Is the promissory note of personality as vulnerability to depression in default? Reply to Zuroff, Mongrain, and Santor. *Psychological Bulletin, 130*, 512–517.

Elliot, A. J., & Church, M. A. (2003). A motivation analysis of defensive pessimism and self-handicapping. *Journal of Personality, 71*, 369–396.

Eronen, S., Nurmi, J. E., & Salmela Aro, K. (1998). Optimistic, defensive-pessimistic, impulsive and self-handicapping strategies in university environments. *Learning and Instruction, 8*, 159–177.

Gagne, F. M., & Norem, J. K. (2005, January). *"Thanks for your support (not)": When partner strategy and social support don't mix.* Paper presented at the Annual Meeting of the Society for Personality and Social Psychology, New Orleans, LA.

Gilbert, P., Clearke, M., Hempel, S., Miles, J. N. V., & Irons, C. (2004). Criticizing and reassuring oneself: An exploration of forms, styles and reasons in female students. *British Journal of Clinical Psychology, 43*, 31–50.

Gollwitzer, P. M. (1999). Implementation intentions: Strong effects of simple plans. *American Psychologist, 54*, 493–503.

Harter, S., Waters, P., & Whitesell, N. R. (1998). Relational self-worth: Differences in perceived worth as a person across interpersonal contexts among adolescents. *Child Development, 69*, 756–766.

Isen, A. M. (1987). Positive affect, cognitive processes, and social behavior. In L. Berkowitz (Ed.), *Advances in experimental social psychology* (Vol. 20, pp. 203–253). San Diego, CA: Academic Press.

Kelly, K., Levanthal, H., Toppmeyer, D., Much, J., Dermody, J., Marvin, M., et al. (2003). Subjective and objective risks of carrying a BRGA1/2 mutation in individuals of Ashkenazi Jewish descent. *Journal of Genetic Counseling, 12,* 351–371.

Martin, L. L., Ward, D. W., Achee, J. W., & Wyer, R. S. (1993). Mood as input: People have to interpret the motivational implications of their moods. *Journal of Personality and Social Psychology, 64,* 315–326.

Norem, J. K. (1988). Strategic realities: Optimism and defense pessimism. *Dissertation Abstracts International, 48*(11-B), 3444–3445.

Norem, J. K. (2001a). Defensive pessimism, optimism, and pessimism. In E. C. Chang (Ed.), *Optimism and pessimism: Implications for theory, research, and practice* (pp. 77–100). Washington, DC: American Psychological Association.

Norem, J. K. (2001b). *The positive power of negative thinking.* New York: Basic Books.

Norem, J. K. (2003). Pessimism: Accentuating the positive possibilities. In E. C. Chang & L. J. Sanna (Eds.), *Virtue, vice, and personality: The complexity of behavior* (pp. 91–104). Washington, DC: American Psychological Association.

Norem, J. K. (2005). [Self-knowledge among defensive pessimists, strategic optimists, and anxious "others"]. Unpublished data, Wellesley College, Wellesley, MA.

Norem, J. K., & Burdzovic Andreas, J. (2007). Understanding journeys: Individual growth analysis as a tool for studying individual differences in change over time. In A. D. Ong & M. Van Dulmen (Eds.), *Handbook of methods in positive psychology* (pp. 477–486). London: Oxford University Press.

Norem, J. K., & Cantor, N. (1986a). Anticipatory and post hoc cushioning strategies: Optimism and defensive pessimism in "risky" situations. *Cognitive Therapy and Research, 10,* 347–362.

Norem, J. K., & Cantor, N. (1986b). Defensive pessimism: Harnessing anxiety as motivation. *Journal of Personality and Social Psychology, 51,* 1208–1217.

Norem, J. K., & Illingworth, K. S. S. (1993). Strategy-dependent effects of reflecting on self and tasks: Some implications of optimism and defensive pessimism. *Journal of Personality and Social Psychology, 65,* 822–835.

Norem, J. K., & Illingworth, K. S. S. (2004). Mood and performance among defensive pessimists and strategic optimists. *Journal of Research in Personality, 38,* 351–366.

Norem, J. K., & Smith, S. (2006). Defensive pessimism: Positive past, anxious present, and pessimistic future. In L. J. Sanna & E. C. Chang (Eds.), *Judgments over time: The interplay of thoughts, feelings, and behaviors* (pp. 34–46). Oxford, England: Oxford University Press.

Peterson, C. (1991). The meaning and measurement of explanatory style. *Psychological Inquiry, 2*(1), 1–10.

Powers, T. A., Keoestner, R., & Topciu, R. A. (2005). Implementation intentions, perfectionism, and goal progress: Perhaps the road to hell *is* paved with good intentions. *Personality and Social Psychology Bulletin, 31*, 902–912.

Robins, C. J., Bagby, R. M., & Rector, N. A. (1997). Sociotropy, autonomy, and patterns of symptoms in patients with major depressions: A comparison of dimensional and categorical approaches. *Cognitive Therapy and Research, 21*, 285–300.

Sanna, L. J. (1996). Defensive pessimism, optimism, and simulating alternatives: Some ups and downs of prefactual and counterfactual thinking. *Journal of Personality and Social Psychology, 71*, 1020–1036.

Sanna, L. J. (1998). Defensive pessimism and optimism: The bitter-sweet influence of mood on performance and prefactual and counterfactual thinking. *Cognition & Emotion, 12*, 635–665.

Schoneman, S. W. (2002). The role of the cognitive coping strategy of defensive pessimism within the social-evaluative continuum. *Dissertation Abstracts International, 63*, 3024.

Shahar, G., Blatt, S. J., Zuroff, D. C., Kuperminc, G. P., & Leadbeater, B. J. (2004). Reciprocal relations between depressive symptoms and self-criticism (but not dependency) among early adolescent girls (but not boys). *Cognitive Therapy and Research, 28*, 85–103.

Showers, C. (1992). The motivational and emotional consequences of considering positive or negative possibilities for an upcoming event. *Journal of Personality and Social Psychology, 63*, 474–484.

Showers, C., & Reuben, C. (1990). Distinguishing defensive pessimism from depression: Negative expectations and positive coping mechanisms. *Cognitive Therapy and Research, 14*, 385–399.

Spencer, S. M., & Norem, J. K. (1996). Reflection and distraction: Defensive pessimism, strategic optimism, and performance. *Personality and Social Psychology Bulletin, 22*, 354–365.

Tomaya, M. (2005). Influence of cognitive strategies on test coping strategies and academic achievement: Defensive pessimism and strategic optimism. *Japanese Journal of Educational Psychology, 53*, 220–229.

Vosberg, S. K. (1998). Mood and the quantity and quality of ideas. *Creativity Research Journal, 11*, 315–331.

Yamawaki, N., Tschanz, B. T., & Feick, D. L. (2004). Defensive pessimism, self-esteem instability and goal strivings. *Cognition & Emotion, 18*, 233–249.

7

THE ROLE OF SELF-CRITICISM IN SELF-IMPROVEMENT AND FACE MAINTENANCE AMONG JAPANESE

TAKESHI HAMAMURA AND STEVEN J. HEINE

A survey found that among all the papers ever published in the *Journal of Personality and Social Psychology*, 92% of them had a first author who was affiliated with a North American institution, and only 1% had first authors affiliated with a non-Western institution (Quiñones-Vidal, Lopez-García, Peñaranda-Ortega, & Tortosa-Gil, 2004). This fact severely limits what can be concluded from social psychological research and human nature. Whether the psychological processes that have been investigated are specific to North Americans or are true of humans more generally is a question regarding which the social psychological database remains largely mute. To go about answering this question, researchers must seriously consider the ways in which they can differentiate those aspects of human psychology that are tethered to particular cultural practices from those that are common to people from all cultures (Norenzayan & Heine, 2005).

In the past few decades an increasing number of studies have been conducted outside of Western cultural contexts, especially in Japan and other East Asian cultures. These studies have revealed the extent to which a number of fundamental psychological phenomena emerge in dramatically different forms across cultures. A good example of this effort is the research program of Nisbett and colleagues on cultural influences on cognition (e.g., Nisbett, Peng, Choi, & Norenzayan, 2001; Peng & Nisbett, 1999). This line of research has demonstrated that some basic cognitive processes, such as perception, attention, memory, and reasoning, are culturally influenced; Easterners tend to engage in more holistic ways of perceiving and attending to objects, whereas Westerners tend to engage in more analytical processes. Furthermore, East Asians have been shown to engage in more dialectical reasoning strategies than do Westerners, in which contradictions are accepted and the world is perceived to exist in flux (e.g., Ji, Nisbett, & Su, 2001; Peng & Nisbett, 1999). These pioneering efforts have demonstrated how a number of fundamental psychological processes do not emerge reflexively, regardless of context, but are shaped by engagement in the particular scripts, practices, and situations that each culture provides.

In this chapter we explore the ways in which the notion of a "good self" is constructed differently across cultures. Toward this objective, we review cross-cultural studies on self-enhancement and suggest the limitation of self-enhancement as a psychological construct in describing East Asians' striving to become a good self. Then we discuss the East Asian way of being a good self, namely through self-criticism in the context of face maintenance.

UNIVERSALITY OF SELF-ENHANCEMENT?

The idea that North Americans and East Asians might differ in how they see themselves has been introduced repeatedly by anthropologists (e.g., Bachnik, 1992; Lebra, 1976). This observation is particularly relevant for social psychology, as the topics of how people see and evaluate themselves are central to the discipline. The observation that one's understanding and evaluation of the self might differ across cultures is provocative, and a number of studies have been conducted in the past few decades to explore this question. As a result, we now have better insights into the ways in which East Asians see and evaluate themselves and how these are similar and different from the ways in which North Americans do.

One focus of research on how the self is shaped by cultural processes has been to explore whether Westerners and East Asians are similar in their motivations to view themselves positively, that is, to self-enhance. Many studies have explored this question over the past decade, using a variety of different measures. The authors of this chapter investigated this literature by conducting a meta-analysis of all the studies that have compared Westerners and East Asians in terms of their self-enhancement motivations (Heine & Hamamura, 2007). We briefly summarize the main findings here.

The meta-analysis consisted of a total of 89 independent comparisons involving more than 28,000 participants and 31 methods of assessing self-enhancing motivations. First, we explored the question of whether East Asians and Westerners self-enhanced to a similar degree. For 30 of the 31 methods in the meta-analysis (the exception being measures of self-esteem according to the Implicit Associations Measure; Kitayama & Uchida, 2003; Kobayashi & Greenwald, 2003), Westerners self-enhanced significantly more than did East Asians. The average effects of these cultural comparisons were large, $d = .84$ (.95 CI = .67, .95), and consistently found. Second, we considered the question of whether people from each culture showed evidence for self-enhancement. It is not surprising that, in light of the attention that the topic of self-enhancement has received in the West, the evidence for self-enhancement among Westerners was strong: average $d = .86$ (.95 CI = .66, 1.07). In contrast, the evidence for self-enhancement among people of Asian descent living in the West was considerably weaker, $d = .33$ (.95 CI = −.05, .72). More striking, the evidence for self-enhancement among East Asians living in Asia was overall lacking: average $d = −.02$ (.95 CI = −.20, .17). Self-enhancing motivations, although routinely observed among Western samples, are difficult to identify among East Asian samples.

However, in several comparisons East Asians showed evidence of self-enhancement, albeit weaker than that of Westerners (e.g., Brown & Kobayashi, 2002; Heine & Lehman, 1995; Sedikides, Gaertner, & Toguchi, 2003). Further analysis has revealed that these instances are limited to two methods, both of which ask participants to compare themselves with the average other: one is the "better than average effect" (BAE) and one is the "one's future is better than average effect" (FBAE). In fact, studies involving these two methods showed clear evidence for East Asian self-enhancement ($d = .25$ and .29 for the BAE and the FBAE, respectively), whereas the weighed average effect size for all the other methods in the meta-analysis was negative, $d = −.22$, providing evidence for self-criticism. It is interesting that the self-enhancement effects from these two methods were also larger for Westerners (average $d = 1.31$, .98 for the BAE and FBAE, respectively) than were those from the other methods (average $d = .66$). Hence, this analysis shows that the self-enhancement effects reported from BAE and FBAE methods are inconsistent with the effects reported from studies that used other methods. Why might this be the case?

We have suggested that this inconsistency resulted because the effect sizes reported from the BAE and FBAE are conflated with a cognitive bias that has little to do with self-enhancement (Heine & Hamamura, 2007). Klar and Giladi (1997) have suggested that in making a comparative judgment between a singular target (e.g., the self or a randomly chosen other) and a generalized target (e.g., average others), people fail to adequately consider the qualities of the generalized target, and their comparison comes to reflect their evaluation of the singular target in absolute terms. For example, when students are asked to compare a randomly chosen student from their university with most other students of the same university, they come to see even a randomly chosen student more positively than they see most other students. Viewing a random other as better than average is a finding parallel to what is seen in the BAE, yet it could not be driven by self-enhancing motivations as the self is not being assessed.

This cognitive bias of failing to consider the qualities of a generalized target is applicable to the comparisons involving the self as well, as the self is another example of a singular target. Thus, what this line of research suggests is that self-enhancement effects reported from the BAE and FBAE methods actually consist of two components: people's motivation to view themselves positively (self-enhancement) and their cognitive bias stemming from comparing a singular target with a generalized target.

Following this rationale, we conducted studies to revisit effect sizes reported from the BAE and FBAE methods in light of this cognitive bias, what Klar and Giladi (1997) referred to as the "everybody is better than their group's average" effect (EBTA; Heine & Hamamura, 2007). In two studies, we asked participants to (a) compare themselves with average others from their university and (b) compare themselves with a fictitious other from their university; we contrasted participants' two types of evaluations in an attempt to assess the self-enhancement effect while circumventing the effect driven by the cognitive bias. The findings revealed that both European-Canadians and Japanese evaluated themselves more positively than they did average others (weighted average effect sizes of 1.35 and .53 for European-Canadians and Japanese, respectively), which is consistent with the pattern that has emerged from previous studies (e.g., Brown & Kobayashi, 2002). However, when people's evaluations of their selves were compared with their evaluations of a random other, a contrast that circumvents the EBTA effect, the magnitude of the bias was much smaller. European-Canadians still showed evidence for self-enhancement ($d = .94$), in that they viewed themselves more positively than they viewed the random other. In contrast, Japanese showed evidence for self-criticism (average $d = -.27$), in that they evaluated themselves more negatively than they evaluated a random other. In sum, these studies show that the methods of BAE and FBAE[1] are conflated with the EBTA effect, and when the EBTA effect is circumvented methodologically, East Asians no longer show evidence for self-enhancing motivations. Combined with our meta-analysis, these studies seem to indicate that self-enhancement motivations are largely absent among East Asians.

---

[1]FBAE is prone to the "everybody is better than their group's average" effect because in estimating the relative likelihood of future life events, people tend to focus just on their own perceived likelihood and ignore the likelihood of the average other (Klar, Medding, & Sarel, 1996). Furthermore, FBAE tends to be larger for less likely future life events. That is, when people estimate the relative likelihood of dying from a plane crash or car accident, what they do is focus on the likelihood of themselves being involved in a plane crash and car accident in their absolute terms and ignore the base rates. As a result, their estimate becomes more strongly biased for events with lower base rates (plane crash) than for those with higher base rates (car accident). For this reason, studies find larger FBAE for negative future life events, as the negative events tend to be less common compared with positive events (Price, Pentecost, & Voth, 2002).

SELF-CRITICISM AND FACE

If East Asians are not motivated to self-enhance, how are they trying to view themselves? Heine and his colleagues (e.g., Heine, 2001, 2005; Heine, Lehman, Markus, & Kitayama, 1999) have articulated how self-criticism plays a key role for East Asians' striving to becoming a good self. Rather than restate these arguments here, in this section we take a slightly different approach by focusing on the constructive role of self-criticism in the context of East Asians' concern for face.

Face, a key concept for understanding social interactions among East Asians, can be defined as

> the respectability and/or deference which a person can claim for himself from others by virtue of the relative position he occupies in his social network and the degree to which he is judged to have functioned adequately in that position as well as acceptably in his general conduct. (Ho, 1976, p. 883)

What we suggest here is that although self-esteem and face are universally familiar (they are existential universals; Norenzayan & Heine, 2005), face is prioritized among East Asians and self-esteem is prioritized among Westerners. We suggest that East Asians use a number of psychological processes to gain and maintain face, just as Westerners use various psychological processes to have and maintain their self-esteem. But before launching a discussion of the psychological processes related to face, we need to further clarify the concept of face.

Face can be understood as a communal property that is loaned from societies to individuals who occupy particular positions in the social network (Mao, 1994). As a communal property, face differs from personal attributes such as reputation in an important way. For example, a CEO's reputation is determined by his or her personal achievements and past behaviors as an individual, but a CEO's face is determined solely by his or her position in the organizational hierarchy. For this reason, two CEOs of similar-size corporations might have different reputations, but they would have face of equal size (Kim & Nam, 1998).

Face comes with a position that one occupies in society, and as each person occupies a number of social roles, each person possesses a number of different faces. For example, a woman might have face as a mother, a wife, and a neighbor, in addition to her face as a CEO. These faces are not equal in size or prestige. That is, one's face as a CEO is probably larger or more prestigious than one's face as a neighbor, because a CEO occupies a much higher position in the social network and has influence on the lives of a greater number of people.

The maintenance of face hinges on others' evaluation of it. One's face is safely protected so long as the occupant is seen as adequately performing what is required of his or her position. If one fails to live up to the minimal standards associated with one's role, one's face is lost. In other words, one is successful in maintaining face only to the extent that one's performance as an occupant of face is favorably evaluated. Hence, the fate of one's face hinges on others' evaluations, and individuals do not have much control over it, aside from making efforts to ensure that they're meeting the minimal standards associated with their role. This is a key point regarding face and the role of self-criticism, on which we elaborate in the following sections.

Furthermore, the more prestigious the face, the more difficult it is to successfully maintain it. For instance, one's faces as a CEO and as a neighbor differ in their prestige because duties and obligations of a CEO have much more impact throughout one's social networks than do the duties and obligations of a neighbor. The broader the social network within which a person's face is implicated, however, the greater the chance that some will judge that person to be failing to live up to his or her role expectations. Roles with more prestigious face mean that a greater number of people have a say in evaluating the occupant of the face. For example, on a typical day as a CEO, one might participate in meetings with subordinates, board members, and bankers, all of whom have at least some say in the evaluation of one's performance as an occupant of a CEO's face. When the evaluations are bad enough, the CEO's face is in jeopardy. In describing the processes of face loss, Ho (1976) used the analogy of overloading a ship. A ship does not sink immediately with overloading, not until the load meets a critical point; however, once the load passes the threshold, the ship sinks. By analogy, a person's face is lost only after evaluations of a person transgress the minimal standards associated with his or her role.

Losing face might not result in the direct and immediate loss of a position. But it will result, for example, in obligations not being reciprocated. Hence, a CEO who has lost face might not be able to make his or her subordinates respect their duties and obligations, which will certainly make his or her job as a CEO difficult. Some scholars have noted that the experience of face loss sometimes triggers intense negative consequences such as feelings of shame, antisocial behavior, and withdrawal from social activities, making the experiences of face loss an important topic in understanding the psychological well-being of East Asians (Kim & Nam, 1998; Zane & Yeh, 2002).

CULTURAL PRACTICES OF FACE MAINTENANCE

East Asian face maintenance is sustained by a number of cultural practices. In this section, we focus on three of these: socialization, communication, and social stability.

Research on East Asian socialization alludes to the idea that from early on East Asian children are socialized with various cultural practices related to face maintenance. For example, Japanese parents and teachers encourage children to identify with socially shared images of an ideal person of the same gender and age group, essentially a face of "good child" (Heine et al., 1999). This fact suggests that Japanese children are brought up to live up to the expectations associated with being a good child. Similar emphasis on proper codes of conduct during socialization is observed in China as well (Ho, 1986; Stover, 1974).

Another characteristic of East Asian socialization is to discourage deviations from what is regarded as appropriate. An example of this characteristic can be seen in school rules. Many Japanese school rules have strict regulations regarding school uniforms (e.g., the length of skirt cannot be too short or long; shoelaces have to be white), hairstyles (e.g., no long hair for boys; no coloring), and how students should spend their afterschool hours (e.g., mandatory participation in club activities; no part-time jobs). Sometimes the discouragement of deviation takes place even among students in the form of bullying, which in Japan is especially targeted toward those who are perceived to be different (Crystal, 1994). With these mechanisms of discouraging deviants, children are brought up to stick to what is considered good and appropriate for them. This evidence suggests that East Asian children are familiarized and encouraged to participate in face-related cultural practices from early on.

Another area in which East Asians' prioritizing of face maintenance can be seen is in daily communication. Two aspects of East Asian communication that seem particularly relevant here are public modesty and debate. Public modesty is perhaps one of the more visible practices that make East Asian cultures appear different from Western cultures. Japanese language, for example, consists of very complex rules of modesty and respect for hierarchy that determine how people refer to themselves. For instance, a student would refer to himself differently depending on whom he is interacting with (e.g., teacher vs. best friend). When used properly, modesty can display one's deference to others (e.g., a student showing respect to a teacher), and it also serves the purpose of concealing any qualities that could be perceived as inappropriate for the face that a person occupies. For a similar reason, when individuals' private needs and wants are in conflict with what is considered to be appropriate for their face, the rules of modesty prescribe individuals to refrain from expressing those needs and wants. In this way, the proper use of modesty works as a shield against the negative evaluation for one's face performance (Hall & Noguchi, 1995).

Debate is another characteristic of East Asian communication that is relevant to face maintenance. Debate creates a forum in which individuals are to express, exchange, justify, and critique opinions, making use of formal logic, with the idea being that the best decisions will be made with this process. Debate is an important social practice of Western civilization, and as such, Western individuals learn to engage in this type of communication from early on. However, a number of cross-cultural researchers have noticed that debate, such as in business meetings or among politicians, is less frequent in East Asian societies (e.g., Becker, 1986; Feldman, 1997; Minami, 1953).

East Asians' concern for face maintenance seems important in understanding why debate might be relatively absent there. Some scholars have suggested that debate is infrequent in East Asia because it necessitates public confrontations that are to be avoided as much as possible (e.g., Becker, 1986; Minami, 1953). Consistent with this idea, cross-cultural studies of conflict resolutions find that East Asians prefer techniques that allow easier restoration of harmonious relations after disputes such as mediation and bargaining (Hamilton & Sanders, 1992; Leung, 1987). The underlying rationale here is that East Asians' priority in conflict resolution is to not damage the faces of the people involved. For this reason, when a conflict involves two individuals with unequal faces, those with lower prestige face are expected to yield to those with more prestigious face. For instance, when a conflict involves a manager and his or her subordinate, the manager's face as someone who makes a decision and makes his or her subordinates respect it would be threatened if the subordinate challenges the decision and tries to resolve it with debate. Instead, in this situation subordinates are expected to yield to the manager's decision. In fact, not yielding to those with higher face might result in negative repercussions (Redding & Wong, 1986). As illustrated in this example, East Asians' concern for face seems to play an important role in accounting for why debate might be relatively absent in East Asia.

Social stability is another characteristic of East Asian society that seems relevant in the discussion of face. One key requirement of face maintenance is for individuals to have an understanding of what is required of their face, and social stability seems to favor this process. Social networks that individuals find themselves in might be very complex, but as long as they are stable, the individual will be able to learn slowly and gradually what is required of particular positions in that social network. However, in a less stable social network, finding out what is required for a particular face would be more difficult. For example, in a corporation that goes through periodic restructuring, people could very well be assigned to a position that nobody else has held before, and finding out what is required of that face would thus be more difficult.

A few characteristics of traditional East Asian workplaces such as lifelong employment and a seniority-based evaluation system seem to reflect the emphasis placed on social stability. In fact, a study on presidential succession in Japanese and American corporations found that the succession in Japanese companies had caused few changes whereas the changes in American companies caused more changes (Sakano & Lewin, 1999). One psychological construct that seems relevant is uncertainty avoidance, or tolerance for unstructured situations (Hofstede, 1991). To the extent that East Asians' face maintenance could be carried out more smoothly in a more stable social network in which uncertainties and unstructured situations are controlled and integrated into the existing system, uncertainty avoidance of East Asians should be relatively high, which is what has been found in this line of research (Hofstede, 1991; Shuper, Sorrentino, Otsubo, Hodson, & Walker, 2004). Hence, social stability seems to be another aspect of East Asian cultures' orientation toward face maintenance.

This section reviewed three East Asian cultural practices—socialization, communication, and social stability—that seem to foster and sustain the environment in which East Asians' face maintenance is practiced. In the next section, we review some psychological processes, especially focusing on self-criticism, that are implicated by East Asians' concerns for face.

PSYCHOLOGICAL PROCESSES FOR FACE MAINTENANCE

We believe that a variety of psychological processes are implicated in the maintenance of face just as a number of psychological processes are implicated in efforts to enhance and maintain self-esteem (see Heine, 2001, 2005). Facing a potentially long list of face-related psychological processes, in this section we focus our discussion on three main areas: (a) individuals' awareness of social expectations associated with a particular face; (b) awareness of others' evaluation of their face; and (c) self-criticism and self-improvement, or individuals' attempts to focus on their shortcomings and work to improve them to secure favorable face from others.

For East Asians to be able to successfully maintain face, it is crucial that they become aware of what is expected of them as occupants of particular positions. However, although a general consensus usually exists about what is expected of each position, the boundaries of those standards typically vary enough so that a new occupant faces some uncertainty. The new occupant must go about determining, to the best of his or her ability, the areas in which they are potentially most vulnerable with regard to expectations. One strategy for doing this might be to learn from someone who has occupied that position before. For instance, one might talk to a predecessor to find out more about the expectations of one's new position. Or one might be able to discern what is appropriate and inappropriate for the position on a trial-and-error basis. In any case, what is required of individuals is to be a keen observer of cues indicating what is and is not appropriate as an occupant of a particular role.

This rationale predicts that when East Asians encounter a new environment in which they don't have clear knowledge of what is expected of them (e.g., a new neighborhood or workplace), they should be particularly sensitive and attentive to social cues that are signaling the norms of the new environment. One line of research that sheds light on this prediction is the study of flexible self-concepts; several studies have found that East

Asians' self-concepts are more context-specific compared with the more cross-situationally stable North American self-concept (Cousins, 1989; Kanagawa, Cross, & Markus, 2001; Suh, 2002). Kanagawa et al. (2001), for example, manipulated the situations in which participants completed a self-description task (e.g., alone in a lab, with another participant, with a professor in his or her office, in a group) and found that Japanese self-concepts were affected more by this manipulation than were those of Americans. This line of research suggests that East Asians are more aware than Americans of what is required of them in particular social settings and adjust themselves accordingly.

Another psychological process that is implicated by East Asians' concern for face is their attentiveness to others' points of view. The rationale is that to the extent that one's successful face maintenance hinges on others having a favorable evaluation of oneself, East Asians should be particularly attentive to the perspectives of others.

A few studies have found support for this idea. For example, cross-cultural studies have been conducted on objective self-awareness, or individuals' awareness of how they appear to others (Duval & Wicklund, 1972). The reasoning from this line of research is that to the extent that East Asians are especially attentive to the perspective of others, they should be more likely to be in a state of objective awareness compared with North Americans. Hence, experimental manipulations for inducing objective self-awareness (e.g., putting oneself in front of a mirror) should have little effect for East Asians. One study compared Japanese and Americans' self-evaluations that were completed either in front of a mirror or not (Heine, Takemoto, Moskalenko, & Lasaleta, 2007). In line with past research, Americans were more self-critical in front of a mirror than they were when no mirror was present. In contrast, Japanese self-evaluations were unaffected by the presence of the mirror. Furthermore, although the Americans were far less self-critical than were the Japanese when no mirror was present, no cultural differences were noted in self-evaluations that were completed in front of the mirror. Perhaps, when Americans are in a position in which Japanese find themselves more frequently—that is, considering themselves from the perspective of an audience—they start to evaluate themselves in ways more typical of Japanese as well. Other research has found that although the likelihood that Canadians will cheat on a test is affected by the presence of a mirror (Diener & Wallbom, 1976), Japanese cheating behavior is unaffected by the mirror (Heine et al., 2007). East Asians appear to habitually consider themselves from the perspective of others.

Furthermore, when participants were asked to recall events in which they were the center of attention (e.g., giving a presentation), the memories of Asian-Canadians were found to be more likely from a third-person perspective compared with European-Canadians (Cohen & Gunz, 2002). That is, Asian-Canadians' recollections were more likely to include imagery of how they might have appeared to others, something that was never accessible to them. In sum, these studies support findings that East Asians are habitually sensitive and aware of how they might be appearing to others (also see Cohen & Hoshino-Browne, 2005).

Because East Asians are also sensitive in detecting what is required of them in particular social settings, their habitual attention to others' perspectives would help them obtain some important insights into others' impressions of their face performance. Nevertheless, for face maintenance to be successful, one also needs to act on others' impressions of oneself, so that others will be more likely to form positive impressions. Hence, it is not enough that individuals know what others are thinking of them. They also need to view themselves in a self-critical manner and make efforts to improve any shortcomings on their part that might make them vulnerable to a critical evaluation by others.

In the remaining section, we focus on the ways in which self-criticism and self-improvement are orienting East Asians' focus toward negative social evaluation and toward improving their shortcomings for preventing potential critical evaluations. Moreover, we discuss how self-criticism and self-improvement might work as overarching goals of East Asians' psychological processes and how their emotions, cognitions, and behaviors are being coordinated accordingly. For this purpose, we draw on the research on regulatory focus by considering its theoretical connection with East Asian self-criticism and face maintenance.

One influential account of the ways in which goals regulate people's emotions, cognitions, and behaviors is regulatory focus theory (Higgins, 1996). Two kinds of regulatory foci have been articulated: promotion and prevention foci. A *promotion focus* is guided by a pursuit for the "ideal" view of the self and a focus on advancement, accomplishments, and aspirations. It is concerned with the presence or absence of positive outcomes. In contrast, a *prevention focus* is guided by a pursuit for the "ought" self and a focus on safety, responsibilities, and obligations. It concerns itself with detecting the presence or absence of negative outcomes (Higgins, 1996). Regulatory foci can be situationally induced, and there are marked individual differences in chronic tendencies to favor one focus over the other. For example, it has been suggested that a child brought up with a socialization characterized by the presence or absence of positive outcomes would have an increased likelihood of being oriented toward a promotion focus, and the reverse pattern of socialization (i.e., characterized by the presence or absence of negative outcomes) would lead to a prevention focus (Higgins, 1996).

In view of the link between socialization and regulatory foci, it seems plausible to predict cultural differences in regulatory foci between East Asians and North Americans. Some research suggests that East Asian children are more likely to have their attention directed toward the presence or absence of negative outcomes (e.g., Lewis, 1995; Miller, Wiley, Fung, & Liang, 1997).

One important distinction between face and self-esteem that might be particularly relevant here is face's vulnerability for loss (Heine, 2005). Compared with self-esteem, face is a resource that is easier to lose than it is to gain. Face is hard to gain because the only way that one can do so is to move up in the social hierarchy. However, face is vulnerable to loss because its maintenance hinges on how the individual is evaluated by relevant others. To the extent East Asians are habitually concerned about protecting this vulnerable resource, it would seem that a self-critical focus would become a more adaptive strategy. That is, East Asians' face maintenance seems to be carried out more smoothly if their focus is oriented toward the presence or absence of negative evaluation by others. In contrast, it seems that self-esteem does not suffer from this same asymmetry. If anything, self-esteem might be easier to be gained than lost, because individuals are in the position to engage in self-deceptive strategies to protect them from self-esteem threats, and can also choose to selectively elaborate on and exaggerate their positive qualities. Hence, if self-esteem is a prioritized resource for North Americans, they would benefit from adopting a greater promotion focus.

A number of studies seem to support this rationale. Lee, Aaker, and Gardner (2000) found that East Asians viewed tennis games that were framed as opportunities to avoid a loss as more important than did North Americans, whereas North Americans viewed the same games as more important when framed as opportunities to secure a win. Elliot, Chirkov, Kim, and Sheldon (2001) contrasted personal goals among Koreans and Americans and found that avoidance personal goals were more commonly identified among the Koreans than they were among the Americans. Heine et al. (2001) found that Japanese were more motivated by failure experiences, whereas North Americans were more motivated by success experiences. Lockwood, Marshall, and Sadler (2005) found that Asian-Canadians were more motivated by negative role models, whereas European-Canadians were more motivated by positive role models. These studies converge in support of the idea that regulatory focus varies across cultures.

A theoretical advantage of drawing on the literature of regulatory focus in better understanding East Asians' self-criticism and face maintenance is the fact that regulatory focus research has documented a divergent set of psychological processes. For example, in one study, prevention-focused individuals were found to initiate tasks earlier than did promotion-focused individuals (Freitas, Liberman, & Salovey, 2002). In another study, when prevention- and promotion-oriented individuals were assigned a proofreading task, prevention-focused individuals were found to be slower but more accurate in detecting errors compared with promotion-focused individuals, who were faster but less accurate (Foerster, Higgins, & Bianco, 2003). To the extent that these divergent psychological processes implicated by two regulatory foci are applicable to cultural differences between North Americans and East Asians, our understanding of East Asians' self-criticism and face-related psychological processes is greatly increased.

In sum, East Asians and North Americans differentially prioritize the two resources of self-esteem and face, and these differences implicate a variety of other psychological processes that also vary across cultures.

In this section we have focused on an awareness of social rules, sensitivity to other's perspectives, and self-criticism as three main areas of face-related psychological processes. This list of psychological processes that are implicated by the face maintenance of East Asians is of course not exhaustive. We anticipate that cultural differences in other psychological processes will emerge that are consistent with efforts to pursue self-esteem or face.

COMPLEXITIES IN STUDY OF FACE

In this section, we consider two issues of research on face that highlight the dynamic nature of this topic. One issue we consider here is the universality of face, and the other issue is the extent to which changing cultural orientations affect East Asians' concern with face.

The idea that one's concern for face is universal could be traced to Goffman's (1955) influential work, in which face is defined as "an image of self delineated in terms of approved social attributes" (p. 213). Goffman's theorizing of face is sometimes described in terms of individuals' theatrical performance wherein individuals are to express themselves, maintain an image appropriate to the current situation, and secure a favorable evaluation from others by using a range of tactics such as being polite or avoiding talking about a sensitive topic (Bond & Hwang, 1986). In essence, in Goffman's framework, face is gained and maintained through social interactions. A number of researchers have asserted that this rather abstract conception of face is applicable across cultures; nevertheless, many of them have also pointed out the need for recognizing culturally specific aspects of face (e.g., Bond & Hwang, 1986; Ho, 1976; Kim & Nam, 1998).

One important way in which East Asians' concern for face, or facework, seems to differ from the facework observed in North American cultures has to do with the cultural differences in how the self is related to others. Markus and Kitayama (1991) proposed that the self-concept among North Americans could be characterized as being largely independent, whereas the self-concept among East Asians could be better described as interdependent. In light of this cultural difference in self-construal, the ways in which individuals engage in facework should differ across cultures as well. For example, for those cultures with independent views of self, one important purpose of social interactions is to express and assert their unique attributes, with others affording opportunities for people to reflect on and affirm their self-concept.

Stover (1974) proposed that a cocktail party is a prototype of North American social interactions. At a typical cocktail party, guests are vying to establish their place and create positive impressions on others, using a number of tactics, and the manner in which individuals express themselves and manage their impression is up to themselves. As this example shows, those with independent selves should have more control over the ways in which they express and present themselves.

Whereas a cocktail party characterizes social interactions of people with independent selves, a Chinese dinner party would characterize social interactions of those with interdependent selves (Stover, 1974). Unlike at a cocktail party, at a Chinese dinner party, the guests are carefully chosen and seated according to a seating plan, and each guest knows his or her standing relative to everybody else and is expected to respect the relationships with appropriate verbal and behavioral rituals (e.g., modesty and bowing). Hence, one's choices for self-expression and impression management are largely determined by the situation. As this example illustrates, face for those with interdependent selves is something over which individuals often do not have much control.

We suggested earlier that face is a universally familiar construct, but as the previous analysis shows, the construct of face does not manifest similarly across cultures. It seems that a fuller understanding of face requires researchers to focus on both cultural similarities and differences (Bond & Hwang, 1986; Kim & Nam, 1998; Ting-Toomey, 1994).

A second issue of face research that we consider here is how East Asians' concern for face comes to accommodate changes in cultural realities. This is an important issue because the past few decades have seen some dramatic changes taking place in East Asian workplaces, wherein facework plays a particularly crucial role. For example, in Japan, the lifetime employment that had characterized employer–employee relations in many firms is now quickly becoming a thing of the past, and more and more corporations have started adapting meritocracy-oriented performance evaluations rather than the seniority-based systems of the past. Rapid economic development and a deluge of foreign capital to China seem to be having a similar impact there.

One might wonder whether these changes will have any lasting impact on East Asians' concern for face. For example, one key requirement of face maintenance, as we saw, is for individuals to have an understanding of what is required of the face that they occupy, and this process can be more smoothly carried out in a socially stable environment. In a less stable social network, finding out what is required of a face would be more difficult. Nevertheless, the changes and restructuring of the workforce in the past few decades have sometimes resulted in many positions being eliminated and many new positions being created, making the process of finding out what is required of a particular face very difficult.

East Asian cultures might accommodate these changes by replacing old strategies of facework with new ones. Alternatively, the changing cultural realities might have a more profound impact on the nature of facework than what the traditional model of facework could accommodate. Future researchers on face seem to have much to learn by considering how cultures accommodate changing realities surrounding face maintenance.

CONCLUSION

Cultural psychological research on the topic of how East Asians see and evaluate themselves has largely focused thus far on self-esteem and self-enhancement strategies (or the lack thereof) among East Asians. In this chapter we explored the essential role of self-criticism and face maintenance in East Asians' striving to secure a good self, and we introduced some of the cultural and psychological processes that are in place to serve face maintenance. As the maintenance of face is likely to implicate a wide variety of psychological processes, our attempt here is only a first step. We hope that future research efforts continue to explore the psychological processes associated with face maintenance as a window to more fully understanding East Asian self-concepts.

REFERENCES

Bachnik, J. M. (1992). The two "faces" of self and society in Japan. *Ethos, 20,* 3–32.

Becker, C. B. (1986). Reasons for the lack of argumentation and debate in the Far East. *International Journal of Intercultural Relations, 10,* 75–92.

Bond, M. H., & Hwang, K. (1986). The social psychology of Chinese people. In M. H. Bond (Ed.), *The psychology of the Chinese people* (pp. 213–264). Hong Kong: Oxford University Press.

Brown, J. D., & Kobayashi, C. (2002). Self-enhancement in Japan and America. *Asian Journal of Social Psychology, 5,* 145–168.

Cohen, D., & Gunz, A. (2002). As seen by the other . . . : Perspectives on the self in the memories and emotional perceptions of Easterners and Westerners. *Psychological Science, 13,* 55–59.

Cohen, D., & Hoshino-Browne, E. (2005). Insider and outsider perspectives on the self and social world. In R. M. Sorrentino, D. Cohen, J. M. Olson, & M. P. Zanna (Eds.), *Culture and social behavior: The tenth Ontario symposium* (pp. 49–76). Hillsdale, NJ: Erlbaum.

Cousins, S. D. (1989). Culture and self-perception in Japan and the United States. *Journal of Personality and Social Psychology, 56,* 124–131.

Crystal, D. (1994). Concepts of deviance in children and adolescents: The case of Japan. *Deviant Behavior, 15,* 241–266.

Diener, E., & Wallbom, M. (1976). Effects of self-awareness on antinormative behavior. *Journal of Research in Personality, 10,* 107–111.

Duval, S., & Wicklund, R. (1972). *A theory of objective self-awareness*. New York: Academic Press.

Elliot, A. J., Chirkov, V. I., Kim, Y., & Sheldon, K. M. (2001). A cross-cultural analysis of avoidance (relative to approach) personal goals. *Psychological Science, 12*, 505–510.

Feldman, O. (1997). Culture, society, and the individual: Cross-cultural political psychology in Japan. *Political Psychology, 18*, 327–351.

Foerster, J., Higgins, E. T., & Bianco, T. A. (2003). Speed/accuracy decisions in task performance: Built-in trade-off or separate strategic concerns? *Organizational Behavior and Human Decision Processes, 90*, 148–164.

Freitas, A. L., Liberman, N., & Salovey, P. (2002). When to begin? Regulatory focus and initiating goal pursuit. *Personality and Social Psychology Bulletin, 28*, 121–130.

Goffman, E. (1955). On facework: An analysis of ritual elements in social interaction. *Psychiatry, 18*, 213–231.

Hall, B., & Noguchi, M. (1995). Engaging in Kenson: An extended case study of one form of "common" sense. *Human Relations, 48*, 1129–1147.

Hamilton, L. V., & Sanders, J. (1992). *Everyday justice: Responsibility and the individual in Japan and the United States*. New Haven, CT: Yale University Press.

Heine, S. J. (2001). Self as cultural product: An examination of East Asian and North American selves. *Journal of Personality, 69*, 881–906.

Heine, S. J. (2005). Constructing good selves in Japan and North America. In R. M. Sorrentino, D. Cohen, J. M. Olson, & M. P. Zanna (Eds.), *Culture and social behavior: The tenth Ontario symposium* (pp. 115–143). Hillsdale, NJ: Erlbaum.

Heine, S. J., & Hamamura, T. (2007). In search of East Asian self-enhancement. *Personality and Social Psychology Review, 11*, 4–27.

Heine, S. J., Kitayama, S., Lehman, D. R., Takata, T., Ide, E., Leung, C., et al. (2001). Divergent consequences of success and failure in Japan and North America: An investigation of self-improving motivations and malleable selves. *Journal of Personality and Social Psychology, 81*, 599–615.

Heine, S. J., & Lehman, D. R. (1995). Cultural variation in unrealistic optimism: Does the West feel more invulnerable than the East? *Journal of Personality and Social Psychology, 68*, 595–607.

Heine, S. J., Lehman, D. R., Markus, H. R., & Kitayama, S. (1999). Is there a universal need for positive self-regard? *Psychological Review, 106*, 766–794.

Heine, S. J., Takemoto, T., Moskalenko, S., & Lasaleta, J. (2007). *Mirrors in the head: Cultural variation in objective self-awareness*. Unpublished manuscript.

Higgins, E. T. (1996). The "self-digest": Self-knowledge serving self-regulatory functions. *Journal of Personality and Social Psychology, 71*, 1062–1083.

Ho, D. Y. F. (1976). On the concept of face. *American Journal of Sociology, 81*, 867–884.

Ho, D. Y. F. (1986). Chinese patterns of socialization: A critical review. In M. H. Bond (Ed.), *The psychology of the Chinese people* (pp. 1–37). Hong Kong: Oxford University Press.

Hofstede, G. (1991). *Cultures and organizations: Software of the mind*. New York: McGraw-Hill.

Ji, L. J., Nisbett, R. E., & Su, Y. (2001). Culture, change, and prediction. *Psychological Science, 12,* 450–456.

Kanagawa, C., Cross, S., & Markus, H. (2001). "Who am I?" The cultural psychology of the conceptual self. *Personality and Social Psychology Bulletin, 27,* 90–103.

Kim, J. Y., & Nam, S. H., (1998). The concept and dynamics of face: Implications for organizational behavior in Asia. *Organizational Science, 9,* 522–534.

Kitayama, S., & Uchida, Y. (2003). Explicit self-criticism and implicit self-regard: Evaluating self and friend in two cultures. *Journal of Experimental Social Psychology, 39,* 476–482.

Klar, Y., & Giladi, E. E. (1997). No one in my group can be below the group's average: A robust positivity bias in favor of anonymous peers. *Journal of Personality and Social Psychology, 73,* 885–901.

Klar, Y., Medding, A., & Sarel, D. (1996). Nonunique invulnerability: Singular versus distributional probabilities and unrealistic optimism in comparative risk judgments. *Organizational Behavior and Human Decision Processes, 67,* 229–245.

Kobayashi, C., & Greenwald, A. G. (2003). Implicit-explicit differences in self-enhancement for Americans and Japanese. *Journal of Cross-Cultural Psychology, 34,* 522–541.

Lebra, T. S. (1976). *Japanese patterns of behavior*. Honolulu: University of Hawaii Press.

Lee, A. Y., Aaker, J. L., & Gardner, W. L. (2000). The pleasures and pains of distinct self-construals: The role of interdependence in regulatory focus. *Journal of Personality and Social Psychology, 78,* 1122–1134.

Leung, K. (1987). Some determinants of reactions to procedural models for conflict resolution: A cross-national study. *Journal of Personality and Social Psychology, 53,* 898–908.

Lewis, C. C. (1995). *Educating hearts and minds*. New York: Cambridge University Press.

Lockwood, P., Marshall, T. C., & Sadler, P. (2005). Promoting success or prevention failure: Cultural differences in motivation by positive and negative role models. *Personality and Social Psychology Bulletin, 31,* 379–392.

Mao, L. R. (1994). Beyond politeness theory: Face revisited and renewed. *Journal of Pragmatics, 21,* 451–486.

Markus, H. R., & Kitayama, S. (1991). Culture and the self: Implications for cognition, emotion, and motivation. *Psychological Review, 98,* 224–253.

Miller, P. J., Wiley, A. R., Fung, H., & Liang, C. (1997). Personal storytelling as a medium of socialization in Chinese and American families. *Child Development, 68,* 557–568.

Minami, H. (1953). *Nihonjin no shinri* [Japanese mind]. Tokyo, Japan: Iwanami Sinsyo.

Nisbett, R. E., Peng, K., Choi, I., & Norenzayan, A. (2001). Culture and systems of thought: Holistic vs. analytic cognition. *Psychological Review, 108,* 291–310.

Norenzayan, A., & Heine, S. J. (2005). Psychological universals: What are they and how can we know? *Psychological Bulletin, 135*, 763–784.

Peng, K., & Nisbett, R. E. (1999). Culture, dialectics, and reasoning about contradiction. *American Psychologist, 54*, 741–754.

Price, P. C., Pentecost, H. C., & Voth, R. D. (2002). Perceived event frequency and the optimistic bias: Evidence for a two-process model of personal risk judgments. *Journal of Experimental Social Psychology, 38*, 242–252.

Quiñones-Vidal, E., Lopez-García, J. J., Peñaranda-Ortega, M., & Tortosa-Gil, F. (2004). The nature of social and personality psychology as reflected in JPSP, 1965–2000. *Journal of Personality and Social Psychology, 86*, 435–452.

Redding, G., & Wong, G. Y. Y. (1986). The psychology of Chinese organization behaviors. In M. H. Bond (Ed.), *The psychology of the Chinese people* (pp. 267–295). Hong Kong: Oxford University Press.

Sakano, T., & Lewin, A. Y. (1999). Impact of CEO succession in Japanese companies: A coevolutionary perspective. *Organization Science: A Journal of the Institute of Management Sciences, 10*, 654–672.

Sedikides, C., Gaertner, L., & Toguchi, Y. (2003). Pancultural self-enhancement. *Journal of Personality and Social Psychology, 84*, 60–79.

Shuper, P. A., Sorrentino, R. M., Otsubo, Y., Hodson, G., & Walker, M. A. (2004). A theory of uncertainty orientation: Implications for the study of individual differences within and across cultures. *Journal of Cross-Cultural Psychology, 35*, 460–480.

Stover, L. E. (1974). *Cultural ecology of Chinese civilization*. New York: New American Library.

Suh, E. M. (2002). Culture, identity consistency, and subjective well-being. *Journal of Personality and Social Psychology, 83*, 1378–1391.

Ting-Toomey, S. (Ed.). (1994). *The challenge of facework: Cross-cultural and interpersonal issues*. Albany: State University of New York Press.

Zane, N., & Yeh, M. (2002). The use of culturally-based variables in assessment: Studies on loss of face. In K. Kurasaki, S. Okazaki, & S. Sue (Eds.). *Asian American mental health: Assessment methods and theories* (pp. 123–138). Dordrecht, the Netherlands: Kluwer Academic.

8

ON THE PSYCHOLOGICAL COSTS OF SELF-ENHANCEMENT

C. RANDALL COLVIN AND ROBERT GRIFFO

Many years ago the first author (Colvin) had a "real job" working for the phone company in the information systems division. He enjoyed working with the latest IBM computers and hard drives the size of washing machines, and liked his coworkers. He did not like his boss, John. John was a first-line manager who wore crooked ties and half-tucked-in shirts, was in his early 40s, and regularly exhibited scary Jack Nicholson–like expressions. John could be an unpleasant person. To new employees, John beamed self-confidence and touted his clout with upper management, indicating that they relied on his expert judgment. John bragged about his expertise with computers and with managing people. One easily got the impression that John single-handedly ran the phone company. John's superior manner quickly gave way to condescending and hostile behavior if he was questioned about a decision. Once he regained the upper hand, he quickly returned to his cocky and overconfident ways. Twenty years later, the first author heard that John had retired from the phone company. It was interesting to learn that John had been repeatedly passed over for promotion, no doubt a serious blow for someone who professed to play such a crucial role in a large corporation.

Our charge for this chapter is to discuss the personality and behavior liabilities associated with people such as John, whom we refer to as *self-enhancers*. One straightforward way to achieve this goal is to conduct a meta-analysis of the published studies on this topic and discuss the results. If researchers used similar conceptual and operational definitions, methods, and analytic approaches, the selection of candidate studies for meta-analysis would be relatively easy. However, the continuing division among self-enhancement researchers, which this volume so clearly highlights, means that different criteria are preferred by different researchers for selecting studies to summarize. The reader must thus wait for the summary of the psychological costs of self-enhancement until after we discuss the various criteria used for selecting studies. In these preliminary steps, we (a) briefly describe the nature of the division between self-enhancement researchers, (b) discuss conceptual definitions of self-enhancement, and (c) evaluate three operational definitions of self-enhancement.

TWO PERSPECTIVES ON SELF-ENHANCEMENT

For more than two millennia, Western philosophy has espoused accurate perceptions of self and the social world and viewed these accurate perceptions to be the ultimate virtue (Copleston, 1957). Many theoretical and clinical psychologists have likewise extolled realistic and accurate self-perception, believing it to be a fundamental feature of mental health (e.g., Jahoda, 1958; Rogers, 1951). A growing body of empirical research indicates that people (a) whose personality characteristics are easily and accurately judged (Colvin, 1993a, 1993b), (b) who possess accurate self-knowledge (Vogt & Colvin, 2005), (c) who accurately judge the personality of others (Vogt & Colvin, 2003), and (d) who refrain from self-distortion (e.g., Colvin, Block, & Funder, 1995; Paulhus, 1998) exhibit higher levels of intrapsychic and interpersonal well-being, respectively, than do individuals who engage in cognitive distortion of self and others' personality traits. From this perspective, mentally healthy people have a relatively accurate sense of self, are willing to present this imperfect self to the social world, and distort reality primarily to maintain manageable levels of anxiety.

In spite of this long tradition, the reality perspective on mental health has encountered a strong challenge. Taylor and Brown (1988) argued that the tendency to maintain overly positive and unrealistic self-perceptions of personality (i.e., positive illusions), as opposed to accurate self-perceptions, is characteristic of most people in general, and mentally healthy people in particular. The illusions perspective has garnered many converts since the publication of Taylor and Brown's review article. It has, however, been questioned on both theoretical and empirical grounds (e.g., Asendorpf & Ostendorf, 1998; Colvin & Block, 1994) and has sparked an ongoing debate over the adaptiveness of self-enhancement that has not yet been resolved. Despite some efforts to reconcile the competing reality and illusions perspectives by integrating them, it appears that both sides have such fundamental differences that a resolution may not be forthcoming any time soon.

CONCEPTUAL DEFINITIONS OF SELF-ENHANCEMENT

In their original formulation, Taylor and Brown (1988) defined *self-enhancement* as a "pervasive, enduring and systematic" (p. 194) tendency to hold unrealistically positive self-evaluations. This definition indicates self-enhancement is a "general, enduring pattern of error" (p. 194) and represents a distortion of reality. Many self-enhancement researchers, including those who hold the reality perspective, have adopted this conceptual definition while further interpreting it to mean that self-enhancement is a traitlike tendency (Paulhus, 1998). Researchers who subscribe to the trait view have demonstrated that self-enhancement (a) exhibits considerable individual differences (John & Robins, 1994), (b) is consistent across highly evaluative traits (Asendorpf & Ostendorf, 1998), and (c) shows rank order stability over 5 years (Colvin, Block, & Funder, 1995).

Some proponents of the illusions perspective have argued for a reconceptualization of self-enhancement, suggesting that it is not a trait but rather a behavior that is situationally responsive and constrained by social norms (Taylor & Armor, 1996; Taylor, Lerner, Sherman, Sage, & McDowell, 2003). The problem with this argument is that it fails to adequately differentiate a situationally dependent behavior from a trait because personality traits always operate in the context of situations and social norms (Funder, 1991). Researchers have also sought to differentiate self-enhancement from defense mechanisms, arguing that "defense mechanisms result in a distortion of reality, while illusions are simply overly positive subjective evaluations" (Taylor, Collins, Skokan, & Aspinwall, 1989, p. 120). This statement is also unclear, indicating that a distortion of reality is somehow different from an overly positive evaluation; many would argue that both reflect an inaccurate self-appraisal. Despite this confusion, one important point to consider is that the process of self-enhancement may consist of both unconscious and conscious processes.

For the purposes of this chapter, *self-enhancement* is defined as an overly positive view of one's own personality traits. This definition implies that an individual is unrealistic about a broad range of trait characteristics (as opposed to a single behavior), that this unrealistic self-view is distorted in a positive direction, and that the assessment of distortion is measured against a reality standard. We acknowledge that relying on a reality standard is both philosophically and methodologically challenging. Nevertheless, we believe that to conduct research on self-enhancement or any area that involves the assessment of accuracy and inaccuracy, researchers must do their best to develop and use proxy measures for reality. We return to this issue later, but essentially the assessment of accuracy uses the logic of construct validity outlined over 50 years ago by Cronbach and Meehl (1955).

Two additional conceptual issues merit discussion. The first pertains to the relationship between self-enhancement and narcissism. The question is whether the two constructs are actually the same construct with different names. This question is not immediately answerable. Some studies have reported low to moderate positive correlations between indices of self-enhancement and the Narcissistic Personality Inventory (NPI; John & Robins, 1994), but this result is difficult to interpret. The NPI is not an appropriate device for measuring narcissistic personality disorder as defined by the *Diagnostic and Statistical Manual of Mental Disorders* (4th ed., text revision [*DSM–IV–TR*]; American Psychiatric Association, 2000), and some research has called into question whether the NPI measures subclinical levels of narcissism or simply positive self-esteem (Edmonds, Colvin, & Roberts, 2005).

At the conceptual level, the two constructs appear to be close cousins. And if one looks closely at the *DSM* diagnostic criteria and compares the criteria with the definition of self-enhancement, the two constructs start to look more like siblings than cousins. Research that includes clinical evaluations of narcissistic personality disorder along with assessments of self-enhancement is needed to establish a clearer connection between the constructs.

The second issue pertains to whether the expected relationship between self-enhancement and mental health is linear or curvilinear. Although the reality and illusions perspectives predict, and find, opposite results between self-enhancement and mental health, both perspectives typically report linear results. The fact that the results are linear is problematic for both approaches. For the positive-illusions perspective, a linear relationship, taken to the extreme, suggests that people who have no contact with reality are the most mentally healthy. The linear relationship is robust despite the more recent suggestion that "mild" distortions of reality are associated with mental health (e.g., Taylor, Kemeny, Reed, Bower, & Gruenewald, 2000). For the reality perspective, a linear relationship, taken to the extreme, suggests that people who self-derogate and dislike themselves are the most mentally healthy. Neither perspective has reported finding these bizarre outliers. The most logical conclusion is that linear relationships are found because the participant samples (mostly college students) are fairly homogenous with respect to psychological adjustment and that more heterogeneous samples might reveal the predicted curvilinear pattern.

In the literature on self-enhancement, it sometimes appears as if researchers from the illusions and reality perspectives are studying two very different constructs. Until the differences between the two perspectives are resolved, it is vitally important for researchers to provide explicit definitions at the conceptual and operational levels, and to report their findings about the (mal)adaptiveness of self-enhancement within the context of these definitions (Robins & John, 1997).

OPERATIONAL DEFINITIONS OF SELF-ENHANCEMENT

Self-enhancement is typically operationally defined in one of three ways. In this section we describe the strengths and weaknesses of each approach.

Self-Report

The assessment of self-enhancement is most often done with self-report measures. Participants typically rate themselves in comparison with the "average" person on a variety of qualities and skills. The majority of participants rate themselves to be above average. Researchers argue that it is logically impossible for most people to be above average and cite this tendency as evidence of self-enhancement (Taylor & Brown, 1988). The "better than average" method was first used to describe group data and has been modified to assess individual tendencies to view oneself as better than average (Taylor et al., 2003).

Once self-reported self-enhancement is assessed, it typically is found to correlate positively with self-reported measures of psychological well-being. Taylor et al. (2003) found that three self-report measures of self-enhancement (How I See Myself [HSM], Taylor & Gollwitzer, 1995; Self-Deceptive Enhancement [SDE], Paulhus, 1998; and Personal Desirability of Traits [PDT], Krueger, 1998) correlated positively with a composite self-report measure of mental health (e.g., the Personal Growth, Autonomy and Purpose in Life scales of the Psychological Health Scale; Ryff, 1989) and psychological resources (e.g., Life Orientation Test, Scheier & Carver, 1985; Rosenberg Self-Esteem Scale, Rosenberg, 1965) but correlated negatively with a composite self-report measure of mental distress (e.g., Beck Depression Inventory, Beck, 1967; Cook–Medley Hostility Scale, Cook & Medley, 1954). These general findings have been frequently replicated (Brown, 1986; Paulhus, 1998; see also Taylor & Brown, 1988, for a review).

Results like these have fostered the belief that self-enhancement is adaptive (Taylor & Brown, 1988). This conclusion is problematic. If individuals self-enhance, or distort reality, when completing the self-enhancement measure, this tendency is likely to carry over to self-report measures of mental health (Colvin & Block, 1994; Shedler, Mayman, & Manis, 1993). We doubt that research participants know, or care, that they should exhibit their most unrealistic and distorted self-views on the self-enhancement measures and be entirely honest on the mental health measures.

This argument suggests that the positive correlation between self-reports of self-enhancement and psychological well-being may represent an artifact of shared method variance (Campbell & Fiske, 1959). This possibility can be eliminated if it is empirically demonstrated that self-reported self-enhancement correlates with measures of psychological well-being and personality that are independent of the self-report domain. The second author (Griffo) conducted a study in which he asked participants to complete nine self-report measures of self-enhancement (e.g., HSM, SDE, PDT) and six measures of psychological well-being (e.g., neuroticism, ego-resiliency, self-esteem) and engage in a videotaped getting-acquainted interaction with a stranger of the opposite sex who was also a participant in the study (Griffo, 2005). Following the interaction, participants rated their partner's personality on a brief measure assessing the five factors of personality (i.e., neuroticism, extraversion, agreeableness, openness to experience, conscientiousness; Vogt & Colvin, 2005) and 12 behaviors that had previously been found to relate to self-enhancement (Colvin, Block, & Funder, 1995). Four trained coders observed the videotaped interactions and rated the participants on the same 12 behaviors on which participants rated each other.

The self-reported self-enhancement and psychological well-being measures, and the partner and judge behavior ratings, were subjected to independent factor analyses for the purpose of data reduction. The results in Table 8.1 are based on the resulting unit-weighted factor scores. As seen in Table 8.1, two of the self-enhancement factors, Unlikely Virtues and Positive Social Comparisons, demonstrate the typical pattern of positive correlations with self-reported psychological well-being, whereas the Self-Perceived Superiority factor was unrelated to self-reported psychological well-being. It is not clear why this factor does not demonstrate the typical pattern of relationships. It is notable that the two measures that comprise this factor are not frequently used as measures of self-enhancement but rather, at least in the case of the NPI, are more likely to be correlated with self-enhancement.

If the relationship between self-enhancement and psychological well-being is more than a method variance artifact, the self-enhancement factors should correlate with non-self-report measures. Table 8.1 shows that of 39 correlation coefficients, only two are significant at the 5% chance level. Despite the fact that the first author (Colvin) has collected and published these same types of data for many years, the lack of relationship could be due to faulty partner and judge ratings. Nevertheless, it can be concluded that in this particular data set there is little evidence of a relationship between self-reported self-enhancement and non-self-report measures of personality and behavior. Similar data have been reported by the primary proponent of the positive illusions perspective (see Table 8.2). These data also show a very strong relationship between self-reported self-enhancement and self-reported psychological well-being (i.e., mental health) but a negligible one between the same self-enhancement measures and peer reports of psychological well-being (Taylor et al., 2003).

The results from these two studies do not provide a conclusive answer to whether an artifact of shared method variance operates in these data. It is

TABLE 8.1
Self-Reported Self-Enhancement Correlated With Ratings of
Psychological Well-Being, Personality, and Behavior

	Self-enhancement factors		
	Unlikely Virtues	Self-Perceived Superiority	Positive Social Comparisons
Self-reported psychological well-being			
Intrapsychic	.55**	−.05*	.41**
Interpersonal	.34**	−.07	.42**
Partner ratings of personality			
Neuroticism	.02	−.07	−.09
Extraversion	−.08	.04	.01
Openness to experience	.01	.02	.12
Agreeableness	.01	.22*	.01
Conscientiousness	−.07	.08	.00
Partner ratings of behavior			
Social enjoyment	−.01	.08	.10
Social skills	.21*	.12	.10
Dominance	.06	−.08	.06
Ambition	−.04	.03	.00
Judge ratings of behavior			
Social enjoyment	−.08	.12	.09
Social skills	−.09	.19+	.03
Dominance	.13	.10	.01
Ambition	−.07	.06	−.03

*Note. N*s range from 99 to 127. Unlikely Virtues = impression management (Paulhus, 1991), Self-Deceptive Denial (Paulhus & Reid, 1991), Self-Deceptive Enhancement (Paulhus, 1991), Minnesota Multiphasic Personality Inventory (MMPI) Lie Scale (Hathaway & McKinley, 1989), Eysenck Personality Inventory (EPI) Lie Scale (Eysenck & Eysenck, 1963). Self-Perceived Superiority = Narcissistic Personality Inventory (Raskin & Terry, 1988), MMPI Ego Inflation Scale (Hathaway & McKinley, 1989). Positive Social Comparisons = How I See Myself (Taylor & Gollwitzer, 1995), Personal Desirability of Traits (Krueger, 1998). Intrapsychic well-being = NEO Five-Factor Inventory (NEO-FFI) Neuoroticism (Costa & McCrae, 1989), California Psychological Inventory (CPI) Well-Being Scale (Gough, 1956), Rosenberg Self-Esteem Scale (Rosenberg, 1965). Interpersonal well-being = NEO-FFI Extraversion (Costa & McCrae, 1989), NEO-FFI Agreeableness (Costa & McCrae, 1989), Block Ego-Resiliency (Block & Kremen, 1996). Social enjoyment = liked partner, enjoyed interacting with partner, interested in what partner said, acted in irritable fashion. Social skills = exhibited social skills, appeared to be relaxed and comfortable, exhibited an awkward interpersonal style. Dominance = tried to control interaction, expressed hostility, talked at rather than with partner. Ambition = displayed ambition, emphasized accomplishments of self and others.
+p < .10. *p < .05. **p < .01 (two-tailed).

always a difficult and time-consuming, and often unrewarding, venture to try to provide evidence for the null hypothesis. And although the null hypothesis in this case remains tenuous, the data suggest that caution is in order when using self-report measures to assess self-enhancement.

Objective Criteria

Some researchers who recognize the limitations of self-report measures of self-enhancement have turned to operational definitions that incorporate objective criteria. With this approach, researchers ask participants to pro-

TABLE 8.2
Correlations Between Self-Enhancement Measures and Mental Health
and Psychological Resources Factors

Mental health measures	HSM	SDE	PDT
Self-report			
Mental Health factor	.66**	.43**	.40**
Mental Distress factor	−.53**	−.33**	−.20
Psychological Resources factor	.71**	.48**	.33**
Peer report			
Peer-judged mental health (interview)	.29**	.10	.11
Clinical ratings of mental health (EMT)	−.01	−.03	.09
Peer ratings of mental health (EMT)	−.06	.01	.09

Note. N = 92. HSM = How I See Myself (Taylor & Gollwitzer, 1995); SDE = Self-Deceptive Enhancement (Paulhus, 1991); PDT = Personal Desirability of Traits (Krueger, 1998); EMT = Early Memory Test (Mayman, 1968). Adapted from "Portrait of the Self-Enhancer: Well Adjusted and Well Liked or Maladjusted and Friendless?" by S. E. Taylor, J. S. Lerner, D. K. Sherman, R. M. Sage, and N. K. McDowell, 2003, *Journal of Personality and Social Psychology, 84*, p. 172. Copyright 2003 by the American Psychological Association.
**p < .01.

vide information about an objectively verifiable attribute. A number of studies have investigated participants' self-reports of, for example, grade point average (GPA) or SAT™ score, which are then compared with the university registrar's records of these data. If participants are found to have exaggerated their scores, they are sometimes characterized as exhibiting self-exaggeration. Moreover, self-exaggeration scores can be related to individual difference measures of psychological well-being to assess its psychological adaptiveness (Gabriel, Critelli, & Ee, 1994; Gramzow, Elliot, Asher, & McGregor, 2003; Robins & Beer, 2001). This approach provides an elegant solution to the shortcomings associated with self-report measures of self-enhancement.

This approach also has its limitations. The conceptual mapping between the broad construct of self-enhancement (i.e., overly positive view of one's personality traits) and the narrow construct of self-exaggeration (e.g., self-reported GPA contrasted with the registrar's records) is unclear. Future research that incorporates assessments of self-enhancement and self-exaggeration may reveal that the latter can be used to index the former. However, it might also reveal that self-exaggeration is an interesting, but independent, construct that is primarily related to the domains of achievement and motivation.

Another unfortunate limitation of this approach is that objective criteria are not abundant. If researchers attempt to move beyond GPA and SAT scores into the domain of personality, they will rediscover the difficulties personality psychologists historically have had selecting behavioral markers for personality traits (e.g., Buss & Craik, 1983; Mischel & Peake, 1982).

Perhaps in the future this point will become moot as advanced neuroimaging techniques provide the necessary objective criteria for the assessment of personality traits. Until then, the objective approach requires additional research to demonstrate its conceptual connection to the broader construct of self-enhancement.

Social Consensus

The assessment of self-enhancement by the social consensus approach compares participants' self-reports of personality with personality ratings by two or more informants who are acquainted with the participant. If participants' self-reports are more favorable than the informants' ratings, the participants are characterized as self-enhancers. However, a social consensus requires two or more people. A consensus of one does not count. The informants must agree about the participant's personality; but agreement does not guarantee validity (Funder & Colvin, 1997). However, the more situations in which the informants have observed the participant, the greater the likelihood that their agreed-upon personality ratings are valid. Even if all of these conditions have been met, there still is no guarantee that this approach will yield a valid assessment of self-enhancement.

This is where the logic of construct validity that we referred to earlier comes into play (Cronbach & Meehl, 1955). In much the same way that early test developers learned that no perfect criterion exists with which to validate a new test, similarly no perfect criterion exists with which to assess a participant's self-rated personality traits. The logic of construct validity acknowledges this limitation and attempts to overcome it by arguing for the use of multiple, and different, criteria. Thus, even if two friends agree about a participant's personality, there may be very good reasons to doubt their "social consensus" represents a reasonable proxy for the truth. However, if unique consensus groups, such as clinical interviewers, parents, significant others, and work associates, provide similar personality portraits based on unique perspectives on the participant's life, it can be argued that a reasonable approximation of truth has been obtained. Colvin et al. (1995) followed this logic when they used two independent sets of clinical examiners and close friends to serve as the social consensus criteria for evaluating participants' self-descriptions of personality. They obtained comparable results across three studies, which supports the usefulness of this approach.

The social consensus approach has received its fair share of criticism. It has been argued that the use of informant ratings (e.g., friends, clinicians) is problematic because they possess limited validity (Taylor et al., 2003). With the exception of informants who are complete strangers, this characterization is not accurate. A study investigating spouse agreement on the five factors of personality demonstrated agreement ranging from .46 (Neuroticism) to .74 (Extraversion; McCrae, Stone, Fagan, & Costa, 1998). In a related study, spouse self-reports on Neuroticism, Extraversion, and Openness correlated substantially with spouse ratings 6 years later (.49, .57, .59, respectively; Costa & McCrae, 1988). The numerous books, chapters, and research articles by Jack and Jeanne Block (Block, 1993) provide numerous examples documenting the validity of personality ratings by clinically trained examiners. Friends' ratings of personality have been shown to predict social behavior (e.g., Colvin & Funder, 1991). When viewed as effect sizes, these informant ratings represent effects that are as strong as they come in the field of social and personality psychology (Funder & Ozer, 1983).

Another criticism centers on the use of difference scores to assess the discrepancy between self- and others' ratings of personality (Zuckerman & Knee, 1996). We encourage readers to evaluate for themselves the existing literature devoted to difference scores (see Colvin, Block, & Funder, 1996). In addition to a conceptual analysis supporting the use of difference scores (Colvin et al., 1996), the criticism appears to be unwarranted from a pragmatic standpoint given the convergence of results obtained from research using both difference scores and residual scores (Paulhus, 1998).

Researchers occasionally use observer ratings to index both self-enhancement and well-being. It is critical that independent sets of observers are used for each type of measure. For example, a study by Kwan et al. (2004) used a round-robin design in which the same group-member ratings were used to assess both self-enhancement and task performance. It was found that self-enhancement correlated negatively with group performance. However, in this case, it is not clear whether these findings were the result of self-enhancement or poor self-presentation, which results in negative evaluations by group members. This ambiguity is a real concern and is related to the self-report method variance issue we discussed earlier. The message is that sound results require the use of independent data sources for the assessment of self-enhancement and psychological well-being (or other relevant constructs).

We have now laid out our logic, rationale, and personal biases for selecting the appropriate set of studies to evaluate the psychological costs of self-enhancement. In summary, our conceptual definition states that self-enhancement is an overly positive view of one's own personality traits. One corollary is that the accuracy of one's self-reported personality characteristics requires comparison with a valid criterion. As a result, the self-report approach is not optimal because of the inherent difficulties in asserting the validity of a self-report measure of self-enhancement. The objective approach is a promising assessment strategy but currently it is unclear how such a narrowband construct, such as exaggeration of GPA or SAT score, conceptually maps onto the much broader construct of self-enhancement. From our perspective, the social consensus approach provides the optimal construct to measurement mapping. It emphasizes the assessment of a wide range of personality traits by self and acquainted others and the use of multiple types of criteria in accordance with the tenets of construct validity, and argues for the use of independent data sources to evaluate the adaptiveness of self-enhancement. Given these stated criteria, we now turn to a discussion of the psychological costs of self-enhancement.

THE PSYCHOLOGICAL COSTS OF SELF-ENHANCEMENT

The selected studies present a very consistent picture that self-enhancing tendencies are associated with narcissism and maladjustment or low levels of psychological well-being. We should also note that several studies have found a positive relationship between self-enhancement and self-reported adjustment. These contrasting findings are discussed in the following sections.

Self-Enhancement and Narcissism

According to the *DSM–IV–TR*, individuals with narcissistic personality disorder "have a grandiose sense of self-importance (Criterion 1). They routinely overestimate their abilities and inflate their accomplishments" (p. 714) and "expect to be recognized as superior without commensurate achievements" (p. 717). Consistent with this description, several studies have demonstrated that the tendency to engage in self-enhancement is associated with narcissism.

Robins and Beer (2001, Study 1) assessed self-enhancement in a group interaction context by comparing participants' rankings of each group member's performance (including the self) with the average of the rankings made by the other group members. Self-enhancement was operationalized as the discrepancy between self-rankings and group-member rankings of performance. Self-enhancement was positively correlated with self-reported narcissism (NPI; Raskin & Terry, 1988).

In light of our earlier caveat about self-enhancement and its relationship to self-reported narcissism, it is noteworthy that a relationship has been found between self-enhancement and an observer-based measure of narcissism. John and Robins (1994) asked participants to rank their own performance and each group member's performance on a group task. Self-enhancement was computed by contrasting self- and group-member rankings of performance. After observing the participants over the course of a weekend assessment program, 11 staff psychologists rated each participant's narcissism using DSM criteria. In addition, composite California Adult Q-set (CAQ; Block, 1961/1978) staff ratings were compared with a CAQ narcissism prototype to create a second index of narcissism. Participants also completed two self-report measures of narcissism. Self-enhancement was correlated positively with the self-reported and staff-based measures of narcissism.

The grandiose nature of narcissism and the overly positive self-view of self-enhancement both provide a common conceptual link between the two constructs. The fact that the two constructs exhibit an empirical link provides additional evidence that the two constructs overlap. This connection provides evidence that self-enhancement is maladaptive.

Self-Enhancement, Personality, and Social Behavior

Research investigating self-enhancement and its relationship to a broad range of personality traits and social behaviors provides additional evidence that self-enhancers are maladjusted. Paulhus (1998) investigated the costs and benefits of self-enhancement during a 7-week group interaction task. Before the first group meeting, self-enhancement was indexed by comparing self-ratings on the NEO Five Factor Inventory (Costa & McCrae, 1989) with the ratings made by two close acquaintances. After the first and seventh group meetings, group members rated self and others on group performance, the five factors of personality, interpersonal behavior, and psychological adjustment.

After the first group interaction, self-enhancers were rated positively by fellow group members, being seen as performing well in the group, having high levels of agreeableness and openness to experience, possessing positive interpersonal characteristics such as being entertaining and warm, and being well adjusted. However, by the seventh group meeting this pattern reversed. Self-enhancers were seen by their fellow group members as being disagreeable, exhibiting poor group performance, acting arrogant, bragging, and being poorly adjusted.

These results were presumed to indicate that self-enhancers make good first impressions but are unable to maintain their favorable impressions over time (Paulhus, 1998). However, the fact that the self and group-member discrepancy score did not correlate with the pretest self and acquaintance discrepancy score until the seventh group meeting might imply that the group members did not, in the early meetings, have enough behavioral information to make valid judgments about their fellow group members.

Across a set of three studies, two longitudinal and one cross-sectional, self-enhancement was again found to be associated with poor adjustment (Colvin et al., 1995). In these studies, self-enhancement was indexed by comparing CAQ self-ratings of personality with a CAQ favorability prototype to index self-rated favorability. Participants' personalities were rated on the CAQ by (a) a team of clinically trained examiners who became familiar with the participants through clinical interviews and observation and (b) two close acquaintances (Study 3). The CAQ ratings were compared with the CAQ favorability prototype to index observer-rated favorability. Self-enhancement was operationalized as the difference between self-rated favorability and observer-rated favorability. Participants' personalities were also described by independent teams of observers 5 years after (Study 1) and 5 years before (Study 2) assessments of self-enhancement at ages 18 and 23, respectively. In addition, participants engaged in a videotaped getting-acquainted dyadic interaction (Study 3) in which a team of trained coders rated the social behavior of each participant using the Riverside Behavioral Q-sort (Funder, Furr, & Colvin, 2000).

Across these three studies a clear pattern emerged. Participants who viewed themselves more favorably than examiners and friends rated them were described by a completely independent group of observers as guileful and deceitful, having a brittle ego-defense, and being distrustful of people, subtly negativistic, hostile, and self-defeating. In contrast, those individuals with relatively accurate self-views were seen as cheerful, having high intellect, productive, sympathetic, and having poise and social presence (Colvin et al., 1995).

Self-Enhancement and Intrapsychic Well-Being

The research presented thus far demonstrates that self-enhancing tendencies are associated with narcissism and poor psychological adjustment. There is, however, an exception to this general finding. Self-enhancement, when assessed by the social consensus approach, tends to be associated with self-reported adjustment. Self-enhancement has been shown to correlate positively with self-reported ego-resiliency (Paulhus, 1998), self-reported self-esteem (Kwan et al., 2004; Paulhus, 1998), self-reported positive affect (Robins & Beer, 2001), and self-reported general adjustment (Kurt & Paulhus, 2005). The finding that self-enhancement is positively related to self-reported adjustment and negatively related to informant-rated adjustment has led some researchers to conclude that self-enhancement is a mixed blessing (Kwan et al., 2004; Paulhus, 1998). That is, self-enhancement may be associated with poor interpersonal well-being but also positive intrapsychic well-being.

The relationship between self-enhancement and self-reported adjustment may be dubious. Recall that for the relationship to be valid, it must be assumed that individuals who hold overly positive views of themselves accurately report high levels of psychological adjustment. This relationship is always open to the alternative explanation that self-enhancers hold unrealistically positive views of their own adjustment (Shedler et al., 1993).

CONCLUSION

We are not ambivalent about the relationship between self-enhancement and psychological well-being. Our review of conceptual and operational definitions and evaluation of the empirical literature led us to the conclusion that self-enhancement is associated with general maladjustment, focused primarily around a syndrome of behaviors similar to narcissistic personality disorder. We argue that the illusions perspective's reliance on self-report measures of self-enhancement, and self-report measures in general, may produce artifactual results as a result of the shared method variance. The research that uses objective criteria is methodologically sound and has produced a number of interesting findings; however, its conceptual connection to the broader self-enhancement construct needs to be demonstrated.

Some researchers have suggested that a little bit of self-enhancement is the optimal amount for good mental health (Baumeister, 1989; Taylor et al., 2000). This statement may ultimately be true, but the current arsenal of methodological techniques does not permit researchers to make absolute assessments, only relative ones. As a result, in any given study, individuals found to score slightly above the mean on self-enhancement may, in an absolute sense, be accurate, self-enhancing, or self-derogating.

Other researchers have indicated that self-enhancement does not operate like a classic defense mechanism, nor should it be considered one (Taylor & Brown, 1988). Again, this statement may be true. When these various issues are considered together, it becomes very clear that although the phenomenon of self-enhancement is interesting, it is not yet well understood. Future efforts need to (a) focus on reaching an agreed-upon definition, or definitions if the phenomenon is deemed to be composed of multiple constructs; (b) consider the various mechanisms that might lead to self-enhancing behaviors (e.g., unconscious vs. conscious, approach vs. avoid strategies); and (c) refine and develop methods to assess self-enhancement. The use of implicit measures may be one way to overcome the shortcomings of self-report.

It is noteworthy that only a handful of studies met our criteria for inclusion in the section on the psychological costs of self-enhancement. We believe it would be a mistake to infer that this means there is little support for the reality perspective, or that errors have been made in choosing criteria for selecting studies. Rather, the lack of studies using the approach we advocate reflects the fact that this approach is time consuming and costly. Although the verdict on our approach is still out, remember that sometimes the hard way is the better way.

REFERENCES

American Psychiatric Association. (2000). *Diagnostic and statistical manual of mental disorders* (4th ed., text rev.). Washington, DC: Author.

Asendorpf, J. B., & Ostendorf, F. (1998). Is self-enhancement healthy? Conceptual, psychometric, and empirical analysis. *Journal of Personality and Social Psychology, 74*, 955–966.

Baumeister, R. F. (1989). The optimal margin of illusion. *Journal of Social and Clinical Psychology, 8*, 176–189.

Beck, A. T. (1967). *Depression: Causes and treatment.* Philadelphia: University of Pennsylvania Press.

Block, J. (1978). *The Q-sort method in personality assessment and psychiatric research.* Palo Alto, CA: Consulting Psychologists Press. (Original work published 1961)

Block, J. (1993). Studying personality the long way. In D. C. Funder & R. D. Parke (Eds.), *Studying lives through time: Personality and development* (pp. 9–41). Washington, DC: American Psychological Association.

Block, J., & Kremen, A. M. (1996). IQ and ego-resiliency: Conceptual and empirical connections and separateness. *Journal of Personality and Social Psychology, 70,* 349–361.

Brown, J. D. (1986). Evaluations of self and others: Self-enhancement biases in social judgments. *Social Cognition, 4,* 353–376.

Buss, D. M., & Craik, K. H. (1983). The act frequency approach to personality. *Psychological Review, 90,* 105–126.

Campbell, D. T., & Fiske, D. W. (1959). Convergent and discriminant validation by the multitrait-multimethod matrix. *Psychological Bulletin, 56,* 81–105.

Colvin, C. R. (1993a). Childhood antecedents of young-adult judgability. *Journal of Personality, 61,* 611–635.

Colvin, C. R. (1993b). "Judgable" people: Personality, behavior, and competing explanations. *Journal of Personality and Social Psychology, 64,* 861–873.

Colvin, C. R., & Block, J. (1994). Do positive illusions foster mental health? An examination of the Taylor and Brown formulation. *Psychological Bulletin, 116,* 3–20.

Colvin, C. R., Block, J., & Funder, D. C. (1995). Overly positive self-evaluations and personality: Negative implications for mental health. *Journal of Personality and Social Psychology, 68,* 1152–1162.

Colvin, C. R., Block, J., & Funder, D. C. (1996). Psychometric truths in the absence of psychological meaning: A reply to Zuckerman and Knee. *Journal of Personality and Social Psychology, 70,* 1252–1255.

Colvin, C. R., & Funder, D. C. (1991). Predicting personality and behavior: A boundary on the acquaintanceship effect. *Journal of Personality and Social Psychology, 60,* 884–894.

Cook, W. W., & Medley, D. M. (1954). Proposed pharisaic-virtue scales for the MMPI. *Journal of Applied Psychology, 38,* 414–418.

Copleston, F. (1957). *A history of philosophy* (Vol. 1). Westminster, MD: Newman Press.

Costa, P. T., & McCrae, R. R. (1988). Personality in adulthood: A six-year longitudinal study of self-reports and spouse ratings on the NEO Personality Inventory. *Journal of Personality and Social Psychology, 54,* 853–863.

Costa, P. T., & McCrae, R. R. (1989). *NEO/FFI manual supplement.* Odessa, FL: Psychological Assessment Resources.

Cronbach, L. J., & Meehl, P. E. (1955). Construct validity in psychological tests. *Psychological Bulletin, 52,* 281–302.

Edmonds, G. W. A., Colvin, C. R., & Roberts, B. W. (2005, January). *Two routes to self-enhancement: The entanglement of narcissism and self-esteem.* Poster session presented at the annual meeting of the Society of Personality and Social Psychology, New Orleans, LA.

Eysenck, H. J., & Eysenck, S. B. G. (1963). *The Eysenck Personality Inventory.* San Diego, CA: Educational and Industrial Testing Service.

Funder, D. C. (1991). Global traits: A neo-Allportian approach to personality. *Psychological Science, 2,* 31–39.

Funder, D. C., & Colvin, C. R. (1997). Congruence of others' and self-judgments of personality. In R. Hogan & J. A. Johnson (Eds.), *Handbook of personality psychology* (pp. 617–647). San Diego, CA: Academic Press.

Funder, D. C., Furr, R. M., & Colvin, C. R. (2000). The Riverside Behavioral Q-sort: A tool for the description of social behavior. *Journal of Personality, 68,* 451–489.

Funder, D. C., & Ozer, D. J. (1983). Behavior as a function of the situation. *Journal of Personality and Social Psychology, 44,* 107–112.

Gabriel, M. T., Critelli, J. W., & Ee, J. S. (1994). Narcissistic illusions in self-evaluations of intelligence and attractiveness. *Journal of Personality, 62,* 143–155.

Gough, H. G. (1956). *California Psychological Inventory.* Palo Alto, CA: Consulting Psychologists Press.

Gramzow, R. H., Elliot, A. J., Asher, E., & McGregor, H. A. (2003). Self-evaluation bias and academic performance: Some ways and some reasons why. *Journal of Research in Personality, 37,* 41–61.

Griffo, R. (2005). *The construct validity of self-reported self-enhancement: A multi-method approach.* Unpublished master's thesis, Northeastern University, Boston.

Hathaway, S. R., & McKinley, J. C. (1989). *The Minnesota Multiphasic Personality Inventory–2.* Minneapolis: University of Minnesota Press.

Jahoda, M. (1958). *Current concepts of positive mental health.* Oxford, England: Basic Books.

John, O. P., & Robins, R. W. (1994). Accuracy and bias in self-perception: Individual differences in self-enhancement and the role of narcissism. *Journal of Personality and Social Psychology, 66,* 206–219.

Krueger, J. (1998). Enhancement bias in descriptions of self and others. *Personality and Social Psychology Bulletin, 24,* 505–516.

Kurt, A., & Paulhus, D. L. (2005). *Moderators of the adaptiveness of self-enhancement: Operationalization, domain, and outcome measures.* Manuscript submitted for publication.

Kwan, V. S. Y., John, O. P., Kenny, D. A., Bond, M. H., & Robins, R. W. (2004). Reconceptualizing individual differences in self-enhancement bias: An interpersonal approach. *Psychological Review, 111,* 94–110.

Mayman, M. (1968). Early memories and character structure. *Journal of Projective Techniques and Personality Assessment, 32,* 303–316.

McCrae, R. R., Stone, S. V., Fagan, P. J., & Costa, P. T. (1998). Identifying causes of disagreement between self-reports and spouse ratings of personality. *Journal of Personality, 66*, 285–313.

Mischel, W., & Peake, P. K. (1982). Analyzing the construction of consistency in personality. In M. M. Page (Ed.), *Nebraska symposium on motivation, 1982: Personality-current theory and research* (Vol. 30, pp. 233–262). Lincoln: University of Nebraska Press.

Paulhus, D. L. (1991). Measurement and control of response bias. In J. P. Robinson, P. R. Shaver, & L. S. Wrightsman (Eds.), *Measures of personality and social psychological attitudes* (pp. 17–59). San Diego, CA: Academic Press.

Paulhus, D. L. (1998). Interpersonal and intrapsychic adaptiveness of trait self-enhancement: A mixed blessing? *Journal of Personality and Social Psychology, 74*, 1197–1208.

Paulhus, D. L., & Reid, D. (1991). Enhancement and denial in socially desirable responding. *Journal of Personality and Social Psychology, 60*, 307–317.

Raskin, R., & Terry, H. (1988). A principal-components analysis of the Narcissistic Personality Inventory and further evidence of its construct validity. *Journal of Personality and Social Psychology, 54*, 890–902.

Robins, R. W., & Beer, J. S. (2001). Positive illusion about the self: Short-term benefits and long-term costs. *Journal of Personality and Social Psychology, 80*, 340–352.

Robins, R. W., & John, O. P. (1997). The quest for self-insight: Theory and research on accuracy and bias in self-perception. In R. Hogan, J. A. Johnson, & S. R. Briggs (Eds.), *Handbook of personality psychology* (pp. 649–679). New York: Academic Press.

Rogers, C. R. (1951). *Client-centered therapy: Its current practice, implications, and theory.* Oxford, England: Houghton Mifflin.

Rosenberg, M. (1965). *Society and the adolescent self-image.* Princeton, NJ: Princeton University Press.

Ryff, C. D. (1989). Happiness is everything, or is it? Explorations on the meaning of psychological well-being. *Journal of Personality and Social Psychology, 57*, 1069–1081.

Scheier, M. F., & Carver, C. S. (1985). Optimism, coping, and health: Assessment and implications of generalized outcome expectancies. *Health Psychology, 4*, 219–247.

Shedler, J., Mayman, M., & Manis, M. (1993). The illusion of mental health. *American Psychologist, 48*, 1117–1131.

Taylor, S. E., & Armor, D. A. (1996). Positive illusions and coping with adversity. *Journal of Personality, 64*, 873–898.

Taylor, S. E., & Brown, J. (1988). Illusion and well-being: A social psychological perspective on mental health. *Psychological Bulletin, 103*, 193–210.

Taylor, S. E., Collins, R. L., Skokan, L. A., & Aspinwall, L. G. (1989). Maintaining positive illusions in the face of negative information: Getting the facts without letting them get to you. *Journal of Social and Clinical Psychology, 8*, 114–129.

Taylor, S. E., & Gollwitzer, P. M. (1995). Effects of mindset on positive illusions. *Journal of Personality and Social Psychology, 69*, 213–226.

Taylor, S. E., Kemeny, M. E., Reed, G. M., Bower, J. E., & Gruenewald, T. L. (2000). Psychological resources, positive illusions, and health. *American Psychologist, 55*, 99–109.

Taylor, S. E., Lerner, J. S., Sherman, D. K., Sage, R. M., & McDowell, N. K. (2003). Portrait of the self-enhancer: Well adjusted and well liked or maladjusted and friendless? *Journal of Personality and Social Psychology, 84*, 165–176.

Vogt, D. S., & Colvin, C. R. (2003). Interpersonal orientation and the accuracy of personality judgments. *Journal of Personality, 71*, 267–295.

Vogt, D. S., & Colvin, C. R. (2005). Assessment of accurate self-knowledge. *Journal of Personality Assessment, 84*, 239–251.

Zuckerman, M., & Knee, C. R. (1996). The relation between overly positive self-evaluations and adjustment: A comment on Colvin, Block, and Funder (1995). *Journal of Personality and Social Psychology, 70*, 1250–1251.

9

ON THE PHYSICAL HEALTH COSTS OF SELF-ENHANCEMENT

WILLIAM M. P. KLEIN AND KATRINA L. COOPER

Most people hold a fairly rosy view of their abilities, future prospects, personality traits, and social status. Individuals believe that they are more moral than their peers (Messick, Bloom, Boldizar, & Samuelson, 1985) and that they possess more positive and fewer negative personality traits (Alicke, 1985). They believe they would be more likely than others to perform desirable acts and less likely to perform undesirable acts (Goethals, Messick, & Allison, 1991) and that they are more immune than are others to negative life events such as divorce and relationship problems (Murray, Holmes, & Griffin, 1996). Self-favoring views are predominant in beliefs about health. People consider their healthy behaviors unique and their unhealthy behaviors common (Suls, Wan, & Sanders, 1988), believe they engage in healthy behaviors more frequently than others do (Weinstein, 1984), and feel they are less likely than others to experience a wide variety of health problems (Helweg-Larsen & Shepperd, 2001). These beliefs hold across many demo-

We thank Erin Cole-Karagory, Nathan Radcliffe, and the Social/Health Psychology Laboratory at the University of Pittsburgh for contributions to the ideas presented in this chapter. Correspondence may be addressed to the first author at Department of Psychology, University of Pittsburgh, 3105 Sennott Square, 210 South Bouquet Street, Pittsburgh, PA 15260; e-mail: wmklein@pitt.edu.

graphic variables, including age and education (Quadrel, Fischhoff, & Davis, 1993; Weinstein, 1987), and are even present among high-risk samples such as smokers (Weinstein, 1998) and prostitutes (e.g., van der Velde, van der Pligt, & Hooykaas, 1994). People sometimes display pessimistic beliefs, such as beliefs about the ability to cope with negative events (Blanton, Axsom, McClive, & Price, 2001), but self-enhancing beliefs are far more common.

Biased beliefs such as these may be adaptive because they might promote positive affect, motivation, and healthy behavior. This notion has been present in the clinical psychology literature for some time, with specific focus on the notion of *depressive realism*—the finding that individuals with depression often maintain a more realistic (and accurate) sense of reality than do individuals without depression (Alloy & Abramson, 1988). In a seminal paper reviewing the broader literature on self-enhancement, Taylor and Brown (1988) took this idea one step further and argued that positive distortions in self-beliefs fostered effective mental health (e.g., the ability to pursue goals and care for others). However, it is also conceivable that these biases undermine rational decision making. If people underestimate their risk of heart disease, they may be less likely to monitor their cholesterol and blood pressure. If homeowners believe that their homes are not contaminated by radon, they will not have their homes tested for radon (Weinstein, Sandman, & Roberts, 1991). It is also possible—and highly likely—that self-enhancement biases are adaptive in some situations and not others. If so, it is important to uncover the latent constructs that best capture these situational differences.

We set out to accomplish three goals in this chapter. First, we review the methodological problems that currently plague the literature on self-enhancement biases and health outcomes, and offer potential solutions. Second, we review extant evidence on the link between self-enhancement biases and various types of health outcomes, focusing on studies that address at least some of these methodological problems. Finally, we step back and consider the likely possibility that self-enhancement biases promote good health under some conditions and not others, and offer possible variables that may be shown in future research to moderate the effects of self-enhancement biases.

METHODOLOGICAL CONSTRAINTS IN LINKING SELF-ENHANCEMENT TO HEALTH OUTCOMES

How might one go about establishing the link between self-enhancement and health outcomes? One must consider a number of significant methodological obstacles. For example, how do we define *self-enhancement*? If we simply define it as believing good things about the self, then measurement of self-enhancement is easy: We simply ask people to rate themselves on a reliable scale and assume that more positive ratings suggest more self-enhancement. Yet the intellectual debate about positive illusions is not about whether positive beliefs are adaptive but whether illusory positive beliefs confer benefits. Thus we need to evaluate the accuracy of a person's judgment before linking that judgment to anything else.

It is notable that the research demonstrating self-enhancement biases has focused on the group rather than the individual as the unit of analysis. It is reasonable to argue that a group is biased if most of its members believe they are better than average. However, it is not possible to determine from such an analysis whether any one group member is biased. A man who has low cholesterol, no family history of heart disease, and a healthy lifestyle is probably accurate if he estimates his heart disease risk to be below average. Indeed, it is possible to be unrealistically optimistic even if one is qualitatively pessimistic. Consider another man who has smoked for 40 years and has a family history of lung cancer. If this man estimates his risk to be slightly above average, which is a pessimistic stance, he will be unrealistically optimistic if his risk turns out to be substantially above average.

Measuring Bias in Self-Judgments

How does one go about determining whether an individual self-evaluation is biased? Perhaps the best method is to determine whether it is consonant with actual events. For example, Klein, Geaghan, and MacDonald (in press) asked college students to estimate their risk of having unplanned sexual intercourse in the next year, and then contacted students again to determine if they indeed had had unplanned sex. Of course, this approach is not feasible in contexts in which the outcome occurs well after the self-evaluation is collected. As a consequence, very few studies take this approach, and when they do, they study short-term outcomes that are usually not related to health (e.g., Buehler, Griffin, & MacDonald, 1997; Dunning & Story, 1991). A related possibility is to ask participants to make predictions about events whose future occurrence is certain. The best example is a study by Taylor et al. (1992) in which HIV-seropositive individuals reported lower perceived risk of getting AIDS—a nearly certain outcome—than did their HIV-seronegative counterparts.

Another approach is to collect information about each participant and use it to make an educated guess about which participants are biased. Wiebe and Black (1997) assessed participants' frequency of having sex and the percentage of time they used condoms to categorize participants as low or high in risk, and participants were identified as illusional if they were at high risk yet perceived low risk (see also Burger & Burns, 1989; Gerrard & Luus, 1995). A clear disadvantage here is that idiosyncratic differences in how two different investigators define the relevance of a given attribute could lead to unfortunate discrepancies in whether a given participant is categorized as biased. An even better approach is to go beyond educated guesses about risk factors and instead use reliable expert models that are based on population prevalence of illnesses and related risk factors. For example, the Harvard Cancer Risk Index computes an individual's chances of experiencing a variety of different types of cancer based on formulas that include weighted combinations of risk factors for which there is substantial medical consensus (Colditz et al., 2000). Actual risk as computed by these models can then be compared with participants' estimates to determine who is biased (Kreuter & Strecher, 1995; Radcliffe & Klein, 2002; Strecher, Kreuter, & Kobrin, 1995).

Other methods to define bias at the level of the individual are available, although none are as desirable as those mentioned earlier. For example, one can compare self-judgments with aggregated judgments made by peers, friends, or family, on the basis of the notion that people are self-enhancing if they rate themselves more positively than do others who know them well (e.g., Kwan, John, Kenny, Bond, & Robins, 2004; Taylor, Lerner, Sherman, Sage, & McDowell, 2003). Although this approach is useful when traits such as leadership ability are being judged, it is less likely to be effective when judging health standing because others in one's life are not necessarily more accurate when judging health risks. A related idea is to have physicians and patients each rate the patient's risk because physicians are likely to have a better sense of a given person's risk. However, research demonstrates that physicians are just as susceptible as laypersons to biases in the evaluation of risk information (Chapman & Elstein, 2000).

Assessing Effects of Bias at the Group Level

All of these methods assume a correlational approach, such that bias is measured at the level of the individual and magnitude (or presence) of bias is then correlated with other variables such as health behavior and anxiety. It is also possible to observe effects of bias when comparing groups that can be assumed a priori to differ in relevant beliefs. Caffeine drinkers are more resistant to evidence linking caffeine consumption to fibrocystic disease, presumably because such evidence threatens the self-enhancing belief that their behaviors will not cause health problems (Kunda, 1987; Liberman & Chaiken, 1992). Guppy (1993) showed that people who speed when driving estimate their risk of having an accident to be lower than do people who do not speed, which is clearly a bias; one can then determine if this group engages in other risky behaviors to make a case that bias is associated with behavior. Klein (1996) informed participants that their health habits were better or worse than those of their peers and found that the group that learned that their habits were worse than average reconstructed their memory (in a self-favoring direction) as to how often they engaged in risky behavior. They also came to see the behaviors as less personally important and less relevant to health.

Problematic Methods of Measuring Bias

Several studies attempt to link self-enhancement biases to health outcomes using definitions of bias that could be problematic. The simplest case is when investigators consider any favorable judgment (e.g., the belief that one's chances of having a health problem are low) to be biased. Significant correlations of such ratings with other variables say nothing about bias—they say only that people who make more favorable ratings fall higher (or lower) on the other variable. An example of this problem may be seen in a study by Dewberry, Ing, James, Nixon, and Richardson (1990), in which participants who estimated lower personal risk of 16 negative events (e.g., breast cancer, losing job) were also less anxious. The investigators concluded that bias reduces anxiety. However, a more plausible interpretation is that people who estimate lower risk are less anxious precisely because they do have lower risk, and they know it.

Other investigators have avoided undue focus on one given judgment by collapsing several self-judgments together, with the inference that people who rate themselves positively across an array of dimensions are more biased. Davidson and Prkachin (1997) asked students to estimate their risk of experiencing 11 health problems, and then collapsed the ratings as a measure of unrealistic optimism. It is plausible that individuals giving low risk estimates for most health problems are more likely to be biased than are those who make favorable ratings regarding a single event (given the greater room for error). However, we would argue that ordinal accuracy is still present such that participants making more favorable ratings across the spectrum are probably healthier and less at risk than are those making decidedly negative ratings across the same spectrum.

A similar argument applies to studies that test cognitive adaptation theory, which argues that illusions such as unrealistic optimism and the illusion of control promote mental and physical health (Taylor, 1983). Helgeson (1999, 2003) administered the Life Orientation Test, a measure of dispositional optimism (Scheier & Carver, 1985); the Rosenberg (1965) Self-Esteem scale, a conventional measure of trait self-esteem; and Pearlin and Schooler's (1978) Mastery scale, a measure of personal control. The sample was a group of men and women with high risk for coronary artery disease who had undergone an angioplasty. High scores on these measures (particularly among men) predicted positive adjustment to disease and lower likelihood of experiencing a cardiac event. These findings are important because they demonstrate quite profoundly that positive beliefs may promote healing and fewer health problems. Yet this study does not speak to the consequences of positively biased beliefs, because the measures tap generic beliefs that cannot be calibrated with any objective criterion. Moreover, the measures used in this study are not reliably correlated with measures of unrealistic optimism (e.g., Davidson & Prkachin, 1997; Radcliffe & Klein, 2002).

In related studies, participants completed the How I See Myself Questionnaire (HSM; Taylor & Gollwitzer, 1995), in which they rated themselves relative to their peers on 21 positive and 21 negative attributes. The authors observed that individuals who rated themselves more favorably had lower mental distress and were in better physical health (e.g., Taylor et al., 2003), and concluded that positive illusions are health promoting. These are crucial findings because they speak to actual physiological outcomes, not just self-reported cognitions and behaviors. However, one can interpret these findings as suggesting that people who view themselves more favorably are in better health, perhaps because they are doing the very things that promote their health and justify their favorable ratings. The one exception is that these authors also looked at how participants' friends rated them on the same dimensions and found that self-serving deviations between self-ratings and other ratings were associated with good mental health. Although using friend ratings introduces other problems, this approach is more persuasive.

Interpreting Cross-Sectional Data

The ability to draw inferences about the link between self-enhancement biases and health outcomes is limited not only by how bias is defined but also by design issues. Cross-sectional studies in which self-enhancement and the health outcome are measured concurrently are common and are characterized by several problems. Third variables (e.g., low levels of education) may promote both biased self-views and negative health outcomes. Risk perceptions and behavior may be correlated because high risk promotes precautionary behavior, or because risk perceptions are an accurate reflection of past behavior (Weinstein, Rothman, & Nicolich, 1998). Prospective and experimental designs are clearly better but far less common. Experimental designs may be difficult because self-enhancement biases are very resistant to change (Weinstein & Klein, 1995). Making matters worse, the relation between self-enhancement bias and a health outcome may not be linear because extreme distortions are likely to be maladaptive (Baumeister, 1989; Wallston, 1994). No studies have addressed possible quadratic relationships between bias and health outcomes.

HEALTH COSTS OF SELF-ENHANCEMENT

In this section we review studies (including cross-sectional investigations) that incorporated what we considered to be a reasonably defensible definition of self-enhancement as well as a health outcome. Most of the relevant studies focus on the link between self-enhancement and risk factors, processing of health information, and health behavior, all of which are proximal determinants of disease. In contrast with the rich literature linking positive beliefs with physical health variables (see Segerstrom & Roach, chap. 3, this volume), there is a dearth of published studies linking biased positive beliefs with such outcomes. Thus, most of our attention is focused on the variables mentioned earlier.

Risk Factors

We begin simply by considering whether people who hold biased self-beliefs also possess risk factors for disease. One study showed that smokers were more likely than nonsmokers to be unrealistically optimistic about their heart attack, cancer, and stroke risks (Strecher et al., 1995), three diseases closely linked with smoking. In a similar manner, individuals who had unrealistically optimistic beliefs concerning their heart attack risk exhibited higher systolic blood pressure and serum cholesterol levels (Radcliffe & Klein, 2002), although these results must be interpreted cautiously because blood pressure and cholesterol levels were used to compute actual risk. Two studies demonstrated that unrealistic optimism was more likely to occur among individuals with lower levels of education (Avis, Smith, & McKinlay, 1989; Kreuter & Strecher, 1996). This finding is important because such individuals are relatively more likely to suffer negative health outcomes (e.g., Winkleby, Jatulis, Frank, & Fortman, 1992). These studies, although small in number, suggest that individuals who are most likely to show an optimistic bias in their health beliefs are those very people who are at an elevated risk for disease. Of course, none of these studies can test for a causal relationship.

Health Information Processing

One component of good health is the effective processing of health information. People who seek out reliable information about self-relevant outcomes, process it carefully and nondefensively, and use it when making important health decisions are likely to experience more positive health outcomes. Several studies demonstrate that people who hold self-enhancing beliefs about their health risks engage in less careful processing of health information. Radcliffe and Klein (2002) found that individuals who were unrealistically optimistic about their risk of suffering a heart attack displayed less knowledge about heart attacks and believed that their standing on risk factors decreased rather than increased their personal risk. In another study, smokers who held unrealistically optimistic beliefs about their lung cancer risk were also more likely to endorse popular myths about lung cancer, believing, for example, that the disease is influenced more by genetics than by smoking and that lung cancer is highly curable (Dillard, McCaul, & Klein, 2006).

Not only do individuals with unrealistically optimistic health beliefs possess less knowledge concerning health risks, they also may actively avoid threatening health information. Individuals in one study who were unrealistically optimistic about their risk for sexually transmitted disease or unintended pregnancy were more likely than unbiased individuals to avoid being exposed to risk-related information and were marginally less interested in learning more about contraception (Wiebe & Black, 1997). In another study, individuals were given a choice of reading about a variety of heart disease risk factors. Those who held unrealistically optimistic assessments of their own heart attack risk preferred to read about a risk factor for which they believed their own standing to be favorable rather than about others for which their standing was unfavorable (Radcliffe & Klein, 2002).

A number of studies suggest that when unrealistically optimistic individuals do receive health-relevant information and test results, they do not process this information carefully and objectively. Participants in the Wiebe and Black (1997) study found pamphlets pertaining to contraception to be less personally relevant if they initially held unrealistically optimistic beliefs concerning their own risk. In the study by Radcliffe and Klein (2002), individuals who had unrealistic beliefs concerning their heart attack risks recalled less information from an essay on heart disease that they had read in the laboratory than did those who did not hold such beliefs.

Biased individuals may also be less likely to believe unfavorable health-related information. Kunda (1987) and Liberman and Chaiken (1992) found that women who consumed caffeine were more critical of information linking caffeine consumption to fibrocystic disease than were individuals for whom this information was irrelevant (women who did not consume caffeine and men). Individuals who received unfavorable medical test results were found to take more time processing such information and were more likely to check the validity of these results than were individuals who did not receive unfavorable results (Ditto, Munro, Apanovitch, Scepansky, & Lockhart, 2003). When people are presented with unfavorable test results, they come to believe that such results are common (Jemmott, Ditto, & Croyle, 1986). This evidence suggests that even if individuals are directly confronted with health-relevant information, they will distort it so it seems less threatening than it is (see also Croyle, Sun, & Louie, 1993).

Several studies demonstrate that people use a variety of related strategies to maintain potentially consequential self-enhancing beliefs. Gerrard, Gibbons, Benthin, and Hessling (1996) found that as adolescents engage in more risky behaviors, they inflate the perceived prevalence of such behaviors, thus encouraging them to participate in still more risky behaviors. When individuals were shown in another set of studies that their estimates for the prevalence of negative health behaviors were exaggerated, they recalibrated estimates of their own behavior to maintain the appearance of it being better than average (Klein, 1996; Klein & Kunda, 1993). If this option was impossible, they instead minimized the relevance of the given behavior to health outcomes (see also Gerrard et al., 1996; Klein, Blier, & Janze, 2001; Radcliffe

& Klein, 2002; Wiebe & Black, 1997). Individuals with high self-esteem—who are more likely to hold exaggeratedly positive beliefs about themselves—may be particularly likely to minimize the effects of their behavior on their health (Boney-McCoy, Gibbons, & Gerrard, 1999). Because minimization of the costs of a health behavior can further promote that behavior (as in the case of smoking; Sayette & Hufford, 1997), this set of findings is important.

Overall, these studies suggest that self-enhancement biases may have a detrimental effect on how people think about health, how they seek out and process health information, and how they interpret diagnostic information about their own health standing. Health messages may often be ignored or distorted to maintain positive illusions about one's health status. Poor processing of health messages is likely to be associated with health-impairing behavior, to which we turn next.

Risky Behavior

Overestimations of one's invulnerability to health risks and ability to control such risks have been shown to influence behavioral intentions. In one study, participants were given a hypothetical choice between two drugs: one that had a lower risk of severe side effects and one that had a higher risk of such side effects but also an opportunity to exert some control over whether the side effects appeared. Participants generally preferred the second drug, not only because the side effects were more controllable, but also because they thought they would be more competent than others at avoiding these side effects (Klein & Kunda, 1994). A similar pattern was observed by these investigators across a variety of hypothetical and real scenarios. In short, self-enhancement led to a preference for more risky alternatives, which in the long run is maladaptive. In another study, smokers who underestimated their risk for developing lung cancer were less likely to intend to quit smoking (Dillard et al., 2006).

What is the impact of self-enhancement biases on actual health behavior? Very few studies have addressed this question. In one study, college students who held unrealistically optimistic beliefs about their risk of engaging in unplanned sex consumed alcohol more frequently and in larger amounts than did students who held more realistic beliefs (Klein et al., in press), which in turn put the first group of students at greater risk of unplanned sex and numerous other negative outcomes. Kreuter and Stretcher (1996) demonstrated that providing accurate health risk assessment information to participants, thereby reducing unrealistic optimism, led to increased exercise and cholesterol screening and decreased fat consumption. However, Segerstrom, McCarthy, Caskey, Gross, and Jarvik (1993) found that smokers who underestimated the tar content of their cigarettes were no more or less likely than were nonbiased smokers to attempt to quit smoking, which suggests that this bias was inconsequential. A study of gay men who were HIV-seropositive and yet reported relatively lower risk of AIDS (representing unrealistic optimism, given the near-certain progression of HIV to AIDS) found that these men engaged in more healthful behaviors than did those who were not unrealistically optimistic, which suggests that unrealistic optimism may in fact lead to positive health outcomes (Taylor et al., 1992; see also Reed, Kemeny, Taylor, Wang, & Visscher, 1994).

Summary

The corpus of studies that link self-enhancement biases with health outcomes is modest in size, and many studies are cross-sectional. Nevertheless, the balance of studies suggests that self-enhancement biases—usually unrealistic optimism about future health outcomes—are associated with higher risk, poorer knowledge of and attention to health risk information, greater use of defensive strategies when processing such information, and more risky behavioral intentions and actual behavior. Our tentative conclusion, then, is that self-enhancement biases generally compromise good health.

These findings stand in marked contrast to other work suggesting that positive beliefs such as optimism are health-promoting. The key difference is that this literature does not usually address the accuracy of such beliefs. The importance of this difference may be seen in the study by Radcliffe and Klein (2002). These investigators showed that participants who were comparatively optimistic (i.e., considered their heart disease risk to be relatively lower than that of their peers, irrespective of accuracy) or dispositionally optimistic (a personality trait) were in better health, more attentive to health information, and less defensive. However, this same study showed a reverse pattern for individuals whose optimism was erroneous. Evidently positive beliefs are healthy, but not when they are misplaced.

RECONCILIATION AND THOUGHTS

On balance, the studies reviewed here paint an unflattering picture of people who hold self-enhancing beliefs. Nevertheless, many studies are cross-sectional, and most take the fairly simplistic approach of linking self-enhancement to a health outcome rather than asking the more interesting question of when self-enhancement might and might not promote good health. Although it is necessary to continue building a body of work that uses defensible definitions of bias and links such bias to a variety of health outcomes, we hope the next generation of research will begin to look at moderators and mediators of this relationship. Armor and Taylor (1998) have suggested, for example, that unrealistic optimism may be adaptive when it promotes the optimistic reinterpretation of negative outcomes and productive efforts to achieve the desired outcome—a self-fulfilling prophecy. Data testing these and other hypotheses are sorely lacking.

Moderation

We suspect a number of important variables may determine whether self-enhancement biases lead to positive or negative health outcomes. Although no studies systematically manipulate such variables, the literature offers hints about what some of these variables might be.

Proactive Versus Retroactive Self-Enhancement Effects

Many studies that illustrate beneficial effects of self-enhancement biases are conducted on samples of individuals who have already experienced a major health event such as breast cancer or an HIV diagnosis (e.g., Taylor et al., 1992). However, studies suggesting a harmful effect of bias tend to involve samples of individuals who may be susceptible to disease in the future but have yet to experience significant health problems. It may be that self-enhancement biases move from being harmful to beneficial as one begins to cope with a major life event, perhaps because of the positive affect and motivation that accompanies these biases (Armor & Taylor, 1998). For example, a smoker's underestimation of lung cancer risk might hinder quit attempts, but if this smoker is diagnosed with lung cancer, unrealistic optimism about future bouts with cancer may strengthen interest and self-efficacy in quitting.

Controllability

Holding biased self-beliefs about highly controllable outcomes is likely to be maladaptive if these biases hinder preventive actions or promote risk-increasing actions (e.g., Klein et al., in press). However, less controllable outcomes such as Huntington's disease—which afflicts 100% of individuals who possess the inherited gene for this disease—might be overwhelming for a person, eliciting intrusive thoughts and depression. In this case, holding mildly distorted views may be beneficial. Unrealistic optimism is far more likely for controllable events (Harris, 1996), so few data speak to the benefits of unrealistic optimism regarding uncontrollable health events.

Reversibility of Outcome

Irrespective of the controllability of the outcome, once the outcome does occur, it may vary in the extent to which it is reversible. Infection with HIV is not currently reversible, yet melanomas can be removed without any future cancer recurrences if caught early. As a consequence, unrealistic optimism regarding HIV risk may be relatively more harmful. In cases in which an outcome is completely reversible, unrealistic optimism may even be beneficial. Unfortunately, it is easier to generate examples of nonhealth events that are reversible (e.g., switching careers in one's mid-20s) than it is to generate such examples of health events.

Relative Likelihood of Outcome

The likelihood of some health outcomes occurring often depends on the likelihood of other health outcomes occurring. For example, the second leading cause of death among Native Americans is unintentional injuries (National Center for Health Statistics, 1997), so many Native Americans do not live long enough to experience common diseases such as cancer. Unrealistic optimism regarding unintentional injuries may then be more consequential in this population. In a similar way, if an outcome is much more likely than are most others, unrealistic optimism about the less likely outcomes may promote motivation and reduce distress so that the person can focus on reducing the high-likelihood risk.

Affective Versus Motivational Consequences

Some self-enhancement biases may exist primarily for affective reasons, yet are unlikely to get in the way of motivation and behavior. In a study of college students, for example, the belief that one's risk of becoming overweight was lower than that of other single individuals (e.g., a best friend) was related to less worry but not to interest in losing weight. However, the belief that one's risk was lower than that of the average student was related to both decreased worry and behavioral intentions (Klein, 2002), which suggests that this belief was more consequential. When self-enhancement biases reduce negative affect with little effect on behavior, they are more adaptive. At present, we know nothing about the variables that differentiate affective and behavioral consequences of self-enhancement biases. A related issue concerns the value placed on life expectancy versus quality of life. If forced to choose between a large number of years with a painful health problem versus a fewer number of years without the health problem, most people choose the latter (e.g., Stalmeier, Bezembinder, & Unic, 1996). If self-enhancement biases promote quality of life and reduce worry and anxiety—as Taylor and Brown (1988) suggested in their review of the literature—then the notion that such biases might hasten the occurrence of disease may be deemed acceptable.

Health Outcomes

The studies reviewed here speak to several proximal predictors of disease including attention to health information and engagement in risky behavior. Nevertheless, there is a clear need for research that links self-enhancement biases directly with physiological outcomes. As noted by Segerstrom and Roach (chap. 3, this volume), many studies have linked optimistic beliefs with measures such as immune system function and cardiovascular reactivity. We are not aware of any studies that link optimistically biased beliefs with these types of measures. Moreover, it would be important to elucidate the mechanisms through which self-enhancement biases might influence subclinical and clinical health outcomes.

CONCLUSION

Many of the leading causes of death—cancer, heart disease, and automobile accidents—are at least partially preventable. Because attitudes, risk perceptions, and other cognitions are key predictors of health behavior, it seems essential to understand whether inaccuracies in these cognitions might increase one's personal risk of experiencing these diseases. Inaccuracy in many domains is more likely to lead to failure than success, so it seems reasonable to expect that inaccuracies in self-related judgments might be health-impairing.

Our goals in this chapter were to discuss some of the methodological issues that must be addressed in attempts to examine the health consequences of self-enhancement biases, review the extant literature on these consequences, and offer ideas for future research that might provide a more comprehensive and theoretically appealing understanding of how self-enhancement biases influence health. We hope to have successfully demonstrated that, if self-enhancement is to be defined as an illusion, it must be measured in the presence of an objective criterion to determine accuracy. Moreover, the best designs to examine the effects of self-enhancement are prospective and experimental.

Because our review of the literature uncovered a fairly small set of studies that used an accuracy criterion, and a still smaller set that used experimental or prospective designs, it is fair to conclude that much more research on this topic is necessary. We hope that such work will transcend the somewhat simplistic hypothesis that self-enhancement biases, when not taken to an extreme, are uniformly good or bad for health. Instead, we hope such work will systematically examine important variables that tell us when self-enhancement is good and when it is bad. We suggested several possible variables, but we are sure many more have not occurred to us. We hope that our optimism that future research will clarify the link between self-enhancement and health will not prove to be unrealistic.

REFERENCES

Alicke, M. D. (1985). Global self evaluation as determined by the desirability and controllability of trait adjectives. *Journal of Personality and Social Psychology, 49*, 1621–1630.

Alloy, L. B., & Abramson, L. Y. (1988). Depressive realism: Four theoretical perspectives. In L. B. Alloy (Ed.), *Cognitive processes in depression* (pp. 223–265). New York: Guilford Press.

Armor, D. A., & Taylor, S. E. (1998). Situated optimism: Specific outcome expectancies and self-regulation. *Advances in Experimental Social Psychology, 30,* 309–379.

Avis, N. E., Smith, K. W., & McKinlay, J. B. (1989). Accuracy of perceptions of heart attack risk: What influences perceptions and can they be changed? *American Journal of Public Health, 79,* 1608–1612.

Baumeister, R. F. (1989). The optimal margin of illusion. *Journal of Social and Clinical Psychology, 8,* 176–189.

Blanton, H., Axsom, D., McClive, K. P., & Price, S. (2001). Pessimistic bias in comparative evaluations: A case of perceived vulnerability to the effects of negative life events. *Personality and Social Psychology Bulletin, 27,* 1627–1636.

Boney-McCoy, S., Gibbons, F. X., & Gerrard, M. (1999). Self-esteem, compensatory self-enhancement, and the consideration of health risk. *Personality and Social Psychology Bulletin, 25,* 954–965.

Buehler, R., Griffin, D., & MacDonald, H. (1997). The role of motivated reasoning in optimistic time predictions. *Personality and Social Psychology Bulletin, 23,* 238–247.

Burger, J. M., & Burns, L. (1989). The illusion of unique invulnerability and the use of effective contraception. *Personality and Social Psychology Bulletin, 14,* 264–270.

Chapman, G. B., & Elstein, A. S. (2000). Cognitive processes and biases in medical decision-making. In G. B. Chapman & F. A. Sonnenberg (Eds.), *Decision-making in health care* (pp. 183–210). New York: Cambridge University Press.

Colditz, G. A., Atwood, K. A., Emmons, K., Monson, R. R., Willett, W. C., Trichopoulos, D., & Hunter, D. J. (2000). Harvard Report on Cancer Prevention Volume 4: Harvard Cancer Risk Index. *Cancer Causes and Control, 11,* 477–488.

Croyle, R. T., Sun, Y., & Louie, D. H. (1993). Psychological minimization of cholesterol test results: Moderators of appraisal in college students and community residents. *Health Psychology, 12,* 503–507.

Davidson, K., & Prkachin, K. (1997). Optimism and unrealistic optimism have an interacting impact on health-promoting behavior and knowledge changes. *Personality and Social Psychology Bulletin, 23,* 617–625.

Dewberry, C., Ing, M., James, S., Nixon, M., & Richardson, S. (1990). Anxiety and unrealistic optimism. *Journal of Social Psychology, 130,* 151–156.

Dillard, A. J., McCaul, K. D., & Klein, W. M. P. (2006). Unrealistic optimism in smokers: Implications for smoking myth endorsement and self-protective motivation. *Journal of Health Communication, 11,* 93–102.

Ditto, P. H., Munro, G. D., Apanovitch, A. M., Scepansky, J. A., & Lockhart, L. K. (2003). Spontaneous skepticism: The interplay of motivation and expectation in responses to favorable and unfavorable medical diagnoses. *Personality and Social Psychology Bulletin, 29,* 1120–1132.

Dunning, D., & Story, A. L. (1991). Depression, realism, and the overconfidence effect: Are the sadder wiser when predicting future actions and events? *Journal of Personality and Social Psychology, 61,* 521–532.

Gerrard, M., Gibbons, F. X., Benthin, A. C., & Hessling, R. M. (1996). A longitudinal study of the reciprocal nature of risk behaviors and cognitions in adolescents: What you do shapes what you think, and vice versa. *Health Psychology, 15,* 344–354.

Gerrard, M., & Luus, C. A. E. (1995). Judgments of vulnerability to pregnancy: The role of risk factors and individual differences. *Personality and Social Psychology Bulletin, 21,* 160–171.

Goethals, G. R., Messick, D. M., & Allison, S. T. (1991). The uniqueness bias: Studies of constructive social comparison. In J. M. Suls & T. A. Wills (Eds.), *Social comparison: Contemporary theory and research* (pp. 149–173). Hillsdale, NJ: Erlbaum.

Guppy, A. (1993). Subjective probability of accident and apprehension in relation to self-other bias, age, and reported behavior. *Accident Analysis and Prevention, 25,* 375–382.

Harris, P. (1996). Sufficient grounds for optimism? The relationship between perceived controllability and optimistic bias. *Journal of Social and Clinical Psychology, 15,* 9–52.

Helgeson, V. S. (1999). Applicability of cognitive adaptation theory to predicting adjustment to heart disease after coronary angioplasty. *Health Psychology, 18,* 561–569.

Helgeson, V. S. (2003). Cognitive adaptation, psychological adjustment, and disease progression among angioplasty patients: 4 years later. *Health Psychology, 22,* 30–38.

Helweg-Larsen, M., & Shepperd, J. A. (2001). Do moderators of the optimistic bias affect personal or target risk estimates? A review of the literature. *Personality and Social Psychology Review, 51,* 74–95.

Jemmott, J. B., Ditto, P. H., & Croyle, R. T. (1986). Judging health status: Effects of perceived prevalence and personal relevance. *Journal of Personality and Social Psychology, 50,* 899–905.

Klein, W. M. (1996). Maintaining self-serving social comparisons: Attenuating the perceived significance of risk-increasing behaviors. *Journal of Social and Clinical Psychology, 15,* 120–142.

Klein, W. M., & Kunda, Z. (1993). Maintaining self-serving social comparisons: Biased reconstruction of one's past behaviors. *Personality and Social Psychology Bulletin, 19,* 732–739.

Klein, W. M., & Kunda, Z. (1994). Exaggerated self-assessments and the preference for controllable risks. *Organizational Behavior and Human Decision Processes, 59,* 410–427.

Klein, W. M. P. (2002). Comparative risk estimates relative to the average peer predict behavioral intentions and concern about absolute risk. *Risk, Decision, and Policy, 7*, 193–202.

Klein, W. M. P., Blier, H. K., & Janze, A. M. (2001). Maintaining positive self-evaluations: Reducing attention to diagnostic but unfavorable social comparison information when general self-regard is salient. *Motivation and Emotion, 25*, 23–40.

Klein, W. M. P., Geaghan, T. R., & MacDonald, T. K. (in press). Unplanned sexual activity as a consequence of alcohol use: A prospective study of risk perceptions and alcohol use among college freshmen. *Journal of American College Health.*

Kreuter, M. W., & Strecher, V. J. (1995). Changing inaccurate perceptions of health risk: Results from a randomized trial. *Health Psychology, 14*, 56–63.

Kreuter, M. W., & Strecher, V. J. (1996). Do tailored behavior change messages enhance the effectiveness of health risk appraisal? Results from a randomized trial. *Health Education Research, 11*, 95–105.

Kunda, Z. (1987). Motivated inference: Self-serving generation and evaluation of causal theories. *Journal of Personality and Social Psychology, 53*, 636–647.

Kwan, V. S. Y., John, O. P., Kenny, D. A., Bond, M. H., & Robins, R. W. (2004). Reconceptualizing individual differences in self-enhancement bias: An interpersonal approach. *Psychological Review, 111*, 94–110.

Liberman, A., & Chaiken, S. (1992). Defensive processing of personally relevant health messages. *Personality and Social Psychology Bulletin, 18*, 669–679.

Messick, D. M., Bloom, S., Boldizar, J. P., & Samuelson, C. D. (1985). Why we are fairer than others. *Journal of Experimental Social Psychology, 21*, 480–500.

Murray, S. L., Holmes, J. G., & Griffin, D. W. (1996). The benefits of positive illusions: Idealization and the construction of satisfaction in close relationships. *Journal of Personality and Social Psychology, 70*, 79–98.

National Center for Health Statistics. (1997). *Health, United States, 1995–1996.* Hyattsville, MD: Public Health Service.

Pearlin, L. I., & Schooler, C. (1978). The structure of coping. *Journal of Health and Social Behavior, 19*, 2–21.

Quadrel, M. J., Fischhoff, B., & Davis, W. (1993). Adolescent (in)vulnerability. *American Psychologist, 48*, 102–117.

Radcliffe, N. M., & Klein, W. M. P. (2002). Dispositional, unrealistic, and comparative optimism: Differential relations with the knowledge and processing of risk information and beliefs about personal risk. *Personality and Social Psychology Bulletin, 28*, 836–846.

Reed, G. M., Kemeny, M. E., Taylor, S. E., Wang, H. Y. J., & Visscher, B. R. (1994). Realistic acceptance as a predictor of decreased survival time in gay men with AIDS. *Health Psychology, 13*, 299–307.

Rosenberg, M. (1965). *Society and the adolescent self-image.* Princeton, NJ: Princeton University Press.

Sayette, M. A., & Hufford, M. R. (1997). Effects of smoking urge on generation of smoking-related information. *Journal of Applied Social Psychology, 27*, 1395–1405.

Scheier, M. F., & Carver, C. S. (1985). Optimism, coping, and health: Assessment and implications of generalized outcome expectancies. *Health Psychology, 4*, 219–247.

Segerstrom, S. C., McCarthy, W. J., Caskey, N. H., Gross, T. M., & Jarvik, M. E. (1993). Optimistic bias among cigarette smokers. *Journal of Applied Social Psychology, 23*, 1606–1618.

Stalmeier, P. F. M., Bezembinder, T. G. G., & Unic, I. J. (1996). Proportional heuristics in time tradeoff and conjoint measurement. *Medical Decision Making, 16*, 36–44.

Strecher, V. J., Kreuter, M. W., & Kobrin, S. C. (1995). Do cigarette smokers have unrealistic perceptions of their heart attack, cancer, and stroke risks? *Journal of Behavioral Medicine, 18*, 45–54.

Suls, J., Wan, C. K., & Sanders, G. S. (1988). False consensus and false uniqueness in estimating the prevalence of health-protective behaviors. *Journal of Applied Social Psychology, 18*, 66–79.

Taylor, S. E. (1983). Adjustment to threatening events: A theory of cognitive adaptation. *American Psychologist, 38*, 1161–1173.

Taylor, S. E., & Brown, J. D. (1988). Illusion and well-being: A social psychological perspective on mental health. *Psychological Bulletin, 103*, 193–210.

Taylor, S. E., & Gollwitzer, P. M. (1995). The effects of mindset on positive illusions. *Journal of Personality and Social Psychology, 69*, 213–226.

Taylor, S. E., Kemeny, M. E., Aspinwall, L. G., Schneider, S. G., Rodriguez, R., & Herbert, M. (1992). Optimism, coping, psychological distress, and high-risk sexual behavior among men at risk for acquired immunodeficiency syndrome (AIDS). *Journal of Personality and Social Psychology, 63*, 460–473.

Taylor, S. E., Lerner, J. S., Sherman, D. K., Sage, R. M., & McDowell, N. K. (2003). Portrait of the self-enhancer: Well-adjusted and well-liked, or maladjusted and friendless? *Journal of Personality and Social Psychology, 84*, 165–176.

van der Velde, F. W., van der Pligt, J., & Hooykaas, C. (1994). Perceiving AIDS-related risk: Accuracy as a function of differences in actual risk. *Health Psychology, 13*, 25–33.

Wallston, K. A. (1994). Cautious optimism vs. cockeyed optimism. *Psychology & Health, 9*, 201–203.

Weinstein, N. D. (1984). Why it won't happen to me: Perceptions of risk factors and illness susceptibility. *Health Psychology, 3*, 431–457.

Weinstein, N. D. (1987). Unrealistic optimism about susceptibility to health problems: Conclusions from a community-wide sample. *Journal of Behavioral Medicine, 10*, 481–500.

Weinstein, N. D. (1998). Accuracy of smokers' risk perceptions. *Annals of Behavioral Medicine, 20*, 135–140.

Weinstein, N. D., & Klein, W. M. (1995). Resistance of personal risk perceptions to debiasing interventions. *Health Psychology, 14,* 132–140.

Weinstein, N. D., Rothman, A. J., & Nicolich, M. (1998). Use of correlational data to examine the effects of risk perception on precautionary behaviors. *Psychology and Health, 13,* 479–501.

Weinstein, N. D., Sandman, P. M., & Roberts, N. E. (1991). Perceived susceptibility and self-protective behavior: A field experiment to encourage home radon testing. *Health Psychology, 10,* 25–33.

Wiebe, D. J., & Black, D. (1997). Illusional beliefs in the context of risky sexual behaviors. *Journal of Applied Social Psychology, 27,* 1727–1749.

Winkleby, M. A., Jatulis, D. E., Frank, E., & Fortman, S. P. (1992). Socioeconomic status and health: How education, income, and occupation contribute to risk factors for cardiovascular disease. *American Journal of Public Health, 82,* 816–820.

III

SELF-CRITICISM AND
SELF-ENHANCEMENT
AS BOTH GOOD AND BAD

10

A FUNCTIONAL APPROACH TO EXPLAINING FLUCTUATIONS IN FUTURE OUTLOOKS: FROM SELF-ENHANCEMENT TO SELF-CRITICISM

JAMES A. SHEPPERD, PATRICK J. CARROLL, AND KATE SWEENY

The end of a marriage ranks among the most painful of psychological experiences, and many people in dissolving marriages have no doubt proclaimed that they will never wed again. Although half of all marriages end in divorce, countless couples exchange marital vows each week secure in the belief that they will defy the odds and their own marriage will last. Are people always so positive about the future? Do people sometimes shelve their positive future outlook in favor of a more negative outlook?

In this chapter, we explore how people think about the future and note that people sometimes fluctuate from moment to moment in their future outlooks. We then address the intriguing question of why people hold positive future outlooks one moment yet hold negative future outlooks another moment. We propose that a fundamental need—the need for preparedness—captures much of the fluctuation in predictions across time (Carroll, Sweeny, & Shepperd, 2006). We suggest that realistic and negative outlooks serve preparedness by advancing self-criticism goals around accurate detection of and protection against imminent environmental threat. As threat passes, however, positive outlooks serve preparedness by advancing self-enhancement goals that mobilize the pursuit and acquisition of environmental opportunity. We also argue that although the natural orientation for most people is toward optimism, people shift their predictions downward for two broad reasons, both of which serve the need of preparedness. We also note that occasionally people move toward a more positive future outlook and discuss reasons for this shift. We conclude with a discussion of the costs and benefits of positive versus negative future outlooks.

FLUCTUATIONS IN FUTURE OUTLOOKS

Considerable evidence suggests that people are optimistic in their future outlooks, believing that their future will be bright, or at least brighter than the future of others. For example, people believe they are more likely than are others to have gifted children, to land their dream job, and to own their own house. In the realm of undesired events, people believe they are less likely than others to experience a variety of ailments, to be the victim of crime, or to have accidents (e.g., Weinstein, 1980). This optimism appears consistent across time and resistant to intervention (Shepperd, Helweg-Larsen, & Ortega, 2003; Weinstein & Klein, 1995).

People do not display optimism only in their predictions of how their outcomes will compare with the outcomes of other people. They also are optimistic in what their future holds for them and what they can accomplish compared with the actual outcomes obtained. For example, lawyers overestimate the likelihood that they will win an upcoming case (Loftus & Wagenaar, 1988). Beginning entrepreneurs overestimate the likelihood that their new businesses will be successful (Cooper, Woo, & Dunkelberg, 1988), stock traders overestimate their ability to successfully pick winning stocks (Odean, 1998), students overestimate how long they can endure pain (Kruger, 1999), and people overestimate the likelihood that they will engage in moral behavior (Epley & Dunning, 2000). Finally, the optimism extends to estimates of the time it will take them to complete tasks, a phenomenon called the *planning fallacy*. For example, people underestimate how long it will take them to write a report (Koole & Spijker, 2000), finish their tax returns (Buehler, Griffin, & MacDonald, 1997), and complete various mundane tasks (Newby-Clark, Ross, Buehler, Koehler, & Griffin, 2000).

Although an optimistic outlook appears commonplace in Western cultures, people are not always optimistic and in some situations favor a more conservative or even negative outlook over a positive one. Several studies in the past decade suggested that people surrender their optimism when they anticipate a challenge to their positive outlook. For example, students in one study estimated their score on a classroom exam on four occasions: once 3 weeks prior to the exam (Time 1), again just after completing the exam (Time 2), again 3 days later and 50 minutes before they were to receive their exam score (Time 3), and one final time just seconds before they received their exam score (Time 4). Although participants were optimistic in their predictions at Time 1, estimating a score higher than they actually received, they became more realistic in their predictions at Time 2 and Time 3, estimating a score that corresponded closely to their actual exam score. At Time 4, however, just moments before receiving their exam score, participants became decidedly pessimistic in their predictions, estimating a score lower than they actually received (Shepperd, Ouellette, & Fernandez, 1996).

Other research finds that as the moment of truth draws near, people shelve their optimism regarding how socially attractive they are rated by peers (Terry & Shepperd, 2004), how they will perform on laboratory tasks (Gilovich, Kerr, & Medvec, 1993), how they will do on a driving test (McKenna & Myers, 1997), and the outcome of a medical test (K. M. Taylor & Shepperd, 1998). For example, participants in one study believed they would or would not soon receive feedback regarding a test for a medical condition. Participants became pessimistic in their predictions (relative to baseline for the medical condition) when they anticipated imminent feedback, particularly when the medical condition was described as severe (K. M. Taylor & Shepperd, 1998).

PREPAREDNESS AND OUTCOME PREDICTIONS

Why do people sometimes hold positive future outlooks one moment yet hold negative future outlooks another moment? We propose that intuitive predictions, as well as shifts between predictions, often occur in response to a larger psychological need: the need to be prepared (Carroll et al., 2006). Preparedness is a goal state of readiness to respond to uncertain outcomes. Sometimes it involves being equipped for setbacks should they occur. Other times it involves a readiness to capitalize on opportunity should it knock. Although the future can never be known with certainty, intuitive prediction allows people to anticipate, plan, and prepare for events before they happen.

Being prepared demands that people be ready for different things at different times. Sometimes preparedness entails embracing an optimistic outlook to organize mental and behavioral activity around the detection and pursuit of opportunity. However, at other times being prepared entails adjusting one's outlook in response to new information and calibrating predictions toward greater accuracy. At still other times, preparedness requires steeling oneself for undesired outcomes.

It is noteworthy that people likely do not prepare at all times or for all conceivable outcomes. Rather, people prepare only when they must and only for outcomes that they perceive as at least somewhat possible. Of course, people will prepare for rare outcomes provided they perceive them as important. For example, a mother will inoculate her child against a rare but deadly disease. However, preparedness requires resources, and a sustained state of preparedness can drain resources unnecessarily and divert resources from other pursuits (Carroll et al., 2006). For example, being continuously on guard against threat is exhausting (Selye, 1976) and can interfere with enjoying life. Moreover, a chronically pessimistic outlook precipitates declines in health and well-being (Peterson & Seligman, 1984; S. E. Taylor, Kemeny, Reed, Bower, & Gruenewald, 2000). People who put all of their money away for the future cannot take pleasure in life in the present. Likewise, preparing for every conceivable outcome is a futile exercise and a poor use of resources. Although it is prudent to save for a rainy day, it is not prudent to prepare for hurricanes when one lives in a region where hurricanes are nonexistent.

Preparedness strivings are activated by changes in the surrounding circumstances that reveal possible threats and possible opportunities. Possible threats are the more powerful of the two types; they imperil one's physical or material resources or one's belief system. Thus, a person taking a car in for repair prepares for the possibility that the repairs will be expensive. Likewise, a student anticipating the return of an exam prepares for a possible threat to his or her self-view. The second of these types of circumstances—possible opportunities—represents chances for growth and increasing one's resources. For example, a reduction in the capital gains tax may prompt people to sell stocks to capitalize on the greater financial return.

Because the future is unknown, people can never fully prepare for what lies ahead. Rather, they can only make a best guess, and this guess may over- or undershoot the mark. Moreover, people sometimes face competing outcomes and have difficulty preparing for both. It is hard for the aspiring professor to prepare for the possibilities of getting tenured and not getting tenured. It is hard for the prisoner to prepare for the possibilities of having parole granted and having it denied. Often preparedness means taking a middle or compromise position, preparing fully for neither outcome, but being somewhat prepared for both.

Giving Priority to Preparing for Setbacks

Although preparedness can entail readiness to respond to possible opportunity, people almost certainly expend most of their preparedness energies preparing for possible setback, perhaps because people are loss averse, finding a loss more aversive than they find a gain of equal value pleasurable (Kahneman & Tversky, 1984). For example, participants in one study read scenarios describing unexpected gains and losses of the same magnitude. Participants reported greater distress over unexpected losses and greater joy over unexpected gains. However, the intensity of distress they reported in response to unexpected losses far exceeded the intensity of joy they reported in response to unexpected gains (Kahneman & Tversky, 1984).

According to cardinal utility theory, the loss aversion stems from the implications losses can have for comfort. Financial resources are extremely important until basic needs are met. Once these needs are met, the need for additional resources drops significantly. A loss of resources, however, could translate into a decrease in comfort and a failure to meet basic needs. The prospect of a loss of resources, compared with the prospect of a gain, is more consequential and thus more likely to prompt preparatory actions (Bernoulli, 1738/1954).

In sum, unexpected bad news carries greater force than does unexpected good news of equal magnitude. Preparing more for setback likely serves an important survival function when one considers the relative consequences of being unprepared for positive outcomes versus being unprepared for negative outcomes (Baumeister, Heatherton, & Tice, 1993). Being unprepared for opportunity means that one's quality of life does not improve when it could have or, at worst, a hardship one is undergoing may be prolonged. However, being unprepared for bad news can be disastrous, as when, for example, businesses in coastal cities fail to board their windows during hurricane weather (or, more generally, when people fail to insure their homes). It can even have consequences for survival, as when hikers fail to bring adequate food and water on long hikes (S. E. Taylor, 1991). If imminent threat is not resolved, being prepared for opportunity may not matter because the organism may not survive to enjoy it. Thus, it seems not only reasonable but also highly adaptive that people orient more toward setbacks and expend more energy preparing for potential losses than they do preparing for potential gains.

The Status Quo of Optimism

In light of the fact that preparedness energies require that people prepare for possible setback before they prepare for opportunity, why are people generally optimistic about the future? Indeed, the ambient state for most people appears to be optimism. We can think of several reasons. First, some evidence suggests that positive and negative events in life are not evenly distributed. Rather, neutral and positive events occur more frequently than do negative events. Or, perhaps more accurately, people evaluate more events in their life as positive than as negative (Kanouse & Hanson, 1972). Thus, people may generally hold a positive future outlook because they experience more positive than negative outcomes or, at the very least, interpret their experiences as more positive than negative. Second, people may simply orient toward what feels good, and a positive future outlook feels good. It feels good to think that the future will turn out well, that one's endeavors will meet with success, and that one's lot in life will improve. Consistent with this perspective, evidence suggests that optimists are happier than their peers

(Alloy & Ahrens, 1987). By contrast, it feels bad and fosters anxiety to think that things will turn out poorly, that one's efforts are in vain, and that one's lot in life will worsen. It is not surprising that people who are less optimistic are more likely to experience depression (Aspinwall & Taylor, 1992).

Third, future outlooks are grounded in plans and intentions, and those plans and intentions are almost always plans for success (Buehler, Griffin, & Ross, 1994). Thus, people typically orient toward what they are striving to achieve—a larger salary, a fun-filled vacation, an early retirement—rather than what they are striving to avoid because it is easier to construct one plausible route to success than to construct the multiple plausible ways one could fail. Fourth, at least in Western cultures, a positive or optimistic outlook is socially encouraged, whereas a negative or pessimistic outlook is discouraged. People are more accepting of others who have an optimistic outlook than they are of those who have a pessimistic outlook (Carver, Kus, & Scheier, 1994; Helweg-Larsen, Sadeghian, & Webb, 2002). Liking from others can be a powerful reward, and people may develop a positive future outlook because they are reinforced for doing so and punished for doing otherwise.

Finally, a variety of cognitive processes (e.g., biased retrieval, inconsistent scrutiny) seem to work toward dampening, muting, and even erasing the existence of negative events, but not positive events, that have transpired (S. E. Taylor, 1991). A consequence of these cognitive processes is that people may have better memory for positive outcomes than for negative outcomes and thus develop a positive future outlook. Consistent with this notion are the results of a review of 52 studies that found that people consistently displayed better (and faster) recall for positive events than for negative events (Matlin & Strang, 1978). In addition, people recall more positive than negative events when remembering events in their life (Linton, 1986).

DOWNWARD SHIFTS IN FUTURE OUTLOOKS

The tendency for optimism aside, we propose two broad categories of reasons why people might shift their predictions downward from optimism, both of which serve the larger need of preparedness. The first category comprises reasons that reflect a response to information. The second category comprises reasons that reflect an attempt to brace for possible bad news.

Responding to Information

Sometimes people shift their predictions downward in response to new information that bears on their predictions or because they have greater clarity about existing information. In such cases, people modify their judgments in light of this information. The information may come from (a) the acquisition of new data bearing directly on the judgments; (b) current mood, which can be a potent source of information; and (c) more careful consideration of existing information.

Acquiring New Data

When events are in the distant future, people often have only vague information on which to base their judgments, and the vagueness of the information permits flexibility in predictions. Over time people often acquire new information that can prompt changes in predictions. Although new information can lead to an upward revision in predictions, it often leads to a downward revision. Indeed, because the ambient state of most people is optimism, people have more room to move downward. For example, sophomores, juniors, and seniors in one study estimated their postgraduation starting salaries. Participants supplied estimates at two points in time: 4 months prior to the seniors' graduation date and 2 weeks prior to the seniors' graduation date. All three groups made optimistic predictions 4 months before the seniors graduated, but only the sophomores and juniors remained optimistic 2 weeks prior to the seniors' graduation date (Shepperd, Morato, & Pbert, 1996). As graduation approached, the seniors presumably gained a wealth of information about the job market both from their own job search experiences and from the experiences of their friends. This new information likely prompted the seniors to revise their predictions downward.

The passage of time can also bring information indicating declining control over those outcomes. In the weeks prior to a sports competition, athletes may predict a sure victory on the basis of their intentions to practice long hours and to scrutinize the strengths and weaknesses of the opposing team. However, on the day of the competition those opportunities have passed, and the athletes must base their predictions on their current readiness rather than on their plans.

Mood as Information

It is noteworthy that people may abandon optimism even when no new information is available. For example, participants in the exam score estimate study described earlier lowered their predictions from Time 3 (50 minutes before receiving their scores) to Time 4 (immediately before receiving their scores) even though they learned nothing about the exam or their performance during the intervening period (Shepperd, Ouellette, et al., 1996). Yet, these participants may have gained other pertinent information across time. Some investigators have proposed that people may rely on their current moods as a source of information about themselves and their outcomes (Schwartz & Clore, 1988). In the exam score example, participants may have noted their increasing feelings of anxiety as feedback drew near and inferred that, if they were feeling so anxious, it must be because they did poorly. Thus, people factor in their anxious feelings as information, even in the absence of more direct data, when judging what a forth-coming outcome is likely to be.

Greater Scrutiny of Existing Data

Even when new information is not available, people may revise their estimates in response to greater scrutiny of existing data. Such revisions can occur in response to accountability pressures (Tetlock, 1992) and because people construe events differently when they are distant than when they are near (Liberman & Trope, 1998).

Accountability pressures, or pressures to defend one's judgments, be-liefs, or actions, may stem from external or internal sources. People may feel pressured to justify or explain their judgments, beliefs, or actions to others, but they may also attempt to justify and explain them to themselves (Tetlock, 1992). Under conditions of intense accountability, people tend to process information with more diligence and complexity. Accountability pressures often reduce perception and decision biases by prompting consideration of relevant issues, contemplation of alternative outcomes, and engagement in self-critical thinking (Tetlock, 1992). As the moment of truth draws near, people are more likely to experience accountability pressures as they antici-pate challenges to their future outlook. Such anticipation leads to less opti-mistic predictions.

According to temporal construal theory (Liberman & Trope, 1998), people mentally construe distant future events in generalized and abstract terms and focus more on what they want to happen (desirability). They con-strue near-future events in specific and concrete terms and focus more on what is likely to happen (feasibility). The difference in focus can lead to greater optimism about events in the distant future than about events in the near future. As events draw near, people shift from focusing on desirability to focusing on feasibility, which leads to a shift away from optimism.

Bracing for Undesired Outcomes

People may shift their predictions for reasons that have little to do with the introduction of new or different information. Often shifts from optimism reflect a response to the possibility of an undesired outcome. That is, people may shift from optimism in an effort to brace themselves for the possibility that things may not turn out as desired (Shepperd, Ouellette, et al., 1996). Bracing has two possible goals (Carroll et al., 2006). The first is to manage the emotional impact of a negative outcome in an attempt to avoid counterfactual emotions such as disappointment. The second is to reduce the likelihood of the negative outcome or to minimize the consequences. Bracing can assume three forms. It can reflect (a) an attempt to avoid disap-pointment (Shepperd, Ouellette, et al., 1996), (b) a form of magical think-ing intended to influence the outcome (Rozin & Nemeroff, 1990), or (c) a mobilization of resources directed at avoiding the undesired outcome or minimizing its consequences (Norem & Cantor, 1986).

Avoiding Disappointment

People's feelings about their outcomes are influenced by both the outcomes themselves and their expectations about the outcomes. As numerous theorists have noted, outcomes that exceed expectations lead to satisfaction, whereas outcomes that fall short of expectations lead to dissatisfaction (e.g., James, 1890; Mellers & McGraw, 2001).

When outcomes are far in the future and one's outlook cannot be easily challenged, people often embrace optimism. However, as events or outcomes draw near, people face the possibility that things may not turn out as hoped for and that their optimism may be disconfirmed. Bad news is unpleasant, particularly when it is unexpected (Shepperd & McNulty, 2002). Having one's expectations disconfirmed leads to disappointment, a particularly powerful and unpleasant counterfactual emotion (van Dijk, Zeelenberg, & van der Pligt, 1999). It is so unpleasant, in fact, that people often lower their expectations as the moment of truth draws near to reduce or avoid disappointment (Shepperd, Ouellette, et al., 1996; K. M. Taylor & Shepperd, 1998).

People may brace to avoid other counterfactual emotions such as regret when their actions or inactions might produce an undesirable outcome. However, we suspect that anticipated disappointment more often drives changes in predictions. Regret results from actions and inactions, whereas disappointment results from outcomes falling short of expectations (van Dijk et al., 1999). Yet people brace even when the outcome has nothing to do with any action or inaction on their part. For example, participants in the medical study described earlier reduced their optimism when expecting feedback even though the medical condition was completely out of their control and provided participants with no actions or inactions to regret (K. M. Taylor & Shepperd, 1998). Thus, although both anticipated regret and anticipated disappointment can produce bracing, we suspect that disappointment is the predominant cause.

Magical Thinking

People sometimes believe that simply voicing an optimistic outlook will influence their outcomes, somehow jinxing them by decreasing the likelihood that their optimistic predictions will be fulfilled. To avoid jinxing themselves, people may make grim predictions in the belief that such predictions will in fact have the opposite effect. Such beliefs reflect a type of magical thinking, or belief in forces outside the realm of normal physical laws (Rozin & Nemeroff, 1990).

People need not actually believe the negative predictions they express publicly. Instead, they may believe that merely by giving voice to negative predictions they diminish the possibility that the negative outcome will transpire. In addition, the conditions (e.g., a decline in primary control over the outcome) that trigger this form of bracing likely increase as the moment of truth draws near. Thus, people are probably most inclined to display this form of superstitious control when all other opportunities to control the outcome have passed.

Consistent with the jinxing idea is research on "tempting fate," by which people believe that outcomes that are out of their control are somehow predicted by, or even influenced by, their actions. For example, participants in one study imagined that they received a Stanford sweatshirt from their mother while they waited to hear their graduate admission decision from Stanford. Participants reported that they believed they were less likely to be accepted into Stanford if they wore the sweatshirt than if they did not wear the sweatshirt (Gilovich, 2005).

Mobilizing Resources

As noted earlier, bracing occasionally represents a mobilization of resources directed at avoiding undesired outcomes or minimizing their consequences. This form of bracing has two types. The first appears as the cognitive strategy of defensive pessimism (Norem & Cantor, 1986). Defensive pessimism entails highly capable people making dire predictions about the future. The predictions create anxiety that then sparks actions geared toward ensuring that the negative predictions are not fulfilled. Defensive pessimists, in effect, harness the anxiety that arises from their gloomy predictions to take preventive measures.

UPWARD SHIFTS IN FUTURE OUTLOOKS

Thus far, we have explored why people shift their predictions downward toward negative future outlooks. As imminent danger passes and as opportunity presents itself, adaptive priorities shift to outlooks that promote the acquisition of resources and growth. People must be able to flexibly exchange a negative outlook that served them well in the face of threat for a positive outlook that reorganizes activity toward pursuit of opportunity once threat passes.

The literature reveals several instances of this upward shift. For example, research on deliberative and implemental mindsets suggests that as people move from a predecision, deliberative mindset to a postdecision, implemental mindset, their future outlook becomes more positive (Gollwitzer & Kinney, 1989). Other research finds that bettors at horse races become more confident that their horse would win after placing their bet than before placing their bet (Knox & Inkster, 1968), a finding that also may reflect a change in mindsets. Finally, people appear to display increases in optimism when they anticipate and imagine future successes (Gregory, Cialdini, & Carpenter, 1982).

People may occasionally shift their predictions upward for reasons that have little to do with preparing for what lies ahead. However, we suspect that the lion's share of the variance in upward shifts stems from the underlying need for preparedness. As with downward shifts from optimism, the upward shift can reflect a response to new information, proactive coping, or an attempt to capitalize on (or, in some instances, create) opportunity.

Responding to New Information

Similar to the information impetus for downward shifts in predictions, people sometimes shift their predictions upward in response to new information that bears on their judgments. The information-based reasons for upward shifts closely parallel the information-based reasons for downward shifts (Carroll et al., 2006). For instance, sometimes people gain new data bearing directly on their judgments and the new data may suggest that more optimistic predictions are in order. A job applicant will undoubtedly become more optimistic about his or her chances of receiving an offer upon learning that no one else applied for the job.

As with the information-based reasons for downward shifts, current mood can be a source of information for upward shifts (Schwartz & Clore, 1988). People rely on their current mood to gauge what's ahead, and they may shift toward greater optimism because their mood suggests to them that good news lies ahead.

Finally, people may shift toward optimism because changing circumstances facilitate access to thoughts about successful goal attainment. The move from a deliberative to an implemental mindset represents one such change in circumstances (Gollwitzer & Kinney, 1989). When people are in a predecision, deliberative mindset, they carefully evaluate strategies for achieving desired goals and tend to be realistic in their orientation as they weigh different plans for action. Once they have selected a plan for action, people move to an implemental mindset in which they are ready to put the selected plan for action into motion. The implemental mindset is characterized by pervasive optimism.

The contrasting outlooks of people in deliberative versus implemental mindsets is illustrated in one study that experimentally induced the two mindsets. In the deliberative mindset condition, participants evaluated the pros and cons of participating in a scavenger hunt in which they had 30 minutes to find a variety of objects. In the implemental mindset condition, participants imagined that they soon would participate in a scavenger hunt and thought about what participation would be like. Participants were more optimistic in their predictions of how they would perform in the scavenger hunt when in the implemental mindset than when in the deliberative mindset

(Armor & Taylor, 2003). The focus on action rather than on planning presumably facilitated thoughts about reaching the goals successfully. It is also noteworthy that these optimistic thoughts may in turn be useful in goal pursuit by directing attention away from extraneous cues toward cues bearing on goal achievement.

Proactive Coping

In some instances the upward shift in predictions reflects proactive coping designed to diminish or avoid an undesired outcome. Similar to defensive pessimism, proactive coping involves acknowledging the possibility of an undesired outcome as an imminent threat and using that acknowledgment to inspire action. In contrast to defensive pessimism, however, proactive coping involves generating positive expectations and perceiving a possible negative outcome as a challenge to be overcome (Aspinwall & Taylor, 1997). This strategy produces positive emotions that promote actions to avoid the outcome or, at the very least, actions to minimize the consequences. In short, proactive copers recognize the threat ahead of them, but respond to the threat with a positive expectancy and with behavior designed to ensure that the positive expectancy is fulfilled.

Capitalizing on (and Creating) Possible Opportunity

Shifts to positive future outlooks may be prompted by more than just new information. Shifts may emerge as people anticipate the future and think about possible opportunities (Gregory et al., 1982). Preparing for an opportunity, from the most significant to the mundane, necessitates the construction of a positive image of oneself achieving that opportunity (a positive possible self). For example, an aspiring undergraduate may imagine herself as a physician who has successfully completed medical school. To the extent that a positive possible self is active in working memory, the representation of the possible self will organize, energize, and direct mental and behavioral activity around the pursuit and enjoyment of the possible opportunity (Ruvolo & Markus, 1992). With time, this positive possible self gains potency, creating feelings of competence, mastery, and optimism as the individual mentally bridges the gap between the present and desired end-state. People come to think of reasons why they might succeed, and these reasons increase feelings of optimism (Campbell & Fairey, 1985). Imagining herself as a physician increases the student's confidence that this future self is possible.

Indeed, the mere anticipation of possible opportunity can prompt an increase in optimism as people construct and project a positive possible self on the future. Such constructions may be particularly likely to occur for transition events such as starting a new school, job, or relationship, moving to a new place, buying a house, or having a baby, in which new possibilities abound and the self is not well defined. These events open the door to growth opportunities, to possible financial and personal gains, and to the prospect that life might change for the better.

COSTS AND BENEFITS OF DIFFERENT FUTURE OUTLOOKS

A common lay perception is that a positive future outlook is beneficial and a negative future outlook is not. To be sure, many benefits are linked to a positive future outlook and many drawbacks are associated with a negative future outlook. However, misplaced optimism can also be problematic, and shifts toward negative outlooks can have adaptive functions.

The Benefits of Negative Future Outlooks

We can think of little benefit to sustained pessimism. However, temporary shifts to pessimism, particularly at the moment of truth, can be quite beneficial. First, considerable evidence suggests that how people feel about their outcomes is influenced by their expectations (Shepperd & McNulty, 2002). People feel satisfied when outcomes exceed expectations and disappointed when outcomes fall short of expectations. Adopting a pessimistic outlook reduces the likelihood of disappointment and thus increases satisfaction with outcomes. Moreover, the more unexpected the outcome, the greater the potential for producing disappointment (van Dijk & van der Pligt, 1997). The benefit of adopting a negative outlook, even if at the 11th hour, is that it diminishes disappointment because the bad news was expected.

A second benefit of shifting to a negative future outlook lies in its ability to inspire action in response. Although we noted this idea in our discussion of defensive pessimism, it can also occur in response to new information. When people expect a negative outcome, they often take action or arrange their circumstances to diminish or address the potential harm. Moreover, evidence suggests that embracing a negative future outlook allows people to recover more quickly when undesired outcomes occur than they could if they persisted in the belief that all will be well (Showers & Ruben, 1990). For example, people who expect financially rough times over the coming months are more likely to watch their spending and delay large purchases in preparation, and thus are better able to weather an economic downturn. In sum, a negative future outlook can prompt actions designed to mitigate the distress associated with an undesired outcome should it occur. As a short-term strategy, a negative outlook can be quite adaptive.

The Benefits of Positive Future Outlooks

Numerous studies document the benefits of optimism. An optimistic outlook is linked to positive affect (Alloy & Ahrens, 1987), greater social acceptance (Helweg-Larsen et al., 2002), greater persistence toward goals (Scheier & Carver, 1988), and better coping and adjustment (Aspinwall & Taylor, 1992; Segerstrom, Taylor, Kemeny, & Fahey, 1998). Research also links an optimistic outlook to a variety of physical health benefits such as bolstered cardiovascular and immune system functioning (Segerstrom et al., 1998) and recovery from coronary events such as a heart attack (Shepperd, Morato, et al., 1996).

Aside from these obvious benefits, theorizing on possible selves suggests another benefit of optimism. As we described earlier, preparing for opportunities necessitates the construction of a positive image of oneself achieving that opportunity (a positive possible self). As the positive possible self becomes activated in memory, it steers mental processing toward goal-relevant information while positive affect associated with the image invigorates and mobilizes action (Ruvolo & Markus, 1992). In time these positive self-images will become increasingly elaborated and the global desired self (e.g., becoming a physician) begins to spawn task-specific desired selves (e.g., taking the requisite classes, studying for the MCAT) that effectively bridge the gap between the present and desired selves and prepare the person to hit the ground running as opportunity arises. In short, an optimistic outlook initiates and sustains the very behavior that will make that optimistic outlook a reality.

Finally, an optimistic outlook may even facilitate the construction of new opportunity. The broaden-and-build theory suggests an intimate link between positive emotions and optimism (Fredrickson, 2001). Positive emotions can give rise to optimism, and optimism can give rise to positive emotions. More important, the positive emotions produced by optimism not only feel good in the moment but also inspire the acquisition of new resources and opportunities in the long run (Fredrickson, 2001). In contrast to negative emotions, which tend to constrict thinking and attention to the immediate situation, positive emotions expand thinking, prompting people to think, for example, about resources at their disposal, opportunities that lie ahead, and possible routes to success. Whereas a pessimistic outlook engendered by negative emotions prepares people to respond to imminent threat in the service of survival, a positive future outlook engendered by positive emotions carries indirect and long-range survival benefits by preparing people to consider and even build enduring personal resources (e.g., proactive coping resources).

In general, positive emotions produced by optimism prepare people to capitalize on possible opportunities by expanding attention and thinking to foresee emerging opportunities and resources. The personal resources accrued during positive emotional states even outlive the positive emotions that produced them (Frederickson, 2001). For example, the acquisition of personal resources may inspire feelings of pride and the imagination of even larger future opportunities ("Why settle with this future when I could have that future?").

In sum, an incidental effect of optimism may be an increase in personal resources that can transcend the emotional context that created them and could be used in subsequent moments and in different contexts (e.g., resilience in times of stress). These effects compound and accumulate across time, fueling an upward spiral toward improved health and well-being (Frederickson, 2001).

The Costs of Positive and Negative Future Outlooks

A positive future outlook, for all its benefits, can be costly to the extent that people are caught flat-footed and are unprepared for threats and setbacks. Moreover, in some instances a Pollyanna view of the future can prove especially disastrous if it causes people to fail to take reasonable precautions. Failure to purchase home insurance or catastrophic health insurance can lead to financial ruin should the family home be destroyed or a calamitous health emergency arise. People need not expect danger at every turn or attempt to prepare for every possible disaster, but a modicum of worry and pessimism can be well worth the stress if it triggers action that mitigates future harm.

However, a negative future outlook presents its own costs. For one, a prolonged negative outlook forfeits the numerous well-documented benefits of optimism. For example, research finds that positive expectancies are linked to a short-term increase in positive affect (Robins & Beer, 2001). By embracing a negative outlook, people deprive themselves of positive affect and a myriad of physical and behavioral benefits. A second cost is that the anxiety and negative affect that accompany a negative future outlook can be debilitating to the extent that people become obsessed with the belief that tragedy lies in wait around every corner and are unable to carry on their daily affairs. Believing that every phone call in the night might announce bad news or that any time one's partner wants to talk it is to declare the end of the relationship is enormously distressing and can divert attention from the innumerable tasks people must complete each day.

A third cost of a negative future outlook is social in nature. As previously stated, research has found that people who have a pessimistic outlook are liked less than are people who have an optimistic outlook (Carver et al., 1994; Helweg-Larsen et al., 2002). Thus, a negative future outlook carries the risk of social rejection. Finally, research documents a reciprocal relationship between depression and pessimism such that depression fosters pessimistic thinking, which cycles back to amplify depressed mood (Peterson & Seligman, 1984). This reciprocal relationship can foster a downward spiral that may eventuate in a prevailing bias in information processing toward the detection and identification threat that overrides the ambient state of optimism and the focus on possible opportunity.

In sum, both positive and negative future outlooks have unique costs and benefits. The trick to effective functioning lies in the ability to exchange one outlook for the other in response to situational demands. A computer analogy used to illustrate the shift between automatic and controlled self-presentations perhaps best captures the process of exchanging positive and negative future outlooks (Schlenker & Pontari, 2000). Much of self-presentation occurs automatically, below awareness, surfacing into conscious attention and becoming controlled only in response to detection of a threat to the desired identity. The analogy is that of a computer virus program that runs quietly in the background. The security-relevant activities of the virus program become activated on the computer screen upon detection of an intruding virus. In the same way, negative future expectations may override the dominant, and perhaps automatic, positive expectation only if the security system detects the emergence of potential threat. These expectations remain maximized until the threat has been resolved, at which point the dominant, positive expectation resumes.

CONCLUSION

Although people tend to embrace a positive future outlook, predictions of outcomes fluctuate across time and across contexts, and people occasionally shelve their positive future outlook for a negative one. We propose that such shifts serve the adaptive need to prepare for possible setbacks or possible opportunities. Although the need to be prepared can prompt upward and downward shifts in future outlooks, the downward shift in which people prepare for possible setback seems more dominant. Its dominance occurs in part because people are loss aversive, and in part because the ambient state of optimism means that people have more room to shift their predictions downward. The downward shift may reflect a response to new information, or it may reflect an effort to brace for the possibility that things may not turn out as hoped for. However, people do occasionally shift their predictions upward. The upward shift may also represent a response to new information, but may sometimes represent proactive coping or a desire to capitalize on or create potential opportunity. A negative future outlook is not uniformly bad nor is a positive future outlook uniformly good. Both have costs and benefits, and effective functioning entails an ability to exchange one outlook for the other in response to situational demands.

REFERENCES

Alloy, L. B., & Ahrens, A. H. (1987). Depression and pessimism for the future: Biased use of statistically relevant information in predictions for self versus others. *Journal of Personality and Social Psychology, 52,* 366–378.

Armor, D. A., & Taylor, S. E. (2003). The effects of mindset on behavior: Self-regulation in deliberative and implemental frames of mind. *Personality and Social Psychological Bulletin, 29*, 86–95.

Aspinwall, L. G., & Taylor, S. E. (1992). Modeling cognitive adaptation: A longitudinal investigation of the impact of individual differences and coping on college adjustment and performance. *Journal of Personality and Social Psychology, 63*, 989–1003.

Aspinwall, L. G., & Taylor, S. E. (1997). A stitch in time: Self-regulation and proactive coping. *Psychological Bulletin, 121*, 417–436.

Baumeister, R. F., Heatherton, T. F., & Tice, D. M. (1993). When ego threats lead to self regulation failure: Negative consequences of high self-esteem. *Journal of Personality and Social Psychology, 64*, 141–156.

Bernoulli, D. (1954). Exposition of a new theory on the measurement of risk (L. Sommer, Trans.). *Econometrica, 22*, 23–36. (Original work published 1738)

Buehler, R., Griffin, D., & MacDonald, H. (1997). The role of motivated reasoning in optimistic time predictions. *Personality and Social Psychological Bulletin, 23*, 238–247.

Buehler, R., Griffin, D., & Ross, M. (1994). Exploring the "planning fallacy": Why people underestimate their task completion times. *Journal of Personality and Social Psychology, 67*, 366–381.

Campbell, J. D., & Fairey, P. J. (1985). Effects of self-esteem, hypothetical explanations, and verbalization of expectancies on future performance. *Journal of Personality and Social Psychology, 48*, 1097–1111.

Carroll, P. J., Sweeny, K., & Shepperd, J. A. (2006). Forsaking optimism. *Review of General Psychology, 10*, 56–73.

Carver, C. S., Kus, L. A., & Scheier, M. F. (1994). Effects of good versus bad mood and optimistic versus pessimistic outlook on social acceptance versus rejection. *Journal of Social and Clinical Psychology, 13*, 138–151.

Cooper, A. C., Woo, C. Y., & Dunkelberg, W. C. (1988). Entrepreneurs' perceived chances for success. *Journal of Business Venturing, 3*, 97–108.

Epley, N., & Dunning, D. (2000). Feeling "holier than thou": Are self-serving assessments produced by errors in self- or social predictions? *Journal of Personality and Social Psychology, 79*, 861–875.

Fredrickson, B. L. (2001). The role of positive emotions in positive psychology: A broaden-and-build theory of positive emotions. *American Psychologist, 35*, 603–618.

Gilovich, T. (2005). *The perceived likelihood of events that "tempt fate."* Paper presented at the annual meeting of the Society of Personality and Social Psychology, New Orleans, LA.

Gilovich, T., Kerr, M., & Medvec, V. H. (1993). Effect of temporal perspective on subjective confidence. *Journal of Personality and Social Psychology, 64*, 552–560.

Gollwitzer, P. M., & Kinney, R. F. (1989). Effects of deliberative and implemental mind-sets on illusions of control. *Journal of Personality and Social Psychology, 56*, 531–542.

Gregory, W. L., Cialdini, R. B., & Carpenter, K. M. (1982). Self-relevant scenarios as mediators of likelihood estimates and compliance: Does imagining make it so? *Journal of Personality and Social Psychology, 43,* 89–99.

Helweg-Larsen, M., Sadeghian, P., & Webb, M. A. (2002). The stigma of being pessimistically biased. *Journal of Social and Clinical Psychology, 21,* 92–107.

James, W. (1890). *The principles of psychology* (Vol. 1). New York: Holt.

Kahneman, D., & Tversky, A. (1984). Choices, values, and frames. *American Psychologist, 39,* 341–350.

Kanouse, E. E., & Hanson, L. R., Jr. (1972). Negativity in evaluations. In E. E. Jones, D. E. Kanouse, H. H. Kelley, R. E. Nisbett, S. Valins, & B. Weiner (Eds.), *Attribution: Perceiving the causes of behavior* (pp. 47–62). Morristown, NJ: General Learning Press.

Knox, R. E., & Inkster, J. A. (1968). Postdecision dissonance at post time. *Journal of Personality and Social Psychology, 8,* 319–323.

Koole, S., & Spijker, M. (2000). Overcoming the planning fallacy through willpower: Effects of implementation intentions on actual and predicted task-completion times. *European Journal of Social Psychology, 30,* 873–888.

Kruger, J. (1999). Lake Wobegon be gone! The "below-average effect" and the egocentric nature of comparative ability judgments. *Journal of Personality and Social Psychology, 77,* 221–232.

Liberman, N., & Trope, Y. (1998). The role of feasibility and desirability considerations in near and distant future decisions: A test of temporal construal theory. *Journal of Personality and Social Psychology, 75,* 5–18.

Linton, M. (1986). Ways of search and the contents of memory. In D. C. Rubin (Ed.), *Autobiographical memory* (pp. 50–67). Cambridge, England: Cambridge University Press.

Loftus, E. F., & Wagenaar, W. A. (1988). Lawyers' predictions of success. *Jurimetrics Journal, 29,* 437–453.

Matlin, M. W., & Strang, D. J. (1978). *The Pollyanna principle: Selectivity in language, memory, and thought.* Cambridge, MA: Schenkman.

McKenna, F. P., & Myers, L. B. (1997). Illusory self-assessments: Can they be reduced? *British Journal of Psychology, 88,* 39–51.

Mellers, B. A., & McGraw, A. P. (2001). Anticipated emotions as guides to choice. *Current Directions in Psychological Science, 10,* 210–214.

Newby-Clark, I. R., Ross, M., Buehler, R., Koehler, D. J., & Griffin, D. (2000). People focus on optimistic scenarios and disregard pessimistic scenarios while predicting completion times. *Journal of Experimental Psychology: Applied, 6,* 171–182.

Norem, J. K., & Cantor, N. (1986). Defensive pessimism: Harnessing anxiety and motivation. *Journal of Personality and Social Psychology, 51,* 1208–1217.

Odean, T. (1998). Volume, volatility, price, and profit when all traders are above average. *Journal of Finance, 8,* 1887–1934.

Peterson, C. P., & Seligman, M. E. P. (1984). Causal explanations as a risk factor in depression: Theory and evidence. *Psychological Review, 91,* 347–374.

Robins, R. W., & Beer, J. S. (2001). Positive illusions about the self: Short-term benefits and long-term costs. *Journal of Personality and Social Psychology, 80,* 340–352.

Rozin, P., & Nemeroff, C. (1990). The laws of sympathetic magic: A psychological analysis of similarity and contagion. In J. W. Stigler, R. A. Shweder, & G. H. Herdt (Eds.), *Cultural psychology: Essays on comparative human development* (pp. 205–232). New York: Cambridge University Press.

Ruvolo, A. P., & Markus, H. R. (1992). Possible selves and performance: The power of self-relevant imagery. *Social Cognition, 10,* 95–124.

Scheier, M. F., & Carver, C. S. (1988). A model of behavioral self-regulation: Translating intention into action. In L. Berkowitz (Ed.), *Advances in experimental social psychology* (Vol. 21, pp. 303–346). New York: Academic Press.

Schlenker, B. R., & Pontari, B. A. (2000). The strategic control of information: Impression management and self-presentation in daily life. In A. Tesser, R. Felson, & J. Suls (Eds.), *Perspectives on self and identity* (pp. 199–232). Washington, DC: American Psychological Association.

Schwartz, N., & Clore, G. L. (1988). How do I feel about it? Informative functions of affective states. In K. Fiedler & J. Forgas (Eds.), *Affect, cognition, and social behavior* (pp. 44–62). Toronto, Ontario, Canada: Hogrefe.

Segerstrom, S. C., Taylor, S. E., Kemeny, M. E., & Fahey, J. L. (1998). Optimism is associated with mood, coping, and immune change in response to stress. *Journal of Personality and Social Psychology, 74,* 1646–1655.

Selye, H. (1976). *Stress in health and disease.* London: Butterworth.

Shepperd, J. A., Helweg-Larsen, M., & Ortega, L. (2003). Are comparative judgments consistent across time and events? *Personality and Social Psychology Bulletin, 29,* 1169–1180.

Shepperd, J. A., & McNulty, J. K. (2002). The affective consequences of expected and unexpected outcomes. *Psychological Science, 13,* 85–88.

Shepperd, J. A., Morato, J. J., & Pbert, L. A. (1996). Dispositional optimism as a predictor of health changes among cardiac patients. *Journal of Research in Personality, 30,* 517–534.

Shepperd, J. A., Ouellette, J. A., & Fernandez, J. K. (1996). Abandoning unrealistic optimism: Performance estimates and the temporal proximity of self-relevant feedback. *Journal of Personality and Social Psychology, 70,* 844–855.

Showers, C., & Ruben, C. (1990). Distinguishing defensive pessimism from depression: Negative expectations and positive coping mechanisms. *Cognitive Therapy and Research, 14,* 385–399.

Taylor, K. M., & Shepperd, J. A. (1998). Bracing for the worst: Severity, testing and feedback as moderators of the optimistic bias. *Personality and Social Psychology Bulletin, 24,* 915–926.

Taylor, S. E. (1991). Asymmetrical effects of positive and negative events: The mobilization-minimization hypothesis. *Psychological Bulletin, 110,* 67–85.

Taylor, S. E., Kemeny, M. E., Reed, G. M., Bower, J. E., & Gruenewald, T. L. (2000). Psychological resources, positive illusions, and health. *American Psychologist, 55,* 99–109.

Terry, M., & Shepperd, J. A. (2004, January). *Changing standards: Adjusting the definition of an acceptable outcome.* Paper presented at the annual meeting of the Society for Personality and Social Psychology, Austin, TX.

Tetlock, P. E. (1992). The impact of accountability on judgment and choice: Toward a social contingency model. In M. P. Zanna (Ed.), *Advances in experimental social psychology* (Vol. 25, pp. 331–376). New York: Academic Press.

van Dijk, W. W., & van der Pligt, J. (1997). The impact of probability and magnitude of outcome on disappointment and elation. *Organizational Behavior and Human Decision Processes, 69,* 277–284.

van Dijk, W. W., Zeelenberg, M., & van der Pligt, J. (1999). Not having what you want versus having what you do not want: The impact of type of negative outcome on the experience of disappointment and related emotions. *Cognition & Emotion, 13,* 127–148.

Weinstein, N. D. (1980). Unrealistic optimism about future life events. *Journal of Personality and Social Psychology, 39,* 806–820.

Weinstein, N. D., & Klein, W. M. (1995). Resistance of personal risk perceptions to debiasing interventions. *Health Psychology, 14,* 132–140.

11

ON WHEN SELF-ENHANCEMENT AND SELF-CRITICISM FUNCTION ADAPTIVELY AND MALADAPTIVELY

CONSTANTINE SEDIKIDES AND MICHELLE LUKE

Self-love seems so often unrequited.
—Anthony Powell, *The Acceptance World* (1956, p. 28)

It would be an understatement of sorts to point out that modern life places excessive demands on the individual. The busyness of the workplace, the necessity or unavoidability of job changes and the accompanying relocation, the ephemerality of friendships, and the expendability of even family relationships contribute to increased nuance and higher plasticity in the interplay between the individual and the social world. The ebb and flow of these demands is bound to exert its toll on a person's emotional fabric, coping resources, and self-concept.

How does the individual manage? How can one maintain the clarity and structural integrity of the self-system in an ocean of social change? How does one summon the motivation to set goals and carry them out? We argue

Preparation of this chapter was supported by British Academy Grant #LRG-37249 to Constantine Sedikides. Correspondence concerning the chapter should be addressed to Constantine Sedikides, School of Psychology, University of Southampton, Highfield Campus, Southampton SO17 1BJ, England; e-mail: cs2@soton.ac.uk.

that two of the many psychological mechanisms that mediate the person–environment interplay are self-enhancement and self-criticism. Indeed, we posit that the continuity and vitality of the self-system depend on the effective and complementary functioning of self-enhancement and self-criticism. In particular, we discuss the ways in which self-enhancement and self-criticism interact both adaptively and maladaptively.

Our analysis is based on a time-honored conceptual and methodological distinction between two self-evaluation motives. The self-enhancement motive propels thought and behavior in the service of maintaining, protecting, or increasing the positivity of the self-concept. In contrast, the self-assessment motive fuels thought and behavior toward maintaining, protecting, or increasing the accuracy of the self-concept (Baumeister, 1998; J. D. Brown, 1998; Sedikides, Green, & Pinter, 2004).

It is worth emphasizing that both motives have ontological and evolutionary significance (Baumeister, 2005; Sedikides & Skowronski, 2000; Sedikides & Strube, 1997). Indeed, these two motives wield a compelling influence on self-referent information processing. This influence is often antagonistic. Assume, for example, that the two motives are activated and compete for the selective (i.e., motive-congruent) processing of information. Furthermore, assume that this information is mixed in valence (some self-referent statements are positive, some negative) and is mixed in accuracy (some self-referent statements are high in accuracy, others low in accuracy). Evidence for the preponderance of the self-enhancement motive would be obtained if participants endorsed as self-descriptive, solicited more information about, or recalled to a greater degree positive rather than negative statements—especially high-accuracy statements. However, evidence for the preponderance of the self-assessment motive would be obtained if participants endorsed as self-descriptive, solicited more information about, or recalled to a greater degree high- rather than low-accuracy statements, regardless of their valence. In these critical experiments, the self-enhancement motive is shown to be more potent, although self-assessment concerns are also operative (Sedikides, 1993; see also Alicke & Govorun, 2005; J. D. Brown & Dutton, 1995; Sedikides & Gregg, 2003).

To sharpen our argument and align it with the objectives of this volume, we refer to self-enhancement not as an unobservable motivational construct, but rather as a psychological tendency. Thus, we conceptualize self-enhancement as the tendency to focus on and emphasize positive aspects of one's self-concept (e.g., traits, abilities, goals); one's life (e.g., likelihood of desirable events happening, capacity to control such events); or incoming self-relevant information (e.g., feedback). We make the important assumption that a consequence of the self-assessment motive is self-criticism. That is, when opting for accuracy rather than positivity of information or self-knowledge, people may question their intentions, go beyond the information given and engage in deep and objective autobiographical searches, ask the hard questions about the kind of person they are, and draw to a close by criticizing themselves. Self-criticism, then, is the tendency to focus on and emphasize negative aspects of one's self-concept, one's life, or feedback.

The central tenet of this chapter is that both self-enhancement and self-criticism can be adaptive or maladaptive. Hence, we discuss what makes the interplay between self-enhancement and self-criticism adaptive or maladaptive. We rely on a broad definition of adaptiveness. Thus, we refer to *adaptive* as involving or precipitating the presence of positive outcomes (e.g., relatively high life satisfaction and self-esteem, optimism, a sense of control, the ability to set and pursue desired goals, the belief in self-improvement) or the absence of negative outcomes (e.g., depressive symptoms, unhappiness, pessimism, low self-esteem, a sense of lack of control over one's life, the inability to set and pursue goals, a feeling of stagnation) for the individual. It follows that *maladaptive* connotes the absence of positive outcomes or the presence of negative outcomes for the individual.

In particular, we advocate two theses. First, self-enhancement and self-criticism are adaptive when they function symbiotically. Second, self-enhancement and self-criticism are maladaptive when they function either parasitically or antisymbiotically. We provide definitions of these terms in the next section and elaborate on the two theses.

SYMBIOSIS, PARASITISM, AND ANTISYMBIOSIS

The *New Oxford Dictionary of English* (1998) defines *symbiosis* as "interaction between two different organisms living in close physical association, typically to the advantage of both" and as "a mutually beneficial relationship between different people or groups." In the context of this chapter, we define *symbiosis* as a mutually beneficial relationship between self-enhancement and self-criticism.

In addition, the *New Oxford Dictionary of English* (1998) defines *parasite* as "an organism which lives in or on another organism (its host) and benefits by deriving nutrients at the other's expense" and "a person who habitually relies on or exploits others and gives nothing in return." In the context of this chapter, self-enhancement and self-criticism are considered as having a parasitic relationship when one undermines the other while coexisting. Furthermore, self-enhancement and self-criticism are considered as having an antisymbiotic relationship when they are antagonistic and preclude each other. We now proceed with illustrations of symbiosis, parasitism, and antisymbiosis.

WHEN DO SELF-ENHANCEMENT AND SELF-CRITICISM FUNCTION SYMBIOTICALLY?

We consider three illustrative cases of a symbiotic relationship between self-enhancement and self-criticism. We present these relationships as an unfolding scenario and then support the scenario with empirical evidence.

Scenario 1

In the first type of a symbiotic relationship, self-enhancement hits a realism roadblock, such as anticipated or received feedback from either an expert or a standardized test. The feedback instigates self-criticism, which in turn culminates in judicious self-enhancement.

An example of such a scenario is found in research linking self-enhancement to accountability (Sedikides, Herbst, Hardin, & Dardis, 2002). In the typical experimental paradigm, participants write an opinion essay (e.g., "Should the United States pursue exploration of the planet Saturn?") and prepare to grade it. Before they grade it, some participants are led to believe that they are accountable to an expert (e.g., a PhD candidate in logic and English literature), whereas other participants are led to believe that they are unaccountable. The grading of the essay follows.

Anticipated feedback curtails self-enhancement: Accountable participants assigned their essays lower grades than did the unaccountable ones (Sedikides et al., 2002, Experiments 1–3). How can this effect be explained? Accountable participants focus on their weaknesses as essay writers (Sedikides & Herbst, 2002). Indeed, in open-thought protocols, accountable participants list doubts about their competence as essay writers, reflect on the hard time they had writing essays in the past, wonder how bad many of their past essays must have been, and remember how critical others were of their essays (Sedikides et al., 2002, Experiment 4). Attentional focus on weaknesses, then, is tantamount to self-criticism.

In summary, anticipated objective feedback (i.e., expert evaluation) instigates self-criticism, which, in turn, tones down self-enhancement (Sedikides & Herbst, 2002; Sedikides et al., 2002). This process involves adaptive outcomes for the individual. One such outcome is a stronger sense of control and self-efficacy and a clearer and more accurate self-concept: The individual has now learned from experience and knows where he or she stands. In essence, participants look at themselves through the eyes of the evaluator and readjust the positivity of their self-views accordingly (Mead, 1934; Wilson & Dunn, 2004). An additional adaptive outcome is clarification of the individual's future goals. Perhaps a career in journalism will now need to be reconsidered, given the pressing need for frequent and deadline-driven essay writing in that profession. All of a sudden, an acting career seems more desirable. Finally, still another adaptive outcome involves the individual's chances for rapport with the evaluator. Self-boasting in essay writing would give the wrong impression to the evaluator and would precipitate additional criticism, whereas temperate self-appraisal would likely endear the individual to the expert and facilitate a pleasant interaction (Godfrey, Jones, & Lord, 1986; Powers & Zuroff, 1988; Schlenker & Leary, 1982).

Scenario 2

In the second type of symbiotic relationship between self-enhancement and self-criticism, the following scenario unfolds: Self-enhancement encounters a realism barrier, which gives way to a somewhat critical self-view, which prompts a self-improvement orientation.

Such a scenario is exemplified by research on trait modifiability. In the typical experimental paradigm, some participants are led to believe that traits (e.g., intelligence, kindness, assertiveness) are modifiable or easily changeable through practice and training. Other participants are led to believe that traits are fixed and unmodifiable—they were born with it and this is who they are. All participants subsequently receive unfavorable, trait-relevant feedback (e.g., "you are unintelligent, unkind, unassertive"). Of interest is the degree to which participants are affected emotionally by the feedback (i.e., level of criticism) and the degree to which participants seek out additional trait-relevant feedback (i.e., level of improvement).

When participants receive unfavorable feedback about a modifiable trait, they report being dejected and disappointed (Dauenheimer, Stahlberg, Spreeman, & Sedikides, 2002). This negative affective state is likely to spawn self-focus and self-questioning (Sedikides, 1992). It is interesting, however, that despite being hurt by the feedback, participants do not abandon their will for improvement. For starters, participants remember surprisingly well the unfavorable feedback, a pattern that suggests the absence of self-protection motivation (Green, Pinter, & Sedikides, 2005). More to the point, participants show a preference for additional unfavorable feedback (Dunning, 1995) and seek out such feedback (Ryan, Gheen, & Midgley, 1998) even when it is highly diagnostic of their weaknesses (Trope, Gervey, & Bolger, 2003). Stated otherwise, when a modifiable (rather than an unmodifiable) trait is at stake, participants turn self-criticism into self-improvement with obvious adaptive implications (e.g., higher optimism, stronger sense of control over the future). In the journalistic example, in the face of failure the individual will pursue useful tips from the expert on essay writing, but only if the individual believes that essay writing is a modifiable skill.

Scenario 3

In the third type of a symbiotic relationship between self-criticism and self-enhancement, the following scenario takes place: Self-criticism is offset by compensating mechanisms such as positive mood, success experiences, and close relationships. The result is an improvement orientation, as manifested by the solicitation of accurate but liability-focused feedback or by the propensity for upward social comparison. This orientation, in turn, gives rise to more defensible and verifiable self-enhancement patterns.

In the typical paradigm, participants in the experimental condition are put in a positive mood (Trope & Pomerantz, 1998), bring to mind success experiences (Trope & Neter, 1994), or consider the benefits of a close-positive relationship (Kumashiro & Sedikides, 2005). Participants in the control condition are put in a neutral mood, bring to mind neutral experiences, or consider their relationship with an acquaintance, respectively. Next, participants engage in a seemingly important task or take an ostensibly validated test about their personality or abilities. Then participants are given unfavorable feedback that dents their self-views; stated otherwise, the feedback activates a momentarily self-critical view. Of interest is the extent to which participants in the experimental (as opposed to the control) condition seek out additional feedback about their presumed liability—feedback that is accurate and has the potential to improve participants' performance.

Participants who were bolstered by positive mood, a success experience, or a close-positive relationship indeed manifested a preference for accurate and potentially improving feedback, despite the fact that such feedback focuses on their intellectual or personality limitations (Kumashiro & Sedikides, 2005; Trope & Neter, 1994; Trope & Pomerantz, 1998). Such an improvement orientation obviously has adaptive consequences: Armed with a better understanding of gaps in their knowledge or weaknesses in their personality, participants may rechannel personal resources (e.g., time, practice, task analysis) in a bid to ameliorate their current level of skill, especially when their goal is salient or personally important (Butler, 1993).

More important, an improvement orientation is likely to generalize to other intellectual or personality domains via such processes as upward social comparison (Wood, 1989). Comparisons between the self and more fortunate others provide an informative and diagnostic basis for one's self-beliefs and aspirations, thus grounding the self-concept in empirical reality (Collins, 1996). A consequence of this process is temperate self-enhancement. The individual will think of the self in ways that are more measured, verifiable, and defensible. A clear sense of direction (perhaps accompanied by higher sense of control, self-esteem, and life satisfaction) will ensue. Let us evoke the journalistic example once more. Shielded by a restorative process (e.g., positive mood, close-positive relationship), individuals solicit additional information on how to improve their essay-writing skills or compare themselves with a seasoned journalist. This process provides individuals with valuable clues about their current status and prompts them to consider either environments in which demands are well-matched to current abilities or environments that hold the promise of achievable social mobility.

WHEN DO SELF-ENHANCEMENT AND SELF-CRITICISM FUNCTION PARASITICALLY AND WHEN DO THEY FUNCTION ANTISYMBIOTICALLY?

Next, we consider three cases of parasitic or antisymbiotic relationships between self-enhancement and self-criticism: neuroticism, perfectionism, and narcissism.

Neuroticism

In a parasitic relationship, the two tendencies coexist, although one enfeebles the other. We consider such a relationship in the context of neuroticism. The defining feature of neuroticism is affective instability. In particular, neuroticism correlates with, and predisposes the individual toward, negative affect (e.g., anxiety, distress, unhappiness; Costa & McCrae, 1980, 1985). For example, neurotics (compared to non-neurotics) manifest heightened reactivity to negative-mood induction procedures, such as imagining a sad autobiographical event (Larsen & Ketelaar, 1991). In addition, neurotics show decreased desire for control following a mortality salience manipulation (i.e., imagining one's death), a pattern that belies a relatively ambivalent investment in cultural meaning systems (Arndt & Solomon, 2003). Finally, they make faster evaluative judgments when they are in a negative rather than a positive mood (Tamir & Robinson, 2004).

How do neurotics cope with potentially stressful input? A study by Schneider (2004) provides some insights. Neurotic and non-neurotic participants underwent a series of physiological (i.e., acoustic startle stimuli) and psychosocial (e.g., vocal mental mathematics) stressors, while their cognitive appraisals, affective reactions, task performance, and physiological responses were assessed. Compared with their non-neurotic counterparts, neurotics perceived these stressors as threatening (i.e., unfavorable to the self) rather than challenging (i.e., favorable to the self). Perceptions of threat mediated the negative affect experienced by neurotics. In addition, threatened participants experienced slower affective recovery, had reduced cardiac output, manifested less heart rate reactivity, and performed worse than did challenged participants.

These findings bolster the theoretical view that level of neuroticism intensifies perceptions of threat in a variety of situations (Craske, 1999). Neurotics tend to construe threat, even if no threat or minimal threat exists. Threat construals may be due to negative biases in information processing (Barrett, Rapee, Dadds, & Ryan, 1996) and retrieval (Rusting, 1999) as well as the tendency to monitor rather than label one's mood and subsequently to engage in rumination (Swinkels & Giuliano, 1995). Such biases are associated with relative lack of emotional and motivational (i.e., goal-relevant) clarity (Salovey, Mayer, Goldman, Turvey, & Palfai, 1995). Indeed, neurotics have low self-clarity, as indicated by their relatively large discrepancies between actual and ideal self-guides (Hafdahl, Panter, Gramzow, Sedikides, & Insko, 2000). Low self-clarity is linked with low psychological well-being (J. D. Campbell, Assanand, & Di Paula, 2003).

It is of no surprise, then, that neuroticism has maladaptive implications for the individual. In particular, neuroticism is negatively correlated with optimism (Wolfe & Grosch, 1990), is uncorrelated with overconfidence (Schaefer, Williams, Goodie, & Campbell, 2004), is negatively correlated with self-esteem (Judge, Erez, Bono, & Thoresen, 2002), and is accompanied by an external locus of control orientation (Judge et al., 2002). In summary, the coexistence of positive and negative self-cognitions in neurotics—along with their ambivalent and unstable emotionality—is relatively debilitating and contributes to maladaptive outcomes.

Perfectionism

In an antisymbiotic relationship, self-criticism and self-enhancement are antagonistic and preclude one another. An illustrative case of such a relationship is perfectionism. Perfectionism has been defined as a private desire for perfection (Frost, Marten, Lahart, & Rosenblate, 1990), the drive to achieve exceedingly high and faultless goals (Brouwers & Wiggum, 1993), and "the striving to be perfect and to avoid error or flaw" (Powers, Zuroff, & Topciu, 2004). Although initially perfectionism was regarded as a unidimensional construct (e.g., Hewitt & Flett, 1990), a distinction has now been established between perfectionists who are rarely, if ever, satisfied with their performance (maladaptive perfectionists) and those who can be satisfied with their performance (Grzegorek, Slaney, Franze, & Rice, 2004). In our discussion, we refer exclusively to the former class of perfectionists.

An experiment by Grzegorek (2002) provides useful glimpses into the manner in which perfectionists process self-relevant information. Perfectionists completed an analogy test and received either bogus success or bogus failure feedback. Those who received success feedback were as likely as those who received failure feedback to claim that they should have performed better on the test. Perfectionists are dissatisfied with their performance even when, according to objective indicators, they should be pretty pleased with it.

Chronic performance dissatisfaction is associated with a variety of maladaptive outcomes. Perfectionism is associated with self-loathing (Blatt, D'Afflitti, & Quinlan, 1976), distress (Frost et al., 1995), depression (Powers et al., 2004), unresponsiveness to therapies for depression (Blatt, Zuroff, Bondi, Sanislow, & Pilkonis, 1998), anorexia in young adults (Tyrka, Waldron, Graber, & Brooks-Gunn, 2002), and bulimia in women with low self-esteem (Vohs, Bardone, Joiner, Abramson, & Heatherton, 1999). Some authors have even suggested that perfectionism is a potent predictor of suicidal behavior

(Shaw & Segal, 1999), and some findings link excessive self-flagellation with the desire to harm the self (Gilbert, Clarke, Hempel, Miles, & Irons, 2004).

In the case of perfectionism, self-criticism outweighs and precludes self-enhancement. Next, we turn our attention to the reverse relationship between the two tendencies: unbridled self-enhancement leaves no room for self-criticism. This is the case of subclinical narcissism.

Narcissism

The final type of an antisymbiotic relationship between self-enhancement and self-criticism that we consider is narcissism. This trait is defined in terms of a self-aggrandizing, self-centered, dominant, and manipulative orientation (Emmons, 1987; Paulhus, 1998). Also, narcissists score high on disagreeableness and extraversion (Costa & McCrae, 1995), and score high on agency but low on communion (W. K. Campbell, Rudich, & Sedikides, 2002). In terms of attachment styles, narcissists have a positive perception of the self and a negative perception of others (Griffin & Bartholomew, 1994).

How do narcissists respond to interpersonal feedback? In a study by Kernis and Sun (1994), participants performed a task and received bogus success or failure feedback. In the case of failure feedback, narcissists (compared to non-narcissists) derogated the evaluator as incompetent and unlikeable and were prepared to convey their impression in a face-to-face encounter with the evaluator. In another study, narcissists who received failure feedback for their performance on an interdependent task blamed the outcome on their partner, even when the partner was a friend (W. K. Campbell, Reeder, Sedikides, & Elliot, 2000). In still another study, narcissists who received failure feedback behaved aggressively toward the evaluator (Bushman & Baumeister, 1998).

Narcissists, then, cannot do wrong in their own eyes and are unforgiving (Exline, Baumeister, Bushman, Campbell, & Finkel, 2004) and vengeful (R. P. Brown, 2004) toward others. Does this entitled and egocentric orientation have negative implications for psychological health? The evidence does not indicate so. Narcissism is inversely related to sadness, loneliness, and depression, and is positively related to subjective well-being. The relation, however, between narcissism and psychological health is mediated by self-esteem: Narcissism is beneficial for psychological health insofar as it is linked with high self-esteem (Sedikides, Rudich, Gregg, Kumashiro, & Rusbult, 2004).

It is paradoxical, then, that an antisymbiotic relationship between self-enhancement and self-criticism confers adaptive outcomes. However, there are reasons to believe that such a relationship also bears maladaptive outcomes. Narcissists report higher variability on positive mood, negative mood, and mood intensity over the course of several days (Emmons, 1987; Rhodewalt, Madrian, & Cheney, 1998). In addition, narcissists experience more negative affect in response to interpersonal stressors (Rhodewalt et al., 1998) and more volatile emotion in romantic relationships (Rhodewalt & Shimoda, 2000). Moreover, narcissists experience more extreme affective reactions to social comparison information; in particular, they report stronger positive affect following downward social comparison and stronger hostility following upward social comparison (Bogart, Benotsch, & Pavlovic, 2004). In addition, narcissism correlates negatively with automatic self-esteem, as assessed by the Go No-Go Association Test (Gregg & Sedikides, 2005), and narcissistic self-esteem varies over time more than does non-narcissistic self-esteem. These findings would suggest that narcissistic self-esteem is unstable (Kernis, 1993) or contingent (Deci & Ryan, 1995). Finally, because of their inability to forgive, narcissists are deprived of the beneficial consequences of forgiveness for psychological health (Coyle & Enright, 1997; Freedman & Enright, 1996). Thus, although narcissism is adaptive in some ways, it is maladaptive in others.

Intrapsychic adaptiveness is not the only form of adaptiveness, however. Adaptiveness can be defined in terms of social relationships. Does self-enhancement or self-criticism benefit close others or the group? In other words, is narcissistic self-enhancement beneficial to others? It is not clear that it is. Narcissists, for example, desire or pursue controlling and Machiavellian social relationships—what Sedikides, Campbell, Reeder, Elliot, and Gregg (2002) termed the "others exist for me" illusion. In other words, narcissists are attracted to prospective partners who offer them admiration rather than intimacy (W. K. Campbell, 1999), favor a game-playing love (W. K. Campbell, Foster, & Finkel, 2002), and report low levels of commitment to dating relationships (W. K. Campbell & Foster, 2002). Also, narcissists are not bound to be popular group members, given that they exhibit in abundance the self-serving bias: They take credit for their successes and displace blame for failures on others (John & Robins, 1994).

What do others think of the narcissist? In the first social encounters, narcissists give off a positive impression, as they appear energetic, intense, and confident. However, as interpersonal interactions accrue (by the seventh weekly social interaction, to be exact), narcissists are increasingly seen as self-centered, conceited, uninteresting, and hostile (Colvin, Block, & Funder, 1995; Paulhus, 1998). Indeed, narcissists may be treated with derision, rejection, and social exclusion (Exline, Single, Lobel, & Geyer, 2004; Leary, Bednarski, Hammon, & Duncan, 1997). In summary, the narcissistic interpersonal style is likely to be particularly costly in the long run. Narcissism is not only damaging to other persons or the group but also maladaptive to the individual's long-term goals.

CONCLUDING REMARKS

As our opening quote from Anthony Powell indicates, self-enhancement and self-criticism are closely intertwined. Although the motive to self-enhance is powerful and universal (Sedikides, Gaertner, & Toguchi, 2003; but see Heine, Lehman, Markus, & Kitayama, 1999), the motive to self-assess is also important. Self-assessment can yield a self-critical tendency toward one's personality traits, behaviors, skills, abilities, habits, or future goals.

We argued that the tendency to self-enhance and self-criticize can be adaptive or maladaptive. In particular, we offered two theses. The first was that self-enhancement and self-criticism are adaptive when they function symbiotically, that is, when they have a mutually beneficial relationship. We presented three illustrative scenarios of symbiotic relationships: (a) self-enhancement hits a realism roadblock (e.g., indisputable feedback), followed by self-criticism and temperate self-enhancement; (b) self-enhancement encounters a realism barrier, followed by self-criticism and self-improvement; and (c) self-criticism is offset by compensating mechanisms (e.g., positive mood, close relationships), resulting in self-improvement and grounded self-enhancement patterns. Accompanying these scenarios were empirical demonstrations from the literatures on accountability, self-conception modifiability, and self-affirmation, respectively. In all three cases, self-enhancement and self-criticism, working in tandem, were likely to result in adaptive outcomes such as stronger sense of control; efficacy or self-improvement; and higher optimism, self-esteem, or life satisfaction.

The second thesis was that self-enhancement and self-criticism are maladaptive when they function either parasitically (one undermining the other) or antisymbiotically (one precluding the other). We discussed neuroticism as an example of a parasitic relationship: The two tendencies coexisted, although one (i.e., self-criticism) sabotaged the other. Furthermore, we discussed perfectionism and narcissism as examples of antisymbiotic relationships. In perfectionism, self-criticism hinders self-enhancement. In narcissism, self-enhancement impedes self-criticism. Both parasitic and antisymbiotic relationships have maladaptive implications. For example, neuroticism is associated with lower life satisfaction, lower self-esteem, and pessimism. Perfectionism is associated with depression. Finally, narcissism is linked with fluctuations in mood and self-esteem, dysfunctional relationships, and indifferent or cynical treatment from others.

As shown in the case of perfectionism (and, to some extent, neuroticism), a preoccupation with self-criticism is maladaptive. There is mounting evidence for the detrimental consequences of self-criticism not only for psychological but also for physical health. Recurrent self-criticism, for instance, is associated with negative mood and hopelessness (Santor & Patterson, 2004) as well as depressive symptoms (Besser & Priel, 2003), major depression (Cox, McWilliams, Enns, & Clara, 2004), and shame (Dickerson, Gruenewald, & Kemeny, 2004). Also, recurrent self-criticism leads to an increase in proinflammatory cytokine activity and cortisol levels, in concert with feelings of shame (Dickerson et al., 2004). Indeed, we do not regard self-criticism as a motive in normal adults. Rather, as we have already stated, self-criticism is an offshoot of the self-assessment motive, and it is adaptive only when it is engaged for relatively brief periods and in the service of adaptive (i.e., self-improving) action.

What is adaptive, anyway, and for whom? In an earlier article (Sedikides & Strube, 1997), we argued that adaptiveness needs to be linked to the relevant situation and the perceiver's characteristics and objectives, although, even then, it is often hard to discern what is or is not adaptive for the individual. Nevertheless, we distinguished between short-term and long-term adaptiveness. Giving up control willingly (Rothbaum, Weisz, & Snyder, 1982) or expressing pessimism regarding one's performance (Norem & Cantor, 1986) appear to be maladaptive in the short term, but may be adaptive in the long run. Likewise, an individual's goal to demonstrate scholarly prowess at a cocktail party may be achieved by an ostentatious display of knowledge, but such a behavior deprives the individual's colleagues of the opportunity to display their own scholarly talent and may alienate them. Thus, the short-term adaptive value of this behavior is high, but its long-term adaptive value is low. In summary, the adaptiveness of self-enhancing behaviors needs to be considered within a temporal frame of reference.

So far, we considered adaptive outcomes for the individual. What predicts adaptive outcomes for others? Research by Sheldon and Bettencourt (2002) sheds some light on this question. Not only intrapersonal factors (e.g., personal autonomy) but also interpersonal relatedness and feelings of inclusion predicted adaptive outcomes for the group. These outcomes were intrinsic motivation for group activities, high positive and low negative mood within the group, and strong commitment to the group. Indeed, we maintain that both intrapersonal and interpersonal adaptiveness is necessary to achieve optimal self-esteem and functioning (Kernis, 2003; Passmore, 2000; Sheldon, 2004).

REFERENCES

Alicke, M. D., & Govorun, O. (2005). The better-than-average effect. In M. D. Alicke, D. A. Dunning, & J. I. Krueger (Eds.), *The self in social judgment* (pp. 85–107). Philadelphia, PA: Psychology Press.

Arndt, J., & Solomon, S. (2003). The control of death and the death of control: The effects of mortality salience, neuroticism, and worldview threat on the desire for control. *Journal of Research in Personality, 37,* 1–22.

Barrett, P. M., Rapee, R. M., Dadds, M. M., & Ryan, S. M. (1996). Family enhancement of cognitive style in anxious and aggressive children. *Journal of Abnormal Child Psychology, 24,* 187–203.

Baumeister, R. F. (1998). The self. In D. T. Gilbert, S. T. Fiske, & G. Lindzey (Eds.), *Handbook of social psychology* (4th ed.; Vol. 1, pp. 680–740). New York: McGraw-Hill.

Baumeister, R. F. (2005). *The cultural animal: Human nature, meaning, and social life.* New York: Oxford University Press.

Besser, A., & Priel, B. (2003). A multisource approach to self-critical vulnerability to depression: The moderating role of attachment. *Journal of Personality, 71,* 515–555.

Blatt, S. J., D'Afflitti, J. P., & Quinlan, D. M. (1976). Experiences of depression in young adults. *Journal of Abnormal Psychology, 85,* 383–389.

Blatt, S. J., Zuroff, D. C., Bondi, C. M., Sanislow, C. A., & Pilkonis, P. A. (1998). When and how perfectionism impedes the brief treatment of depression: Further analyses of the National Institute of Mental Health Treatment of Depression Collaborative Research Program. *Journal of Consulting and Clinical Psychology, 66,* 423–428.

Bogart, L. M., Benotsch, E. G., & Pavlovic, J. D. (2004). Feeling superior but threatened: The relation of narcissism to social comparison. *Basic and Applied Social Psychology, 26,* 35–44.

Brouwers, M., & Wiggum, C. D. (1993). Bulimia and perfectionism: Developing the courage to be imperfect. *Journal of Mental Health Counseling, 15,* 141–149.

Brown, J. D. (1998). *The self.* Boston: McGraw-Hill.

Brown, J. D., & Dutton, K. A. (1995). Truth and consequences: The costs and benefits of accurate self-knowledge. *Personality and Social Psychology Bulletin, 21,* 1288–1296.

Brown, R. P. (2004). Vengeance is mine: Narcissism, vengeance, and the tendency to forgive. *Journal of Research in Personality, 38,* 576–584.

Bushman, B. J., & Baumeister, R. F. (1998). Threatened egotism, narcissism, self-esteem, and direct and displaced aggression: Does self-love or self-hate lead to violence? *Journal of Personality and Social Psychology, 75,* 219–229.

Butler, R. (1993). Effects of task- and ego-achievement goals on information seeking during task engagement. *Journal of Personality and Social Psychology, 65,* 18–31.

Campbell, J. D., Assanand, S., & Di Paula, A. (2003). The structure of the self-concept and its relation to psychological adjustment. *Journal of Personality, 71,* 115–140.

Campbell, W. K. (1999). Narcissism and romantic attraction. *Journal of Personality and Social Psychology, 77,* 1254–1270.

Campbell, W. K., & Foster, C. A. (2002). Narcissism and commitment in romantic relationships: An investment model analysis. *Personality and Social Psychology Bulletin, 28,* 484–495.

Campbell, W. K., Foster, C. A., & Finkel, E. J. (2002). Does self-love lead to love for others? A story of narcissistic game-playing. *Journal of Personality and Social Psychology, 83,* 340–354.

Campbell, W. K., Reeder, G., Sedikides, C., & Elliot, A. J. (2000). Narcissism and comparative self-enhancement strategies. *Journal of Research in Personality, 34,* 329–347.

Campbell, W. K., Rudich, E. A., & Sedikides, C. (2002). Narcissism, self-esteem, and the positivity of self-views: Two portraits of self-love. *Personality and Social Psychology Bulletin, 28,* 358–368.

Collins, R. L. (1996). For better or worse: The impact of upward social comparison on self-evaluations. *Psychological Bulletin, 119,* 51–69.

Colvin, C. R., Block, J., & Funder, D. C. (1995). Overly positive self-evaluations and personality: Negative implications for mental health. *Journal of Personality and Social Psychology, 68,* 1151–1162.

Costa, P. T., & McCrae, R. R. (1980). Influence of extraversion and neuroticism on subjective well-being: Happy and unhappy people. *Journal of Personality and Social Psychology, 38,* 668–678.

Costa, P. T., & McCrae, R. R. (1985). *NEO Five-Factor Inventory: Form S.* Odessa, FL: Psychological Assessment Resources.

Costa, P. T., & McCrae, R. P. (1995). Domains and factors: Hierarchical personality assessment using the NEO Personality Inventory. *Journal of Personality Assessment, 64,* 21–50.

Cox, B. J., McWilliams, L. A., Enns, M. W., & Clara, I. P. (2004). Broad and specific personality dimensions associated with major depression in a nationally representative sample. *Comprehensive Psychiatry, 45,* 246–253.

Coyle, C. T., & Enright, R. D. (1997). Forgiveness intervention with post-abortion men. *Journal of Consulting and Clinical Psychology, 65,* 1042–1046.

Craske, M. G. (1999). *Anxiety disorders: Psychological approaches to theory and treatment.* Boulder, CO: Westview Press.

Dauenheimer, D. G., Stahlberg, D., Spreeman, S., & Sedikides, C. (2002). Self-enhancement, self-assessment, or self-verification? The intricate role of trait modifiability in the self-evaluation process. *Revue Internationale de Psychologie Sociale, 15,* 89–112.

Deci, E. L., & Ryan, R. M. (1995). Human agency: The basis for true self-esteem. In M. H. Kernis (Ed.), *Efficacy, agency, and self-esteem* (pp. 31–50). New York: Plenum Press.

Dickerson, S. S., Gruenewald, T. L., & Kemeny, M. E. (2004). When the social self is threatened: Shame, physiology, and health. *Journal of Personality, 72,* 1191–1216.

Dunning, D. (1995). Trait importance and modifiability as factors influencing self-assessment and self-enhancement motives. *Personality and Social Psychology Bulletin, 21,* 1297–1306.

Emmons, R. A. (1987). Narcissism: Theory and measurement. *Journal of Personality and Social Psychology, 52,* 11–17.

Exline, J. J., Baumeister, R. F., Bushman, B. J., Campbell, W. K., & Finkel, E. J. (2004). Too proud to let go: Narcissistic entitlement as a barrier to forgiveness. *Journal of Personality and Social Psychology, 87,* 894–912.

Exline, J. J., Single, P. B., Lobel, M., & Geyer, A. L. (2004). Glowing praise and the envious gaze: Social dilemmas surrounding the public recognition of achievement. *Basic and Applied Social Psychology, 26,* 119–130.

Freedman, S. R., & Enright, R. D. (1996). Forgiveness as an intervention goal with incest survivors. *Journal of Consulting and Clinical Psychology, 64,* 983–992.

Frost, R. O., Marten, P., Lahart, C., & Rosenblate, R. (1990). The dimensions of perfectionism. *Cognitive Therapy and Research, 14,* 449–468.

Frost, R. O., Turcotte, T. A., Heimberg, R. G., Mattia, J. I., Holt, C. S., & Hope, D. A. (1995). Reactions to mistakes among subjects high and low in perfectionistic concern over mistakes. *Cognitive Therapy and Research, 19,* 195–205.

Gilbert, P., Clarke, M., Hempel, S., Miles, J. N. V., & Irons, C. (2004). Criticizing and reassuring oneself: An exploration of forms, styles and reasons in female students. *British Journal of Clinical Psychology, 43,* 31–50.

Godfrey, D. K., Jones, E. E., & Lord, C. G. (1986). Self-promotion is not ingratiating. *Journal of Personality and Social Psychology, 50,* 106–113.

Green, J. D., Pinter, B., & Sedikides, C. (2005). Mnemic neglect and self-threat: Trait modifiability moderates self-protection. *European Journal of Social Psychology, 35,* 225–235.

Gregg, A. P., & Sedikides, C. (2005). *Am I gnasty or gnice?: Unmasking the fragility of narcissistic self-regard with the GNAT.* Unpublished manuscript, University of Southampton, Southampton, England.

Griffin, D. W., & Bartholomew, K. (1994). Models of the self and other: Fundamental dimensions underlying measures of adult attachment. *Journal of Personality and Social Psychology, 67,* 430–445.

Grzegorek, J. L. (2002). *Perfectionists' cognitive and affective reactions to self-relevant evaluative feedback.* Unpublished doctoral dissertation, Pennsylvania State University, University Park.

Grzegorek, J. L., Slaney, R. B., Franze, S., & Rice, K. G. (2004). Self-criticism, dependency, self-esteem, and grade point average satisfaction among clusters of perfectionists and nonperfectionists. *Journal of Counseling Psychology, 51,* 192–200.

Hafdahl, A. R., Panter, A. T., Gramzow, R. H., Sedikides, C., & Insko, C. A. (2000). Free-response self-discrepancies across, among, and within FFM personality dimensions. *Journal of Personality, 68,* 111–151.

Heine, S. J., Lehman, D. R., Markus, H. R., & Kitayama, S. (1999). Is there a universal need for positive self-regard? *Psychological Review, 106,* 766–794.

Hewitt, P. L., & Flett, G. L. (1990). Perfectionism and depression: A multidimensional analysis. *Journal of Social Behavior and Personality, 5,* 423–438.

John, O. P., & Robins, R. W. (1994). Accuracy and bias in self-perception: Individual differences in self-enhancement and the role of narcissism. *Journal of Personality and Social Psychology, 66,* 206–219.

Judge, T. A., Erez, A., Bono, J. E., & Thoresen, C. J. (2002). Are measures of self-esteem, neuroticism, locus of control, and generalized self-efficacy indicators of a common core construct? *Journal of Personality and Social Psychology, 83,* 693–710.

Kernis, M. H. (1993). The roles of stability and level of self-esteem in psychological functioning. In R. F. Baumeister (Ed.), *Self-esteem: The puzzle of low self-regard* (pp. 167–182). New York: Plenum Press.

Kernis, M. H. (2003). Toward a conceptualization of optimal self-esteem. *Psychological Inquiry, 14,* 1–26.

Kernis, M. H., & Sun, C. (1994). Narcissism and reactions to interpersonal feedback. *Journal of Research in Personality, 28,* 4–13.

Kumashiro, M., & Sedikides, C. (2005). Taking on board liability-focused feedback: Close positive relationships as a self-bolstering resource. *Psychological Science, 16,* 732–739.

Larsen, R., & Ketelaar, T. (1991). Personality and susceptibility to positive and negative emotional states. *Journal of Personality and Social Psychology, 61,* 132–140.

Leary, M. R., Bednarski, R., Hammon, D., & Duncan, T. (1997). Blowhards, snobs, and narcissists: Interpersonal reactions to excessive egotism. In R. M. Kowalski (Ed.), *Aversive interpersonal behaviors* (pp. 111–131). New York: Plenum Press.

Mead, G. H. (1934). *Mind, self, and society from the standpoint of a social behaviorist.* Chicago: University of Chicago Press.

The New Oxford Dictionary of English. (1998). J. Pearsall (Ed.). Oxford, England: Oxford University Press.

Norem, J. K., & Cantor, N. (1986). Anticipatory and post hoc cushioning strategies: Optimism and defensive pessimism in "risky" situations. *Cognitive Therapy and Research, 10,* 347–362.

Passmore, J. (2000). *The perfectibility of man* (3rd ed.). Indianapolis, IN: Liberty Fund.

Paulhus, D. L. (1998). Interpersonal and intrapsychic adaptiveness of trait self-enhancement: A mixed blessing? *Journal of Personality and Social Psychology, 74,* 1197–1208.

Powell, A. (1956). *The acceptance world.* London: Penguin Books.

Powers, T. A., & Zuroff, D. C. (1988). Interpersonal consequences of overt criticism: A comparison with neutral and self-enhancing presentations of self. *Journal of Personality and Social Psychology, 54,* 1054–1062.

Powers, T. A., Zuroff, D. C., & Topciu, R. A. (2004). Covert and overt expressions of self-criticism and perfectionism and their relation to depression. *European Journal of Personality, 18,* 61–72.

Rhodewalt, F., Madrian, J. C., & Cheney, S. (1998). Narcissism, self-knowledge organization, and emotional reactivity: The effect of daily experiences on self-esteem and affect. *Personality and Social Psychology Bulletin, 24,* 75–87.

Rhodewalt, F., & Shimoda, V. (2000). *What's love got to do with it? Narcissism and romantic relationships.* Unpublished data, University of Utah.

Rothbaum, F., Weisz, J. R., & Snyder, S. S. (1982). Changing the world and changing the self: A two-process model of perceived control. *Journal of Personality and Social Psychology, 42,* 5–37.

Rusting, C. L. (1999). Interactive effects of personality and mood on emotion-congruent memory and judgment. *Journal of Personality and Social Psychology, 77,* 1073–1086.

Ryan, A. M., Gheen, M. H., & Midgley, C. (1998). Why do some students avoid asking for help? An examination of the interplay among students' academic efficacy, teachers' social-emotional role, and the classroom goal structure. *Journal of Educational Psychology, 90,* 528–535.

Salovey, P., Mayer, J. D., Goldman, S. L., Turvey, C., & Palfai, T. P. (1995). Emotional attention, clarity, and repair: Exploring emotional intelligence using the Trait Meta-Mood Scale. In J. W. Pennebaker (Ed.), *Emotion, disclosure, and health* (pp. 125–154). Washington, DC: American Psychological Association.

Santor, D. A., & Patterson, R. L. (2004). Frequency and duration of mood fluctuations: Effects of dependency, self-criticism, and negative events. *Personality and Individual Differences, 37,* 1667-1680.

Schaefer, P., Williams, C. C., Goodie, A. S., & Campbell, W. K. (2004). Overconfidence and the Big Five. *Journal of Research in Personality, 38,* 473–480.

Schlenker, B. R., & Leary, M. R. (1982). Audiences' reactions to self-enhancing, self-denigrating, and accurate self-presentations. *Journal of Experimental Social Psychology, 18,* 89–104.

Schneider, T. R. (2004). The role of neuroticism on psychological and physiological stress responses. *Journal of Experimental Social Psychology, 40,* 795–804.

Sedikides, C. (1992). Mood as a determinant of attentional focus. *Cognition and Emotion, 6,* 129–148.

Sedikides, C. (1993). Assessment, enhancement, and verification determinants of the self-evaluation process. *Journal of Personality and Social Psychology, 65,* 317–338.

Sedikides, C., Campbell, W. K., Reeder, G., Elliot, A. J., & Gregg, A. P. (2002). Do others bring out the worst in narcissists? The "others exist for me" illusion. In Y. Kashima, M. Foddy, & M. Platow (Eds.), *Self and identity: Personal, social, and symbolic* (pp. 103–123). Mahwah, NJ: Erlbaum.

Sedikides, C., Gaertner, L., & Toguchi, Y. (2003). Pancultural self-enhancement. *Journal of Personality and Social Psychology, 84,* 60–70.

Sedikides, C., Green, J. D., & Pinter, B. (2004). Self-protective memory. In D. R. Beike, J. M. Lampinen, & D. A. Behrend (Eds.), *The self and memory* (pp. 161–179). Philadelphia: Psychology Press.

Sedikides, C., & Gregg, A. P. (2003). Portraits of the self. In M. A. Hogg & J. Cooper (Eds.), *Sage handbook of social psychology* (pp. 110–138). London: Sage.

Sedikides, C., & Herbst, K. (2002). How does accountability reduce self-enhancement? The role of self-focus. *Revue Internationale de Psychologie Sociale, 15,* 113–128.

Sedikides, C., Herbst, K. C., Hardin, D. P., & Dardis, G. J. (2002). Accountability as a deterrent to self-enhancement: The search for mechanisms. *Journal of Personality and Social Psychology, 83,* 592–605.

Sedikides, C., Rudich, E. A., Gregg, A. P., Kumashiro, M., & Rusbult, C. (2004). Are normal narcissists psychologically healthy? Self-esteem matters. *Journal of Personality and Social Psychology, 87,* 400–416.

Sedikides, C., & Skowronski, J. J. (2000). On the evolutionary functions of the symbolic self: The emergence of self-evaluation motives. In A. Tesser, R. Felson, &

J. Suls (Eds.), *Psychological perspectives on self and identity* (pp. 91–117). Washington, DC: American Psychological Association.

Sedikides, C., & Strube, M. J. (1997). Self-evaluation: To thine own self be good, to thine own self be sure, to thine own self be true, and to thine own self be better. In M. P. Zanna (Ed.), *Advances in experimental social psychology* (Vol. 29, pp. 209–269). New York: Academic Press.

Shaw, B. F., & Segal, Z. V. (1999). Efficacy, indications, and mechanisms of action of cognitive therapy of depression. In D. S. Janowsky (Ed.), *Psychotherapy indications and outcomes* (pp. 173–195). Washington, DC: American Psychological Association.

Sheldon, K. M. (2004). *Optimal human being: An integrated multi-level perspective.* Mahwah, NJ: Erlbaum.

Sheldon, K. M., & Bettencourt, B. A. (2002). Psychological need-satisfaction and subjective well-being within social groups. *British Journal of Social Psychology, 41,* 25–38.

Swinkels, A., & Giuliano, T. A. (1995). The measurement and conceptualization of mood awareness: Monitoring and labelling one's mood states. *Personality and Social Psychology Bulletin, 21,* 934–949.

Tamir, M., & Robinson, M. D. (2004). Knowing good from bad: The paradox of neuroticism, negative affect, and evaluative processing. *Journal of Personality and Social Psychology, 87,* 913–925.

Trope, Y., Gervey, B., & Bolger, N. (2003). The role of perceived control in overcoming defensive self-evaluation. *Journal of Experimental Social Psychology, 39,* 407–419.

Trope, Y., & Neter, E. (1994). Reconciling competing motives in self-evaluation: The role of self-control in feedback seeking. *Journal of Personality and Social Psychology, 66,* 646–657.

Trope, Y., & Pomerantz, E. M. (1998). Resolving conflicts among self-evaluation motives: Positive experiences as a resource for overcoming defensiveness. *Motivation and Emotion, 22,* 53–72.

Tyrka, A. R., Waldron, I., Graber, J. A., & Brooks-Gunn, J. (2002). Prospective predictors of the onset of anorexic and bulimic symptoms. *International Journal of Eating Disorders, 32,* 282–290.

Vohs, K. D., Bardone, A. M., Joiner, T. E., Jr., Abramson, L. Y., & Heatherton, T. F. (1999). Perfectionism, perceived weight status, and self-esteem interact to predict bulimic symptoms: A model of bulimic symptom development. *Journal of Abnormal Psychology, 108,* 695–700.

Wilson, T. D., & Dunn, E. W. (2004). Self-knowledge: Its limits, value, and potential for improvement. *Annual Review of Psychology, 55,* 493–518.

Wolfe, R. N., & Grosch, J. W. (1990). Personality correlates of confidence in one's decision. *Journal of Personality, 58,* 515–534.

Wood, J. V. (1989). Theory and research concerning social comparisons of personal attributes. *Psychological Bulletin, 106,* 231–248.

IV

CLINICAL IMPLICATIONS OF SELF-ENHANCEMENT AND SELF-CRITICISM

12

ON PROMOTING ADAPTIVE SELF-ENHANCEMENT IN PSYCHOTHERAPY

JAMES L. PRETZER

At one time, low self-esteem was seen as the root of many of society's ills and the enhancement of self-esteem was seen as a central goal for psychotherapy, education, and public policy. Today there is debate regarding whether we should promote self-enhancement at all. One review concluded, "We have not found evidence that boosting self-esteem (by therapeutic interventions or school programs) causes benefits. Our findings do not support continued widespread efforts to boost self-esteem in the hope that it will by itself foster improved outcomes" (Baumeister, Campbell, Krueger, & Vohs, 2003, p. 1). This determination creates a problem for clinicians when clients complain of low self-esteem or present problems for which low self-esteem seems to be a contributing factor. When (if ever) and how should therapists promote self-enhancement in psychotherapy?

Additional research is needed, but the practitioner cannot wait for more research when faced with the task of choosing therapeutic interventions today. In this chapter we discuss how to decide whether to promote self-

Address correspondence to James Pretzer, PhD, Director, Cleveland Center for Cognitive Therapy, 24400 Highpoint Road, Suite 9, Beachwood, Ohio 44122 or e-mail jimpretz@sbcglobal.net.

enhancement in psychotherapy and describe possible approaches to doing so while recognizing that these methods have not received the amount of empirical investigation that would be preferred.

SHOULD WE PROMOTE SELF-ENHANCEMENT IN PSYCHOTHERAPY?

It is important for the therapist to use his or her knowledge and professional judgment in discussing the goals of therapy with the client. If the client seeks self-enhancement as a result of unrealistic beliefs regarding the value of high self-esteem, it would be appropriate for the therapist to advocate a more realistic view of self-esteem and to encourage the client to consider other goals for treatment. However, if low self-esteem presents a real-life problem for the client or if it contributes to problems such as depression, avoidance, or lack of assertion, then working to promote adaptive self-enhancement may be quite appropriate. In light of the evidence that low self-esteem leads to depression under some conditions and that high self-esteem leads to greater happiness (see Baumeister et al., 2003), interventions designed to promote adaptive self-enhancement may be quite relevant to psychotherapy clients who present depression as one of their problems. The available evidence (e.g., Baumeister et al., 2003) does not support the idea that therapists should indiscriminately seek to enhance self-esteem. However, it is compatible with the idea of selectively working to promote self-enhancement when low self-esteem is a problem.

DEVELOPING AN UNDERSTANDING OF A CLIENT'S SELF-ESTEEM PROBLEMS

When psychotherapy focuses on an abstract concept such as self-esteem or self-acceptance, there is a risk of therapist and client slipping into an abstract intellectual discussion that has little impact on the client's real-life difficulties. This risk can be minimized if therapist and client focus on specific problem situations rather than discussing issues in general terms and use the detailed information that they obtain to develop an understanding of the client's problems. Consider the following case example:

> "Fred" is a 46-year-old married man with three daughters in high school. He had been a successful salesman until he was laid off during a recession. At first he was optimistic about finding a new job but became frustrated when he found that job hunting was more difficult than he anticipated. He became quite self-critical and began to view himself as a failure. He then became depressed and anxious, and began having a serious problem with procrastination about job hunting. At the time of his initial

visit with me he was quite depressed, complained of low self-esteem, and manifested a very negative view of himself, saying "I'm not good enough," "I've never really been successful," "Nothing ever works out for me," "I'll never get anywhere," and "I'll fail."

How can the therapist develop an understanding of Fred's low self-esteem and promote adaptive self-enhancement? For example, rather than responding to the client's complaint "I just feel so lousy about myself all the time" with a nondirective prompt such as "Tell me more," the therapist can encourage the client to focus on a specific, concrete example of a time this problem occurred.

> *Fred:*   I just feel so lousy about myself all the time.
>
> *Therapist:*   That sounds really important for us to focus on. Can you think of a good example of a recent time when you felt really lousy about yourself?
>
> *Fred:*   I feel that way all the time.
>
> *Therapist:*   I understand that you feel that way a lot, but it will be easier for us to get a handle on it if we take a look at a couple of concrete examples one at a time. Can you think of a time when feeling lousy about yourself was a problem?
>
> *Fred:*   Well, I guess yesterday when I was looking through the mail would be a good example. I was feeling really bad.
>
> *Therapist:*   Great. Fill me in on the details. What led up to the time when you remember feeling so lousy about yourself? . . .

When therapist and client focus on specific situations in which the client's problems are manifested, it is easier to obtain detailed information (see Exhibit 12.1). As a consequence, it is easier for therapist and client to develop a clear understanding of the client's problems and identify promising interventions.

Fennell (see Fennell & Jenkins, 2004) has proposed a cognitive–behavioral understanding of low self-esteem that provides the foundation for the model shown graphically in Figure 12.1. In this model, early experiences lead the growing child to develop negative core beliefs such as "I'm not good enough," "I'm inadequate," "I'm unlovable," and so on. In addition, the child develops specific dysfunctional beliefs that may include rules for living (e.g., "Don't try anything you're not good at"), standards for judging one's worth (e.g., "If I make a mistake that shows I'm a failure"), and interpersonal strategies (e.g., "Don't ask for help or they'll know I'm inadequate"). These beliefs and assumptions may lie dormant for extended periods if the individual is confident that his or her performance is adequate. However, when a critical incident occurs in which the individual fails or fears that he or she will fail, these beliefs and assumptions are activated. This activation results in

EXHIBIT 12.1
Guidelines for Developing an Understanding of Self-Esteem Problems

1. Ask about specific incidents one at a time rather than talking in general terms.
2. Treat your preconceptions, intuitions, and hunches as hypotheses to be tested; don't assume that they are true.
3. Ask for specific information about specific events, then look for general patterns. Don't start off with generalities. Find out about any events that triggered low self-esteem, the thoughts that coincided with low self-esteem, and the individual's response to the situation:
   a) Precipitants
      "What led up to the situation?"
      "When did you start feeling really lousy about yourself? What was going on right before that?"
   b) Thoughts that coincide with low self-esteem.
      "What was your immediate reaction when [the precipitating event] happened?"
      "What thoughts ran through your head?"
      "Were there any other thoughts?"
   c) Responses
      "What did you do then?"
      "Would you have done anything differently if you hadn't felt so lousy about yourself?"
4. Also find out if there are similar situations in which low self-esteem is not a problem. If so, find out what is different about those situations.

anticipations regarding the responses of significant others, in anxiety, and in maladaptive behavior. If the individual's behavior elicits responses from others that seem to confirm the dysfunctional beliefs, these responses reinforce the beliefs and can result in self-criticism and depression that further contribute to the problem. This model can provide a useful starting place when developing an individualized conceptualization.

When interventions are selected and implemented on the basis of the therapist's conceptualization, therapy becomes a self-correcting process. If the interventions work as expected, the therapist has evidence that the conceptualization possesses sufficient validity to provide a basis for effective intervention. If the interventions are ineffective or produce unexpected results, the therapist has an indication that the conceptualization needs further refinement (or a complete revision).

OPTIONS FOR PROMOTING SELF-ENHANCEMENT IN PSYCHOTHERAPY

Many of the interventions used in contemporary psychotherapy can be used to enhance self-esteem to some extent. However, a number of interventions appear to be particularly promising. These interventions are all "general purpose" interventions that can be used for purposes other than self-

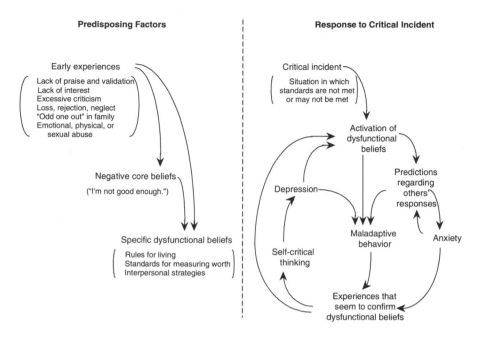

Predisposing Factors | Response to Critical Incident

Early experiences
- Lack of praise and validation
- Lack of interest
- Excessive criticism
- Loss, rejection, neglect
- "Odd one out" in family
- Emotional, physical, or sexual abuse

Negative core beliefs
("I'm not good enough.")

Specific dysfunctional beliefs
- Rules for living
- Standards for measuring worth
- Interpersonal strategies

Critical incident
- Situation in which standards are not met or may not be met

Activation of dysfunctional beliefs

Depression

Predictions regarding others' responses

Self-critical thinking

Maladaptive behavior

Anxiety

Experiences that seem to confirm dysfunctional beliefs

Figure 12.1. A cognitive–behavioral model of low self-esteem. From "Low Self-Esteem" by M. Fennell and H. Jenkins in *Oxford Guide to Behavioural Experiments in Cognitive Therapy* (pp. 414–430), edited by J. Bennett-Levy, G. Butler, M. Fennell, A. Hackman, M. Mueller, and D. Westbrook, 2004, New York: Oxford University Press. Copyright 2004 by Oxford University Press. Adapted with permission.

enhancement; however, they appear to be particularly useful for promoting adaptive self-enhancement.

Nonspecific Aspects of Psychotherapy That May Promote Self-Enhancement

A number of studies on the importance of the therapeutic relationship in behavior therapy have found that the personal relationship between therapist and client contributes significantly to treatment outcome. Posttreatment ratings provide evidence of the importance of the therapist's understanding, interest, respect, sympathy, and encouragement (Matthews et al., 1976; Rabavilas, Boulougouris, & Perisaki, 1979). These findings are quite compatible with the more traditional view that the therapist's empathy and warmth are essential in fostering self-acceptance. Although the importance of the therapeutic relationship can be understood in many different ways (see Safran & Segal, 1990), it seems clear that the therapeutic relationship itself can have important beneficial effects.

If a good therapeutic relationship were enough to effectively promote adaptive self-enhancement, the remainder of this chapter would be unnecessary. However, many authors (e.g., Beck, Rush, Shaw, & Emery, 1979) have argued that a good therapeutic relationship is necessary, but not sufficient, for therapeutic change. For example, Fred responded well to warmth, understanding, and empathy but his low self-esteem and constant self-criticism persisted despite a good therapeutic relationship.

Addressing Negative Thoughts

It can be argued that low self-esteem is the product of negative self-evaluation. In Fred's case, thoughts such as "I'm not good enough," "I've never really been successful," "Nothing ever works out for me," "I'll never get anywhere," and "I'll fail" played a major role both in his low self-esteem and in his depression. One option for addressing such thoughts is for the therapist to work to identify the specific thoughts occurring in problem situations and then help the client to come up with more adaptive alternatives (A. T. Beck, Rush, Shaw, & Emery, 1979; J. S. Beck, 1995; Freeman, Pretzer, Fleming, & Simon, 2004; Greenberger & Padesky, 1995).

Table 12.1 presents the results of a therapy session in which Fred and the therapist focused on addressing the negative thoughts he had experienced in two different situations. At the end of the previous therapy session, the therapist had asked Fred to take notes on problem situations using a simple thought record that provided columns for recording the situation, emotions, and spontaneous thoughts. When Fred returned with a completed thought record, the therapist helped Fred look critically at his spontaneous thoughts, to consider whether the thoughts were consistent with the available evidence, to recognize thoughts that were unrealistically negative, and to identify adaptive alternatives to unrealistic thoughts.

After devoting most of a therapy session to developing the responses shown in Table 12.1, Fred reported feeling significantly less anxious and hopeless. The therapist then introduced the idea that, with practice, Fred could become more skilled at spotting dysfunctional thoughts as they occurred and generating adaptive responses on his own. The therapist was careful to make it clear that this process is complex and that practice is required for one to become skilled at it. Otherwise, Fred might have criticized himself for not immediately mastering this complex task.

Another option for dealing with negative thoughts is for the therapist to help the client devise behavioral experiments in which the client tests the validity of the thoughts in real-life situations. For example, when Fred was faced with simple, day-to-day tasks he frequently found himself thinking "I'll fail" and subsequently avoided the task as much as possible. One option is to frame "I'll fail" as a prediction that might or might not be true, choose a specific task to use in testing this prediction, clarify the criteria for success or failure, and plan how Fred can test the prediction. In addition to providing a simple method for testing the validity of the thought, this approach creates a no-lose situation. If Fred attempts a task to test the thought "I'll fail" and performs it successfully, he has succeeded in demonstrating that the thought is not valid. If he is unable to perform the task, he has succeeded in discovering that the thought is valid. Neither outcome is a failure. See Fennell and Jenkins (2004) for examples of using behavioral experiments to increase self-esteem.

Encouraging Positive Self-Evaluation

Early cognitive–behavioral approaches conceptualized low self-esteem in terms of negative self-evaluations and tended to presume that one simply needs to eliminate negative thoughts to increase self-esteem. However, it has been argued more recently that the ratio of negative self-evaluations to positive self-evaluations may be more important than the absolute number of negative self-evaluations (see Schwartz, 1986). One can change this ratio by decreasing the frequency of negative self-evaluations or by increasing the frequency of positive self-evaluations.

The therapist can encourage positive self-evaluations by asking questions that focus the client's attention on opportunities for legitimate positive self-evaluation and guiding the client toward more positive evaluations:

Fred: (after describing the results of a week's work on job hunting): Breaking it down into more manageable steps helped, but I didn't accomplish nearly as much as I hoped.

Therapist: My bet is that you'd normally give yourself a hard time about not accomplishing as much as you expected.

Fred: Yeah.

Therapist: And how would that leave you feeling?

Fred: Like a failure.

Therapist: And once you're feeling like a failure, what effect does that have?

Fred: I get really discouraged and don't get much done.

Therapist: Now, if it's really true that you're a failure, we'll have to figure out how to deal with that. But first, let's take a look at whether accomplishing less than you expected means you're a failure. . . . As you remember it, what was the point to trying out the idea of breaking your job hunting into more manageable steps?

Fred: To make it easier and get more done.

Therapist: And, if I remember right, to test whether breaking it into manageable steps helped or not.

Fred: Yeah, that too.

Therapist: How did it turn out?

TABLE 12.1
Fred's Initial Thought Record

Situation	Moods	Automatic thoughts (images)	Evidence that supports the hot thought	Evidence that does not support the hot thought	Alternative/ balanced thoughts	Rate moods now
Looking at bills, insurance bill in particular.	Anxious; scared. (70%)	I don't know enough and am not good enough to get a job and make enough money to pay my bills. (80%)	I got fired.	Phil says I probably know enough. I didn't get laid off because of lack of knowledge; it was because of the company's problems. A big company could provide some training. I could work my way up. If I keep interviewing, I'll find out whether I know enough at this level. Phil was willing to offer me a position. (100%)	It's not easy but I probably can get another job and do well at it if I try. (90%)	Anxious. (50%) Hopeless. (30%)
Sitting down at table (with want ads and bills on it) to look for job or take follow-up steps on ads in paper.	Anxious; about to cry; hopeless. (80%)	You'll never get anywhere. (100%)				

208   JAMES L. PRETZER

Who were you with? What were you doing? When was it? Where were you?	Describe each mood in one word. Rate intensity of mood. (0–100%)	What was going through my mind just before I started to feel this way? What does this say about me? What does this mean about me? My life? My future? What am I afraid might happen? What is the worst thing that could happen if this is true? What does this mean about how the other person(s) feel(s)/ think(s) about me? What does this mean about the other person(s) or people in general? What images or memories do I have in this situation?	Circle hot thought in previous column for which you are looking for evidence. Write factual evidence to support this conclusion. (Try to avoid mind reading and interpretation of facts.)	Ask yourself the questions in the hint box (p. 70 of Mind Over Mood) to help discover evidence that does not support your hot thought.	(a) Write an alternative or balance thought. (b) Rate how much you believe in each alternative or balanced thought. (0–100%)	Rerate moods listed in Column 2 as well as new moods. (0–100%)

Fred:	I got some job hunting done, but I could have done a lot more.
Therapist:	Let's take it one step at a time. . . . When you tried to break job hunting into smaller steps, did it make it easier?
Fred:	Yeah. It wasn't always easy to do, but when I managed to take it one step at a time it wasn't nearly as overwhelming.
Therapist:	Now, you were saying that you could have gotten more done this week, but you also said that you found several promising ads and responded to them. How does that compare with the amount you got done the week before?
Fred:	That's a lot more than I got done last week.
Therapist:	So it wasn't easy but you tested whether breaking job hunting down into smaller steps was a good idea, discovered that it was, and accomplished more this week than you did last week. How does that sound to you?
Fred:	When you put it that way, it sounds pretty good.
Therapist:	If you had a friend who was job hunting and he told you that he could have accomplished more but he'd tried out some advice he'd been given even though it was hard, learned that it was a good idea, and got more job hunting done than during the previous week, what would you say to him? Would you tell him that he's a miserable failure because he could have done more or would you tell him that he's doing well and encourage him to keep it up?

Clients can also be asked to actively watch for legitimate opportunities to give themselves a pat on the back or can be asked to keep a running list of accomplishments, steps in the right direction, and good tries. Clients often are less harsh in evaluating others' performance than they are in evaluating themselves. When this is the case, it can be useful to prompt them to consider evaluating themselves in the same way as they evaluate others.

In working to increase the frequency of positive self-evaluations, the therapist has a choice regarding whether to focus on self-evaluations regarding performance in specific situations ("I did well in that interview") or on more global self-evaluations ("I'm a success"). The therapist has a similar choice between working toward realistic positive self-evaluations ("I'm doing better at getting myself to follow through on job hunting") and between working toward more extremely positive ones ("I'm the greatest"). Focusing on performance in specific situations and working toward realistic positive self-evaluations will likely have significant practical advantages.

If the client is reluctant to endorse positive self-evaluations, it can be important to identify his or her fears and beliefs about the consequences of doing so. It is not unusual to encounter clients who believe that positive self-evaluations are egotistical and will alienate others, that positive self-evaluations will provoke criticism from others, or that positive self-evaluations will increase the risk of failure. Concerns of this sort can often be addressed by examining the client's grounds (if any) for believing this, drawing a distinction between positive self-evaluation and boasting or overconfidence, identifying experiences that are not consistent with the client's fears, and then experimenting with positive self-evaluation and observing the actual results.

Modifying Dysfunctional Beliefs About the Self

One alternative to conceptualizing self-esteem simply in terms of an ongoing stream of positive and negative self-evaluations is to see it as the product of generalized beliefs about the self. For example, at the time he sought treatment, Fred's primary view of himself was "I'm a failure." It has been argued that humans experience what has been termed the *confirmatory bias*. Once a belief has been acquired, people tend to selectively attend to experiences that confirm that belief and to overlook or discount experiences that would disconfirm that belief (Mahoney & DeMonbreun, 1977). Fred's belief that "I'm a failure" shaped his perception of events so that he automatically focused on experiences consistent with his view of himself as a failure and tended to discount observations that should have contradicted this belief. In such cases, interventions that simply address specific self-evaluations are likely to prove insufficient. It can be important to modify any dysfunctional beliefs about the self that are present.

The first step in effectively modifying dysfunctional beliefs is to get them explicitly stated in the client's own words. With Fred, this step was fairly simple because he directly stated his conviction "I'm a failure" quite frequently. Often, the client's dysfunctional beliefs are implicit rather than explicitly stated and considerable work on the part of therapist and client is needed to identify them and get them stated explicitly. See J. S. Beck (1995), Freeman et al. (2004), or Greenberger and Padesky (1995) for discussions of methods for identifying dysfunctional beliefs and getting them stated explicitly.

Once dysfunctional beliefs have been stated explicitly, they can be addressed in much the same way as dysfunctional thoughts are addressed. A typical method involves looking critically at the belief, developing more adaptive alternatives, and testing both the old belief and the alternative view(s) against the available evidence (see J. S. Beck, 1995; Freeman et al., 2004; or Greenberger & Padesky, 1995). It is important to note that if the therapist relies solely on verbal interventions, intellectual insight that is not accompanied by substantial change in emotions and behavior is likely to result. It is important for verbal interventions to be accompanied by interventions that identify concrete, real-life evidence that contradicts the dysfunctional belief and supports the adaptive alternative.

In Fred's case, interventions that challenged his view of himself as a failure (such as the thought record shown in Figure 12.2) were accompanied by persistent attention to evidence that contradicted his view of himself as a failure, assignments in which challenging tasks were broken down into manageable steps, and experiments in which he chose to perform tasks less than perfectly and observed the results. Although he found the verbal interventions to be quite useful, his experience of attempting challenging tasks and succeeding despite imperfect performance had even more impact. A number of structured formats for effectively testing dysfunctional beliefs against experience have been developed (e.g., J. S. Beck, 1995, pp. 176–182; Greenberger & Padesky, 1995, pp. 143–144).

A particularly useful approach is for therapist and client to work together to find ways to directly test dysfunctional beliefs in real-life situations. For example,

Therapist: (recapping) So it sounds as though the basic idea is "I'm a failure" and that belief has a big impact. . . . What do you think of that idea? Do you think it's true?

Fred: Well, it sure feels like it.

Therapist: And it sounds like you've been feeling that way a lot. . . . Suppose it were true that someone was a failure; how would that show in real life? What would we see that would show that they were a failure?

Fred: They'd fail at whatever they try.

Therapist: At *everything* they try?

Fred: Yeah, a failure fails at whatever they try.

Therapist: So if you're a failure, we'd expect it to be that you fail at whatever you try? How does that fit with your track record?

Fred: I've certainly been failing at everything lately. I can't even get a job letter written.

Therapist: Has it been that you try writing the letter and fail at it or that you expect to fail and therefore can't get yourself to give it a try?

Fred: I guess it's really that I'm so sure I'll fail that I don't really try.

Therapist: So it sounds as though your problems getting things done don't really tell us whether you're a failure or not. They tell us that if you expect to fail at something, it's hard for you to get yourself to try.

Fred: Yeah.

Therapist: So how could we test out whether you're a failure or not?

Fred:	I guess I could actually write a job letter and see how it turns out.
Therapist:	And if you're a failure, how would it turn out?
Fred:	I wouldn't be able to write a job letter even if I try.
Therapist:	Suppose you're not a failure. How would it turn out then?
Fred:	I'd be able to write the letter.
Therapist:	Now, is a person who's not a failure going to succeed at everything they try?
Fred:	No, nobody succeeds at everything they try.
Therapist:	So, even if you're not a failure, you'll fail at some of the things you try.
Fred:	Yeah, I guess so.
Therapist:	I like the idea of testing out whether you're a total failure or not. Let's work out the details of when and how you'll test it out. . . .

When Fred returned for the next session he had discovered that when he made an attempt, despite his anticipation of failure, he often was successful. This observation contracted his belief "I'm a failure" and supported his alternative view "It's hard for me to get myself to do things when I'm depressed, but when I try, I often do OK."

ADDRESSING ISSUES THAT INTERFERE
WITH SELF-ENHANCEMENT

It might seem that interventions that decrease negative self-evaluations, that increase positive self-evaluations, and that modify the individual's negative beliefs about himself or herself would be sufficient to produce adaptive self-enhancement. However, a number of issues commonly undercut attempts to boost self-esteem. It can be important for the therapist to address these issues as well.

Decreasing Self-Criticism

In Fred's case, constant self-criticism undercut his self-esteem. Although Fred could have tried to develop adaptive responses to each self-critical thought, the sheer volume of self-criticism would have made this difficult. Interventions that decrease the flow of self-critical thoughts should help increase self-esteem.

Examining the Pros and Cons of Self-Criticism

Often it is useful to start by explicitly examining the pros and cons of self-criticism. Clients initially may not recognize the drawbacks of constant self-criticism or may overestimate the benefits of self-criticism. In Fred's case, his long-standing tendency to set high standards for himself and push hard to achieve them had resulted in a high level of academic achievement and job performance. Unfortunately, it also resulted in his setting unrealistically high standards for himself, being chronically dissatisfied with performance that actually was quite good, seeing himself as a failure despite above-average performance, and being prone to depression whenever he encountered job difficulties.

Once the pros and cons of self-criticism were examined, it became clear to Fred that the drawbacks of his self-criticism greatly outweighed the benefits. Of course, this realization did not make his self-criticism spontaneously cease. However, until Fred realized the drawbacks of his self-criticism, he was not motivated to work on reducing it. Indeed, he saw his high standards for himself as one of his good points.

Addressing Fears About the Consequences of Relaxing Self-Criticism

Clients may have strong fears about the consequences of being less self-critical. For example, at this point in therapy Fred began having a recurrent nightmare of ending up as a vagrant living on the street. Upon exploration, he and his therapist discovered that Fred feared that he would become a total failure if he relaxed his standards at all.

Once Fred's fears regarding the effects of relaxing his self-criticism were clear, it was possible to help him reevaluate those fears. For example, Fred and his therapist explored whether it is true that all those who are not constantly self-critical become total failures, examined the likely consequences of a less self-critical approach to life, and considered the effects of trying a less self-critical approach in real-life situations.

Identifying Adaptive Alternatives to Constant Self-Criticism

Many individuals who have learned to use self-criticism as a strategy for improving performance or avoiding mistakes have little idea of what alternative strategies they might consider. Adaptive alternatives can be identified in a variety of ways. Therapist and client can jointly brainstorm alternatives, the therapist can ask the client to think of examples of people they know who do well without constant self-criticism, or the therapist can propose an alternative strategy. Some possible alternatives include moderating the amount of self-criticism, using self-criticism selectively, balancing attention to one's flaws and shortcomings with an equal amount of attention to one's strengths and accomplishments, or asking "Am I accomplishing what I need to?" rather than "Am I screwing up?" Fred decided to try moderating his self-criticism and paying more attention to his strengths and accomplishments.

Putting Adaptive Alternatives Into Practice

Verbal discussion alone usually is not sufficient to reduce the amount of self-criticism. It can be important to explicitly plan how the client can put adaptive alternatives into practice and to test them in real-life situations. Behavioral experiments can be a particularly useful way of doing this (see J. S. Beck, 1995; Fennell & Jenkins, 2004; Greenberger & Padesky, 1995). Fred initially was quite hesitant about trying a less self-critical approach. However, when he eventually did try it on small, unimportant tasks he discovered that he did at least as well while experiencing less stress and frustration. He then was willing to gradually adopt a less critical approach in a broad range of situations.

Addressing Dysfunctional Interactions With Significant Others

If an individual regularly faces significant others who are harshly critical, who are demeaning, or who are protective and helpful in a way that implies that the client is incompetent, this situation can contribute substantially to low self-esteem and can undermine the therapist's attempts to promote adaptive self-enhancement. The therapist then is faced with a choice between working to modify dysfunctional interactions or working to help the individual to cope effectively with the dysfunctional relationship. When it is possible either to modify dysfunctional interaction patterns or to help the client extricate him- or herself from a dysfunctional relationship, this approach usually is preferable. When a client seeks help in tolerating relationships that undercut his or her self-esteem, the therapist should explore the client's reasons for wanting to cope with the relationship rather than working to improve the relationship or leaving the relationship. Individuals with low self-esteem may believe that they must tolerate dysfunctional or abusive relationships, thinking, "I don't deserve a good relationship," "This is the best I can do," or "I don't dare leave. I can't make it without him." A realistic look at the pros and cons of tolerating the relationship as it is, working to improve the relationship, or leaving the relationship can help the client make a good choice regarding this important decision.

When there are good reasons for the client to focus on maintaining self-esteem in the face of a dysfunctional relationship, a number of interventions can be useful. Often, the negative evaluations expressed by others contribute to low self-esteem. In this case, it can be useful to help the client to look critically at the other person's opinions and to draw a distinction between that individual's opinions and his or her own opinions. For example,

> Magdalena was a divorced mother of two who was temporarily living with her mother. According to Magdalena's report, her mother had al-

ways been harsh, critical, and demanding. When Magdalena, as a child, had spilled her milk or made a mistake, her mother often had responded by screaming that Magdalena was "an embarrassment" and by declaring that the mistake showed how much of a failure Magdalena was. Now that Magdalena was an adult, her mother responded in very much the same way whenever Magdalena disagreed with her.

At first, Magdalena talked as though her mother's criticisms were valid. The therapist focused on helping her look critically at her mother's views ("So it sounds as though your mother's opinion is that only a neglectful mother would let her daughter go to school dressed like that. What do *you* think? Is there something inappropriate about letting your daughter wear blue jeans and a T-shirt to school? How do the other children dress?").

Once Magdalena was able distinguish her own views from her mother's, she had a choice regarding whether to openly disagree with her mother, to comply with her mother's demands, or to quietly do what she believed was best without openly disagreeing. She also found it useful to limit the amount of time she spent with her mother, to be selective about which topics she discussed with her mother, to spend time with supportive friends, and to move out as soon as she could afford to do so.

It can be quite useful to instruct the client to watch for times when the other individual criticizes him or her but the client does not agree. In this case, the client's task is to rate the validity of the other person's opinion on a 0 to 10 scale and to rate the validity of his or her own opinion on the same scale (without overtly questioning the validity of the criticism or expressing his or her own disagreement). The expectation is that, with the therapist's help, the client will discover that the other individual's criticisms are not always completely valid and that the client's own opinions often are quite valid.

If an individual's low self-esteem results in his or her interacting with others in ways that elicit criticism, disrespect, or overprotection, and these responses further diminish the individual's self-esteem, the results can be particularly problematic. Once established, this type of self-reinforcing interaction between the individual's cognitions, his or her interpersonal behavior, and the responses of significant others can be quite persistent. Strategies for intervening in these complex situations are beyond the scope of this chapter. Interested readers may find that Fleming's discussion of the treatment of dependent personality disorder (Freeman et al., 2004) presents a promising approach to intervening in this complex situation.

Modifying Factors That Indirectly Reduce Self-Esteem and Self-Acceptance

For some individuals, factors such as depression, perfectionism, or pessimism have a major impact on self-esteem and self-acceptance. When this is the case, effective treatment can result in adaptive self-enhancement even though the interventions used are not necessarily intended to directly promote self-enhancement.

Depression

A negative view of oneself, of one's day-to-day experience, and of the future is a hallmark of depression (A. T. Beck et al., 1979), and it is interesting to note that whether depression is treated through psychotherapy or pharmacotherapy or remits spontaneously, the individual's negative thinking tends to improve as his or her level of depression decreases (see Ingram, Miranda, & Segal, 1998). This observation suggests that when low self-esteem, pessimism, and a globally negative view of experience are manifestations of a clinical depression, treatment for depression may be the most appropriate way to increase self-esteem.

Many different options are available for treating depression. These include a variety of antidepressant medications, several empirically supported psychotherapy approaches, and medical procedures such as electroconvulsive therapy. At this point, none of the empirically supported treatments for depression has been found to be consistently superior to the other empirically supported treatments. However, it is important to note that generic psychotherapy isn't necessarily effective as a treatment for depression. In fact, when an individual with depression is simply encouraged to express his or her feelings while the therapist listens sympathetically, the client may experience little relief or may actually become more depressed.

Perfectionism

Some individuals believe that it is necessary for them to strive to perform tasks perfectly. Such individuals typically set high standards and react with harsh criticism when those standards are not met. As a result, they often fall short of their standards for themselves, criticize themselves harshly, and have low self-esteem in response to perceived failures.

Many individuals enter treatment seeing their perfectionism as one of their good points, not as a problem to work on. Therefore, it is important to begin treatment by explicitly examining the pros and cons of perfectionism. It usually is easy to demonstrate that perfectionism has major drawbacks and that there would be substantial advantages to adopting more moderate standards. It might seem that individuals would be motivated to relinquish their perfectionism once the drawbacks are clear. However, individuals often harbor extreme fears regarding the consequences of becoming less perfectionistic. For example, Fred believed "If I ever relax my standards for myself, I will become a complete failure." It can be important to identify these fears and address them explicitly. It then is possible for therapist and client to explore alternatives to perfectionism and experiment with putting these alternatives into practice in real-life situations. One useful way to reduce the client's fears regarding the consequences of doing things imperfectly is to have him or her experiment with intentionally making small mistakes and observing the actual consequences.

Pessimism

When an individual applies a pessimistic outlook to his or her own efforts, the individual's self-esteem can be significantly affected. For example, if an individual is pessimistic about the likelihood of succeeding at an endeavor, he or she may be less likely to attempt it. If the individual does not make an attempt, he or she will not have a chance to succeed at it and will not have that success and the resulting feedback as a basis for self-esteem. For detailed discussions of methods for reducing pessimism, see Pretzer and Walsh (2001) and Gillham, Reivich, and Shatté (2001).

ADDITIONAL OPTIONS FOR DIRECTLY PROMOTING SELF-ENHANCEMENT

A number of additional interventions can be useful in increasing self-esteem. Although these interventions can be implemented independently of the interventions discussed thus far, my experience has been that they often are most effective if used in conjunction with interventions that directly challenge negative self-evaluations, encourage more positive self-evaluations, decrease self-criticism, and modify dysfunctional interpersonal interactions.

Increasing Positive Feedback

Realistic positive feedback from others can be quite useful in promoting self-enhancement. One option is for the therapist to make a point of providing the client with positive feedback regarding accomplishments, progress, steps in the right direction, and so on. However, it can be important for the therapist to be judicious in directly providing positive feedback. If there is too large a discrepancy between the therapist's feedback and the client's self-perception, the client may reject or discount the therapist's feedback ("You're just saying that to make me feel better").

Honest positive feedback from significant others can be particularly effective. If the client avoids situations in which feedback from others is likely or discounts positive feedback when it is given, the therapist can encourage the client to risk facing feedback from others, help him or her plan ways of doing this, and help him or her accept positive feedback when it is received. Of course, if some of the client's significant others tend to be harshly critical or to have a globally negative outlook, they may not be promising as sources of positive feedback. Marital, family, or group therapy often provides the therapist with valuable opportunities to encourage greater expression of positive feedback and honest appreciation.

Increasing Involvement in Activities That Raise Self-Esteem

Often, clients report that certain activities, such as spending time with supportive friends or performing tasks they are skilled at, increase their self-esteem. Simply increasing the amount of time spent in activities that raise self-esteem can be quite useful. The therapist may need to help the client find time for such activities or may need to address cognitions that discourage him or her from doing so. If the idea that spending time engaged with friends or hobbies is a waste of time interferes with attempts to increase involvement in these activities, a discussion of the tangible benefits of doing so often makes it clear that such time is not wasted.

Engineering Success Experiences

Individuals with low self-esteem may be reluctant to face challenges or try new activities for fear that they won't do well enough. Individuals who do this usually intend to minimize the risk of failure. They may unintentionally also limit their opportunities for success and positive evaluation. It can be useful to address this issue by helping clients to face challenges in ways that are not too scary and that are likely to result in success. It is important to be realistic about the client's abilities, to help them choose activities for which positive experiences are likely, and to help them use appropriate standards for self-evaluation. It is possible to set up many situations as "no lose" by framing them as an experiment in which the goal is to find out if the activity is something that the client enjoys and can master with practice. This way, if the client tries the activity and finds that he or she enjoys it and is getting better at it, the client has succeeded in discovering that the activity is a good match for him or her. However, if the client tries the activity and discovers that he or she does not enjoy it or has difficulty mastering it, the client has succeeded in discovering that the activity is not a good match for him or her. The focus is on evaluating the activity, not on evaluating the client.

Fixed Role Therapy

This intervention, initially developed as part of personal construct theory (Kelly, 1955), involves the therapist helping the client spell out the ways in which higher self-esteem would change the client's behavior and then introducing the idea of the client's experimenting with intentionally acting as though he or she had higher self-esteem. For example,

> LaShanna was a college student whose primary complaint was low self-esteem. The initial six sessions of therapy had focused on establishing a warm, accepting therapeutic relationship; identifying and addressing specific cognitions that reduced her self-esteem; reevaluating her standards for self-evaluation; and encouraging positive self-evaluation. LaShanna's

response to these interventions was "I believe all this in my head, but I don't feel it in my heart." Her therapist then applied fixed role therapy in the following way:

Therapist: Let's try approaching it a little differently. . . . Suppose, poof! you suddenly had plenty of self-esteem. In your head and your heart you knew that you were an OK person. . . . What difference would it make? How would you do things differently? How would you say things differently?

LaShanna: Umm. . . . I guess I'd speak up more in class. I don't usually raise my hand when I have a question because I don't want to bother anybody.

Therapist: (writing the client's answer down) Great. You'd raise your hand and ask when you had a question in class. What else would be different if you knew you were OK? Would this apply to expressing opinions in class too?

LaShanna: Yeah. I never speak up in class discussions. It wouldn't just be in class either. I never stay to talk to the prof after class or go to office hours even when I have something I'd really like to talk about.

Therapist: (writing these down as well) So, speak up in class discussions, stay after class to talk with the prof, go by office hours to talk to the prof. . . . Would anything be different outside of class?

LaShanna: I guess I'd speak up more there too. A group of us ordered a pizza last night and I didn't say anything when they ordered sausage and mushrooms even though that doesn't agree with me. . . . I had gas all night.

Therapist: What would you say in a situation like that if you knew you were OK?

LaShanna: I'd say, "Guys, could we get half pepperoni? Sausage gives me gas."

Therapist: How do you think that would go?

LaShanna: It would be fine. They're real nice.

Therapist: So let me recap. If you knew in your head and in your heart that you were OK, you'd raise your hand in class when you had a question, you'd speak up in discussions and express your opinion, you'd stay after class or go by office hours to talk to the prof, and you'd speak up for what you wanted with your friends. . . . Is that it?

LaShanna: Yeah, I would.

Therapist:	What would you think of a little experiment? Suppose, even though you don't feel OK, you were to intentionally act the way you would if you knew you were OK. Raising your hand in class, speaking up for the kind of pizza you like, and so on. . . . What do you think that would be like?
LaShanna:	It would be a little scary.
Therapist:	Sure it would. This is something you don't normally do. How do you think people would react?
LaShanna:	It would be fine. My profs like it when people ask questions or stay after to talk and my friends are real nice.
Therapist:	The idea is that one way to get feelings to change is to try acting the way you would if you felt different. It gives you a chance to try it on for size, to see how you feel about it, and to see how people react.
LaShanna:	OK.
Therapist:	Here's the list I wrote down of the things you'd do differently. . . . Is there anything else we should add?

At her next session, LaShanna reported that she'd tried speaking up in class and with friends on several different occasions. Her professors had reacted as though it was fine for her to speak up in class, and she had gotten useful information by asking questions. With friends, she hadn't always gotten what she asked for, but her requests had been taken seriously and, if anything, it seemed like her friends were more considerate than usual. LaShanna had been nervous at first, but when people reacted as though it was OK for her to speak up, she became more comfortable. In discussing this experience she said, "I guess maybe I'm OK after all."

This technique does not presume that acting as though one has high self-esteem will miraculously bring it forth. Rather, fixed role therapy can provide a promising way for the client to experiment with an unfamiliar social role, to test the effects of interacting with others in a more confident way, to face his or her own fears, and to obtain feedback from others.

ALTERNATIVES TO PROMOTING SELF-ENHANCEMENT

Working to directly promote self-enhancement is one option, but other interventions are worth considering as well. One alternative is to work toward self-acceptance. Adopting a view such as "I've got strengths and weaknesses but all-in-all, I'm OK" could be a promising alternative to constant self-evaluation. A growing body of theorists and innovators has been emphasizing the importance of acceptance in psychotherapy (see Hayes, Jacobson,

Follette, & Dougher, 1993, for a variety of perspectives on the role of acceptance in psychotherapy). Although self-acceptance is conceptually quite different from self-enhancement, proponents of acceptance-based approaches in psychotherapy argue that self-acceptance has significant advantages over self-evaluation.

Another alternative to self-enhancement is a modification of the "feel the fear and do it anyway" approach that is used with anxiety problems. If an individual who feels inadequate chooses to go ahead and face challenges in manageable steps anyway, the benefits are often substantial. Individuals are often surprised to discover that they are more adequate than they expected, that they become more adequate with practice, and that others can accept them despite their shortcomings.

Finally, some individuals have low self-esteem because of repeated negative experiences in interpersonal relationships. When these negative experiences are due to poor social skills, working to improve social skills and social problem-solving skills can be quite useful. Increased success in interpersonal interactions can have a substantial impact on the individual's self-esteem. However, it can take some delicacy to implement these interventions so that the individual concludes "If I do better at relating to people, they get to know me and accept me" rather than "If I try hard enough, I can get people to accept me." The latter conclusion risks the individual feeling that he or she must constantly strive for acceptance.

CONCLUSIONS

Although the idea of promoting self-enhancement through psychotherapy is an important topic, clinicians do not yet have a sound base of empirical research to guide them in deciding whether to work toward self-enhancement or in choosing methods for doing so. Although additional research is needed, practitioners face those decisions today and cannot wait for the research to be done. My recommendations are as follows:

- If the client is depressed, is abusing substances, or is involved in dysfunctional relationships, address those problems first. Once those problems have been resolved, additional work on self-enhancement may not be needed.
- Establish a therapeutic relationship characterized by empathy, warmth, understanding, interest, respect, sympathy, and encouragement. Communicate acceptance both verbally and nonverbally.
- Focus on specific situations in which low self-esteem is a problem rather than talking about self-esteem in general terms.
- Identify and address unrealistic cognitions that suppress self-esteem and self-acceptance.

- Increase realistic positive feedback from self, from the therapist, and from significant others if possible.
- Identify and modify any beliefs that block self-enhancement.
- Put new beliefs compatible with self-enhancement into practice in real-life situations. You can use techniques such as behavioral experiments, fixed role therapy, and so on.

Although the available research on the outcome of attempts to promote self-enhancement and the lack of empirically supported methods for promoting self-enhancement through psychotherapy support the need for caution, clinical experience is encouraging. For example, Fred responded to treatment quite quickly. After four 1-hour sessions of treatment, he no longer saw himself as a failure, was able to recognize his strengths as well as his weaknesses, was able to actively pursue job hunting despite his insecurities, and found a new job that he was approaching with a reasonable degree of confidence.

Of course, case examples such as this do not provide evidence that the interventions proposed in this chapter are effective. Fred's response to treatment is not necessarily typical, and it is possible that his improvement was due to factors other than psychotherapy. The interventions presented in this chapter are widely used as components of empirically supported treatments for problems other than low self-esteem. However, until researchers take a more detailed look at these interventions' relevance to promoting self-enhancement, clinicians will need to take an individualized approach to treatment and carefully observe the results of their interventions. By taking a pragmatic approach whereby we as clinicians persist with the interventions that work and learn from the interventions that don't, we can provide effective treatment even though empirically supported treatment protocols are not yet available.

REFERENCES

Baumeister, R. F., Campbell, J. D., Krueger, J. I., & Vohs, K. D. (2003). Does high self-esteem cause better performance, interpersonal success, happiness, or healthier lifestyles? *Psychological Science in the Public Interest, 4*(1), 1–44.

Beck, A. T., Rush, A. J., Shaw, B. F., & Emery, G. (1979). *Cognitive therapy of depression.* New York: Guilford Press.

Beck, J. S. (1995). *Cognitive therapy: Basics and beyond.* New York: Guilford Press.

Fennell, M., & Jenkins, H. (2004). Low self-esteem. In J. Bennett-Levy, G. Butler, M. Fennell, A. Hackman, M. Mueller, & D. Westbrook (Eds.), *Oxford guide to behavioural experiments in cognitive therapy* (pp. 414–430). New York: Oxford University Press.

Freeman, A., Pretzer, J. L., Fleming, B., & Simon, K. M. (2004). *Clinical applications of cognitive therapy* (2nd ed.). New York: Kluwer Academic.

Gillham, J. E., Reivich, K. J., & Shatté, A. J. (2001). Building optimism and preventing depressive symptoms in children. In E. C. Chang (Ed.), *Optimism and pessimism: Implications for theory, research, and practice* (pp. 301–320). Washington, DC: American Psychological Association.

Greenberger, D., & Padesky, C. A. (1995). *Mind over mood.* New York: Guilford Press.

Hayes, S. C., Jacobson, N. S., Follette, V. M., & Dougher, M. J. (Eds.). (1993). *Acceptance and change: Content and context in psychotherapy.* Reno, NV: Context Press.

Ingram, R. E., Miranda, J., & Segal, Z. V. (1998). *Cognitive vulnerability to depression.* New York: Guilford Press.

Kelly, G. A. (1955). *The psychology of personal constructs* (Vols. 1 & 2). New York: Norton.

Mahoney, M. J., & DeMonbreun, B. G. (1977). Psychology of the scientist: An analysis of problem-solving bias. *Cognitive Therapy and Research, 1,* 229–238.

Matthews, A. M., Johnston D. W., Lancashire, M., Munby, M., Shaw P. M., & Gelder, M. G. (1976). Imaginal flooding and exposure to real phobic situations: Treatment outcomes with agoraphobic patients. *British Journal of Psychiatry, 129,* 362–371.

Pretzer, J. L., & Walsh, C. A. (2001). Optimism, pessimism, and psychotherapy: Implications for clinical practice. In E. C. Chang (Ed.), *Optimism and pessimism: Implications for theory, research, and practice* (pp. 321–346). Washington, DC: American Psychological Association.

Rabavilas, A. D., Boulougouris, J. C., & Perisaki, C. (1979). Therapist qualities related to outcome with exposure in-vivo in neurotic patients. *Journal of Behavior Therapy and Experimental Psychiatry, 10,* 293–299.

Safran, J. D., & Segal, Z. V. (1990). *Interpersonal process in cognitive therapy.* New York: Basic Books.

Schwartz, R. M. (1986). The internal dialogue: On the asymmetry between positive and negative coping thoughts. *Cognitive Therapy and Research, 10,* 591–605.

13

ON PROMOTING ADAPTIVE SELF-CRITICISM IN PSYCHOTHERAPY

RAYMOND M. BERGNER

When it comes to criticizing other persons, it seems a widely shared understanding that such criticism should benefit the individual criticized. When the English teacher criticizes the student's essay, the parent appraises the child's action, or the coach evaluates the athlete's technique, the general consensus is that such criticism ought to be constructive. It ought, for example, to inform its recipient that something is wrong, what precisely about it is wrong, and how this something might be changed in the future. It ought, in sum, to be adaptive—to assist the individuals criticized in adjusting their behavior in such a way that they can function more successfully in their worlds. When criticism fails this understood requirement, it is typically regarded as failing its task. We say that it was "unconstructive," "unhelpful," "failed to provide its recipient with any information about how to change," and the like.

When it comes to criticizing themselves, however, countless therapy clients seem to not have this basic understanding regarding the constructive

I wish to thank Laura Nichols for her invaluable assistance in searching the clinical and research literature for this chapter.

functions of criticism. Furthermore, and more important, they fail repeatedly in their self-critical actions to conduct themselves in ways that are self-enhancing or beneficial. Instead, they resort to self-critical practices that are not merely unhelpful but are quite damaging to their behavioral capabilities, self-esteem, emotional well-being, ability to change problematic matters in their lives, and more. In many cases, the extent of this injury is so great that the practices may be considered pathogenic; that is, they engender very significant functional impairments in these persons with respect to their ability to participate well and meaningfully in their worlds. If I may borrow a phrase from Freud, these practices severely damage their ability "to love and to work."

Such destructive, maladaptive, and even pathogenic self-criticism is the subject of this chapter. In it, I (a) describe patterns of such criticism most commonly observed in clinical practice, as well as their consequences; (b) provide a set of therapeutic strategies for helping clients to abandon such patterns in favor of more adaptive alternatives; and (c) relate some therapeutic responses to common resistances that clients present when urged to change their self-critical ways.

COMMON DESTRUCTIVE SELF-CRITICAL PATTERNS

The following are the most common patterns of pathogenic self-criticism that my clinical colleagues and I have observed in our clients.

Pattern #1: Private Self-Degradation Ceremonies

"Shannon," a 20-year-old college student, reported at intake that she continued to experience repercussions from an event that had occurred many years earlier. While in eighth grade at a parochial school, her class had held a graduation party at a state park. During this party, a boy to whom she was strongly attracted asked her to walk with him alone in a wooded area. In the course of this walk, the boy suddenly thrust his hand into her pants and touched her vaginal area. Shocked and confused, Shannon froze. Before she could recover and say or do anything (a period she estimated at perhaps 5 seconds), the boy removed his hand. Nothing further transpired between the two. As a result of this single, brief incident, Shannon branded herself a "slut." She continued to characterize herself with this label throughout her adolescence, despite the fact that she scrupulously avoided all further sexual contact during this period. Furthermore, she believed that everyone in her social circle knew of the incident, regarded her as a slut, and talked about her behind her back. The result of all of this was an extremely lonely and painful adolescence.

Although Shannon's example represents an extreme one, it nonetheless exemplifies a kind of self-criticism observed in many clients. In reaction to perceived transgressions, mistakes, and failures, these individuals brand themselves with disqualifying labels such as "mentally disturbed," "unlovable," "stupid," "insignificant," "bad," and the like. Although others might level similar self-accusations in a moment of pique without really meaning them, these individuals stand fully and deeply behind their indictments. The effects of such critic acts, particularly when persons stamp the same destructive labels on themselves time after time, can be devastating.

A helpful concept for articulating the precise nature and implications of such critic acts is one formulated many years ago by Harold Garfinkel (1957), that of a "degradation ceremony" (see also Bergner, 1999; Ossorio, 1976, 2005). This concept may be explicated by the hypothetical example of a lieutenant in the military who has been found guilty of a grave breach of his military duties. One morning, his company is assembled on the parade grounds, and he is brought before them. The company commander steps forward, faces the lieutenant, and before the entire assemblage makes a formal pronouncement to the effect that the lieutenant has engaged in conduct unbecoming an officer, that this conduct is a reflection of the lieutenant's character, and that for these reasons the lieutenant is hereby stripped of his rank and demoted to the rank of private (from Ossorio, 1976).

In this ceremony, the lieutenant is literally "de-graded;" that is, he is removed from one grade or status in his community, relocated to a lesser one, and with this relocation experiences a severe reduction in his eligibility to participate in his community. Whereas once he could give orders to most of the men and women on the base, reside in special quarters, and in general enjoy a wide range of officers' privileges, he now can do none of these. His community status, and with it his behavioral eligibilities, have been radically diminished.

In this paradigm case, one person formally degrades another before witnesses. In the derivative case known as a private self-degradation ceremony (Bergner, 1999; Ossorio, 1976, 2005), one person informally enacts all three roles: He or she serves as denouncer, as witness, and as denounced. This individual privately declares himself or herself to be a certain sort of degraded person (e.g., a "slut" or a "selfish, loveless narcissist"). These persons are responding to things going wrong by declaring in effect that not only were they deficient on this occasion, they are also the kind of person who, by dint of their defective character, incompetence, or moral blemish (a) merit diminished standing in the human community and (b) are disqualified from ever doing any better (cf. Goffman, 1963, on stigmatizing labels).

Finally, compounding the damage just recounted is the fact that degrading labels that persons assign to themselves tend to be impervious to contradictory empirical evidence (Bergner, 1999; Ossorio, 1976, 2005). Once individuals brand themselves with these labels, they tend, in the face of such evidence, not to alter the label but to assimilate new facts to it (Abramson,

Seligman, & Teasdale, 1978, on the insidious attributional style; cf. Beck & Weishaar, 2005, on prejudicial self-schemas). Thus, these labels, as in Shannon's case, often prove quite enduring and resistant to change, even in the face of massive evidence of their invalidity.

Pattern #2: Using Perfection as a Standard, Not an Ideal

Jack, a tax accountant in his early 30s, related the following self-critical scenario:

> On those rare occasions when a finished return looks good to me, I focus on how it wasn't done on time. If it was done on time, I focus on how inefficient I was in preparing it and how I've wasted money for my client and my firm. If all that is okay, I focus on how I should have found a better way to do it. I always find something wrong. The standard is perfection, and if I achieve it, I get a 10. If I fail to achieve it, I get a zero. There are no 9.5's here like in Olympic figure skating.

Many years ago, the theologian Reinhold Niebuhr raised the question of the intent of the biblical injunction "Be ye perfect!" (Niebuhr, 1956). Was perfection intended, he inquired, to be something that people could actually achieve and were expected to achieve? If so, the standard was quite impossible and therefore foolish. However, he suggested, perfection was being posed, not as a standard of adequacy, but as an ideal—as a destination or guide star that persons should strive toward even while knowing that they can never reach it. Failures to achieve this ideal would be inevitable, and the desired reaction in the face of such failures would be not self-laceration but humility and an unflagging commitment to strive toward the ideal.

The contrast between this perspective and the one contained in Jack's quote is stark. For Jack, perfection is a standard of adequacy. Failure to achieve it is not occasion for mere disappointment, humble acknowledgment, and renewed efforts. It is occasion to "give oneself a zero" and declare oneself a complete failure (cf. Sorotzkin, 1998). One should achieve perfection (the note of grandiosity is unmistakeable here), and failure to do so is grounds for recriminations against oneself (including often the sorts of self-degradations discussed earlier). In my clinical experience, it is not the pursuit of perfection per se but its use as an all-or-nothing standard of adequacy that proves so destructive to clients.

With respect to its consequences, perfectionism dooms its practitioners to a chronic sense of failure and misery (Ellis, 2002). Success is for the most part impossible, and so the individual is forever "getting a zero." Demoralization and even behavioral paralysis set in when virtually nothing he or she does ever results in a sense of pride, appreciation, or accomplishment. Finally, the individual who uses perfectionistic standards typically exhibits a highly negative focus. What draws his or her attention are deficits from the standard upheld, not any positive actions or accomplishments that might be appreciated (Bergner, 1981).

Pattern #3: The Hanging Judge

Randy, a 22-year-old college student, missed his highway turnoff one day. The mistake was not a costly one, as the next turnoff, an alternative route to his destination, was only a mile down the road, and he was under no time pressure. However, upon recognizing his mistake, he had what he described as a "screaming fit" in which he pounded his fist on his dashboard in a fit of rage at himself, shook his steering wheel violently, and screamed a long series of obscenities at himself.

The image of the "hanging judge" (Driscoll, 1981, 1989; Ossorio, 1976) is the image from the old Western frontier of the judge who, for any offense, no matter how minor, would sentence the defendant to death by hanging. It is the image of someone bent, not on observing the basic principle that the punishment should fit the crime, but on accomplishing the angry and vindictive destruction of the accused. Thus, what distinguishes this form of self-criticism is its excessively harsh, scathing, vindictive quality. Indeed, the intense anger, hatred, and assaultiveness toward oneself exhibited in this pattern have led previous authors to describe these persons as "abusive" critics and even as "killer" critics (Stone & Stone, 1993). Finally, as Randy's example illustrates, the interest in this scenario is not in changing or improving oneself but in punishing and reviling oneself.

In conclusion, it should be noted that the listing of the preceding three patterns is not intended to be exhaustive. Other, less frequently observed patterns also exist. A more comprehensive list of these may be found in Bergner (1995).

GENERAL CONSEQUENCES OF DESTRUCTIVE SELF-CRITICISM

In most cases, some positive benefits derive from treating oneself in the self-critical ways described earlier (Flett & Hewitt, 2002). For example, the sort of "reading oneself the riot act" entailed in the hanging judge scenario might for a time prove an effective goad to make oneself pursue an important goal. However, the self-critical patterns described are all, on balance, damaging to the individual's ability to function well. Their costs outweigh their benefits. Earlier, a few consequences unique to each self-critical scenario were noted. In this section, several general consequences that tend to result from all three of these maladaptive patterns are discussed.

Damaged Self-Esteem

A person's self-esteem is that person's summary appraisal of his or her own worth or goodness (Bergner, 1995). As such, it is clearly and directly a product of the individual's functioning as a critic of self. If persons repeatedly brand themselves "unlovable," "selfish," "screwed-up," and the like; repeatedly declare themselves failures for not living up to impossible standards; repeatedly attack themselves in hateful, abusive ways; or engage in other injurious self-critical practices, their self-esteem will be abysmal.

Personal Ineligibility

When persons criticize themselves destructively, they are making evaluations that affect profoundly their sense of eligibility to act in the world. If they appraise themselves as "unlovable," they are essentially saying that they are ineligible to be loved; if "stupid," that they are ineligible for the myriad things in life that call for intelligence; or if "insignificant nothings," that they are ineligible to have relationships with the worthy "somethings" of the world. Appraising themselves thus, they will find it enormously difficult to pursue desired relationships, jobs, and other life opportunities.

Negative Emotional States

When individuals engage repeatedly in such actions as branding themselves with disqualifying labels, declaring themselves ineligible, and judging themselves failures vis-à-vis impossible standards, they are likely to be depressed (Brown & Beck, 2002; Mongrain, 1998). When they appraise themselves in such a way that the situations they must confront seem too much for them, they will be anxious (Bergner, 2003; Cox, Walker, Enns, & Karpinski, 2002). When they judge themselves the bearers of highly stigmatizing, socially discrediting characteristics, they will experience shame (Bergner, 2003; Goffman, 1963). When they repeatedly evaluate themselves as morally deficient and blameworthy, they will experience guilt (Beck & Weishaar, 2005; Bergner, 2003; Ossorio, 1976). In these and other ways, destructive self-criticism culminates in negative emotional states.

Vulnerability to the Criticisms of Others

When, as critics of themselves, individuals believe the worst, they will be all too ready to concur with the negative criticisms of others. When others criticize them, they cannot defend themselves, and their experience will be that they are highly vulnerable to being devastated and defined by these others: "They must be right; if they find me lacking, I must be lacking." Furthermore, because the bad opinion of others brings with it such helplessness and devastation, these individuals must live their lives saddled with an inordinate concern about what other people think. They will say with some frequency that they are too desperate for external validation from others, and that because of this they find it very hard to be themselves and act in conformance with their own beliefs and desires.

Inability to Change

A final hallmark of destructive self-criticism is that, even when it represents a response to truly problematic actions or characteristics, it contains little that the person rendering it might use to change his or her behavior in the future. In the quotations given earlier, denunciatory labels, impositions of impossible standards, and harsh prosecutorial attacks abound. However, there is little in the way of useful problem diagnoses or of implementable prescriptions that the individual might use to bring about change.

PSYCHOTHERAPY TO ALTER SELF-CRITICAL BEHAVIOR

The basic goal of psychotherapy for critic problems, as conceived here, is to enable persons to abandon destructive, maladaptive modes of self-criticism in favor of more adaptive and humane ones. In this section, I describe a number of therapeutic interventions that I and others have found to be highly effective in bringing about these ends.

Helping Individuals to Recognize Their Self-Directed Critic Acts

Many clients are substantially unable to observe themselves as critics. In their reports about themselves, they are able to report the consequences of their self-critical acts (e.g., "I came away feeling so inferior" or "I just got this horrible sinking feeling that I am so insignificant to others") but not the acts themselves. The sense created in them is that their pain emanates from unknown sources, or that it "comes from out of nowhere."

Such individuals are in a poor position from which to change. They have a serious problem but are unacquainted with what might be termed its *business end*. They know the effects, but not the causes of these effects. Thus, the therapist must help them to recognize both the fact that they are the producers of their own misery and the details regarding the precise nature of their self-critical acts. The following represent three means of assisting clients in this regard.

Self-Monitoring

An excellent technique for helping persons to become better observers of themselves is one widely used by cognitive–behavioral therapists, that of self-monitoring (Beck, Rush, Shaw, & Emery, 1979; Beck & Weishaar, 2005; Haaga & Beck, 1992). For example, a therapist might suggest that clients carry around a small index card. At those times when they realize that they are feeling emotionally upset, or perhaps that they are engaging in some problematic behavior (withdrawing, lashing out angrily, etc.), they are to try to track what they were thinking immediately before the troublesome emotion or behavior. If they can identify their thoughts, they are to make a brief note on the index card regarding their nature. Such notes may serve three functions. First, clients who meet with some success in this activity become better observers of their own self-critical behaviors, and thus more cognizant of the fact that their problems come from them and not from out of the blue. Second, these notes may be brought to therapy for discussion with the therapist regarding their contents. Here, important themes regarding both the form and the content of self-criticism may be discerned. Third, when clients have attained some competence at more constructive self-critical practices, they might be directed to catch themselves in the act of destructive self-criticism and attempt immediately to counteract this by implementing more beneficial modes of criticizing themselves (cf. Beck et al., 1979; Beck & Weishaar, 2005, on the daily record of dysfunctional thoughts technique).

Logical Reconstruction

Where destructive critic acts consist of instantaneous, automatic appraisals enacted with little awareness, an effective therapeutic tactic can be that of logical reconstruction. The work here is analogous to that of a detective who must start with the facts of the accomplished crime and then work backward to reconstruct what must have happened. Thus, a therapist might reason with a client that "Although you have little awareness of doing so, from the withdrawal, depression, and despair you are describing, it sounds like you must have judged that you were inferior to her and that there could be no possibility of her being interested in you." Such critic appraisals may be hypothesized and discussed with the client, and in this way their likely content and nature discerned. When such collaborative work bears fruit, clients can become aware of the nature of their self-critical acts, can see how they are the perpetrators of these acts, and can take an essential first step toward removing them from their instantaneous, "automatic pilot" mode of perpetration.

"Be Your Critic"

A third technique, both for clinically assessing and for helping clients to recognize their self-critical acts, entails asking them to be their self-critics, and to speak from this position during the therapy hour. The basic technique here involves asking clients to take a third-person critical stance (e.g., "Beth, I'd like to ask you to sort of step back and be Beth's critic; tell me what you think of her just as you would if she were someone else"). The client is interviewed, not as himself or herself ("I felt depressed . . ."), but as his or her critic ("Beth infuriates me when she sits around watching TV when there are still important things to be done").

Getting the Client to "Own" the Critic

In some cases, clients will get to a point at which they recognize that self-criticism is at the root of their problems but, when conveying their understanding of this, they will use expressions such as "my critic" or "critical parent part," as if the behavior in question issued from some dissociated entity within them, not from them. In the same vein, they may say things such as, "She [the critic] has been quiet lately, but I'm always afraid she'll come back." Not only do such statements convey that the critic is "not me" but they also convey a sense of lack of control—a sense that "This isn't my behavior that I can elect to do or not do; it issues from some part of me that I do not control."

Such persons must be helped to "own" their critic acts; that is, they must be helped to come to a full recognition that they are the authors or perpetrators of these acts—a full sense that "*I* do this, *I* am its author, *I* am its perpetrator." Clients who fully appreciate this fact occupy positions of far greater control from which change is more possible. In essence, from this position, desisting from destructive criticism and implementing other more adaptive forms becomes an active possibility. The following two strategies are very helpful in achieving these (as well as other) ends.

Establishing What the Client Is Trying to Accomplish

I, along with a number of previous practitioners (Driscoll, 1981, 1989; McKay & Fanning, 1992), have found it beneficial to explore with clients what they are trying to accomplish with their self-critical behaviors. In addition to helping them to own these behaviors, knowing what they are trying to accomplish by them creates a number of further therapeutic benefits. First, clients realize that they are not crazy, foolish, or arbitrarily malicious for behaving as they do; rather, they see that their behavior constitutes an effort to secure understandable and often laudable human ends. Second, if they are clear about their purposes, clients are in a better position to evaluate their operating premise that "criticizing myself this way will get me these benefits." Were they correct, or has treating themselves this way not been very successful in getting them what they want? Third, the therapist may use clients' existing motivations (e.g., for self-improvement) in the service of positive change by showing them how alternative forms of self-criticism might do a more effective, less costly, and less painful job of getting them what they have been seeking all along. As the architect Buckminster Fuller once advocated, "use existing forces; don't oppose them" (as quoted in Seldes, 1985). Among the more common reasons that clients engage in problematic self-criticism are the following.

Self-Improvement

Many clients believe that their favored modes of self-criticism will result in self-improvement and that failure to implement them will result in complacency and stagnation. If they do not hold themselves to the highest standards, or denounce themselves roundly for failures, or bring home to themselves the "truth" about what deficient creatures they are, they believe they will never become any better (Driscoll, 1981, 1989; Ossorio, 1976).

To Avoid Egotism

Many persons believe that it is wrong to think well of themselves. To do so amounts to an unacceptable egotism, boastfulness, or self-aggrandizement. Thus, to maintain the virtue of humility, they are required to think ill of themselves (Driscoll, 1981, 1989).

To Protect Themselves From Dangers

Often, clients sense that certain dangers would ensue were they to abandon their current self-critical practices (Driscoll, 1981, 1989; McKay & Fanning, 1992). For example, for some perfectionistic clients, their avid pursuit of flawlessness may be seen as an attempt to avoid the danger of being subjected to the painful criticisms of others (Burns & Beck, 1978; Habke & Flynn, 2002; Hewitt & Flett, 2002). For these individuals, to be perfect is to be beyond reproach—to be safe from the dreaded negative opinions of others. In a related vein, other clients believe that if they were to think more positively of themselves, they would be raising themselves up and would thereby run the risk of being "shot down" and humiliated; however, if they deprecate themselves to others, they run no such risk.

To Achieve Interpersonal Ends

Self-criticism may be used as a tactic to secure various ends in relationships (Driscoll, 1981, 1989; Ossorio, 1976). Some individuals, for example, may use it to secure reassurance and sympathy; they find that when they criticize themselves, others (at least for a while) tend to pay attention, to console them, and to counter their self-criticisms with positive reassurances. Other persons, by way of a second example, may criticize themselves because they fear that others will hold them responsible or expect too much of them. If they run themselves down, others may not expect too much from them or not be too harsh with them should they fail (cf. Higgins, Snyder, & Berglas, 1990, on self-handicapping).

Prescribing Problematic Self-Critical Behaviors

The following therapeutic intervention is one of the most powerful in this chapter. When the groundwork procedures discussed earlier have been executed carefully and thoroughly, sudden and radical changes often result, not merely in the client's ownership of self-critical behaviors but also in his or her actual discontinuation of them. This intervention is the seemingly paradoxical one of recommending to clients that, for a prescribed period, they continue to engage in their maladaptive self-critical behaviors, but consciously and deliberately.

Because this recommendation to perpetuate their destructive self-critical actions will seem to most clients both strange and ill-advised, it should be supported with some discussion of its rationale. The best policy here, rather than engage in the deception advocated in many symptom prescription approaches, is simply to share with the client the actual therapeutic rationales for the directive. For me, these rationales are as follows: (a) "Engaging in your problematic critic behaviors consciously and deliberately is a way to take control of them." The client is informed that removing them from his or her reflex, automatic mode of perpetration, which has resulted in the client having insufficient awareness and control over them, will greatly enhance his or her control. (b) "It will help you to gather vital information." Clients may be informed that deliberately enacting old critic behaviors provides an opportunity to monitor carefully a number of matters that will later be essential for making a full and considered decision to continue or discontinue them. Is the behavior in fact securing its desired ends? Does the client notice any negative side effects that attend pursuing his or her ends in this way? Does the client experience a sense that certain dangers would ensue from stopping the behavior? (c) "Never trust overnight changes." Clients may be informed that it is generally not desirable to make radical overnight changes, as doing so usually amounts to an insufficiently considered, impulsive act. In contrast, the conservative approach of continuing to enact the old critic behaviors deliberately, while giving careful consideration to the sorts of matters just noted, is a way to proceed slowly and responsibly toward a decision about their continuance that will rest on a firmer foundation.

Responding to Noncompliance

Clients will typically react to the directive to continue their destructive self-critical practices in one of two ways. The first (and less therapeutically desirable) response is that they will decline to implement it. Because this response entails a cessation of their problematic self-critical behaviors, the client will typically report feeling better. However, this response may also entail a fearful avoidance of these behaviors, and thus less of a sense of ultimate ownership and control. For this reason, the suggested therapeutic response to such refusal is to attempt one additional time to secure compliance with the directive. In my experience, even when the client again does not comply, this additional refusal seems to solidify the therapeutic gain.

Responding to Compliance

The second response to this directive is implementation. In response to such compliance, recommended therapeutic procedures include (a) expressing appreciation for clients' efforts; (b) clarifying precisely what they did; (c) exploring the results of their self-monitoring efforts (e.g., "Did it seem like treating yourself this way last week led to self-improvement, or not?"); (d) underscoring any new sense of control over self-critical behaviors that they report; and (e) recommending that they repeat the directive for 1 additional week.

The results of successful compliance with this directive are typically greater senses of ownership and control over the critic behaviors, and thus an enhanced sense of choice in the matter of whether or not to abandon them. In my experience, the majority of clients who comply and meet with reasonable success in their attempts to take control of destructive critic behaviors abandon these behaviors over a period ranging from several days to several weeks. The modal report is that they cannot continue to perpetrate such actions consciously and deliberately once they have appreciated fully the exact nature of what they have been doing to themselves (Bergner, 1993).

Presenting Positive Concepts and Modes of Self-Criticism

When clients cease engaging in their old, maladaptive critical acts, they report significant changes in how they feel and behave. However, merely eliminating these destructive forms is not a sufficient therapeutic outcome. Self-criticism is a vital and necessary human function. It is at the heart of human self-regulation and adaptation, and we cannot function optimally as human beings if we cannot perform well the job of the critic—if we cannot (a) recognize and appreciate when things are going right and leave them alone and (b) recognize when they are going wrong and generate useful diagnoses and prescriptions for change (Bergner, 1995; Ossorio, 1976). Thus, it is strongly in clients' interests not merely to desist from destructive self-criticism but to become the most competent critics that they can be.

An essential part of the present psychotherapy thus becomes that of helping clients acquire concepts and skills pertaining to effective, adaptive forms of self-criticism. There are many ways of accomplishing this goal, most of which involve simple presentation, discussion, and practice of these more adaptive modes both within the therapy hour and in homework assignments (see, e.g., Beck & Weishaar, 2005; Bergner, 1995; McKay & Fanning, 1992). In this section, one method for accomplishing this goal is highlighted.

Using Social Role Images

Therapists may convey virtually anything pertinent to competent critic function by using social role images such as those of parent, teacher, coach, or boss or supervisor. The primary reason for use of such images is that most clients with critic problems, although they lack a concept of constructive self-criticism, do possess skills and understandings regarding how a person operating in one of these roles would constructively criticize another. Thus, the therapist is able to use and build on resources that the client already possesses (cf. O'Hanlon & Weiner-Davis, 2003, on the principle of utilization).

By way of illustration, a therapist might be interested in conveying the core perspective contained in this chapter, namely, that the primary function of criticism should be to enhance the quality of the behavior, and thus the quality of life, of the person criticized. Whereas few clients will exhibit a command of this perspective in the case of self-criticism, almost all will understand it in the case of one person criticizing another. Thus, the latter case becomes an excellent vehicle through which to communicate the perspective. For example, almost all clients easily recognize that if a dance instructor degrades a student ("You clumsy oaf!"), the criticism is poor because it disqualifies the dancer and renders him or her less able, not more able, to dance. In contrast, they recognize that a dance instructor who appreciates it when things go right ("Yes! That's it. Well done!") and who corrects with constructive, implementable prescriptions when things go wrong ("Not that way, Susie. Now watch me. Turn your foot this way") is doing a good job as a critic precisely because such criticism is likely to benefit the performance of the dancer.

Image: Parent

Perhaps the most generally useful social role image is that of parent. The concept of parent is a complex one, but may be thought of for present purposes as comprising two basic elements. The first of these is a commitment to the best interests of one's child—an enduring commitment to doing those things that will help this child develop into a competent, moral, participating adult. The second element is that of competently undertaking certain tasks or functions in the raising of one's child such as discipline, nurturance, guidance, protection, acceptance, appreciation, and support (Hardison, 1991).

When this image is used with destructively self-critical clients who understand and value this role, numerous therapeutic options become possible. Such individuals might be asked if, as a parent, they would criticize their children as they do themselves. Would they always focus on negatives and never appreciate positives? Crucify their children for anything less than perfection? Brand them with disqualifying labels? Never let them succeed in their parents' eyes? What would they do if their children were attacked by hostile critics—would they join the chorus of the critics as they do in their own case? Should their children do something problematic, what sorts of parental criticisms would they use to help them to change their behavior?

These lines of questioning and discussion are largely concerned with extending existing parental skills into the domain of self-criticism. As noted, however, the parental role also implies a commitment to act in the best interests of one's child, a commitment that transcends and informs the behavioral execution of all of its various tasks. Not only specific behaviors but also this entire relational commitment can be proposed to clients as an alternative to their current, self-abusive ones. Their current agendas (e.g., "My job is to rub your nose in the ugly truth about yourself;" "My job is never to give you any approval until you shape up") can be articulated and contrasted with the parental one. Finally, the merits of making a new personal commitment to oneself along the lines of the parental one can be discussed.

In these and other ways, the image of the parent who is acting in the best interests of a child, which the client already possesses, becomes the model for something he or she does not possess: the concept of a competent, effective, constructive self-critic. As the role of parent is a broader and more complex one than that of critic (the role of critic being just one part of the parental role), in principle all that a person needs to be a competent self-critic has a parallel in the parental role. This role can therefore be an avenue to everything that the client might need to alter his or her approach to self.

The images of teacher, coach, boss, supervisor, dance instructor, or any other social role calling for competent criticism of one person by another may also be used in psychotherapy with self-critical clients. Although these roles are more limited, the logic and tactics of using them are substantially similar to those for using the image of parent and thus are not discussed separately.

Encouraging Active Practice

Clients should be urged to practice actively the new, more constructive and competent modes of self-criticism that are discussed in therapy. When clinical judgment indicates that the individual is able to do something new, and when he or she exhibits a readiness to do so, various assignments may be made for the client to carry out both in and out of the therapy hour. Because a rich clinical literature already exists regarding such skill-enhancing interventions as behavior rehearsal, empty-chair exercises, and the assignment of homework, these techniques are not described further here.

Some Common Resistances and Other Obstacles

Despite our best efforts as therapists, most clients present resistances both to abandoning their current self-critical practices and to adopting alternative practices. Confronted with the prospect of change, these individuals have genuine reservations, concerns, fears, and doubts. Although these clients have strong reason to try something new, in their minds they often have stronger reason not to do so. In the following discussion, I describe six common client resistances and some effective therapeutic responses to each.

Objection: "It's Too Weak to Be Effective"

When the constructive approaches to self-criticism described earlier are related to some clients, their reaction is that they find them weak, insufficient responses to their own mistakes and failings. If they are to change their shortcomings, they believe, they must bring serious negative consequences to bear upon themselves, and the present approaches seem to them mere slaps on the wrist that will not get the job done.

A recommended first therapeutic response to this objection (and to all subsequent ones) is to reflect it and to demonstrate an understanding of its intuitive, common-sense logic. The individual's objection is heard and appreciated as a sensible, indeed quite plausible one.

After this first approach, various approaches are possible. One of these is to note for clients how this objection embodies precisely the logic behind their current approaches to themselves—that is, that they must be extremely harsh and punitive with themselves to get results. They may be asked if this approach has worked to date. If it has not, might experimenting with some other approach be worth a try? Or, might they perhaps need to become even more harsh and punitive to see if this approach could work if practiced more assiduously; a homework assignment along these lines might then be devised and clients be urged to perform an "experiment" on their "hypothesis."

Another approach is to raise counterarguments with the client. One of the most useful and compelling of these is a thought experiment that once again draws on the client's understanding of two-person systems:

> Think of two people who want you to correct a mistake that you've made. The first of them is someone who in general has your best interests in mind, treats you well, is supportive of you, and appreciates your good points and your achievements; when you make a mistake, he or she points it out to you clearly, makes no bones about the fact that it was a mistake, relates the reasons why, and urges a change. The second person is someone who in general treats you poorly, never supports you, never seems to notice anything positive about you, and reads you the riot act whenever you make a mistake [details here should be custom-tailored to the client's self-critical modus operandi]. With which of these two critics are you going to be more inclined to cooperate?

Objection: "But It's the Truth!"

Clients repeatedly lock themselves into destructive self-critical practices by mistakenly regarding the whole matter as a truth issue. They do not see themselves as active critics with choices in such matters as what standards to uphold or how to respond to personal failings. Rather, they see themselves as victims—as persons compelled by the evidence to recognize factual, inescapable truths about themselves.

In response to such an objection, clients may be reminded that although facts may constrain what appraisals a person can make realistically, they do not dictate specific appraisals. For example, they might be urged to consider an object far simpler than a person: a rock. Although the facts about a rock might constrain what appraisals can be made realistically (e.g., one cannot carry off behaviorally an assertion that it is a calculator), it is possible to regard and to treat it as a container of a geologic record, an object that obeys the law of gravity, a potential paperweight, and much more. Furthermore, the facts about the rock could not constrain clients from, should they care to, passing what amount to personal "laws" about rocks—for example, that they will count them "good rocks" if and only if they possess certain characteristics or meet certain standards of perfection of their choosing. Persons are quintessentially status assigners—beings who can and routinely do pass personal laws, set personal standards, assign things to various places or positions in their worlds, and thus give those things more or less value. When they are appraising rocks and when they are appraising persons, including themselves, the facts do not lock them into any one uniquely correct appraisal or any one uniquely correct mode of response.

Thus, even when clients must contend with admittedly negative facts about themselves, they are not limited to any one way to look at these facts or any one way to treat themselves in response to them. The facts do not dictate that they be cruel to themselves (e.g., the fact that a man is unattractive does not compel a person to tell him repeatedly that he is ugly). The facts do not dictate that they systematically choose the least charitable interpretation possible (e.g., the fact that a woman is concerned about her appearance does not dictate that a person regard her as "vain" rather than "insecure about her attractiveness"). The facts do not dictate that they systematically choose the least heuristic or solution-generative appraisal possible (e.g., the fact that a young boy is performing beneath his ability in school does not compel a person to regard him as a "lazy bum" rather than as "alienated" or "resisting what he sees as parental coercion"). The facts do not dictate that they select any given quality (e.g., beauty, brilliance, achievement, or popularity) and declare it an absolute requirement for personal worth. The facts do not dictate that one should never forgive oneself.

Objection: "It's morally wrong"

Morality is an important matter for many persons who are destructive critics of themselves. Indeed, as mentioned earlier, one of the reasons some persist in their self-lacerating ways is because they believe it is virtuous to do so and it is immorally egotistical to appraise themselves in more positive ways. These beliefs may be called into question profitably with many persons. The following moral questions are beneficial ones to raise with certain clients: (a) Is it any more virtuous to abuse oneself psychologically than it is to do so physically with alcohol, tobacco, or other harmful substances? (b) Because destructive self-criticism is so damaging to one's ability to function, does one have a moral obligation to others such as one's children or families not to destroy one's ability to relate to and care for them? (c) Do not destructive self-critical practices fail a critical moral test insofar as they damage one's ability to responsibly change one's behavior? (d) Is it morally acceptable to treat any human being the way a critical person treats him- or herself? Exploring such questions often makes it possible to use the client's existing motive to be moral in the service of treating him- or herself more humanely.

Objection: "I'm Afraid I'll Get a Big Head"

This is one of the more common reservations that clients have about refraining from their accustomed self-critical practices and adopting new, more adaptive ones. They fear that they will become arrogant and egotistical. Furthermore, they anticipate that others will detect this arrogance, will "shoot them down" in a painful and humiliating way, and will ultimately reject them.

Several avenues of response are often helpful here. The first of these is a clarification of what is being advocated in the present approach. Some who fear that they will become arrogant mishear what is being said and believe that the therapist is promoting a completely non-self-critical, "everything about me is wonderful," approach that would lead to an inflated self-evaluation. Such a misinterpretation should be corrected by the therapist, and the client should be reminded that what is being advocated is a constructive self-critical approach in which part of the person's job is to identify faults and mistakes and to correct these.

A second basis for clients' fears of egotism lies in the fact that one of the jobs of the critic consists in recognizing, acknowledging, and affirming one's own successes, competencies, and other positive attributes. Individuals are frightened that this behavior will prove a route to arrogance. Several lines of response are often helpful in dispelling such fears: (a) Clients might be reminded of the notion of an objective self-assessment wherein a person concludes something on the following general order: "Well, I believe that my strengths lie in X, Y, and Z; my weaknesses in A, B, and C; and my so-so areas in D, E, and F." Such an example is helpful to pose to clients because in it they can see a person who is acknowledging positives but who does not strike most observers as egotistical. (b) The notion of self-efficacy beliefs as developed by Bandura (1997) is a helpful one to share with clients in the present context. These are beliefs of individuals that, in specific areas of life such as athletics or academics, they have the ability to be successful if they exert the necessary efforts. Clients may be informed that research has shown that such beliefs are virtually indispensable if persons are to feel the personal confidence they need to undertake important things in life and to persist in them in the face of obstacles (Bandura, 1997). Thus, such beliefs are more like basic human needs than they are instances of unacceptable egotism. (c) Finally, clients may be asked to consider the opposite state of affairs, in which all positive criticism is withheld. Again, the use of two-person images is helpful for making this point. For example, a client who is a dedicated teacher might be asked: "What would happen if you withheld all acknowledgments of your students' successes, strengths, and competencies from them? What would you be doing to them? Is it really any different in your own case?"

Obstacle: Other Critics

Many clients with critic problems report that they are devastated by the negative appraisals of others and find themselves helplessly defined by these appraisals. One young woman expressed this issue in the following way: "When my father criticizes me, I am absolutely crushed; to me it's like God is speaking, and I just can't bring myself to believe anything other than what he is telling me." An important obstacle to these clients treating themselves in more constructive ways, then, becomes the fact that others are criticizing them, and they find themselves unable to do anything but concur with these criticisms.

Eleanor Roosevelt once stated that "No one can make you feel inferior without your consent" (Bright, 1988, p. 159). I have found it useful to share this quote with clients and to discuss at length its basic contention that criticism can devastate and control a person only when that person provides his or her own consent. When individuals listen to the criticisms of others and conclude, often automatically and unthinkingly, that the other must be right, and when they further concur that the matter is indeed the "federal case" that the other alleges it is, then they are most deeply affected. When, however, they refuse to provide such consent, they are far less vulnerable to others' criticisms. Thus, if clients can find ways to cease their reflex concurrence with the criticisms of others, and can instead assume control of their own ultimate appraisals, they can mute considerably the power of these criticisms to devastate and control them.

A helpful prescription in such cases is to recommend to clients, at a point when they have made some progress in becoming more constructive critics of themselves, that they insert their own critic between themselves and others. If others offer a criticism, they are to use the following procedure in the handling of such criticism. First, as a matter of the strictest policy, they are to suspend judgment regarding its merits. Rather than maintaining their customary, reflex concurrence, they are to say to themselves, "That person may be right, partially right, or wrong. I will consent to nothing until I have personally considered the matter; I will be the final judge." Second, they are to give the criticism the consideration due it and come to an independent, personal decision regarding its worth. Do they believe, on the basis of their own best reflection, that the criticism has some merit or no merit at all? Third, if they make the personal judgment that the criticism has merit, they are to handle the matter of what does or does not need to be done in their own way. For the external critic, the matter may be a "hanging offense," but this person's opinion should in no way bind the individual from handling it in the more humane ways that he or she has been acquiring.

The central function of this prescription is the absolutely essential one of restoring clients to being their own ultimate critics. When they are successful, they retain an openness to the criticisms of others, but are no longer at their mercy. Although the prescription may be described fairly simply and straightforwardly, its implementation is for most clients quite difficult. Furthermore, it usually requires a great deal of supportive discussion about such matters as the supposed superiority or infallibility of their detractors and the eligibility of clients to criticize themselves competently and authoritatively.

FINAL THOUGHTS

The goal of individuals becoming competent, constructive critics of themselves is of the utmost importance to their ability to lead full, satisfying, participatory lives. Possessed of such critic competencies, they become far more able to live their lives in ways that are expressive of their genuine loves, interests, and values; and to do so unrestricted by crippling senses of ineligibility, disabling emotional states, excessive concern about the reactions of others, and other impediments. I hope that the ideas contained in this chapter, which have been exceptionally helpful to me in securing such benefits for clients, will be of similar usefulness to the reader.

REFERENCES

Abramson, L., Seligman, M., & Teasdale, J. (1978). Learned helplessness in humans: Critique and reformulation. *Journal of Abnormal Psychology, 87*, 32–48.

Bandura, A. (1997). *Self-efficacy: The exercise of control.* New York: Freeman.

Beck, A., Rush, A., Shaw, B., & Emery, G. (1979). *Cognitive therapy and the emotional disorders.* New York: Guilford Press.

Beck, A., & Weishaar, M. (2005). Cognitive therapy. In R. Corsini & D. Wedding (Eds.), *Current psychotherapies* (7th ed., pp. 238–268). Itasca, IL: Peacock.

Bergner, R. (1981). The overseer regime: A descriptive and practical study of the obsessive-compulsive personality style. In K. Davis (Ed.), *Advances in descriptive psychology* (Vol. 1, pp. 245–272). Greenwich, CT: JAI Press.

Bergner, R. (1993). Victims into perpetrators. *Psychotherapy, 30*, 452–462.

Bergner, R. (1995). *Pathological self-criticism: Assessment and treatment.* New York: Plenum Press.

Bergner, R. (1999). Status enhancement: A further path to therapeutic change. *American Journal of Psychotherapy, 53*, 201–214.

Bergner, R. (2003). Emotions: A relational view and its clinical applications. *American Journal of Psychotherapy, 57*, 471–490.

Bright, D. (1988). *Criticism in your life.* New York: Master Media.

Brown, G., & Beck, A. (2002). Dysfunctional attitudes, perfectionism, and models of vulnerability to depression. In G. Flett & P. Hewitt (Eds.), *Perfectionism:*

Theory, research, and treatment (pp. 231–252). Washington, DC: American Psychological Association.

Burns, T., & Beck, A. (1978). Cognitive behavior modification of mood disorders. In J. Foreyt & D. Rathjen (Eds.), *Cognitive behavior therapy* (pp. 109–134). New York: Plenum Press.

Cox, B., Walker, J., Enns, M., & Karpinski, D. (2002). Self-criticism in generalized social phobia and response to cognitive-behavioral treatment. *Behavior Therapy, 33*, 479–491.

Driscoll, R. (1981). Self-criticism: Analysis and treatment. In K. Davis (Ed.), *Advances in descriptive psychology* (Vol. 1, pp. 273–278). Greenwich, CT: JAI Press.

Driscoll, R. (1989). Self-condemnation: A comprehensive framework for assessment and treatment. *Psychotherapy, 26*, 104–111.

Ellis, A. (2002). The role of irrational beliefs in perfectionism. In G. Flett & P. Hewitt (Eds.), *Perfectionism: Theory, research, and treatment* (pp. 217–229). Washington, DC: American Psychological Association.

Flett, G., & Hewitt, P. (2002). Perfectionism and maladjustment: An overview of theoretical, definitional, and treatment issues. In G. Flett & P. Hewitt (Eds.), *Perfectionism: Theory, research, and treatment* (pp. 5–32). Washington, DC: American Psychological Association.

Garfinkel, H. (1957). Conditions of successful degradation ceremonies. *American Journal of Sociology, 63*, 420–424.

Goffman, E. (1963). *Stigma: Notes on the management of spoiled identity.* Englewood Cliffs, NJ: Prentice-Hall.

Haaga, D., & Beck, A. (1992). Cognitive therapy. In F. Paykel (Ed.), *Handbook of affective disorders* (2nd ed.). New York: Guilford Press.

Habke, A., & Flynn, C. (2002). Interpersonal aspects of trait perfectionism. In G. Flett & P. Hewitt (Eds.), *Perfectionism: Theory, research, and treatment* (pp. 151–180). Washington, DC: American Psychological Association.

Hardison, E. (1991). *Development of a comprehensive model of parenting: Six dimensions of parental responsibility.* Unpublished master's thesis, Illinois State University, Normal.

Hewitt, P., & Flett, G. (2002). Perfectionism and stress processes in psychopathology. In G. Flett & P. Hewitt (Eds.), *Perfectionism: Theory, research, and treatment* (pp. 255–284). Washington, DC: American Psychological Association.

Higgins, R., Snyder, C. R., & Berglas, S. (1990). *Self-handicapping: The paradox that isn't.* New York: Plenum Press.

McKay, M., & Fanning, P. (1992). *Self-esteem* (2nd ed.). Oakland, CA: New Harbinger.

Mongrain, M. (1998). Parental representations and support seeking behaviors related to dependency and self-criticism. *Journal of Personality, 66*, 151–173.

Niebuhr, R. (1956). *An interpretation of Christian ethics.* New York: Meridian.

O'Hanlon, W., & Weiner-Davis, M. (2003). *In search of solutions.* New York: Norton.

Ossorio, P. (1976). *Clinical topics* (LRI Report #11). Boulder, CO: Linguistic Research Institute.

Ossorio, P. (2005). *"What actually happens": The representation of real world phenomena*. Ann Arbor, MI: Descriptive Psychology Press.

Seldes, G. (Ed.). *The great thoughts*. New York: Ballantine Books.

Sorotzkin, B. (1998). Understanding and treating perfectionism in religious adolescents. *Psychotherapy, 35*, 87–95.

Stone, H., & Stone, S. (1993). *Embracing your inner critic*. San Francisco: HarperCollins.

14

SELF-CRITICISM AND SELF-ENHANCEMENT: FROM COMPLEXITIES OF THE PRESENT TO A COMPLEX FUTURE

EDWARD C. CHANG, RITA CHANG, LAWRENCE J. SANNA,
AND ALLISON M. KADE

We, the authors of this chapter, end this volume by taking a look at where we are now and where we can or may be heading in the study of self-criticism and self-enhancement. First, we begin with a brief review of some of the key points made by contributors to the present work. Next, we look at two interesting areas of research that may help us expand our appreciation for the study of self-criticism and self-enhancement, namely, perfectionism and self-worth. Finally, we end this chapter with a look toward the future and highlight some of the challenges and promises that may lie ahead for researchers and practitioners interested in these broad and robust constructs.

WHERE WE ARE NOW

This section focuses on reviewing some of the major points raised earlier in this volume and then focuses on a discussion of emerging lines of research on perfectionism and contingencies of self-worth to highlight ways in which more inclusive models of self-criticism and self-enhancement can be developed.

Everyone Is Right, No One Is Wrong: Taking a More Critical Look

A central goal of this volume was to underscore the idea that self-criticism and self-enhancement are not stagnant constructs, but rather dynamic ones. As metamotives tied to fundamental notions of the self, their meaning and function are fluid and impact people's lives in a variety of ways, from helping us feel good about ourselves to protecting us from being foolhardy. Indeed, the contributors of this volume have collectively made it clear that self-criticism is not simply maladaptive or adaptive, but can be both. In a similar way, self-enhancement is not simply adaptive or maladaptive, but it too can be both. Let us recap some of the key points made thus far. In doing so, let us also reexamine some questions that follow on the present discussion of self-criticism and self-enhancement.

Is self-enhancement good for a person? On the basis of several of the chapters in this volume, the answer to that question is yes. Self-enhancement is involved in feeling good about oneself, having positive relationships with others, engaging in useful coping strategies (see chap. 2, this volume), protecting against stress experiences, helping with physical recovery from medical procedures, and extending a person's longevity (see chap. 3, this volume). Yet, several of the other chapters in this volume would have readers believe that the answer to that same question is no. Self-enhancement is involved in narcissism and poor psychological adjustment (see chap. 8, this volume), problems in processing health-related information, and behaviors that in turn may ultimately put one's health at risk (see chap. 9, this volume).

However, one might ask, is self-criticism bad for a person? On the basis of several of the chapters in this volume, the answer to that question is yes. Self-criticism is involved in the development or maintenance of negative affective conditions such as depression and anxiety (see chap. 4, this volume) and generating problematic situations with others (see chap. 5, this volume). Again, however, several of the other chapters in this volume would have readers believe that the answer to that same question is no. Self-criticism can represent a positive tool used to effectively reach important goals (see chap. 6, this volume) and can be involved in critical ways to improve oneself (see chap. 7, this volume). So, it seems that everyone is right and no one is wrong. That is, self-criticism is both good and bad. Self-enhancement is also both good and bad. Is this just another case of collective self-enhancement among scientists and practitioners? We think not. All of the contributors recognized the complexity of what they were talking about and were careful to contextualize their discussion of self-criticism and self-enhancement accordingly. Thus, although there may be some disagreements in how some researchers interpret certain findings or how some research methodologies are viewed as more useful or limiting than others, all of the contributors appreciated that complex constructs are involved. With that in mind, we next focus our attention on two areas of research that appear to be undergoing important transformations that may in turn help direct us to novel ways for understanding the complexities of self-criticism and self-enhancement. We begin with a look at perfectionism. Indeed, our examination of perfectionism in the context of the present volume is not completely fortuitous. As discussed in chapter 11 (this volume), researchers have found a reliable link between perfectionism and self-criticism. What is more, some researchers have even considered self-criticism to represent a necessary, if not sufficient, hallmark of (maladaptive) perfectionism (e.g., Dunkley, Zuroff, & Blankstein, 2003; Frost, Marten, Lahart, & Rosenblate, 1990; Shahar, Blatt, Zuroff, & Pilkonis, 2003; cf. Dunkley, Zuroff, & Blankstein, 2006).

Pushing for More Inclusive and Specific Models: Looking at Emerging Research on Performance Perfectionism and Contingencies of Self-Worth

Moving Beyond Unidimensional and Unifunctional Models: A Look at the Pursuit of Perfectionism Across the Ages

In the following sections we discuss how perfectionism has been historically considered as a positive attribute, how it has been considered in more recent times as a negative attribute, and how newer studies are now seeking to consider perfectionism neither as a positive nor as a negative attribute, but as both. Specifically, we look at emerging works on performance perfectionism as a multidimensional and multifunctional construct and discuss how a more inclusive model of self-criticism and self-enhancement may be developed.

A Historical Look at Perfectionism. Long before modern views linked perfectionism to potentially hazardous pursuits, a very different notion of perfectionism dominated. During the Middle Kingdom (1991–1778 BCE) in Egypt, the perfect individual was defined as one who was "*effective because his life [was] in harmonious attunement to society and nature, the universal order*" (La Rondelle, 1971, p. 8). Thus, the perfect individual lived a life that was in step with the world around him or her. Although perfection was not linked to any clear moral notions in ancient Egyptian culture, it became a key concept linked to seeking the good life (*summum bonum*) in ancient Greek thought. For example, in Plato's *The Republic*, the good or just life is attained when the soul is in perfect harmony with itself. And hence, the perfect individual is also the just or virtuous individual. Likewise, in the *Nicomachean Ethics*, Aristotle defined the supreme goal of all human activity as *eudaemonia*, or happiness linked to the perfection of one's nature. The notion that perfection and the process of trying to perfect oneself was a good is also found in the ancient and classical writings within Mahāyāna Buddhism and Christianity (Aitken, 1994; Milosh, 1966; Ratnayaka, 1978). Yet, studies on perfectionism over the past 2 decades have shown that there may be more reasons to consider this personality process a vice rather than a virtue.

Modern Views of (Pathological) Perfectionism: On Two Popular Multidimensional Models and Measures. Initially, researchers once held the view that perfectionism represented a unidimensional construct (Burns, 1980). However, findings from more recent studies have supported a multidimensional view of perfectionism. Indeed, over the past decade and even before, two multidimensional models and measures have come to dominate and drive the extant research on perfectionism. First is the conceptualization of perfectionism presented by Frost and his colleagues (Frost, Heimberg, Holt, Mattia, & Neubauer, 1993; Frost et al., 1990). According to Frost et al. (1990), perfectionism is conceptualized as an individual differences variable involving excessive self-criticism associated with high personal standards, doubts about the effectiveness of one's actions, concerns about meeting social expectations (typically those of the parents), and an excessive focus on organization and neatness. To assess for this conceptualization of perfectionism, Frost et al. (1990) developed the Frost Multidimensional Perfectionism Scale (FMPS). The FMPS is a 35-item multidimensional measure of perfectionism consisting of six scales that assess for the dimensions of concern over mistakes, personal standards, parental expectations, parental criticism, doubts about actions, and organization. It is worth noting that in studies of perfectionism with the FMPS, both aggregate FMPS scores and separate FMPS subscale scores have been used. In general, higher aggregate FMPS scores and higher FMPS subscale scores reflect greater perfectionism.

A second important conceptualization of perfectionism represented in the extant literature is the one presented by Hewitt and Flett (1991). According to them, perfectionism refers to a multidimensional phenomenon composed of three relatively distinct dimensions, namely, self-oriented, other-oriented, and socially prescribed perfectionism. *Self-oriented perfectionism* refers to the tendency of an individual to set and seek high self-standards of performance. *Other-oriented perfectionism* refers to the tendency of an individual to expect that others should or will be perfect in their performance. *Socially prescribed perfectionism* refers to the tendency of an individual to believe that others expect perfection from him or her. To assess for these dimensions of perfectionism, Hewitt and Flett (1991) developed the Multidimensional Perfectionism Scale (MPS). The MPS is a 45-item measure of perfectionism consisting of three theoretically distinct scales. Higher scores on each scale reflect greater levels of perfectionism. As one might surmise in light of the obvious conceptual similarities underlying the FMPS and the

MPS, scores on the two scales have been found to correlate with one another (Frost et al., 1993).

Modern Research on Perfectionism: Perfectionism Is Hazardous to One's Psychological Health. Findings from a large number of studies have shown that perfectionism represents a concomitant of psychological maladjustment at best and a liability associated with the development of maladjustment at worst (Hewitt & Flett, 2002; Shafran & Mansell, 2001). For example, studies with the FMPS have shown that both higher global or aggregate scores and higher subscale scores on the FMPS are associated with greater depressive symptoms (Frost et al., 1990; Kawamura, Hunt, Frost, & DiBartolo, 2001; Stöber, 1998), greater psychological symptoms (Frost et al., 1990), greater obsessive–compulsive behaviors (Frost & Steketee, 1997), greater worry across different life domains (E. C. Chang et al., in press), greater social anxiety (Saboonchi, Lundh, & Öst, 1999), less self-esteem (Rice, Ashby, & Slaney, 1998), greater perceived stress (E. C. Chang, 2006b), greater suicidal ideation (E. C. Chang, 1998), and less psychological well-being (E. C. Chang, 2006a; E. C. Chang, Watkins, & Banks, 2004). Likewise, studies with the MPS have also shown that higher scores on some of the three dimensions of perfectionism tapped by this instrument are associated with greater depressive symptoms (E. C. Chang & Sanna, 2001; Hewitt & Flett, 1993; Hewitt, Flett, & Ediger, 1996), less self-esteem (Flett, Hewitt, Blankstein, & O'Brien, 1991), greater fears and phobias (Blankstein, Flett, Hewitt, & Eng, 1993), greater eating disturbances (Downey & Chang, in press), greater neuroticism (Hewitt, Flett, & Blankstein, 1991), less sexual satisfaction between spouses (Habke, Hewitt, & Flett, 1999), greater perceived stress (E. C. Chang & Rand, 2000), and less psychological well-being (E. C. Chang, 2006b).

In light of these compelling findings linking perfectionism with psychological maladjustment, it should be of little surprise that there has been a growing trend to look at perfectionism as a destructive and dysfunctional condition (Blatt, 1995) and as a condition that appears to necessitate clinical attention and treatment (Halgin & Leahy, 1989; Hirsh & Hayward, 1998). However, it is not clear if perfectionism, like self-criticism, should be viewed as largely detrimental and hazardous to one's psychological adjustment as some of these findings would seem to indicate. Indeed, growing evidence is supporting a more inclusive view of the functions of perfectionism.

A Revised Look at Perfectionism: Not Just Multidimensional but Also Multifunctional. Decades before researchers conducted numerous empirical studies linking perfectionism to maladjustment, Hamachek (1978) made an important distinction between neurotic and normal perfectionism.

> Persons who might fit under the label "normal perfectionists" (whom we could just as easily refer to as skilled artists or careful workers or masters of their craft) are those who derive a very real sense of pleasure from the labors of a painstaking effort and *who feel free to be less precise as the situation permits.*

This is not, however, apt to be true for neurotic perfectionists. Here we have the sort of people whose efforts—even their best ones—never seem quite good enough, at least in their own eyes. It always seems to these persons that they could—and should—do better. Of course, what this does is to rob them of the satisfaction which might ordinarily accompany a superior achievement or at least a well-done job. And this is also why neurotic perfectionists are neurotic. They are unable to feel satisfaction because in their own eyes they *never seem to do things good enough to warrant that feeling.* (p. 27)

Hamachek's (1978) distinction is useful for many reasons but is especially important because the distinction helps to reconcile a key conundrum faced by researchers and scholars alike: namely, how can perfectionism always be bad when it is also obvious that as a society we often seek and desire perfectionism within society? The answer to this conundrum is that we may have failed to realize that not all people with perfectionism (or those dominant on perfectionistic processes) look or act alike and, perhaps more important, we may have failed to also consider the coexistence of two distinct functions of perfectionism, one adaptive (positive) and the other maladaptive (negative). Indeed, findings from some studies increasingly support a conceptual distinction between adaptive and maladaptive perfectionism. For example, recognizing the need to get beyond past theoretical frameworks that have tended to largely emphasize the maladaptive aspects of perfectionism as reflected in measures such as the FMPS and the MPS, several researchers have distinguished between positive and negative attributes of perfectionism (e.g., Bieling, Israeli, & Antony, 2004; Frost et al., 1993; Hill et al., 2004; Slaney, Rice, Mobley, Trippi, & Ashby, 2001; Terry-Short, Owens, Slade, & Dewey, 1995).

Performance Perfectionism: When High Standards of Performance Meet Outcome Cognitions. The lead author, E. C. Chang (2006a), has more recently proposed a model of perfectionism that integrates research and theory on outcome cognitions with high standards of performance. Indeed, the notion that activation of high standards of performance may operate in conjunction with the activation of outcome cognitions to determine behavior is not at all new. For some time, researchers have proposed self-regulation models that implicate the importance of goal-related standards that may sometimes lead to discrepancy experiences and of outcome cognitions that may direct or motivate behavior in such situations (e.g., Bandura, 1977; Rotter, 1954). When an individual perceives a discrepancy between some standard and a goal, positive and negative outcome cognitions are believed to play a powerful role in determining approach and avoidance behaviors, respectively (Carver & Scheier, 1982; Scheier & Carver, 1985). Therefore, it seems reasonable to expect that positive and negative outcome cognitions would naturally come into play when perceptions of high standards of performance are involved.

The first author, E. C. Chang (2006a), termed high standards of performance involving positive and negative outcome cognitions as *performance perfectionism*. Performance perfectionism is believed to represent a multifaceted construct that is determined not only by the presence of positive versus negative outcome cognitions but also by the source of high standards of performance, namely, self (for example) versus other (for example). Indeed, beyond high standards of performance, a number of different models of perfectionism have all pointed to the importance of distinguishing between self-oriented and socially prescribed sources. Therefore, because performance perfectionism may be determined by the valence (positive vs. negative) of the outcome cognitions involved and by the source of high standards of performance (self-oriented vs. socially prescribed), four distinguishable aspects of performance perfectionism can be considered. Within Chang's framework, two aspects of performance perfectionism are considered to be adaptive and two aspects of performance perfectionism are considered to be maladaptive. *Positive self-oriented performance perfectionism* is defined by high personal standards of performance that involve positive outcome cognitions for the individual. *Negative self-oriented performance perfectionism* is defined by high personal standards of performance that involve negative outcome cognitions for the individual. *Positive socially prescribed performance perfectionism* is defined by high standards of performance placed on an individual by others that involve positive outcome cognitions for the individual. *Negative socially prescribed performance perfectionism* is defined by high standards of performance placed on an individual by others that involve negative outcome cognitions for the individual. The Performance Perfectionism Scale (PPS) has been found to be a reliable and valid measure of these four dimensions (E. C. Chang, 2006a).

Consistent with expectations that performance perfectionism represents not only a multidimensional construct (E. C. Chang, 2006a, Study 1a & 1b) but also a multifunctional construct, studies with the PPS have shown that negative self-oriented and socially prescribed perfectionism are positively associated with measures of maladjustment (e.g., depressive symptoms, worry, stress; E. C. Chang, 2006a, Study 3a), whereas positive self-oriented and socially prescribed perfectionism are negatively associated with these measures of maladjustment. Alternatively, positive self-oriented and socially prescribed perfectionism have been found to be positively associated with measures of adjustment (e.g., life satisfaction, positive relations with others, purpose in life, personal growth; E. C. Chang, 2006a, Study 3b), whereas negative self-oriented and socially prescribed perfectionism have been found to be negatively associated with these measures of maladjustment. Moreover, the first author, E. C. Chang (2006a, Study 4) found positive self-oriented performance perfectionism to be the most robust unique positive predictor of college academic performance (viz., exam scores, course grade) even after intellectual ability was controlled for. Thus, these findings for performance perfectionism with the PPS underscore the importance of developing inclusive conceptual frameworks and measures that allow for new questions and answers to emerge. Indeed, if researchers studying perfectionism focused primarily on asking when or how perfectionism is maladaptive, then little progress could or would be made regarding the idea of perfectionism as also potentially adaptive.

Including Outcome Cognitions in the Study of Self-Criticism and Self-Enhancement: A Sketch of a Model. On the basis of emerging works on perfectionism, especially more recent works on performance perfectionism, an expanded view of self-criticism and self-enhancement can be considered. As noted earlier, popularized notions have typically held the idea that self-criticism is bad and self-enhancement is good. If we modify the framework to accommodate positive and negative outcome cognitions, then we may be able to consider self-criticism as involving both adaptive and maladaptive components, and self-enhancement as also involving both adaptive and maladaptive components (see Figure 14.1). As the figure shows, researchers can obtain support for what may have been popularly viewed as contradictory hypotheses (e.g., self-criticism is harmful to one's psychological well-being vs. self-criticism is beneficial to one's psychological well-being). This is because the potential functions of self-criticism and self-enhancement are neither singular nor mutually exclusive. Similar to what has been proposed in the first author's, E. C. Chang's (2006a), model of performance perfectionism, four possibilities for self-criticism and self-enhancement can be entertained. *Positive self-criticism* may be defined by negative self-referent thoughts that are associated with positive outcome cognitions (e.g., "I'm not very smart, but if I study harder I should do better on my next exam"). *Negative self-criticism* may be defined by negative self-referent thoughts that are associated with negative outcome cognitions (e.g., "I'm not very smart, so it is useless to even try to study for the next exam"). *Positive self-enhancement* may be defined by positive self-referent thoughts that are associated with positive outcome cognitions (e.g., "I'm smarter than most people, but I know if I study I'll ace the next exam no matter how hard it is"). Last, *negative self-enhancement* may be defined by positive self-referent thoughts that are associated with negative outcome cognitions (e.g., "I'm smarter than most people, but the teacher's exams are made to fail everyone so what's the use of studying?"). Indeed, a careful reading of the present volume shows that these theoretical possibilities not only are possible but may even have some initial empirical support. As stated earlier, self-criticism and self-enhancement are dynamic constructs and their function and dominance within an individual often do and will change across time and varying situations (see chaps. 10 and 11, this volume). And if self-criticism and self-enhancement are not amenable to change or some degree of self-regulation, then these processes can be modified through constructive interventions (see chaps. 12 and 13, this volume).

	Positive Outcomes	Negative Outcomes
Self-Criticism	Adaptive	Maladaptive
Self-Enhancement	Adaptive	Maladaptive

Figure 14.1. A multifunctional model of self-criticism and self-enhancement as a function of outcome cognitions.

Building Greater Depth and Breadth in Future Models: A Look at Stability and Contingencies of Self-Worth

In addition to considering a multidimensional and multifunctional model of self-criticism and self-enhancement, we believe that emerging research and theory on stability of self-esteem and contingencies of self-worth represent fruitful points of integration in future studies on self-criticism and self-enhancement.

Self-Esteem: Level and Stability Matter. Self-esteem is defined by a person's general sense of self-worth (Rosenberg, 1965). Thousands of studies over the past several decades have shown that self-esteem is an important and reliable hallmark of a wide variety of important psychological outcomes and conditions (Branden, 1994; Mruk, 1995). In general, individuals with high self-esteem have been found to be healthier and happier. In contrast, studies have shown that individuals with low self-esteem are at greater risk for maladjustment. For example, in one study, Trzesniewski et al. (2006) found that low self-esteem scores (as assessed at 11–13 years of age) uniquely predicted a wide range of negative outcomes at age 26, including major depressive disorder, poor cardiorespiratory health, perceived level of unfitness, and violent crime convictions, even after controlling for gender, socioeconomic status, and level of depression during adolescence.

Yet, findings from some studies on self-esteem have shown that high self-esteem alone may not always be sufficient to foster positive adjustment (e.g., Kernis, Cornell, Sun, Berry, & Harlow, 1993; Kernis, Grannemann, & Barclay, 1992). Indeed, some researchers have even pointed to potential links between high self-esteem and negative outcomes and conditions, including greater aggression (Baumeister, Campbell, Krueger, & Vohs, 2003; Baumeister, Smart, & Boden, 1996). As a consequence, researchers have begun to focus not only on level of self-esteem but also on stability of self-esteem. According to Kernis (2005), findings from a number of studies indicate that negative outcomes (e.g., greater anger and hostility proneness, greater reactivity to daily events, increase in depressive symptoms) are often associated with individuals who display unstable (fragile) high self-esteem compared with those with stable (secure) high self-esteem.

Contingencies of Self-Worth: Appreciating Sources of Self-Esteem. Beyond a look at level and stability of self-criticism and self-enhancement, emerging research on contingencies of self-worth highlights the potential value of also clarifying sources of these core constructs—namely, what areas of personal relevance drive a person's trait (or state) assessment of self-criticism and self-enhancement?

According to Crocker and Wolfe (2001), research on self-esteem has been dominated by global conceptualizations of this trait. As a result, these investigators argue that the lack of contextualization in past studies of self-esteem has led to inconsistencies in the research and theory (e.g., is self-esteem a trait or state?). In their view, some of these inconsistencies can be accounted for from within a framework that considers self-esteem in terms of *contingencies of self-worth*, that is, domains or categories of outcomes on which a person has staked his or her self-esteem. Building on earlier research on contingent self-worth, Crocker and her colleagues (Crocker & Luhtanen, 2003; Crocker, Luhtanen, Cooper, & Bouvrette, 2003; Crocker, Sommers, & Luhtanen, 2002; Crocker & Wolfe, 2001) identified seven distinct contingencies of self-worth (measured by the Contingencies of Self-Worth Scale [CSWS]; Crocker et al., 2003), namely, those involving others' approval (e.g., "My self-esteem depends on the opinions others hold of me"), appearance ("My self-esteem is influenced by how attractive I think my face or facial features are"), competition ("Doing better than others gives me a sense of self-respect"), competence ("My self-esteem is influenced by my academic performance"), family support ("It is important to my self-respect that I have a family that cares about me"), virtue ("My self-esteem depends on whether or not I follow my moral or ethical principles"), and faith ("My self-esteem goes up when I feel that God loves me"). Thus, within this model, a person's contingencies of self-worth are believed to impact fluctuations in state self-esteem, which rises or falls around its trait level when positive or negative outcomes emerge in domains most valued by the individual. Consistent with this view, findings from a number of studies with the CSWS have shown that when negative outcomes occurred for individuals in domains most valued by them (e.g., academic performance), their self-esteem levels dropped (e.g., Crocker et al., 2002; see Crocker & Knight, 2005, for a review).

Considering Trait Versus State and Sources of Self-Criticism and Self-Enhancement: Adding to a Sketch of a Model. Given our discussion of self-esteem, we believe there may be some value in looking not only for trait levels of self-criticism and self-enhancement among individuals but also for the stability of these constructs among individuals across time. Likewise, our brief look at emerging research on contingencies of self-worth suggests some possible value to contextualizing relevant sources of self-criticism and self-enhancement in individuals. Together, such a framework can help us attain a better sense of how and why different varieties of self-criticism and self-enhancement may remain high versus low and stable versus unstable, across different groups and goals (see Figure 14.2). The figure identifies, within this framework, varieties of self-criticism and self-enhancement associated with broad outcome cognitions in both trait (e.g., "I typically don't feel good about myself, so I know I will not reach any goals I pursue") and state forms (e.g., "Right now, I don't feel good about myself, so it's not likely that I'll be able to reach my goal"). In a similar way, we can look at specific contingencies of the self that may impact both trait and state dimensions of self-criticism and self-enhancement in individuals. For example, some students may strongly base how they think about themselves on their academic performance. One self-critical student may think in positive terms (e.g., "Doing well academically is important to me. If I don't do well, then it's probably because I'm not very smart. But, if I work harder, then I should at least do better next time"). Another self-critical student may think in more negative terms (e.g., "Doing well academically is important to me. If I don't do well, then it's probably because I'm not very smart. But, with this teacher, there's no way I can do very well in his class"). And, as the figure shows for competence, it is possible to hold positive and negative self-critical and self-enhancing thoughts because, for example, one can always deconstruct academic dimensions of competence involving the self to even more specific domains (e.g., math vs. English; Marsh, 1990; Marsh, Trautwein, Lüdtke, Köller, & Baumert, 2005). An appreciation of the different sources that may affect a person's trait and state experiences of self-criticism and self-enhancement may make it easier to see how an individual may embody multiple self-critical and self-enhancing selves in the aggregate form, even if one aspect is dominant within a particular domain. At the very least, we believe new models of self-criticism and self-enhancement are needed that can address and accommodate the complex findings that continue to emerge in the extant literature (e.g., Stapel & Van der Zee, 2006). In turn, such models may be useful in guiding the development of instruments that can be used in the assessment and treatment of different forms of self-criticism and self-enhancement in select populations (e.g., patients with clinical depression).

WHERE ARE WE GOING?

We end this chapter by discussing some of the ongoing challenges that remain to be addressed in the research on self-criticism and self-enhancement. Also, the first author of this chapter returns to follow up on the self-critical patient and student introduced earlier in this volume.

	Self-Criticism		Self-Enhancement	
	Positive	Negative	Positive	Negative
Trait	Adaptive	Maladaptive	Adaptive	Maladaptive
State		Maladaptive	Adaptive	
Appearance		Maladaptive	Adaptive	
Others' Approval	Adaptive			Maladaptive
Competition	Adaptive			Maladaptive
Virtue	Adaptive		Adaptive	
Family Support	Adaptive			Maladaptive
Competence	Adaptive	Maladaptive	Adaptive	Maladaptive
Faith		Maladaptive		Maladaptive

Figure 14.2. A hypothetical example of integrating a multifunctional model of self-criticism and self-enhancement within a framework of contingencies of self-worth.

Some Lingering Questions to Consider in Future Research

Thus far, we have examined how emerging research and theory on perfectionism and self-worth may hold some promise for the development of more inclusive and complex models of self-criticism and self-enhancement. Yet, many more questions still need to be answered. Among them are questions about developmental factors, variations across more diverse populations, and methodology.

First, consistent with the concern that temporal factors have often been neglected by researchers (Sanna & Chang, 2006), little research exists that focuses on identifying developmental factors linked to self-criticism and self-enhancement. Thus, it is not clear when one learns to be self-critical, self-enhancing, or both. Likewise, little is known about the sorts of conditions or experiences that help reinforce and establish trait self-criticism and self-enhancement (Grusec & Ezrin, 1972). However, if self-criticism and self-enhancement are not the result of learning, then do they reflect the workings of basic biological systems (e.g., behavioral inhibition and behavioral activation; Carver & White, 1994; Gray, 1990) or the unfolding of genetic influences (Neiss, Sedikides, & Stevenson, 2002)?

Second, much of the cross-cultural research looking at self-criticism and self-enhancement has focused on East versus West differences in young adults. Does this focus mean that self-criticism cannot function to improve the self for non-Asians (e.g., defensive pessimists)? Alternatively, is self-enhancement absent in Easterners compared with Westerners (E. C. Chang &

Asakawa, 2003; E. C. Chang, Asakawa, & Sanna, 2001; Sedikides, Gaertner, & Toguchi, 2003)? And what can be said about self-criticism and self-enhancement in other diverse groups, broadly defined, including different racial or ethnic and age groups?

Last, as mentioned by contributors of this volume, the answer to the question of what represents a useful methodology to best assess for self-criticism and self-enhancement is complex and in need of greater examination. On the basis of their review of the literature, Kwan, John, Kenny, Bond, and Robins (2004) argued that studies of self-enhancement have used methodologies drawn from either social comparison theory (e.g., a participant might be asked if the likelihood of failing a major exam is more likely, less likely, or about the same, compared with others) or models of self-insight (e.g., a participant's self-perception and perceptions of the participant by others are compared). Yet, these two approaches do not always yield convergent results. These researchers accordingly pointed to a need to consider newer methodologies that took into account three key components in the assessment of self-enhancement, namely, measurements of self-perceptions, perceptions of others, and perceptions by others. We think this promising approach should also be considered in future studies of self-criticism.

The Self-Critical Patient and Student: Some Hope for the Future

We end this chapter with a return to Ms. X and Mr. Y. What happened to these two self-critical individuals? Recall that Ms. X was the highly successful but self-critical artist that the first author was treating as an outpatient during his internship at Bellevue. The first author did not believe that dysthymia was an accurate diagnosis for the patient in light of a careful review of her records, direct and multiple assessments with the patient, and clear counterindicators, including great professional successes and involvement in a good long-term relationship with her partner. In essence, this person was doing more than just reaching for the American dream; she was making it happen for herself. Her main problem was that she had convinced herself, and perhaps even past interns, that her self-criticism must be maladaptive given the way everyone views negative self-focused thinking as problematic, if not pathological. So, after careful consideration of the case and discussions with the supervisor, the first author developed a plan to help Ms. X gain greater appreciation for all of her successes, while not working directly to alleviate or eliminate her self-critical ways. After more than 4 months in which Ms. X chronically complained about how therapeutically useless and ineffective the first author was in reducing her self-critical ways, she missed her appointment for the first time since she began treatment at Bellevue more than 4 years prior. Of course, the first author was very concerned, and when he made contact with her over the phone the following day, he was relieved to find that she was okay. She had been so busy setting up for a new gallery showing that she had forgotten and missed her appointment. And when Ms. X was asked to reschedule for the following week, she indicated that she was too busy to do so. To the first author's great surprise, Ms. X added that she was not getting much in therapy from the first author and she was too busy to see him or anyone else to continue her treatment. She further added that if things should ever get "bad" enough for her, she knew how to get a hold of someone at the hospital. Trained to focus on follow-up assessments, the first author contacted Ms. X 1 month and 6 months by phone after their last session together. Was she still self-critical? Yes. Was she still very successful in her profession and involved in a happy and growing relationship? Yes. During the last conversation with Ms. X, she admitted that she had learned to live with her self-criticism rather than see it as something that she needed to get rid of. In fact, she reflected on the possibility that it was her ability to appreciate her self-criticism in constructive ways that allowed her to be as successful as she has been and continued to be. It is interesting to note that, in Japan, Morita therapy has long been used to treat individuals who present with various psychological problems (e.g., anxiety); this treatment is not directly focused on eliminating these problems, per se, but rather on helping individuals learn to constructively live with them in their daily lives (S. C. Chang, 1974). It is ironic that what the first author viewed as a potential clinical success was received by some of his clinical peers as an unfortunate loss.

And, what happed to Mr. Y, the self-critical graduate school applicant? After some concerns were raised about Mr. Y, the first author reminded others on the admissions committee that in this case, Mr. Y's self-criticism was associated with fewer, not greater, signs or samples of problematic behavior. The positive association between Mr. Y's self-criticism and his achievements clearly did not point to the expected self-punitive individual others might have imagined was at high risk for developing major depressive disorder. So, Mr. Y was invited for an interview and to the delight of the committee, impressed all of us with his high intellect, genuine scientific curiosity, high emotional maturity, and overall high positive energy. We did not see any signs of the self-criticism Mr. Y had mentioned in his own self-statements. Several weeks after the interview, Mr. Y was notified that he was one of the best applicants the panel had seen in a while and that the panel would be delighted if he would decide to attend the clinical doctoral psychology program at the university. He did and has continued to be successful and highly regarded by his peers and those who work with him.

In closing, the constructs of self-criticism and self-enhancement are central not only to understanding oneself but also to improving one's life. And because human behavior is dynamic and complex, why should it be a surprise that these constructs demand representations that reflect dynamic and complex processes? Indeed, as the chapters of this volume have collectively shown, the constructs of self-criticism and self-enhancement affect and are affected by a variety of causal mechanisms, contextual factors, and outcomes that continuously shape and determine people's everyday interactions with themselves and with the world around them. Bold new models, measures, and methods are now needed to better map these complexities. In turn, the fruits of such developments may one day help modern scientists and practitioners alike to slowly move away from popular but limiting models of self-criticism and self-enhancement.

REFERENCES

Aitken, R. (1994). *The practice of perfection: The Pāramitās from a Zen Buddhist perspective*. New York: Pantheon Books.

Bandura, A. (1977). Self-efficacy: Toward a unifying theory of behavioral change. *Psychological Review, 84*, 191–215.

Baumeister, R. F., Campbell, J. D., Krueger, J. I., & Vohs, K. E. (2003). Does high self-esteem cause better performance, interpersonal success, happiness, or healthier lifestyles? *Psychological Science in the Public Interest, 4*, 1–44.

Baumeister, R. F., Smart, L., & Boden, J. M. (1996). Relation of threatened egotism to violence and aggression: The dark side of high self-esteem. *Psychological Review, 103*, 5–33.

Bieling, P. J., Israeli, A. L., & Antony, M. M. (2004). Is perfectionism good, bad, or both? Examining models of the perfectionism construct. *Personality and Individual Differences, 36*, 1373–1385.

Blankstein, K. R., Flett, G. L., Hewitt, P. L., & Eng, A. (1993). Dimensions of perfectionism and irrational fears: An examination with the Fear Survey Schedule. *Personality and Individual Differences, 15*, 323–328.

Blatt, S. J. (1995). The destructiveness of perfectionism: Implications for the treatment of depression. *American Psychologist, 50*, 1003–1020.

Branden, N. (1994). *The six pillars of self-esteem*. New York: Bantam Books.

Burns, D. D. (1980, November). The perfectionist's script for self-defeat. *Psychology Today, 14*, 34–52.

Carver, C. S., & Scheier, M. F. (1982). Control theory: A useful conceptual framework for personality–social, clinical, and health psychology. *Psychological Bulletin, 92*, 111–135.

Carver, C. S., & White, T. L. (1994). Behavioral inhibition, behavioral activation, and affective responses to impending reward and punishment: The BIS/BAS scales. *Journal of Personality and Social Psychology, 67*, 319–333.

Chang, E. C. (1998). Cultural differences, perfectionism, and suicidal risk: Does social problem solving still matter? *Cognitive Therapy and Research, 22*, 237–254.

Chang, E. C. (2006a). Conceptualization and measurement of adaptive and maladaptive aspects of performance perfectionism: Relations to personality, psychological functioning, and academic achievement. *Cognitive Therapy and Research, 30*, 677–697.

Chang, E. C. (2006b). Perfectionism and dimensions of psychological well-being in a college student sample: A test of a stress-mediation model. *Journal of Social and Clinical Psychology, 25*, 1021–1042.

Chang, E. C., & Asakawa, K. (2003). Cultural variations on optimistic and pessimistic bias for self versus a sibling: Is there evidence for self-enhancement in the West and self-criticism in the East when the referent group is specified? *Journal of Personality and Social Psychology, 84*, 569–581.

Chang, E. C., Asakawa, K., & Sanna, L. J. (2001). Cultural variations in optimistic and pessimistic bias: Do Easterners really expect the worst and Westerners really expect the best when predicting future life events? *Journal of Personality and Social Psychology, 81*, 476–491.

Chang, E. C., & Rand, K. L. (2000). Perfectionism as a predictor of subsequent adjustment: Evidence for a specific diathesis-stress mechanism among college students. *Journal of Counseling Psychology, 47*, 129–137.

Chang, E. C., & Sanna, L. J. (2001). Negative attributional style as a moderator of the link between perfectionism and depressive symptoms: Preliminary evidence for an integrative model. *Journal of Counseling Psychology, 48*, 490–495.

Chang, E. C., Watkins, A. F., & Banks, K. H. (2004). How adaptive and maladaptive perfectionism relate to positive and negative psychological functioning: Testing a stress-mediation model in Black and White female college students. *Journal of Counseling Psychology, 51*, 93–102.

Chang, E. C., Zumberg, K. M., Sanna, L. J., Girz, L. P., Kade, A. M., Shair, S. R., et al. (in press). Relationship between perfectionism and domains of worry in a college student population: Considering the role of BIS/BAS motives. *Personality and Individual Differences*.

Chang, S. C. (1974). Morita therapy. *American Journal of Psychotherapy, 28*, 208–211.

Crocker, J., & Knight, K. M. (2005). Contingencies of self-worth. *Current Directions in Psychological Science, 14*, 200–203.

Crocker, J., & Luhtanen, R. K. (2003). Level of self-esteem and contingencies of self-worth: Unique effects on academic, social, and financial problems in college students. *Personality and Social Psychology Bulletin, 29*, 701–712.

Crocker, J., Luhtanen, R. K., Cooper, M. L., & Bouvrette, A. (2003). Contingencies of self-worth in college students: Theory and measurement. *Journal of Personality and Social Psychology, 85*, 894–908.

Crocker, J., Sommers, S. R., & Luhtanen, R. K. (2002). Hopes dashed and dreams fulfilled: Contingencies of self-worth and graduate school admissions. *Personality and Social Psychology Bulletin, 28*, 1275–1286.

Crocker, J., & Wolfe, C. T. (2001). Contingencies of self-worth. *Psychological Review, 108*, 593–623.

Downey, C. A., & Chang, E. C. (in press). Perfectionism and symptoms of eating disturbances in female college students: Considering the role of negative affect and body dissatisfaction. *Eating Behaviors*.

Dunkley, D. M., Zuroff, D. C., & Blankstein, K. R. (2003). Self-critical perfection-ism and daily affect: Dispositional and situational influences on stress and cop-ing. *Journal of Personality and Social Psychology, 84,* 234–252.

Dunkley, D. M., Zuroff, D. C., & Blankstein, K. R. (2006). Specific perfectionism components versus self-criticism in predicting maladjustment. *Personality and Individual Differences, 40,* 665–676.

Flett, G. L., Hewitt, P. L., Blankstein, K. R., & O'Brien, S. (1991). Perfectionism and learned resourcefulness in depression and self-esteem. *Personality and Individual Differences, 12,* 61–68.

Frost, R. O., Heimberg, R. G., Holt, C. S., Mattia, J. I., & Neubauer, A. L. (1993). A comparison of two measures of perfectionism. *Personality and Individual Differences, 14,* 119–126.

Frost, R. O., Marten, P., Lahart, C., & Rosenblate, R. (1990). The dimensions of perfectionism. *Cognitive Therapy and Research, 14,* 449–468.

Frost, R. O., & Steketee, G. (1997). Perfectionism in obsessive-compulsive disorder patients. *Behaviour Research and Therapy, 35,* 291–296.

Gray, J. A. (1990). Brain systems that mediate both emotion and cognition. *Cognition and Emotion, 4,* 269–288.

Grusec, J. E., & Ezrin, S. A. (1972). Techniques of punishment and the development of self-criticism. *Child Development, 43,* 1273–1288.

Habke, A. M., Hewitt, P. L., & Flett, G. L. (1999). Perfectionism and sexual satisfac-tion in intimate relationships. *Journal of Psychopathology and Behavioral Assess-ment, 21,* 307–322.

Halgin, R. P., & Leahy, P. M. (1989). Understanding and treating perfectionistic college students. *Journal of Counseling and Development, 68,* 222–225.

Hamachek, D. E. (1978). Psychodynamics of normal and neurotic perfectionism. *Psychology, 15,* 27–33.

Hewitt, P. L., & Flett, G. L. (1991). Perfectionism in the self and social contexts: Conceptualization, assessment, and association with psychopathology. *Journal of Personality and Social Psychology, 60,* 456–470.

Hewitt, P. L., & Flett, G. L. (1993). Dimensions of perfectionism, daily stress, and depression: A test of the specific vulnerability hypothesis. *Journal of Abnormal Psychology, 102,* 58–65.

Hewitt, P. L., & Flett, G. L. (Eds.). (2002). *Perfectionism: Theory, research, and treat-ment.* Washington, DC: American Psychological Association.

Hewitt, P. L., Flett, G. L., & Blankstein, K. R. (1991). Perfectionism and neuroti-cism in psychiatric patients and college students. *Personality and Individual Dif-ferences, 12,* 273–279.

Hewitt, P. L., Flett, G. L., & Ediger, E. (1996). Perfectionism and depression: Longi-tudinal assessment of a specific vulnerability hypothesis. *Journal of Abnormal Psychology, 105,* 276–280.

Hill, R. W., Huelsman, T. J., Furr, R. M., Kibler, J., Vicente, B. B., & Kennedy, C. (2004). A new measure of perfectionism: The Perfectionism Inventory. *Journal of Personality Assessment, 82,* 80–91.

Hirsh, C. R., & Hayward, P. (1998). The perfect patient: Cognitive-behavioural therapy for perfectionism. *Behavioural and Cognitive Psychotherapy, 26,* 359–364.

Kawamura, K. Y., Hunt, S. L., Frost, R. O., & DiBartolo, P. M. (2001). Perfectionism, anxiety, and depression: Are the relationships independent? *Cognitive Therapy and Research, 25,* 291–301.

Kernis, M. H. (2005). Measuring self-esteem in context: The importance of stability of self-esteem in psychological functioning. *Journal of Personality, 73,* 1–37.

Kernis, M. H., Cornell, D. P., Sun, C. R., Berry, A. J., & Harlow, T. (1993). There's more to self-esteem than whether it is high or low: The importance of stability of self-esteem. *Journal of Personality and Social Psychology, 65,* 1190–1204.

Kernis, M. H., Grannemann, B. D., & Barclay, L. C. (1992). Stability of self-esteem: Assessment, correlates, and excuse making. *Journal of Personality and Social Psychology, 56,* 1013–1023.

Kwan, V. S. Y., John, O. P., Kenny, D. A., Bond, M. H., & Robins, R. W. (2004). Reconceptualizing individual differences in self-enhancement bias: An interpersonal approach. *Psychological Review, 111,* 94–110.

La Rondelle, H. K. (1971). *Perfection and perfectionism: A dogmatic-ethical study of biblical perfection and phenomenal perfectionism.* Berrien Spring, MI: Andrews University Press.

Marsh, H. W. (1990). The structure of academic self-concept: The Marsh/Shavelson model. *Journal of Educational Psychology, 82,* 623–636.

Marsh, H. W., Trautwein, U., Lüdtke, O., Köller, O., & Baumert, J. (2005). Academic self-concept, interest, grades, and standardized test scores: Reciprocal effects models of causal ordering. *Child Development, 76,* 397–416.

Milosh, J. E. (1966). *The scale of perfection and the English mystical tradition.* Madison, WI: University of Wisconsin Press.

Mruk, C. J. (1995). *Self-esteem: Research, theory, and practice.* New York: Springer.

Neiss, M. B., Sedikides, C., & Stevenson, J. (2002). Self-esteem: A behaviour genetic perspective. *European Journal of Personality, 16,* 351–368.

Ratnayaka, S. (1978). *Two ways of perfection: Buddhist and Christian.* Sri Lanka, India: Lake House Printers and Publishers.

Rice, K. G., Ashby, J. S., & Slaney, R. B. (1998). Self-esteem as a mediator between perfectionism and depression: A structural equations analysis. *Journal of Counseling Psychology, 45,* 304–314.

Rosenberg, M. (1965). *Society and the adolescent self-image.* Princeton, NJ: Princeton University Press.

Rotter, J. B. (1954). *Social learning and clinical psychology.* Englewood Cliffs, NJ: Prentice Hall.

Saboonchi, F., Lundh, L.-G., & Öst, L.-G. (1999). Perfectionism and self-consciousness in social phobia and panic disorder with agoraphobia. *Behaviour Research and Therapy, 37,* 799–808.

Sanna, L. J., & Chang, E. C. (Eds.). (2006). *Judgments over time: The interplay of thoughts, feelings, and behaviors.* New York: Oxford University Press.

Scheier, M. F., & Carver, C. S. (1985). Optimism, coping, and health: Assessment and implications of generalized outcome expectancies. *Health Psychology, 4,* 219–247.

Sedikides, C., Gaertner, L., & Toguchi, Y. (2003). Pancultural self-enhancement. *Journal of Personality and Social Psychology, 84,* 60–79.

Shafran, R., & Mansell, W. (2001). Perfectionism and psychopathology: A review of research and treatment. *Clinical Psychology Review, 21,* 879–906.

Shahar, G., Blatt, S. J., Zuroff, D. C., & Pilkonis, P. A. (2003). Role of perfectionism and personality disorder features in response to brief treatment for depression. *Journal of Consulting and Clinical Psychology, 71,* 629–633.

Slaney, R. B., Rice, K. G., Mobley, M., Trippi, J., & Ashby, J. S. (2001). The Revised Almost Perfect Scale. *Measurement and Evaluation in Counseling and Development, 34,* 130–145.

Stapel, D. A., & Van der Zee, K. I. (2006). The self-salience of other-to-self effects: Integrating principles of self-enhancement, complementarity, and imitation. *Journal of Personality and Social Psychology, 90,* 258–271.

Stöber, J. (1998). The Frost Multidimensional Perfectionism Scale revisited: More perfect with four (instead of six) dimensions? *Personality and Individual Differences, 24,* 481–491.

Terry-Short, L. A., Owens, R. G., Slade, P. D., & Dewey, M. E. (1995). Positive and negative perfectionism. *Personality and Individual Differences, 18,* 663–668.

Trzesniewski, K. H., Donnellan, M. B., Moffitt, T. E., Robins, R. W., Poulton, R., & Caspi, A. (2006). Low self-esteem during adolescence predicts poor health, criminal behavior, and limited economic prospects during adulthood. *Developmental Psychology, 42,* 381–390.

AUTHOR INDEX

Numbers in italics refer to listings in the references.

Clara, I. P., 91, *102*, 191, *194*
Clark, D. A., 60, 67
Clark, L. A., 55, 67, 79, 83
Clarke, G., 58, 69
Clarke, M., 189, *195*
Clearke, M., 100, *102*
Clore, G. L., 167, 171, *179*
Coates, D., 23, *31*
Cobi, J., *50*
Cohen, D., 114, 115, *119*
Cohen, F., 42, *50*
Cohen, S., 23, *31*
Colditz, G. A., 144, *154*
Colligan, R. C., 47, *51*
Collins, R. L., 125, *139*, 186, *194*
Colvin, C. R., 19, 20, 25, 28, *31*, *32*, 124,
    125, 126, 127, 128, 131, 132, 134,
    135, *137*, *138*, *140*, 190, *194*
Contrada, R. J., 41, *50*
Cook, K. E., 28, *30*
Cook, W. W., 127, *137*
Cooper, A. C., 162, *177*
Cooper, M. L., 256, *262*
Copleston, F., 124, *137*
Cornell, D. P., 255, *264*
Costa, P. T., 131, 132, 134, *137*, *139*, 187,
    189, *194*
Costello, N., *50*
Cote, S., 75, 86
Cousins, S. D., 114, *119*
Cox, B., 64, 68, 230, *244*
Cox, B. J., 80, 81, 83, 84, 91, *102*, 191, *194*
Coyle, C. T., 190, *194*
Coyne, J. C., 76, 78, 81, 82, 84, 101, *102*
Craig, J. A., 76, 86
Craighead, W. E., 59, 69
Craik, K. H., 130, *137*
Craske, M. G., 187, *194*
Critelli, J. W., 130, *138*
Crocker, J., 256, *262*
Cronbach, L. J., 126, 131, *137*
Cross, S., 114, *121*
Croyle, R. T., 148, *154*, *155*
Crystal, D., 111, *119*
Csikszentmihalyi, M., 8, *15*, 21, *34*
Cummings, N., 42, 53

Dadds, M. M., 187, *192*
D'Afflitti, J. P., 60, 61, 66, 79, 83, 188, *193*
Dalgard, O., 44, *50*
Danner, D. D., 22, *32*
Dardis, G. J., 184, *197*

Dauenheimer, D. G., 185, *194*
Davidson, K., 145, *154*
Davis, W., 142, *156*
Deci, E. L., 190, *194*
Decker, S., 23, *34*
Deich, J., 45, *50*
Dekel, S., 23, *30*
DeMonbreun, B. G., 211, *224*
Dent, J., 56, *70*
de Ridder, D., 27, *32*
Dermody, J., *103*
DeRubeis, R. J., 39, *54*, 56, 58, 60, 66, 67,
    68
DeVincent, C. J., 41, *51*
de Vries, T., *50*
Dewberry, C., 145, *154*
Dewey, M. E., 252, *265*
DiBartolo, P. M., 251, *264*
Dickerson, S. S., 191, *194*
Diener, E., 21, 22, 23, *32*, *33*, 114, *119*
Diener, M., 21, *32*
Dillard, A. J., 147, 149, *154*
Di Paula, A., 188, *193*
Ditto, P. H., 148, *154*, *155*
Dobson, K., 56, 59, 60, 63, 67, 68, 69, *70*
Dohr, K. B., 63, 68
Doi, T., 9, *13*
Donnellan, M. B., 26, *32*, *265*
Doren, B., 63, 68
Dougall, A. L., 26, *32*
Dougher, M. J., 222, *224*
Downey, C. A., 251, *262*
Driscoll, R., 229, 233, 234, *244*
Duncan, N., 61, *71*, 74, 76, 78, 86
Duncan, T., 190, *196*
Dunkelberg, W. C., 162, *177*
Dunkel-Schetter, C., 41, *52*
Dunkley, D. M., 61, 64, 68, 249, *263*
Dunn, E. W., 184, *198*
Dunning, D., 143, *155*, 162, *177*, 185, *194*
Dutton, K. A., 28, *32*, 182, *193*
Duval, S., 114, *120*
Dwyer, J., 48, *51*
Dyck, M. J., 60, 68

Ediger, E., 251, *263*
Edmonds, G. W. A., 126, *138*
Ee, J. S., 130, *138*
Efantis-Potter, J., *50*
Elliot, A. J., 90, *102*, 116, *120*, 130, *138*,
    189, 190, *193*, *197*
Ellis, A., 7, *14*, 228, *244*

Elstein, A. S., 144, *154*
Emery, G., 57, 66, 206, *223*, 231, *243*
Emmons, K., *154*
Emmons, R. A., 189, *194*
Endo, Y., 22, *32*
Eng, A., 251, *261*
Enns, M., 64, 68, 80, *84*, 91, *102*, 191, *194*, 230, *244*
Enright, R. D., 190, *194*
Epley, N., 162, *177*
Erez, A., 188, *195*
Ernst, D., 60, 68
Eronen, S., 90, *102*
Evans, M. D., 59, 67, 68
Exline, J. J., 189, 190, *194*
Eyre, S. L., 55, 67
Eysenck, H. J., *138*
Eysenck, M., 56, 69
Eysenck, S. B. G., *138*
Ezrin, S. A., 258, *263*

Fagan, P. J., 131, *139*
Fahey, J. L., 43, *53*, 174, *179*
Fairey, P. J., 172, *177*
Fanning, P., 233, 234, 236, *244*
Fazaa, N., 79, *84*
Federenko, I., *51*
Feeley, M., 58, 67
Feick, D. L., 93, *104*
Feldman, O., 112, *120*
Feldman, P. J., *53*
Felsen, I., 62, 66
Fennell, M., 203, 207, 215, *223*
Fenton-O'Creevy, M., 26, *32*
Fernandez, J. K., 163, *179*
Fichman, L., 74, 75, 79, *84*
Field, N. P., 24, *30*
Finkel, E. J., 189, 190, *193*, *194*
Fischhoff, B., 142, *156*
Fiske, D. W., 127, *137*
Fitzgerald, T. E., 41, *50*
Fitzpatrick, D. K., 76, *86*
Fleming, B., 206, *223*
Fletcher, B., 42, *53*
Flett, G., 63, 64, 68, 76, *84*, 188, *195*, 229, 234, *244*, 250, 251, *261*, *263*
Flory, J. D., 41, *52*
Flynn, C., 234, *244*
Foerster, J., 116, *120*
Folkman, S., 22, 24, *32*, *33*
Follette, V. M., 222, *224*
Ford, R. Q., 62, 66

Fortman, S. P., 147, *158*
Foster, C. A., 190, *193*
Fournier, M., 27, *32*
Fowers, B. J., 22, *32*
Franche, R. L., 60, 68
Frank, C., 42, *53*
Frank, E., 147, *158*
Franklin, J., 63, 69
Franko, D. L., 76, *86*
Franze, S., 188, *195*
Fredrickson, B. L., 22, *32*, 174, 175, *177*
Freedman, S. R., 190, *194*
Freeman, A., 206, 211, 216, *223*
Freitas, A. L., 116, *120*
Freud, S., 6, *14*
Frick, P. J., 28, *30*
Friedman, H. S., 47, *52*
Friesen, W. V., 22, *32*
Frist, W. H., 41, *51*
Frost, R. O., 63, 64, 68, 188, *195*, 249, 250, 251, 252, *263*, *264*
Fuchs, C. Z., 58, 70
Funder, D. C., 25, 28, *32*, 124, 125, 128, 131, 132, 135, *137*, *138*, 190, *194*
Fung, H., 115, *121*
Fung, K., 41, 49
Furr, R. M., 135, *138*, *264*

Gaab, J., *51*
Gabriel, M. T., 130, *138*
Gaertner, L., 27, *34*, 107, *122*, 191, *197*, 259, *265*
Gagné, F. M., 22, *32*, 93, *102*
Ganellen, R., 63, 67
Garber, J., 7, *14*
Gardner, W. L., 116, *121*
Garfinkel, H., 227, *244*
Garvey, M. J., 67
Gauvin, L., 55, 70
Geaghan, T. R., 143, *156*
Gelder, M. G., *224*
Gergen, K., 78, 82, *84*
Gerin, W., 45, 46, *50*
Gerrard, M., 143, 148, 149, *154*, *155*
Gervey, B., 185, *198*
Geyer, A. L., 190, *194*
Gheen, M. H., 185, *196*
Gibbons, F. X., 148, 149, *154*, *155*
Gibson, B., 26, *33*
Gidron, Y., 44, 48, *50*
Giladi, E. E., 107, 108, *121*
Gilain, L., 41, 49

Gilbert, P., 100, *102*, 189, *195*
Gillham, J. E., 218, *224*
Gilovich, T., 163, 170, *177*
Gilutz, H., 44, *50*
Girdler, S. S., *50*
Girz, L. P., *262*
Giuliano, T. A., 187, *198*
Godaert, G. L., *50*
Godfrey, D. K., 185, *195*
Goethals, G. R., 141, *155*
Goffman, E., 84, 117, *120*, 227, 230, *244*
Goldman, S. L., 187, *197*
Gollan, J. K., 69
Gollwitzer, P. M., 96, *102*, 127, *140*, 146,
        157, 170, 171, *177*
Goodie, A. S., 188, *197*
Goodkin, K., *50*
Gordon, L., 74, *84*
Gotlib, I. H., 59, 68
Gough, H. G., *138*
Govorun, O., 182, *192*
Goyal, T. M., *50*
Graber, J. A., 188, *198*
Gramzow, R. H., 130, *138*, 188, *195*
Grannemann, B. D., 255, *264*
Gray, J. A., 258, *263*
Green, J. D., 182, 185, *195*, *197*
Greenberger, D., 206, 211, 212, 215, *224*
Greenspan, S. L., *52*
Greenwald, A. G., 8, *14*, 107, *121*
Gregg, A. P., 28, *34*, 182, 189, 190, *195*, *197*
Gregory, W. L., 171, 172, *178*
Grewen, K., 47, 48, *50*
Griffin, D., *34*, 141, 143, *154*, *156*, 162, 166,
        177, *178*, 189, *195*
Griffo, R., 128, *138*
Grosch, J. W., 188, *198*
Gross, T. M., 149, *157*
Grove, M. J., 68
Grove, W. M., 67
Gruenewald, T. L., 23, *35*, 126, *140*, 164,
        179, 191, *194*
Grusec, J. E., 258, *263*
Grzegorek, J. L., 188, *195*
Gudleski, G. D., 79, *84*
Guichard, C., 41, *49*
Gulanski, B. I., *52*
Gump, B., 41, 46, *50*, *52*
Gunz, A., 114, *119*
Guppy, A., 144, *155*

Haaga, D. A., 60, 68, 231, *244*

Habke, A., 234, *244*, 251, *263*
Hafdahl, A. R., 188, *195*
Haheim, L., 44, *50*
Halgin, R. P., *263*
Hall, B., 111, *120*
Hamachek, D. E., 251, 252, *263*
Hamamura, T., 106, 107, 108, *120*
Hamann, S., 45, 49
Hamilton, L. V., 112, *120*
Hammon, D., 190, *196*
Hankin, B. L., 27, *33*
Hanson, L. R., Jr., 165, *178*
Hardin, D. P., 184, *197*
Hardison, E., 237, *244*
Harlow, T., 255, *264*
Harris, M. J., 70
Harris, P., 151, *155*
Harris, S. D., *31*
Harter, S., 100, *102*
Hasher, L., 63, 68
Hathaway, S. R., *138*
Hayes, S. C., 221, *224*
Hayward, M. C., 26, *32*
Hayward, P., *264*
Heatherton, T. F., 26, *33*, *35*, 165, *177*, 188,
        198
Heaton, T. B., 19, *33*
Heidegger, M., 4, *14*
Heimberg, R. G., 64, 68, *195*, 250, *263*
Heine, S. J., 22, *32*, 105, 106, 107, 108, 109,
        111, 113, 114, 116, *120*, *122*, 191,
        195
Held, B. S., 8, *14*
Helgeson, V. S., 42, 46, *50*, 76, 79, *84*, 145,
        155
Hellhammer, D. H., 39, *52*
Helweg-Larsen, M., 141, *155*, 162, 166, 174,
        175, *178*, *179*
Hempel, S., 100, *102*, 189, *195*
Hengeveld, M. W., *50*
Herbert, M., 24, *35*, *157*
Herbst, K., 184, *197*
Hessling, R. M., 148, *155*
Hewitt, P., 63, 64, 68, 76, *84*, 188, *195*, 229,
        234, *244*, 250, 251, 261, *263*
Higgins, E. T., 115, 116, *120*
Higgins, R., 234, *244*
Hill, R. W., 252, *264*
Hillel, A., 47, *51*
Hirsh, C. R., *264*
Ho, D. Y. F., 110, 111, 117, *120*
Hodson, G., 113, *122*

Niebuhr, R., 228, *244*
Niedenthal, P. M., 97, *102*
Nietzel, M. T., *70*
Nisbett, R. E., 106, *121*, *122*
Nixon, M., 145, *154*
Noguchi, M., 111, *120*
Nolen-Hoeksema, S., 7, *14*
Norasakkunkit, V., 8, *14*
Norem, J. K., 90, 91, 92, 93, 94, 95, 96, 97, 99, 100, *102*, *103*, *104*, 169, 170, *178*, *192*, *196*
Norenzayan, A., 105, 106, 109, *121*, *122*
Noriega, V., *31*
Nurmi, J. E., 90, *102*

O'Brien, P., *52*
O'Brien, S., 251, *263*
O'Connor, B. P., 39, *51*
Odean, T., 162, *178*
Offord, K. P., 47, *51*
O'Hanlon, W., 236, *244*
Olff, M., *50*
Ortega, L., 162, *179*
Ortega, S., 42, *53*
Osaka, E., 8, *15*
Ossorio, P., 227, 229, 230, 234, 236, *245*
Öst, L.-G., 251, *264*
Ostendorf, F., 124, 125, *136*
Otsubo, Y., 113, *122*
Ouellette, J. A., 163, 167, 168, 169, *179*
Owen, N., *53*
Owens, J. F., *34*, 41, *52*
Owens, R. G., 252, *265*
Ozer, D. J., 132, *138*

Padesky, C., 206, 211, 212, 215, *224*
Page, S., 79, *84*
Palfai, T. P., 187, *197*
Panter, A. T., 188, *195*
Passmore, J., 192, *196*
Patterson, R. L., 191, *197*
Paulhus, D. L., 25, 26, 28, 29, *34*, 124, 125, 127, 132, 134, 135, *138*, *139*, 189, 190, *196*
Pavlovic, J. D., 190, *193*
Pbert, L. A., 167, *179*
Peake, P. K., 130, *139*
Pearlin, L. I., 44, *51*, 145, *156*
Peñaranda-Ortega, M., 105, *122*
Peng, K., 106, *121*, *122*
Pennebaker, J. W., 38, *54*
Pentecost, H. C., 108n1, *122*

Perisaki, C., 205, *224*
Peterson, C., 7, 8, *15*, 43, 47, 48, *51*, *52*, 96, *103*, 164, 175, *178*
Pham, L. B., 44, *52*
Piasecki, J. M., 68
Pickering, T., 45, *50*
Pilkonis, P. A., 67, 188, *193*, 249, *265*
Pinter, B., 182, 185, *195*, *197*
Pittman, T. S., 82, 84
Platt, B., 78, 82, 85
Pomerantz, E. M., 186, *198*
Pontari, B. A., 176, *179*
Potthoff, J. G., 79, 82, 85
Poulin, F., 25, *30*
Poulton, R., *265*
Powell, A., *196*
Powers, T. A., 74, 76, 78, 79, 81, 82, 85, 86, 101, *104*, 185, 188, *196*
Pozo, C., *31*
Pransky, G. S., 41, *50*
Pretzer, J. L., 206, 218, 223, *224*
Price, P. C., 108n1, *122*
Price, S., 142, *154*
Priel, B., 61, *70*, 76, 79, 85, 191, *193*
Prilleltensky, I., 9, *15*
Pringle, J. D., 77, 86
Prkachin, K., 145, *154*
Pruessner, J. C., 39, 40, *51*, *52*

Quadrel, M. J., 142, *156*
Quinlan, D. M., 60, 61, 66, 67, 79, 83, 188, *193*
Quiñones-Vidal, E., 105, *122*

Rabavilas, A. D., 205, *224*
Radcliffe, N. M., 144, 145, 147, 148–149, 150, *156*
Rafalson, L., *50*
Räikkönen, K., 41, *52*
Rand, K. L., 251, *262*
Rapee, R. M., 187, *192*
Raskin, R., 26, *34*, 133, *139*
Ratnayaka, S., *264*
Rector, N. A., 74, *83*, 101, *104*
Redding, G., 112, *122*
Redei, E., 39, *54*
Reed, G. M., 23, *35*, 41, 42, 43, 48, *52*, *53*, 126, *140*, 150, *156*, 164, *179*
Reeder, G., 189, 190, *193*, *197*
Rehm, L. P., 58, 63, *70*
Reid, D., *139*
Reinecke, M. A., 26, *35*

Reivich, K. J., 218, *224*
Rennicke, C., 23, *30*
Reuben, C., 90, 92, 97, *104*
Rhodewalt, F., 189, 190, *196*
Rice, K. G., 65, *70*, 188, *195*, 251, 252, *264*, *265*
Richardson, J., 41, 45, *51*, *52*
Richardson, S., 145, *154*
Richter, L., 27, *30*
Ridgeway, V., 56, 69
Rini, C. K., 41, *52*
Robbins, R. J., *52*
Roberts, B. W., 126, *138*
Roberts, N. E., 142, *158*
Robins, C. J., 76, 79, 85, 101, *104*
Robins, R. W., 20, 25, 26, 28, 29, *32*, *33*, *34*, 125, 126, 130, 133, 135, *138*, *139*, 144, *156*, 175, *179*, 190, *195*, 259, *264*, *265*
Robinson, D. S., *31*
Robinson, M. D., 187, *198*
Rodin, J., 42, 43, 46, 48, *51*, *52*, *53*, 55, 69
Rodriguez, R., 24, *35*, *157*
Rogers, C., 6, 8, *15*, 124, *139*
Romano, J. M., 58, *70*
Rose, K. C., 63, 68
Rosenberg, M., 127, *139*, 145, *156*, 255, *264*
Rosenblate, R., 63, 68, 188, *195*, 249, *263*
Rosenfarb, I. S., 74, 75, 86
Ross, M., 162, 166, *177*, *178*
Roth, D. L., 60, *70*
Roth, D. M., 58, *70*
Rothbaum, F., 8, *15*, 192, *196*
Rothman, A. J., 146, *158*
Rotter, J. B., 44, *52*, 252, *264*
Rounsaville, B., 55, *67*
Rozin, P., 168, 169, *179*
Ruben, C., 173, *179*
Rudich, E. A., 28, *34*, 189, *193*, *197*
Rusbult, C., 22, 28, *34*, 189, *197*
Rush, A., 57, 63, 66, 68, 206, *223*, 231, *243*
Rusting, C. L., 187, *196*
Ruvolo, A. P., 172, 174, *179*
Ryan, A. M., 185, *196*
Ryan, R. M., 190, *194*
Ryan, S. M., 187, *192*
Ryff, C. D., 127, *139*

Saboonchi, F., 251, *264*
Sackeim, H. A., 59, *70*
Sadeghian, P., 166, *178*
Sadler, P., 116, *121*

Safran, J. D., 205, *224*
Sage, R. M., 26, 27, *35*, 39, *53*, 125, *140*, 144, *157*
Sakano, T., 112, *122*
Salmela Aro, K., 90, *102*
Salovey, P., 116, *120*, 187, *197*
Samuelson, C. D., 141, *156*
Sanbonmatsu, D. M., 26, *33*
Sanders, G. S., 141, *157*
Sanders, J., 112, *120*
Sandman, C. A., 41, *52*
Sandman, P. M., 142, *158*
Sanft, H., 63, 68
Sanislow, C., 67, 188, *193*
Sanna, L. J., 8, *13*, 90, 91, 92, 97, *104*, 251, 258, 259, *262*, *265*
Santor, D. A., 61, *70*, 75, 77, 86, 191, *197*
Sapolsky, R. M., 39, *52*
Sarason, S. B., 9, *15*
Sarel, D., 108n1, *121*
Sasseville, T. M., 75, 86
Sayette, M. A., 149, *157*
Scepansky, J. A., 148, *154*
Schaefer, P., 188, *197*
Scheier, M. F., 23, 24, 25, *31*, *34*, 40, 41, 42, 50, *52*, 63, 67, 127, *139*, 145, *157*, 166, 174, *177*, *179*, 252, *261*, *265*
Schlenker, B. R., 176, *179*, 185, *197*
Schneider, S. G., 24, *35*, *157*
Schneider, T. R., 187, *197*
Schofield, P., 41, *52*
Schommer, D., *51*
Schoneman, S. W., 90, 92, *104*
Schooler, C., 44, *51*, 145, *156*
Schulz, R., 23, *34*, 41, 50, *52*
Schwartz, N., 167, 171, *179*
Schwartz, R. M., 207, *224*
Sedikides, C., 27, 28, *34*, 107, *122*, 182, 184, 185, 186, 188, 189, 190, 191, 192, *193*, *194*, *195*, *196*, *197*, *198*, 258, 259, *264*, *265*
Seeman, T. E., 39, 44, *52*
Seery, M. D., 40, *53*
Segal, Z. V., 56, 57, 63, 69, *70*, 189, *198*, 205, 217, *224*
Segerstrom, S. C., 41, 42, 43, 48, 49, *53*, 149, *157*, 174, *179*
Seguin, J., 55, *70*
Seldes, G., 233, *245*
Seligman, M., 7, 8, *14*, *15*, 21, *34*, 47, 48, *51*, *52*, 56, 66, 164, 175, *178*, 228, *243*

Selye, H., 164, *179*
Sephton, S. E., *53*
Shafran, R., 251, *265*
Shahar, G., 76, 79, 80, *85*, 86, 100, *104*, 249, *265*
Shair, S. R., *262*
Shaked, N., 22, *32*
Shatté, A. J., 218, *224*
Shaw, B., 57, 63, 66, 68, 189, *198*, 206, *223*, 231, *243*
Shaw, P. M., *224*
Shea, T. M., *67*
Shean, G. D., 79, *84*
Shedler, J., 20, *34*, 127, 135, *139*
Sheldon, K. M., 8, *15*, 21, *35*, 116, *120*, 192, *198*
Shelton, R. C., 59, *69*
Shepperd, J. A., 141, *155*, 161, 162, 163, 167, 168, 169, 173, 174, *177, 179, 180*
Sherman, D. K., 26, 27, *35*, 39, *53*, 125, *140*, 144, *157*
Shichman, S., 61, *67*, 74, 75, *83*
Shimoda, V., 190, *196*
Showers, C., 90, 92, 97, *104*, 173, *179*
Shuper, P. A., 113, *122*
Shuster, B., 78, *85*
Sieber, W. J., 42, 44, 45, 46, *53*
Silver, C., 26, *35*
Simon, K. M., 206, *223*
Simon, T., *50*
Single, P. B., 190, *194*
Sivam, R. W., 90, *102*
Skokan, L. A., 125, *139*
Skowronski, J. J., 182, *197*
Slade, M., 38, *51*
Slade, P. D., 252, *265*
Slaney, R. B., 65, *70*, 188, *195*, 251, 252, *264, 265*
Smart, L., 26, *30*, 40, *49*, 255, *261*
Smith, J. G., *52*
Smith, K. W., 147, *154*
Smith, S., 99, *103*
Snedeker, J. L., 41, *53*
Snowdon, D. A., 22, *32*
Snyder, C. R., 8, *14, 15*, 234, *244*
Snyder, S. S., 192, *196*
Soane, E., 26, *32*
Solberg Nes, L., 41, 42, *53*
Solomon, S., 187, *192*
Sommers, S. R., 256, *262*
Sorotzkin, B., 228, *245*
Sorrentino, R. M., 113, *122*

Spencer, S. M., 90, *104*
Spencer, T. E., 41, 42, *53*
Spijker, M., 162, *178*
Spreeman, S., 185, *194*
Stahlberg, D., 185, *194*
Stalmeier, P. F. M., 152, *157*
Stapel, D. A., 257, *265*
Staudinger, U. M., 8, *13, 27, 30*
Steiger, H., 55, *70*
Steinmetz, J. L., 63, *69*
Steketee, G., *263*
Steptoe, A., 47, *53*
Stevenson, J., 258, *264*
Stites, D. P., *50*
Stöber, J., 251, *265*
Stone, A. A., *51*
Stone, H., 229, *245*
Stone, S., 131, *139*, 229, *245*
Story, A. L., 143, *155*
Stotland, S., 55, *70*, 76, *86*
Stover, L. E., 111, 118, *122*
Strang, D. J., 166, *178*
Strecher, V. J., 144, 147, 149, *156, 157*
Strube, M. J., 182, 192, *198*
Struthers, W., 61, *69*
Su, Y., 106, *121*
Suh, E. M., *122*
Suls, J., 42, *53*, 141, *157*
Sun, C., 189, *196*, 255, *264*
Sun, Y., 148, *154*
Swann, W. B., 77, *86*
Sweeny, K., 161, *177*
Sweetman, E., 76, *86*
Swinkels, A., 187, *198*
Swinson, R. P., *83*

Takano, Y., 8, *15*
Takata, T., *120*
Takemoto, T., 114, *120*
Tamir, M., 187, *198*
Taylor, K. M., 163, 169, *179*
Taylor, S. E., 7, 9, *15*, 19, 20, 22, 23, 24, 25, 27, 28, *30, 35*, 37, 38, 39, 41, 42, 43, 44, 48, *52, 53*, 124, 125, 126, 127, 128, 131, 136, *139, 140*, 142, 143, 144, 145, 146, 150, 151, 152, *154, 156, 157*, 164, 165, 166, 172, 174, *177, 179*
Teasdale, J., 56, 58, 59, 66, *70*, 228, *243*
Tennen, H., 41, *50*
Terry, H., 26, *34*, 133, *139*
Terry, M., 163, *180*

Terry-Short, L. A., 252, *265*
Tetlock, P. E., 168, *180*
Theorell, T., 43, *51*
Thompson, J., 78, *86*
Thompson, R., 61, *70*, 101, *102*
Thoresen, C. J., 188, *195*
Tice, D. M., 165, *177*
Ting-Toomey, S., 118, *122*
Toguchi, Y., 27, *34*, 107, *122*, 191, *197*, 259, *265*
Tomakowsky, J., 42, 48, *53*
Tomaya, M., 90, *104*
Topciu, R. A., 79, *85*, 101, *104*, 188, *196*
Toppmeyer, D., *103*
Tortosa-Gil, F., 105, *122*
Tracy, J. L., 28, *34*
Trautwein, U., 257, *264*
Trichopoulos, D., *154*
Trippi, J., 252, *265*
Trope, Y., 168, *178*, 185, 186, *198*
Truax, P. A., 69
Trzesniewski, K. H., 26, 28, *32*, *34*, 255, *265*
Tschanz, B. T., 93, *104*
Tuason, V. B., 67, *68*
Turcotte, T. A., *195*
Turgeon, L., 25, *30*
Turvey, C., 187, *197*
Tversky, A., 164, 165, *178*
Tyrka, A. R., 188, *198*

Uchida, Y., 107, *121*
Unic, I. J., 152, *157*

Vaillant, G. E., 47, *51*
Vallerand, R. J., 39, *51*
van de Loo, F., *50*
van der Eijnden, R. J. J. M., 22, *31*
van der Pligt, J., 142, *157*, 169, 173, *180*
van der Velde, F. W., 142, *157*
Van der Zee, K. I., 257, *265*
van Dijk, W. W., 169, 173, *180*
Van Lange, P. A. M., 22, *34*
Verette, J., 22, *34*
Vettese, L. C., 77, 78, 80, *85*, *86*
Vicente, B. B., *264*
Vick, S. B., 40, *53*
Visscher, B. R., 41, 42, 48, *52*, *53*, 150, *156*
Vitaro, F., 25, *30*
Vogt, D. S., 124, 128, *140*
Vohs, K., 26, *33*, *35*, 38, *49*, 188, *198*, 201, *223*, 255, *261*
Vosberg, S. K., 95, *104*

Voth, R. D., 108n1, *122*

Wadhwa, P. D., 41, *52*
Wagenaar, W. A., 162, *178*
Waldron, I., 188, *198*
Walker, E. F., 45, *49*
Walker, J., 80, *84*, 230, *244*
Walker, M. A., 113, *122*
Wallbom, M., 114, *119*
Wallston, K. A., 45, *51*, 146, *157*
Walsh, C. A., 218, *224*
Walter, R. A., 47, *51*
Wan, C. K., 141, *157*
Wang, H. Y. J., 42, *52*, 150, *156*
Wanner, B., 25, *30*
Ward, D. W., 97, *103*
Washburn, J. J., 26, *35*
Waters, P., 100, *102*
Watkins, A. F., 251, *262*
Watson, D., 38, *54*, 55, 67, 79, 83
Watts, F. N., 56, 59, *70*
Webb, M. A., 166, *178*
Weinberger, A. D., 58, *71*
Weiner-Davis, M., 236, *244*
Weinstein, N. D., 141, 142, 146, *157*, *158*, 162, *180*
Weintraub, J. K., 25, *34*
Weisbuch, M., 40, *53*
Weishaar, M., 59, *71*, 228, 230, 231, 232, 236, *243*
Weisz, J. R., 8, *15*, 192, *196*
West, S. G., *50*
Whiffen, V., 75, 76, 77, 78, 83, 84, 86, 101, *102*
White, T. L., 258, *261*
Whitehead, A. N., 4, *15*
Whitesell, N. R., 100, *102*
Wicklund, R., 114, *120*
Wiebe, D. J., 143, 148, 149, *158*
Wiedenfeld, S. A., 47, *51*
Wielgus, M. S., 76, *86*
Wiggum, C. D., 188, *193*
Wilber, C., 55, *67*
Wildschut, T., 22, *34*
Wiley, A. R., 115, *121*
Willemsen, G., *53*
Willett, W. C., *154*
Williams, C. C., 188, *197*
Williams, J. M., 56, 57, 59, *70*
Williamson, D. A., 56, *69*
Williamson, G. M., 41, *52*
Willman, P., 26, *32*

SUBJECT INDEX

of cross-cultural self-enhancement, 106–108

of self-enhancement studies, 124–136

Methodological issues, 259

in linking self-enhancement to health outcomes, 142–146

in measurement of self-enhancement, 28–29

Minnesota Multiphasic Personality Inventory, 47

Moderating factors, in studies of self-enhancement and physical health, 151–153

Modesty, 25–26

in East Asian cultures, 111

Modifying factors, for self-esteem and self-acceptance, 216–218

Mongrain, M., 77

Mood-as-information model, 97, 167–168, 171

Morality, and self-criticism, 240–241

Morita therapy, 260

Moskowitz, D. S., 75

Multidimensional Perfectionism Scale, 64, 250–251

Narcissism, 189–190

and positive illusions, 26

and self-enhancement, 126, 133–134

Narcissistic Personality Inventory, 26, 126

Native Americans, 152

Negative affect, use of, 97–99

Negative cognitive triad, 57

Negative emotional states, 230

Negative mood, use of, 95–97

Negative thoughts, 206–207

Negativity, and defensive pessimism, 90–92

NEO Five Factor Inventory, 134

Neubauer, A. L., 64

Neuroticism, 187–188

Niebuhr, Reinhold, 228

Nisbett, R. E., 106

Nixon, M., 145

Noncompliance, with therapeutic intervention, 235

Norem, J. K., 97

Nursing home studies, 43–44

Objective criteria, for self-report of self-enhancement, 129–131, 136

Observer ratings, in assessment of self-enhancement, 132

Obsessive–compulsive disorder, 80

Opportunity, possible, 172–173

Optimism, 162–163

benefits of, 40–41, 173–175

and coping, 24–25

costs of, 175–176

downshift from, 166–170

limits of, 41–42

and self-enhancement, 38

shift toward, 170–173

as status quo, 165–166

Optimism, big, 43

Optimism, little, 43

Optimism, strategic, 90–94. *See also* pessimism, defensive

"Others Exist for Me" illusion, 190

Outcome predictions, and preparedness, 163–166

Overloading, and self-criticism, 76

Padesky, C. A., 211

Parasitism, 183

of self-enhancement and self-criticism, 187–190

Parent, as social role image, 237–238

Parenting, and origin of self-criticism, 74–75

Paulhus, D. L., 134

Pearlin and Schooler's Mastery scale, 145

Peer relationships, and self-criticism, 78–79

Perfectionism, 56, 62–65, 101, 188–189, 228–229, 249–257

adaptive and maladaptive, 64–65, 74

ancient views of, 249–250

destructive, 251

multidimensional view, 250–251

multifunctional, 251–252

neurotic and normal, 251–252

personal standards, 64

and self-criticism, 64, 82

and self-esteem, 217–218

self-oriented and other-oriented, 64, 250

socially prescribed, 64, 250

Perfectionism, performance, 252–254

Performance Perfectionism Scale (PPS), 253–254

Persistence, and optimism, 42

Personal construct theory, 219

Personal Desirability of Traits (PDT), 127

Personal factors, and self-criticism, 100

Personal ineligibility, 230

dysfunctional beliefs about, 211–213
ideal, 115
interdependent, 9, 118
"ought," 115
possible, 172, 174
Self-acceptance
    as alternative to self-enhancement, 221–222
    modifying factors, 216–218
Self-assessment, objective, 241
Self-assessment motive, 182, 190–192
Self-awareness, objective, and face maintenance, 114–115
Self-change, and defensive pessimism, 91–95, 97–99
Self-concept
    cultural factors, 117
    and expert evaluation, 184–185
    flexible, 113–114
    negative, 28
    positive, 28
"Self-critical," used for introjective depression, 61
Self-criticism, 182–183. *See also* depression
    accuracy of, 59–60
    active, 101
    adaptive, 225–243
    in Beck's cognitive model of depression, 56–58
    as both good and bad, 248–249
    comparison of approaches, 62–65
    complexity of, 100–102
    conscious/deliberate, 234–236
    costs of, 91
    decreasing, 213–215
    and defensive pessimism, 89–102
    destructive, 226–232
    as dynamic construct, 248
    etiology and function of, 74–75
    expanded view of, 254
    and face, 109–110, 115–117
    general context for, 73–74
    hazards of, 55–65
    identifying goals of, 233–234
    influences on, 99–100
    interpersonal correlates of, 75–76
    as interpersonally maladaptive, 73–83
    as interpersonally positive, 81–82
    mediating models, 76–77
    moderating models, 76–77
    modern views on, 6–7
    negative, 254

Plato's view of, 4–5
positive, 254
positive concepts and modes, 236–238
psychodynamic approaches to, 60–62
and self-improvement, 185
and self-understanding, 4–5
and social phobia, 80–81
sources of, 256–257
specificity in, 95–97
as therapeutic intervention, 234–236
Self-Deceptive Enhancement (SDE), 127
Self-degradation, private ceremonies of, 226–228
Self-efficacy, and control, 45–46
Self-efficacy beliefs, 241
Self-enhancement
    adaptive, 127, 201–223
    Aristotelian view of, 5–6
    as both good and bad, 248–249
    conceptual definitions of, 125–127
    and defensive pessimism, 101
    degree of, 37–38
    as dynamic construct, 248
    expanded view of, 254
    flexibility of, 27
    global, 46–48
    modern views on, 7–8
    and narcissism, 126, 133–134
    negative, 254
    operational definitions of, 127–133
    and personality, 134–135
    and physical health, 37–49, 141–153
    positive, 254
    psychological costs of, 123–136
    and social behavior, 134–135
    sources of, 256–257
    temperate, 186
    two perspectives on, 124–125
    universality of, 106–108
    and well-being, 135
Self-enhancement index, 28–29
Self-enhancement motive, 182, 190–192
Self-enhancers, 124
Self-esteem, 37–38
    benefits of, 38–40
    damaged, 229–230
    and defensive pessimism, 92–95
    dynamics of, 40
    and face, 109, 116–117
    level and stability of, 255–256
    limits of, 40
    modifying factors, 216–218

ABOUT THE EDITOR

Edward C. Chang, PhD, is an associate professor of clinical psychology and a faculty associate in Asian/Pacific Islander American Studies at the University of Michigan, Ann Arbor. He received his BA in psychology and philosophy from the State University of New York at Buffalo and his MA and PhD degrees from the State University of New York at Stony Brook. He completed his American Psychological Association–accredited clinical internship at Bellevue Hospital Center–New York University Medical Center in New York. He serves as an associate editor of the *Journal of Social and Clinical Psychology* and *Cognitive Therapy and Research* and is on the editorial boards of several leading journals, including the *Journal of Personality and Social Psychology* and the *Asian Journal of Social Psychology*. He has published numerous works on optimism and pessimism, perfectionism, social problem solving, and cultural influences on behavior. Dr. Chang is the editor of the book *Optimism and Pessimism: Implications for Theory, Research, and Practice* (American Psychological Association, 2001) and is a coeditor of *Virtue, Vice, and Personality: The Complexity of Behavior* (American Psychological Association, 2003); *Social Problem Solving: Theory, Research, and Training* (American Psychological Association, 2004); *Judgments Over Time: The Interplay of Thoughts, Feelings, and Behaviors* (American Psychological Association, 2006); and the *Handbook of Mental Health in Racial/Ethnic Groups: Understanding Changes Across the Lifespan* (forthcoming). He is currently working on an authored book that takes a critical look at adaptive and maladaptive perfectionism.